GENDERING WAR TALK

GENDERING WAR TALK

Edited by

MIRIAM COOKE AND ANGELA WOOLLACOTT

PRINCETON UNIVERSITY PRESS

PRINCETON, NEW JERSEY

Library of Congress Cataloging-in-Publication Data

Gendering war talk / edited by Miriam Cooke and Angela Woollacott.
p. cm.
Essays written during and immediately after a ten-week institute
held at Dartmouth College during the spring of 1990.
Includes bibliographical references and index.
ISBN 0-691-06980-8 (cloth) — ISBN 0-691-01542-2 (pbk.)
1. War and society.   2. Peace—Social aspects.   3. Sex role.
I. Cooke, Miriam.   II. Woollacott, Angela, 1955– .
U21.2.G45   1993   92-27190   303.6'6—dc20   CIP

This book has been composed in Adobe Sabon

The following essays have been published previously in slightly
different form: Lynn A. Higgins, "Sexual Fantasies and War Memo-
ries: Claude Simon's Narratology," as "Gender and War
Narrative in *La Route des Flandres*" in *L'Esprit Createur* 27, no. 4
(Winter 1987); and Sonya Michel, "Danger on the Home Front:
Motherhood, Sexuality, and Disabled Veterans in American Postwar
Films," in *Journal of the History of Sexuality*, © 1992 by The
University of Chicago. All rights reserved.

Princeton University Press books are printed
on acid-free paper and meet the guidelines for
permanence and durability of the Committee on
Production Guidelines for Book Longevity
of the Council on Library Resources

Printed in the United States of America

10   9   8   7   6   5   4   3   2   1

10   9   8   7   6   5   4   3   2   1

CONTENTS

PREFACE

GENDER AND WAR? Gender? Much to our surprise, as we began to plan an institute on gender and war to be held at Dartmouth College in the spring of 1990, the very concept of gender immediately proved problematic. On several occasions, when we explained to colleagues that we were organizing a research seminar on the subject, the response was, "Yes, women have always participated in war," or "Women are no less warlike than men. (Look at Margaret Thatcher.)" No, we got used to responding, we are not talking just about women; we are talking about gender: how it is constructed in and through war and, conversely, how warlike values are reinforced through the behavior normally expected of women . . . and men. It would seem not only that "gender" for many people still means "women," but, as we wrote in our proposal for the institute, "although gender and war have been subjects of prescription and representation in Western culture since antiquity, academic inquiry has only recently come to focus on the intersections of these topics."

An opportunity to explore these intersections arose when Dartmouth created a series of humanities institutes, funded with resources provided by the A. W. Mellon Foundation and the National Endowment for the Humanities. The goal of these institutes was to provide a forum for faculty from Dartmouth and other universities to pursue individual research under a multidisciplinary umbrella, research that would then be shared both through publications and in the classroom. Each institute would include a senior fellow, who would serve as a resource for the group, and twelve participating scholars.

When five faculty members at Dartmouth—Lynda Boose, Lynn Higgins, Marianne Hirsch, Albert LaValley, and Brenda Silver, representing different fields within English, French, comparative literature, and film studies—learned about the institutes, we recognized the perfect format to pursue our common interests in gender studies and in cultural representations of war. We were all just beginning to explore the interconnections of these areas in our research and our teaching. We had begun to read important new scholarship by Carol Cohn, Barbara Ehrenreich, Susan Jeffords, Claudia Koonz, Sara Ruddick, Elaine Scarry, Klaus Theweleit, and others, and we were eager to devote more concentrated attention to expanding and defining this exciting new field. The result was the Institute we named "Gender and War: Roles and Representations."

We felt extremely fortunate that Klaus Theweleit, author of the controversial and widely acclaimed two-volume work *Male Fantasies*, our choice for senior fellow, was able to come from Freiburg with his family and that we could bring together scholars from a wide variety of institutions and of disciplinary, methodological, and ideological perspectives. In addition to the individual research projects documented in this volume, other participants studied the mythology of heroes and heroines in Rajput culture (Lindsey Harlan), the representation of women in Nazi films (LaValley), the languages of gender and pacifism in 1930s Britain (Silver), and gender and the ethics of nuclear deterrence (Walter Sinott-Armstrong). The institute, and this volume, were also enriched by seminars with several visitors: Carol Cohn examined the language and thinking of nuclear defense intellectuals and their role in American political culture; Sara Ruddick spoke about her philosophy of maternal work and peace politics; and Margaret Higonnet and Sonya Michel, co-editors with Jane Jenson and Margaret Collins Weitz of *Behind the Lines: Gender and the Two World Wars*, shared their recent work on words and images in cultural representations of war and its aftermath. Jessica Wolfe, who works with trauma survivors through the Boston Veterans Administration Medical Center, introduced us to the research and theory on gender differences in post-traumatic stress disorder.

As co-directors of the institute, we speak for all the participants in expressing our thanks to the Mellon Foundation, the NEH, and Dartmouth College for their funding, and to Dartmouth College for its practical and moral support. One of the nicest things about the experience was the chance to interact with the college course and the faculty seminar on War/Peace Studies and with the many individual colleagues whose work provided additional theoretical perspectives and case studies in different historical periods and cultures. Responses from beyond the academy, from those who heard or read about the institute in the media, indicate that increasing numbers of people recognize the need to understand the connections between gender and war. For, as recent events once again made clear, the impact of these issues is far from abstract; rather, it is felt in the reality of lives lost and families uprooted. If understanding the gendered roles and cultural representations that contribute to war can help denaturalize its "inevitability," then we might just begin to imagine a peaceful future for our sons and our daughters.

Lynn A. Higgins
Brenda R. Silver
Hanover, New Hampshire
June 1991

INTRODUCTION

MIRIAM COOKE AND ANGELA WOOLLACOTT

G*ENDERING WAR TALK* is a volume of essays that were written during and immediately after a ten-week institute on gender and war that was held at Dartmouth College during the spring of 1990. In their proposal for the institute, Lynda Boose, Lynn Higgins, Marianne Hirsch, Al LaValley, and Brenda Silver wrote:

> A culturally produced activity that is as rigidly defined by sex differentiation and as committed to sexual exclusion as is war points to a crucial site where meanings about gender are being produced, reproduced, and circulated back into society. After biological reproduction, war is perhaps the arena where division of labor along gender lines has been the most obvious, and thus where sexual difference has seemed the most absolute and natural. The separation of "front" and "home front" has not only been the consequence of war but has also been used as its justification. Arguably, this remains true despite the experiences of our own wartorn century, during which civilian bombing, wars of national liberation, civil wars, and genocide have challenged the distinctions between these fronts and the gender relations they enforce.

It is only since the 1980s that scholars have undertaken the academic project of analyzing these intersections between war and gender. Several monographs and anthologies have addressed the role of women in primarily Euro-American wars. A very few have dealt with discourse, war, and gender. The essays in *Gendering War Talk* are broadly cross-cultural and multidisciplinary. They test European and American models of the warrior and the waging of war against alternative, less familiar examples from the Middle East and Latin America. The disciplines represented include literature, film and drama, history, psychology, and philosophy. The essays elaborate connections between these disciplines as well as between cultural, social, economic, and political representations.

Our discussions of the roles and representations of women and men in war both confirm and challenge existing images, for example, that women are pacifists, or that they are Patriotic Mothers; that men are essentially aggressive, or that they are threatened by their lack of aggressivity. Essays examine the dynamic intersections between men's and women's experience of war and its articulation in language and images. They expose the historical constructedness of the war story that must eliminate the feminine to survive.

Each essay uses violence in some way as an analytical category and focuses on the immediate experience of war. Some examine the metaphorization of violence, equating epistemic with physical violence. Others highlight the dangers inherent in such a strategy, which may allow for numbness in anomie; they insist on the importance of restricting discussion of violence to its physical manifestations. Essayists analyze the implications of the different forms of violence perpetrated against men as opposed to against women; they evoke the theatricalization of torture and terrorism to serve political ends. Many of the essays wrestle with the problem of how to evaluate the representation of violence. What are the ramifications of watching and remaining unmoved by "cool" yet pornographic enactments of violence, as in the film *The Cook, the Thief, His Wife, and Her Lover*? Although there is substantial agreement that war produces change for women, as also for other marginalized groups, there is disagreement on the nature of the change. Klaus Theweleit and Lynda Boose, for example, argue that war holds no lasting, and certainly no positive, changes for women. For Theweleit, the only good war is the lost war that is embraced as a lost war. Some contributors, the editors included, contend that the fluidity of war allows for linguistic and social renegotiations. Few of the writers define themselves as being engaged in an explicitly pacifist enterprise, yet all are agreed that the project of analyzing violence connotes an ethical stance that is part of any peace process.

Unlike most other anthologies that bring together papers read at a conference or solicited among colleagues, this volume actually grew out of our discussions. During numerous meetings in seminar rooms as well as in homes, bars, and gyms we debated, argued and analyzed preliminary drafts, unfamiliar pieces of literature, war films and plays. We had come to the institute each with an individual project; we left with the knowledge that these other projects had become part of our own and that each one of us had become in some way part of everyone else's project. It was this knowledge, as well as our wish to continue to work together, that made this book possible.

.   .   .   .   .

Gendering War Talk is divided into five thematic sections: Presenting the Unpresentable, War Mythopoeia, Home/Front?, Engendering Language, and The Politics of Representation. The interpretive essay by Klaus Theweleit, the senior fellow at the institute, raises issues addressed during the Institute and incorporates the work of all contributors. Each section explores how cultural conceptions of gender as well as discursive and iconographic representation reshape the experience and meaning of war.

∠The volume is concerned with twentieth-century wars. As became clear during the Gulf War, the role of technology, not only in the manufacture of armaments but also in the universal coverage of hot spots through the electronic media, has become central to the understanding of modern and postmodern wars. Essays reveal that war is beginning to undo the binary structures that it originally put in place: peace and war; home (female space) and front (male space); combatant and civilian. Women's inclusion as participants in wars of this century has blurred distinctions between gender roles in peace and in war. War has become a terrain in which gender is negotiated. As we reinterpret and redefine gender roles and identities in war, it becomes clear that war also has become negotiable. The certainties constructed by binary thinking are revealed to be subject to question. Although the entire volume is concerned with these issues, it strives for definitions that do not create a closed discourse. ⟩×ⁱ

Each war story confronts the dilemma of how to describe events and emotions for which no language seems sufficient. Who has the right to speak? And for whom? How can the survivor bear witness, present the lived experience of pain, terror, and disgust without falling into repetition or, worse, cliché? How can the victim and discourse on the victim sustain an identity that is differentiated in terms of gender, race, and humanity? Marianne Hirsch and Leo Spitzer argue that the representation of victims as undifferentiated by sex in fact serves to obliterate women. In what ways do memory, with its inadvertent or deliberate retrospective distortion, and myth interact to present the unpresentable? Does the aestheticizing of violence further or undercut its presentability? Diana Taylor's essay on theater and the Dirty War in Argentina shows how purportedly artistic representations of violence can in fact be the commission of yet another kind of violence.

Definitions of twentieth-century wars must take into account the persistence of archetypal narratives. Each experience of war is consciously or unconsciously articulated in terms of a founding myth, whether it be that of *The Iliad* or of the *Mahabharata*. The experience of contemporary wars with their changes in strategies and hardware and in gender roles and identities would seem to challenge myths of male bonding and heroism, and of glorious victories. Stan Rosenberg's analysis of the narratives of American pilots in Vietnam attests to the need for the mythology of male heroism and bravery despite a blatantly contradictory reality. Lynda Boose's study of the ideal of masculinity in contemporary American culture examines the re-emergence of militarism in the wake of the emasculating war in Vietnam.

Through individual essays and their cumulative message, we challenge the assumption that war is removed from civilian society, from women and children. Even when it does not overtly involve civilians, war transforms the relationships between family members as well as between male combatants and the women to whom they are related or attached. As the essays by Irene Matthews and Angela Woollacott show, gender patterns formed in the crucible of family relationships are susceptible to the exigencies of war. Women's new responsibilities in "civil" society that is in fact "war" society create a sense of autonomy and privilege. Women's participation in "war" society that may in fact be "civil" society creates a sense of belonging and responsibility. War transforms motherhood from a social to a political factor. As Sara Ruddick demonstrates, the practice of mothering contains prescriptions and potential for peace activism. To the extent that boundaries between home and front can be deconstructed, unprecedented modes of gendered thinking become possible.

⟨ New realities emerge when one accepts that war experience is constructed according to culturally distinct gender expectations. It is not only in explicitly fictitious genres but also in apparently factual and objective discourse that desire and archetypal convention shape and change this experience. Language used to describe or discuss war becomes itself the vehicle of, as well as the potential challenge to, assumptions about appropriate gender roles in relation to war. Language transforms experience into consciousness. This process can be seen in Miriam Cooke's essay, which traces through the connections between women's writing and "fighting" as interdependent aspects of transformed feminist consciousness.⟩ Yet this transformation is not easy. Society censors those who write outside of what is considered to be their gender-specific experience: women should not write about the front as a lived experience; men should not describe threatened masculinity. Margaret Higonnet shows how the battle over women's discursive presence was enacted in the very language of World War I fiction. Carol Cohn dissects the gender assumptions in contemporary language and demonstrates how those assumptions structure national security discourse.

Representation often replaces lived reality. Lynn Higgins illustrates how men's inclusion of women in representations of war can erase them as anything other than fantasy. The experience of war once inscribed, constructed, and transmitted empowers institutions as well as individuals. In the aftermath of war, the work of public policymakers seems to mesh with that of the media and filmmakers in reinstating social norms, particularly as they relate to questions of gender. Sonya Michel's comparative analysis of women's sexual as opposed to maternal powers in restoring manhood to disabled World War II and Vietnam veterans demonstrates how the film industry may be instrumental in winning lost wars.

Klaus Theweleit argues that wars cannot be separated from each other, that both lost and won wars must be continually rewon. He contends that men have used war and violence to rival women's power to give birth. To stop this recycling, he says, we must confront all the dimensions to war that perpetuate men's attempts to create. We must instead recognize the value of caring labor.

In mapping multiple sites where gender and war intersect as cultural formations, the essays present points at which both are open. The interrogation of the authors exposes the negotiable binarisms of war/peace, masculinity/femininity. Far from reinforcing rigid gender distinctions, these essays show that war is an arena in which gender constructions and deconstructions are culturally encoded.

CONTRIBUTORS

LYNDA E. BOOSE is Associate Professor of English and a Shakespearean scholar at Dartmouth College. She is the co-editor of *Daughters and Fathers* (1988). Her personal background includes three years of living in the Vietnam War theater, where her civilian job involved shipping back the personal effects and, when there were any, the remains of U.S. Naval airmen shot down over Vietnam.

CAROL COHN is a Senior Research Scholar at the Center for Psychological Studies in the Nuclear Age, an affiliate of the Harvard Medical School. Her publications include "Sex and Death in the Rational World of Defense Intellectuals" (*Signs* 12, no. 4 [Summer 1987]). She is currently at work on a book entitled *Deconstructing National Security Discourse and Reconstructing Security*.

MIRIAM COOKE teaches Arabic language and literature at Duke University, where she is Director of Asian and African Languages and Literature. Her books include *War's Other Voices: Women Writers on the Lebanese Civil War* (1988), *Opening the Gates: A Century of Arab Feminist Writing* (co-edited with Margot Badran, 1990), and the forthcoming *Arab Women, Arab Wars*.

LYNN A. HIGGINS is Professor of French and Comparative Literature at Dartmouth College, where she also teaches film studies. She is the author of *Parables of Theory: Jean Ricardou's Metafiction* and the forthcoming *New Novel, New Wave, New Politics*. She is editor with Brenda Silver of *Rape and Representation* (1991).

MARGARET R. HIGONNET is Professor of English and Comparative Literature at the University of Connecticut. She has co-edited *Behind the Lines: Gender and the Two World Wars* (1987) and *The Representation of Women in Fiction* (1983); she has also edited *The Sense of Sex: Feminist Perspectives on Hardy* (1992) and several volumes of the journal *Children's Literature*.

MARIANNE HIRSCH, Professor of French and Comparative Literature, and LEO SPITZER, Professor of History, teach an interdisciplinary course on Holocaust representation at Dartmouth College. Most recently, Hirsch published *The Mother/Daughter Plot: Narrative, Psychoanalysis, Feminism* (1989), and Spitzer published *Lives in Between: Assimilation and Marginality in Austria, Brazil, West Africa, 1780–1945* (1990). Hirsch is working on *Family Pictures: Photography and Narratives of Loss*, and Spitzer is writing a book called *Surviving Memory*.

IRENE MATTHEWS is Assistant Professor of Comparative Literature in the English Department of Northern Arizona University and is still wishfully hoping that understanding war will eventually lead to its elimination.

SONYA MICHEL teaches the history of women and gender at the University of Illinois at Urbana-Champaign. She is a co-editor of *Behind the Lines: Gender and the Two World Wars* (1987).

STANLEY D. ROSENBERG is Professor of Psychiatry at Dartmouth Medical School and Chief Psychologist and Director of Psychology Training. His interests include psychodynamic psychotherapy and social psychological research on adult development, posttraumatic stress disorders, and language pathology. Books include *The Cold Fire* (with Bernard Bergen) and *Men at Mid-Life* (with Michael Farrell).

SARA RUDDICK teaches philosophy and feminist studies at the New School for Social Research in New York City. She is the author of *Maternal Thinking: Toward a Politics of Peace* (1989).

DIANA TAYLOR is Associate Professor of Spanish and Comparative Literature at Dartmouth. She is the author of *Theatre of Crisis: Drama and Politics in Latin America* (1991) and editor of three volumes of critical essays on Latin American and Spanish playwrights. Since 1982 she has been director of Dartmouth's Hispanic theater group, "Primer Acto."

KLAUS THEWELEIT, free-lance writer and househusband, lives in Freiburg, Germany. His publications include *Ein Aspirin von der Grösse der Sonne* (1990); *Objektwahl: "All You Need Is Love"* (1990); *Buch der Könige*, vol. 1: *Orpheus Eurydike* (1988); *Male Fantasies*, vols. 1 and 2 (1987 and 1989); and *Männerphantasien*, 2 vols. (1977 and 1978).

ANGELA WOOLLACOTT is Assistant Professor of History and Director of the Women's Studies Program at Case Western Reserve University. She is author of the forthcoming book *On Her Their Lives Depend: Munitions Workers in the Great War*.

PART I

PRESENTING THE UNPRESENTABLE

Chapter 1

GENDERED TRANSLATIONS:

CLAUDE LANZMANN'S *SHOAH*

MARIANNE HIRSCH AND LEO SPITZER

> The film is made around my own obsessions.
> (*Claude Lanzmann*)

> To live, as well as to die, a Jewish father needs to know that
> the future of his child is secure.
> (*Sigmund Freud*)

> The cinema is the medium that reaches far into Hades.
> (*Klaus Theweleit*)

THERE ARE MOMENTS when gender does not impose itself as a category of analysis, when, displaced by other factors, it virtually disappears from view. The Holocaust is such a moment. While the experience and the representation of war generally places women and men in radically different positions—on the home- and battlefronts, for example—the Holocaust, at least for its victims, seems to be a moment that recognizes no gender differences, that erases gender as a category. Nazism would exterminate all Jews, regardless of gender, class, nationality, professional, or economic status. If Jews are vermin, as Hitler insisted, then distinctions among Jews normally applied in social interaction become irrelevant. In the elaborate "final solution" devised by the Nazis during the early 1940s, all victims were to be stripped of difference and rendered powerless. The Holocaust's victims were thus to be "degendered" by the process of persecution and extermination.

The opening scene of Claude Lanzmann's *Shoah* offers an ironic illustration of the representational divergences between gender and war, on the one hand, and gender and the Holocaust, on the other.[1] His nine-and-a-half-hour cinematic oral history of the Holocaust begins as Simon Srebnik, one of the only two survivors of the massive exterminations in the Polish village of Chelmno, reenacts for the camera an event that villagers there still remember to this day: his regular trip down the Narew

River on a flat-bottomed rowboat when, at the prodding of his German guards, he sang Polish folk tunes and Prussian military songs in his beautiful tenor voice. In the mouth of the chained thirteen-year-old Jewish orphan boy, condemned to death, the immense gulf between the experience of Jewish males and the rewards and disappointments of a wartime masculinity emerges with pointed irony: "A mug of red wine, a slice of roast," he was taught to sing. "That's what the girls give their soldiers. When the soldiers march through town, the girls open their windows and their doors." [*Wenn die Soldaten durch die Stadt marschieren, öffnen die Mädchen die Fenster und die Türen.*][2]

Shoah's numerous witnesses attest to the erasure of gender as one of the prime instruments of Nazi dehumanization and extermination. As victims are shaved, stripped down or clad in identical striped uniforms, starved, screamed at, beaten, tormented; as they are reduced by the thousands to bodies (referred to not as "victims" or "corpses" but as *Figuren* and *Schmattes*, "figures," "junk"); as they are piled into wagons "like sardines," laid out in mass graves "like herrings"; as their flesh starts crumbling in the ground where they are dumped; as they fall out of gas vans and gas chambers "like potatoes"; as they become a "load," converted, within the space of hours, to ashes—gender, with humanity, gets erased. "It was not a world," the Polish courier Jan Karski insists as he describes his Dantesque journey through the Warsaw ghetto at the end of *Shoah*: "There was not humanity. . . . Women with their babies, publicly feeding their babies, but they have no . . . no breast, just flat."[3]

Ironically, however, Claude Lanzmann's film itself *also* eradicates gender differences among the victims of the Final Solution. The almost obsessive thrust of *Shoah*, its primary goal, is to bring to memory and to record the workings of the Nazi machinery of destruction: to detail its operations and lethal course, from the ghettos, to the transports and trains, to the selection in the extermination camps, to mass murder in gas vans and gas chambers, to the burial and burning of the corpses. The film penetrates both the procedural and psychic dimension of this process: the secrecy that enabled it to work, the collusions of a world that stood by in silence and allowed it to happen. Lanzmann's primary witnesses for this daunting project—the persons he interviews and interrogates most fully—are those who were closest to the process and mechanics of extermination: some survivors of the special work details in the concentration camps, several German perpetrators, and a few Polish bystanders who lived and worked near the killing centers. Among the Jewish victims, those who were at once closest to the death machine and able to survive and to testify were, by selection, men. But *Shoah* elicits other voices as well. Lanzmann interviews some survivors of the Warsaw ghetto, a few Auschwitz survivors from the Jewish community of Corfu, two survivors of the Riga ghetto who appear in the film to sing a ghetto song, a woman who spent the war in hiding in Berlin, and one survivor of the Theresienstadt "family camp" in Auschwitz. Even among *these* witnesses, however, Lanzmann clearly privileges testimonies from men. Although the experience of Jewish women is described in the Jewish men's and the bystanders' and perpetrators' narratives—although they are talked about and represented by others—they themselves appear on-screen on only a few, and extremely brief, occasions. And even when they do appear, even when their voices are heard, the camera seems to shy away from sustained focus on their faces.

Some of the women who are seen and heard in the course of the film act as mediaries and interpreters from Polish, Hebrew, and Yiddish, carrying the words and the information of the narrators to Lanzmann, and the questions from Lanzmann, who is the only interviewer and the central presence in the film. A number of the Polish "bystander" witnesses are women as well, as is one of the German informants. The perpetrators and bystanders, inasmuch as they figure in the film, represent a range of groups, male and female, farmers and tradespeople. But among the Jewish survivors who speak and give their accounts in the film, the erasure of differences and, particularly, the almost complete absence of women are striking.

For Lanzmann, gender is irrelevant to the death machinery on which he focuses with such relentless energy: a machinery that is designed to render subject into object, to degender, to declass, to dehumanize, to exterminate, and to destroy the traces. But in focusing so resolutely on this machinery and privileging the detailed explanation of its operation, Lanzmann backgrounds the *subjective* experience of its victims—the differentiated individual realm within which, according to other survivor accounts, significant gender differences do emerge.[4] Indeed, women's Holocaust narratives and testimonies do bring out a gendered experience. In accounts collected by Lewin, Laska, Heinemann, Katz, and Ringelheim, women speak of the effects of their ceasing to menstruate and the fear that their fertility would never return; they speak of rape, sexual humiliation, sexual exchange, abuse, enforced abortions, and the necessity of killing their own and other women's babies. They speak of the extermination selection process in which maternity becomes a much greater liability than paternity. They describe most extensively and analyze most deeply the relationships and friendships that developed between women in concentration camps. Controversially, some even argue that women showed greater survival skills than men.[5]

These, however, are not the accounts we hear in *Shoah*.

This, then, is the paradox: From the perspective of the oppressor, the victim lacks subjectivity. If the critic scrutinizes that perspective, concentrating the focus on the machine that fulfills and implements the oppressor's deepest desires, he or she also risks an erasure of the subjective. Such an unintentional and ironic replication does emerge in *Shoah* when we interrogate gender as an inherent element of subjectivity. And yet, despite the erasure of women that Lanzmann performs through the focus and method of his inquiry, traces of gender difference are nonetheless reinscribed in his film. Perhaps unwittingly, they sustain and motivate much of the energy driving this monumental oral history. Our endeavor to uncover these traces, to excavate the feminine buried within the layered structure of the film's testimonies—a feminine cast in the archetypal roles of a Persephone, a Eurydice, a Medusa—is what we are calling "gendered translation."

.　.　.　.　.

Jewish women survivors do not themselves advance the central inquiry of *Shoah;* they do not further Lanzmann's investigation into the machine of death with information detailing its operations. They exist in the film for different purposes. The first Jewish woman to be seen on-screen is Hannah Zaïdel, the daughter of Motke Zaïdel, survivor of Vilna. She appears as a curious listener obsessed with her father's story: "I never stopped questioning him," she states in the film, "until I got at the scraps of truth he couldn't tell me. It came out haltingly. I had to tear the details out of him, and finally, when Mr. Lanzmann came, I heard the whole story for the second time."[6] But in the film it is Claude Lanzmann, not Hannah Zaïdel, who asks the questions. Indeed, as one of the few screened female listeners who is not also an interpreter, Hannah sits in a faded background, smoking a cigarette, when her father and his fellow survivors describe being forced to uncover mass graves and dig up bodies, including those of Zaïdel's mother and sisters, in order to burn them and eradicate their traces. Paula Biren appears next, a survivor of the Lodz ghetto who responds, briefly, in the negative, to the only question she is asked ("You never returned to Poland since?"). Unlike most of the male witnesses who speak in the film on repeated occasions, Biren and the other Jewish women disappear after only one brief interview.[7]

While a great deal of energy is spent in the film to bring some of the men back to the scenes of extermination—to have them relive, intensely and relentlessly, the experience *in the present* so as to be able to remember and testify about *the past*—only one woman goes through this process. She is Inge Deutschkron, who returns to her native Berlin from Israel and declares, "This is no longer home." Her brief narrative recalls the day Jews were deported from the city while she herself remained behind in hiding, and relates how, throughout the rest of the war, she felt "utterly alone" and "terribly guilty" not to have departed on the transports with the rest. Her position—in hiding and removed from the central destiny of her people, a destiny Lanzmann interrogates through the Sonderkommando survivors and other men—emblematizes the position of women in the film as a whole. Unlike most of the male witnesses whose faces fill the screen for long periods of time, Inge Deutschkron is little more than a disembodied voice: her narrative is largely presented in voice-over as scenes of Berlin and departing trains occupy the space of the screen; her face and name appear only at the very end of her brief account.[8] And unlike most of the other male witnesses, she never returns in the film.

At a very important moment in *Shoah*, in the midst of Rudolf Vrba's and Filip Müller's narratives of the failed uprisings in Auschwitz, another Jewish female informant appears briefly. Her role in the film is also symptomatic. Ruth Elias initiates the narrative about the Theresienstadt "family camp" brought to Auschwitz by the Nazis for propaganda purposes— about the group that became a focus of resistance activities during the months of its cynical "reprieve," before almost all of its members were sent to the gas chambers. But Elias's story in the film is limited to the Theresienstadt group's transport to Auschwitz only, and to her disbelief at the news that she had arrived at an extermination camp. Details about the group's six-month stay in Auschwitz, about relations between its members, about the possibilities of resistance, about feelings generated by warnings of imminent gassing, about the exterminations themselves: these we receive not from Theresienstadt family camp member Elias, who quickly disappears from the film entirely without ever enlightening us about the means of her own escape from death, but from Rudolf Vrba and Filip Müller, who observed the Theresienstadt group as outsiders. This female witness, whose face, like Inge Deutschkron's, appears on-screen only at the very end of her brief voice-over narration, is merely allowed to start the story, which is then taken over by the two men.[9]

Elias's role—to set the scene, provide the atmosphere, the affect, and not the facts or the details—allows us to understand one way in which *Shoah* uses women. We can gain additional insight from the last two Jewish women to be seen in the film, who immediately precede its final sequence recalling the Warsaw ghetto uprising. Gertrud Schneider and her mother (who remains nameless in the film) come on-screen to sing a ghetto song, "Asoi muss seyn"—"Because that's how it must be."[10] Their broken voices are first heard in the background as we watch an unidentified barren landscape. Several measures into the song, the two women come into view, but only one, the daughter, carries the song. The mother becomes yet another of the film's emblems of gender distinction. She cannot sing the entire song; her voice breaks and she starts crying. But in crying and covering her face in lament, fingernails painted red, she acts out its words. This song is the only untranslated text in the film: its meaning for the non-Yiddish speaking viewer must be translated by the mother's gestures: "The best years, are finished / And gone—never to be recovered. / It's difficult to repair what has been destroyed. / . . . Because that's how it must be / That's how it must be, that's how it must be."[11] Besides expressing passivity and resignation, the film's staging of the "Asoi muss seyn" also demonstrates the double speechlessness of women: Gertrud Schneider sings but does not speak, and her nameless mother, overcome with the emotional weight of memory and the event captured by the camera, gestures but neither sings nor speaks. Such iconic moments, in which meaning is conveyed not through words but through images or music, structure the emotional texture of the film. They provide the background weave to the relentless factual fabric of Lanzmann's inquisitive project. And it is women who are most often relegated to that background.

The roles women act out in the film—hiding, passivity, lament, invisibility—are for the most part supported in the men's narratives about women. The image of the mother and child who jump from a train, resulting in the mother's being shot in the heart (its still-horrified male Polish peasant narrator repeating "in the heart"), serves to underscore emotionally the callousness of the oppressors and the hopelessness of escape. But other moments of female resistance introduce another element: the association of femininity with danger and death. Rudolf Vrba describes how secrecy became the key to the efficiency of the final solution. Panic, he explains, would have been a "hitch in the machinery," and panic was especially feared from women with small children. The film's male narrators recall how women unleashed several frightening scenes of destruction: how, at a transport stop, for instance, one woman threw her empty cup at a guard who refused to give her water, which led him to shoot senselessly and indiscriminately at the entire wagon. In Filip Müller's account, another woman, warned by a friend in the Sonderkommandos that she and her group would be gassed, tried to warn everyone but was not believed. In a gesture of anguish and desperation, she scratched her whole face and started to scream. She was tortured and the man who warned her was thrown into the oven alive. The story of her tormented rebellion releases some of the emotional pressure built up in the film in account after account of death and killing. Yet the pathos of Filip Müller's moving narrative is also rendered all the more powerfully poignant by her helplessness, and by the ultimate futility of her action.[12]

The male narratives, moreover, tend to reach a greater emotional power when encounters with women and memories of family and domesticity are evoked. Thus Michael Podchlebnik reports that he had asked to be killed after he unloaded his wife and children from a gas van in

Chelmno. And, in what is one of the most frequently discussed scenes in the film, Abraham Bomba describes at length his job as a barber who had to cut the hair of women inside the undressing room of Treblinka's gas chamber: he testifies insistently that he felt nothing in carrying out his task, that in such situations it is impossible to have any feelings at all. But as he begins to tell how a friend of his, also a barber, met his own wife and sister in that room, his narrative breaks down, and he begins to cry and asks to be permitted to stop his account. When he resumes talking, at Lanzmann's insistence, his English turns into phrases mumbled in Yiddish. For Bomba, as for the others, encounters with women threaten whatever precarious emotional distance, whatever control and denial of feelings they had attempted to establish in order to survive.[13] Indeed, the interruption within the powerful scene with Bomba demonstrates that the evocation of these encounters on-screen endangers even the very continuity of the film's narrative flow.

. . . . .

In a film set on making distinctions in details (Were they Poles or Czechs? Were there forty thousand or four hundred thousand? How many glasses of beer? How far? How long? How many minutes did it take? How many hours? How many bodies?), Lanzmann refuses to recognize or acknowledge differences in role or experience among the Jewish victims, irrespective of whether these relate to gender, age, or other social demarcations. "Eine Masse" (one pile)—the phrase uttered by Richard Glazar in his descriptions of the crowd of naked victims waiting to be gassed, and of the piles of belongings that had to be disposed of, like their owners, with speed and efficiency—describes not only the Jews as they were treated by the Nazis, but, ironically, also the Jews as they are represented in the film. For Lanzmann, distinctions among Jewish victims are ultimately either irrelevant or outright disturbing. When, for example, Polish peasants point to different treatment of Jews on the basis of class by describing how some Central European Jews arrived in passenger instead of freight or cattle trains, Lanzmann insists that such class discriminations were not very frequent. He includes a narrative about Jews who tried to trade diamonds for water to show that, of course, it did not matter whether you had diamonds: the guards took the diamonds and did not bring water. And when the German SS Unterscharführer, Franz Suchomel, describes the experiences of the Treblinka "funnel," Lanzmann seems uncomfortable with the gender distinctions that emerge. The men were gassed first, Suchomel explains, and the women had to wait, for extended periods of time, in the funnel outside the gas chambers. Describing the fear of death and the physical evacuation it often provoked in the victims, Suchomel connects these reactions to those of his own mother on her deathbed. But when he insists that the men were beaten and the women were not, Lanzmann refuses this distinguishing "humanity" on the part of the guards and presses Suchomel to admit that, probably, the women were beaten as well.[14]

Shoah's equalization of victims, its reluctance to explore differences among them, extends to the realm of morality as well. Many of Lanzmann's informants, for example, actually belonged to that area that Primo Levi identified as the moral "gray zone"—a zone inhabited by Jews who ultimately survived because they participated as Kapos or in the work details of the death machines.[15] Lanzmann does not contemplate the implications of this participation. Nor does he encourage or include stories that would exalt his informants or make them heroic. Thus we never find out how Rudolf Vrba escaped from Auschwitz, merely that he did so. We never hear about Richard Glazar's role in the Treblinka uprising, merely that such an uprising was planned. If important differences emerge among persons whom we get to know within the film, these are due primarily to individual variations in storytelling talent, to differences in insight and analytical skill, to the amount of prodding and manipulation required to jolt memories and elicit recollections.

Lanzmann, in effect, allows differences in testimony to emerge and develop but downplays differences in experience. The story of the victims, as revealed in Shoah, is one story. Might Lanzmann fear that any detailed exploration of distinctions would replay and recall the divide-and-conquer tactic by which Nazis persuaded Jewish councils and individuals to help the work of the death machine? Might any focus on real differences unduly echo the illusion of difference encouraged by the Nazis that led some Jews to believe that if they collaborated, they might be saved, that the death of some might save the lives of others?[16] Might distinctions appear trivial within the "giant crime," the unparalleled devastation of the Holocaust?[17] Whatever the explanation, it is clear that Lanzmann's general discomfort and uneasiness concerning discussions of distinctions—his resolute unwillingness to contemplate and explore differences among the victims in Shoah—is most vehement when it comes to gender.

· · · · ·

Women's presences do more than to punctuate Shoah with emotional power and pathos. At the end of the film, Simha Rottem, one of two Warsaw ghetto survivors interviewed by Lanzmann in Israel, recalls walking through the abandoned ghetto after his emergence from the underground sewers. His lengthy narrative concludes with his evocation of a disembodied, haunting and dangerous female voice. "I suddenly heard a woman calling from the ruins," he recalls.

> It was darkest night, no lights, you saw nothing. All the houses were in ruins, and I heard only one voice. I thought some evil spell had been cast on me, a woman's voice talking from the rubble. I circled the ruins. I didn't look at my watch, but I must have spent half an hour exploring, trying to find the woman whose voice guided me, but unfortunately I didn't find her. . . . Except for that woman's voice and a man I met as I came out of the sewers, I was alone throughout my tour of the ghetto. I didn't meet a living soul. At one point I recall feeling a kind of peace, of serenity. I said to myself: "I'm the last Jew. I'll wait for morning, and for the Germans."[18]

This image of the "last Jew" spoken by Rottem at the very end of the film echoes the final words of *Shoah*'s first part,[19] uttered by Simon Srebnik:

> But I dreamed too that if I survive, I'll be the only one left in the world, not another soul. Just me. One. Only me left in the world if I get out of here.[20]

The mysterious female voice heard by Simha Rottem (which in Hebrew he describes as emanating from a "fata morgana") and the feelings of abandonment that Rottem shares with Srebnik summarize *Shoah*'s representations of femininity—the danger of women, their helplessness and passivity, their emotional power, and their disembodied haunting presence. But the conclusions Rottem and Srebnik draw from their own sense of desertion allow us to see yet another dimension of femininity in the film: its connection to death without hope of rebirth, to destruction without a parallel generativity. Rottem, like Srebnik, is the "last Jew alive." His failure to locate and to identify the distant female voice—a woman in need of help, or an evil spell luring him toward destruction—echoes the finality of the final solution, a process of extermination designed to erase all trace of Jewish existence, past, present, and future. As *Shoah*'s witnesses make devastatingly clear, in the Holocaust mothers cannot protect or nourish their children, they cannot keep them alive, and they cannot produce more. Within this context of hopelessness, Rottem and Srebnik see themselves each as the last Jew, forever cut off from his future, the terminus of Judaism. And Lanzmann places both their voices at climactic moments in the film—at the very end of each of its two parts—reinforcing, with devastating and conclusive effect, the impact of total death built up during *Shoah*'s nine-and-a-half hours.

It would appear, then, that despite its effort to scrutinize the workings and details surrounding the Nazi machinery of death and extermination, this film cannot fathom the particular conjunction between femininity and the absence of generativity. Its inability to do so is underscored in two significant scenes of male suicide, which dominate the second part of

Shoah. The first, the untimely suicide of Freddy Hirsch, considered by many as "the moral leader" of the Theresienstadt family camp in Auschwitz, is recalled with great sympathy by Rudolf Vrba. When it became certain that his group would be gassed the next morning, Hirsch was asked by the underground resisters to lead them in an uprising. "If we make the uprising," Hirsch inquired, "what is going to happen to the children? Who is going to take care of them?" Vrba, his contact, responded that the children would probably die in any case, "that there is no way out for them." This direct and undoubtedly truthful assessment proved to be paralyzing for Hirsch. According to Vrba: "He [Hirsch] explains to me that he understands the situation, that it is extremely difficult for him to make any decisions because of the children, and that he cannot see how he can just leave those children to their fate. He was sort of their father. I mean he was only thirty at the time, but the relationship between him and those children was very strong." An hour after proposing the uprising to Hirsch, Vrba found him dying of an overdose of barbiturates. The uprising, consequently, never took place.[21]

Hirsch's suicide, a direct result of his perceived failed paternity, is echoed at the end of the film by an uncannily similar description of what caused the suicide of Adam Czerniakow, the leader of the Warsaw ghetto Jewish council. In the film, Raul Hilberg summarizes relevant passages from the final pages of the diary Czerniakow left behind. According to Hilberg, Czerniakow "is terribly worried that the orphans will be deported [from the Warsaw ghetto], and repeatedly brings up the orphans. . . . Now if he cannot be the caretaker of the orphans, then he has lost his war, he has lost his struggle. *Why the orphans?* They are the most helpless element in the community. They are the little children, its future, who have lost their parents. . . . If he cannot take care of the children, what else can he do?" Hilberg, in apparent identification with Czerniakow's assessment, adds, "Some people report that he wrote a note after he closed the book on the diary in which he said: 'They want me to kill the children with my own hands.' "[22]

The suicides of Hirsch and Czerniakow, placed as prominently in the film as they are and echoing each other in the similarity of their presumed motivations, can be useful in explaining the film's relation to the category of gender. Hirsch and Czerniakow take the masculine role of responsible paternity extremely seriously. Both see in the children the possibility of a future, and cut off from that future, impeded from exercising their own power to insure continuity into that future, they cannot go on.[23] Hirsch and Czerniakow act out the masculine response to the realization that there is no future left, a realization repeated in the film's last words by Simha Rottem. They can neither face nor suppress that insight, and are unable to remain with the children to offer them adult support and solace in their final moments.[24] In privileging these incidents and their masculine perspectives, the film itself resonates their evasion.[25] In contrast, *Shoah*'s much briefer recollections of female suicide—of women who slash their own wrists and those of their children, of women who poison themselves and their daughters and sons—offer a poignant alternative response. Although we learn neither the name nor story of these women, their suicide/killings reveal equally despondent but less self-centered motivations than those of Hirsch and Czerniakow. For these women, death is an act of final resistance: escape for themselves and their offspring from prolonged suffering at the hands of their oppressors. It is a chosen end that reveals the women's more local and modest confrontation with death as opposed to the global ambition and ultimate denial of Hirsch and Czerniakow.

· · · · ·

In his analysis of different cultures' responses to death, the anthropologist Maurice Bloch demonstrates a deep connection between death and femininity, a connection that, he argues, is cross-culturally present. But most cultures, Bloch explains, go further. Women not only manage rituals connected with death, thereby representing death, but they also occupy the space of regeneration, rebirth, and continuity, signifying the conquest of death.[26] In Greek and Roman mythology, certainly, Persephone, the goddess of the underworld, is also a symbol of spring, renewal, and generativity—represented both as the daughter of Demeter, goddess of the grain, and the mother of Demoophon. In the exploration of the genocidal machinery of destruction that is the subject of *Shoah*, that second position, the feminine connection to generativity, is eradicated, which seems to make the first, connection to destruction, doubly terrifying. Within the context of this film, women come to represent death without regeneration. Could it be, therefore, that women figure the Nazi destruction of the Jews so unbearably that they must virtually be excised from representation altogether?

· · · · ·

"Is it possible to literally *speak from inside the Holocaust*—to bear witness from the very *burning* of the witness?" Shoshana Felman asks in her essay "The Return of the Voice: Claude Lanzmann's *Shoah*." Exploring the act of testifying about the the event-without-a-witness, Felman elaborates: "In what ways, by what creative means (and at what price) would it become possible *for us* to witness the event-without-a-witness? A question which translates into the following terms of the film: Is it possible to witness *Shoah* (the Holocaust and/or the film) from inside?"[27]

As Felman insists, *Shoah* is a film about the act of witnessing and about the process of survival. Since *Shoah* uses no documentary footage from the period, the Jewish witnesses we see on-screen are all Holocaust survivors, and since Lanzmann interrogates primarily those who have been in the deepest pits of the death machine, who have been farthest within the crypts of extermination, they are survivors who have literally been *inside* Hades. Not only have they been inside the camps and the ghettos, inside the gas chambers and the crematoriums, but some have also been left for dead, shot by bullets that failed to reach their vital organs. Against all odds, and certainly against the Nazi design for the final solution, they have literally come out again to testify. Thus Filip Müller, the Sonderkommando crematorium worker who wanted to die, was sent out of the gas chamber by the women of his village so that he might bear witness. In the words of Richard Glazar, "It was normal that for everyone behind whom the gate of Treblinka closed, there was death, had to be death, for no one was supposed to be left to bear witness. I already knew that, three hours after arriving at Treblinka"[28] This paradox, presented by Felman as the paradox of "witnessing about the event without witness," emerges in this film as a process marked by gender distinction.

Only men are in the position of descending into this underworld, the place that the modern imagination has most closely associated with a vision of Hades, and of coming out again to testify. And the power of their testimonies is heightened by the women they meet and are forced to leave behind. In this sense they are like Orpheus, the witness: the one who has come out of Hades alive, and whose song is made hauntingly beautiful by an encounter no other living human has been able to experience and to speak about. Like Orpheus, *Shoah*'s Jewish male witnesses have all survived intimate confrontations with death. If we read *Shoah* as an Orphic text in the terms of Klaus Theweleit's *Buch der Könige*, we can further illuminate the gendering of testimony and of survival that motivates the distinctive creative energies driving this monumental cinematic document.[29]

The essential elements of Theweleit's elaborate model of "Orphic creation" are acted out within *Shoah*: Orpheus's descent and reemergence from Hades after his encounter with Eurydice, the dead woman who herself cannot come out and speak, the power and beauty of his song, and the interdiction against looking at the dead woman's face. In Theweleit's terms, Orphic creation—the birth of human art forms, social institutions, and technological inventions—results from descent *and emergence*, a possibility denied to Eurydice. It is thus an artificial "birth" produced by men: by male couples able to bypass the generativity of women. In this process, women play the role of "media," of intermediaries—voices and translators—not of primary creators or witnesses. This type of masculine collaboration and historical creation, dependent on the intermediary role of women, is reflected in *Shoah*, where the masculine anxiety about the curtailment of female reproduction, about the cessation of Jewish transmission through the female line, gives rise to an alternate form of reproduction: to creation in which Lanzmann and Raul Hilberg, Lanzmann and each of his articulate male witnesses, together, "give birth" to the story that was never supposed to have come to light, never to have been heard. We see the pleasure of this collaborative relationship in the scene where Lanzmann and Hilberg together reconstruct, by means of Nazi train schedules and records, "Fahrplanordnung 587," the route of a particular transport train from its origin to Auschwitz.[30] We see it also in the obvious rapport and apparent common cause—in the pleasurable ease of exchange characterizing the conversations between Lanzmann and Richard Glazar, Filip Müller, and Rudolf Vrba. In a modern manifestation of Orphic creation, together with these "Orphic" male survivors of the journey to Hell, Lanzmann circumvents women and mothers, and initiates a new form of transmission for modern Jewish history.

As in Theweleit's Orphic model, *Shoah*'s women, whose faces can virtually not be seen, become the midwives of male creation, the mediators who deliver the stories' words from one male to another. Indeed, the film relies on a process of "gendered translation" to make its inquiry comprehensible. As memory enters speech in the witnessess, female translators are the midwives of a multilingual process of signification, repeating, through mimicry, the act of remembering itself. Listening to questions and answers, they carry words back and forth, transform and reformulate them, often significantly, and render them understandable and acceptable. Through their tedious and repetitive work, they become essential supplements to the film's project of exploration. Not only do they act out its search for an intelligible language with which to convey the unspeakable, but they are the shadowy intermediary voices between language and silence, between what is articulated and what must remain unspeakable.

Shoah's primary interlocutors, then, are truly Orphic voices, literally talking heads, whose song is as transgressive, as endangering, as the song of the poet whose body was torn asunder by angry Maenads. All have literally *sur*vived—lived *too* long, lived *beyond* the limits of their lives. Ultimately, of course, it is the film itself that *is* Orpheus, and we as view-

ers are implicated in its creative agenda, also cast as witnesses in an endless chain of bearing witness, also impeded, if not forbidden, to *look* at
the faces of dead women.

In fact, the determination and consistency with which women's faces
are avoided in the film evoke the Medusa, another female underworld
figure, more threatening than Eurydice. If gazing at Eurydice will definitively kill *her*, gazing at Medusa will kill the one who looks. Medusa is the
absolute other, the figure for the encounter with total death. According to
Jean-Pierre Vernant's study, *La mort dans les yeux*, she combines "facial-
ity" with monstrousness: what threatens to kill, what turns to stone, is
the act of *looking* at her face.[31] Thus, in the *Odyssey*, Medusa's face is the
guardian of the realm of death, whose radical otherness she maintains
against all the living. She is also a figure associated with war and, in that
context, she signifies the absence of generativity. Medusa only gives birth
(unnaturally, from the neck) at the moment when she is decapitated by
Perseus. To look at Medusa is to enter a world where all boundaries are
erased: to look is also to be looked at; her eyes are mirrors in which her
monstrousness is reflected back to the viewer. She calls into question the
very act of looking: to look is to be possessed, to lose oneself, to find
oneself pulled into the absolute alterity of death. In that sense, Medusa is
the figure most endangering for cinema, especially for the cinematic evocation and representation of death. If women's faces are indeed associated not only with Eurydice but also with Medusa, their absence from the
screen of *Shoah* undergirds the film's mythic structure.

And yet Inge Deutschkron, Ruth Elias, Gertrud Schneider, and her
mother do offer their own examples of survival, curtailed as they are by
Lanzmann's mythic vision. Together with the translators, they disrupt the
film's relentless pursuit with traces of alternate stories. Their presence,
minimal as it is, serves as a reminder of the *price* this film pays for its
remarkable ability to make possible the testimony from the *inside*. And
the *inside* here is not only the underworld of the death machinery, it is
also the hell created by the encounter between past and present, an encounter that makes the past present with unexpected and unbearable
force. What would it have meant to include women in that encounter, to
confront masculine and feminine modes of survival and remembrance?
Shoah does not permit us to answer this question.[32]

Lanzmann insists that his film is not a documentary but a performance.
He hires the trains, asks the engineer to drive them, takes Srebnik back to
Chelmno, places Bomba in the barbershop. Like an analyst, he brings
each of them to the point of reexperiencing their most profound encounter with the Nazi death machinery. Women are left out of these remarkable performances. While Lanzmann's film—in bearing witness to the
event-without-a-witness and erasing the distance between past and pre-

sent—has the mythic and artistic force of Orphic creation, it also reveals the politics of this mythology by replicating the sacrifice of Eurydice and the slaying of Medusa.

NOTES

1. All references are to *Shoah* (1985) written and directed by Claude Lanzmann, distributed by New Yorker Films, and to *Shoah: An Oral History of the Holocaust*, the complete text of the film by Claude Lanzmann, preface by Simone de Beauvoir (New York: Pantheon, 1985). The authors wish to thank the participants of the humanities institute Gender and War: Roles and Representations at Dartmouth College as well as the members of the Dartmouth faculty seminar Domination, Subordination, and Consciousness for insightful comments on earlier versions of this paper. We are also grateful to Jane Caplan, Michael Ermarth, Claudia Koonz, Miranda Pollard, Paula Schwartz, Linda Williams, and Marilyn Young for their suggestions.

2. Lanzmann, *Shoah*, p. 6.

3. Ibid., pp. 172–74.

4. Among the many accounts, see for example: Rudolf Vrba and Alan Bestic, *44070: The Conspiracy of the Twentieth Century* (Bellingham, Wash., 1989); Ruth Schwertfeger, *Women of Theresienstadt: Voices from a Concentration Camp* (Oxford, 1989); Rhoda G. Lewin, ed., *Witnesses to the Holocaust* (Boston, 1990); Vera Laska, ed., *Women in the Resistance and in the Holocaust: The Voices of Eyewitnesses* (Westport, Conn., 1983); Marlene E. Heinemann, *Gender and Destiny: Women Writers and the Holocaust* (New York, 1986); Fania Fénelon (with Marcelle Routier), *Playing for Time* (New York, 1977); Julie Heifetz, *Too Young to Remember* (Detroit, 1989).

5. See Esther Katz and Joan Miriam Ringelheim, eds., *Proceedings of the Conference, Women Surviving: The Holocaust* (New York: Institute for Research in History, 1983); Joan Miriam Ringelheim, "The Unethical and the Unspeakable: Women and the Holocaust," *Simon Wiesenthal Annual* 1 (1984): 69–87, and "Women and the Holocaust: A Reconsideration of Research," *Signs: Journal of Women in Culture and Society* 10, no. 4 (Summer 1985): 741–61. Also see Sybil Milton, "Women and the Holocaust: The Case of German and German-Jewish Women," in Renate Bridenthal, Atina Grossman, and Marion Kaplan, eds., *When Biology Became Destiny: Women in Weimar and Nazi Germany* (New York, 1984), pp. 297–333; Schwertfeger, *Women of Theresienstadt*; Lewin, *Witnesses to the Holocaust*; Laska, *Women in the Resistance and in the Holocaust*.

6. Lanzmann, *Shoah*, p. 8.

7. Ibid., p. 16.

8. Ibid., pp. 50–51. For Deutschkron's memoir of her survival in Berlin during the war, see Inge Deutschkron, *Ich trug den gelben Stern* (Munich, 1985). It is interesting to compare Lanzmann's evocation of disembodied female voices with Kaja Silverman's analysis of embodied female voices in classic Hollywood cinema in *The Acoustic Mirror: The Female Voice in Psychoanalysis and Cinema* (Bloom-

ington, Ind., 1988). Dissociating body from voice in Hollywood film increases authority; it is a tactic generally reserved for men, a tactic that masks the precariousness of male subjectivity. Folding the voice inside the image, as is done for women, diminishes authority; women, Silverman suggests, need to be freed from their claustral confinement in their bodies. Lanzmann's approach is the opposite: the male voices are both embodied and authoritative, while the female voices carry little substantive information.

9. Lanzmann, *Shoah*, pp. 154–66. For Vrba's more detailed account of the first Theresienstadt group in Auschwitz, see Vrba and Bestic, *44070*, pp. 180–96.

10. Lanzmann, *Shoah*, pp. 194–95.

11. Ibid., p. 195.

12. Ibid., pp. 29, 123, 30, 126.

13. Ibid., pp. 11, 116–17.

14. Ibid., pp. 35–36, 40, 111. It is interesting to compare this sequence of the film with Saul Friedländer's account of a conversation with Lanzmann as the film was being shot: " 'Tell me, sir,' Claude asks the officer from Treblinka, 'which burn faster, men's bodies or women's?' and the SS officer calmly begins to expatiate." See *When Memory Comes*, trans. Helen R. Lane (New York, 1979), pp. 116–18. Does Friedländer misremember the conversation, or did this question of Lanzmann's remain on the cutting-room floor?

15. Primo Levi, *The Drowned and the Saved*, trans. Raymond Rosenthal (New York, 1989).

16. See Zygmund Bauman, *Modernity and the Holocaust* (Cambridge, 1989), esp. chap. 5, "Soliciting the Co-operation of Victims."

17. See Terence des Pres, *The Survivor* (Oxford, 1976).

18. Lanzmann, *Shoah*, pp. 199–200.

19. When projected in theaters, the film is normally shown in two parts, each with an intermission.

20. Lanzmann, *Shoah*, p. 103.

21. Ibid., pp. 161–62. For a fuller account of the resistance within Auschwitz and of Freddy Hirsch's suicide, see Vrba and Bestic, *44070*, pp. 167–96.

22. Lanzmann, *Shoah*, pp. 188–90.

23. Inadvertently, Simon Srebnik echoes their realization when he subtly changes the refrain of the military song he had been taught by the Nazi soldiers. Instead of singing "Ei warum, Ei darum / Ei bloss wegen dem / Tschindarassa-bumdarassa -sa" ("Oh why, oh because / Only because of the / Tschindarassa-bumdarassa -sa"), he sings "Warum-darum / Warum-darum / Wegen der Kinderrasse, Kinderhasser, Bum" ("Why-because, why-because / Because of the race of children, the child-haters, Bum"). With his flat "warum-darum," Srebnik echoes the tone and message of the "Asoi muss seyn," and with his shift from the sounds that mimic the sexual encounter between the girls and the soldiers to his interpretation of those sounds—the intercourse between the "child-haters," whose procreation eradicates the "race of children"—Srebnik, himself a child, underscores the feelings of being the last Jew alive. See Anne-Lise Stern, "Ei Warum, Ei Darum: O pourquoi," in E. Didier, A.-M. Houdebine, and J.-J. Moscovitz, eds., *Shoah, le film: Des psychanalystes parlent* (Paris, 1990).

24. For a contrasting male response, see Betty Jean Lifton, *The King of Children: A Biography of Janucz Korczak* (New York, 1988).

25. Saul Friedländer mentions another account filmed by Lanzmann but curiously not included in the film, the story of the two hundred children of Bialystok who were deported to Theresienstadt, kept there for two months, used in negotiations that fell through, and eventually killed. See *When Memory Comes*, p. 117.

26. Maurice Bloch, Introduction, in Maurice Bloch and Jonathan Parry, eds., *Death and the Regeneration of Life* (New York, 1982).

27. Shoshana Felman, "The Return of the Voice: Claude Lanzmann's *Shoah*," in Shoshana Felman and Dori Laub, *Testimony: Crises of Witnessing in Literature, Psychoanalysis, and History* (New York: 1991), p. 227. See also Felman's "A l'age du témoignage: *Shoah* de Claude Lanzmann," in Michel Deguy, ed., *Au Sujet de* Shoah (Paris, 1989), p. 81.

28. Lanzmann, *Shoah*, p. 50.

29. Klaus Theweleit, *Buch der Könige: Orpheus und Euridike* (Frankfurt, 1988). For an English translation and condensation of his argument, see "The Politics of Orpheus between Women, Hades, Political Power and the Media: Some Thoughts on the Configuration of the European Artist, Starting with the Figure of Gottfried Benn, or: What Happened to Eurydice?" *New German Critique* 36 (Fall 1985): 133–56.

30. Lanzmann, *Shoah*, pp. 138–45. Lanzmann has credited Hilberg's massive study *The Destruction of the European Jews* (New York, 1961) with inspiring his own project. On male collaboration, see also Wayne Koestenbaum, *Double Talk* (New York, 1989). See Klaus Theweleit's essay in this volume for further suggestions about the attractions of masculine collaboration and the concomitant exclusion of women.

31. Jean-Pierre Vernant, *La mort dans les yeux: Figures de l'autre en Grèce ancienne* (Paris, 1985).

32. See Klaus Theweleit's essay in this volume for a suggestive discussion of gendered models of memory.

Chapter 2

SPECTACULAR BODIES: GENDER, TERROR,

AND ARGENTINA'S "DIRTY WAR"

Diana Taylor

O
N MARCH 24, 1976, the Argentine Armed Forces overthrew the constitutional government headed by Perón's widow, María Estela Martínez de Perón. The first military junta to hold power after this coup, consisting of Jorge Rafael Videla (army), Emilio Eduardo Massera (navy), and Orlando Ramón Agosti (air force), issued three documents on the day they seized power, one proclamation and two decrees, in which they vowed to reconstruct the nation by means of a "process of national reorganization." The process, now known simply as the *proceso* in Spanish, or the "dirty war" in English, lasted through three military juntas until its collapse in 1983. By that time more than thirty thousand Argentine civilians had been abducted or tortured, had died or "disappeared."

Beginning with their first pronouncements of March 24, the military leaders declared themselves the "supreme organ of the Nation" (T, 112), determined to "fill the void of power" (T, 107) embodied by Perón's widow and, through a show of muscle, transform the "infirm," inert Argentine masses into a functioning, harmonious (albeit abstract) Patria (motherland).[1] The exercise in national bodybuilding was aimed at producing an authentic "national being" (T, 108). María Estela Martínez de Perón's government was sick; its "productive apparatus" (T, 107) was exhausted; "natural" solutions were no longer sufficient to insure a full "recuperation" (T, 107).[2] The antisocial disease was hidden, invisible to the naked eye; it was pernicious, lurking in the interior interstices, not readily accessible to sight or control.[3] But, as the junta leaders made clear from their first utterance, both open and hidden subversion would be eradicated (T, 108).

The military's representation of its task through these initial texts centered on the semanticization of the political as body. Given the intensely patriarchal military framework, the social body was gendered. The female occupied the two extreme poles—at one end the profoundly rotten bitch, or *puta*, who gave birth to Argentina's bad children. She, like

Freud's castrated woman, represented nothing but lack ("ausencia total" in the junta's words, T, 107), the loss of grandeur, principles, and faith. At the other end of the spectrum was the good, desexualized, virginal mother, the Patria.[4] She too lacked the penis. If anything, her lack was even more acute than the *puta*'s. Not only was she anatomically without a penis, she could not even borrow one. The Patria, although disembodied, still retained some of the dreadful feminine characteristics of the castrated woman that scholars such as Klaus Theweleit associate with male fears and fantasies: the red floods and collapsible boundaries. As President Videla stated in August, when faced with Argentina's escalating violence, the Patria was "bleeding to death. When it most urgently needs her children, more and more of them are submerged in her blood" (T, 59). The Patria, like the *puta*, was still represented as a bleeding wound or gap. Yet this was the blood of sacrifice—hence potentially redemptive. Still, as the junta's first proclamation of March 24, 1976, had made clear, its decision to take power "was a decision made for the Patria" (T, 108). What made the Patria acceptable, perhaps even necessary, within this discourse was that she was not credited with giving birth to her children—on the contrary, the glorious military men gave birth to her. The Patria was empowered by her heroic sons. The genealogy of these men, as Massera spelled out in a speech on June 22 of the same year, was entirely patrilinear, handed down "through the blood of our heroes . . . for the good of our Patria and our sons' future" (T, 40). Good, pure (male) blood protected the Patria against the bad, polluted, dangerous blood of the woman (menstruation, childbirth), traditionally held at bay by taboo and ritual. The heroes gave birth to military men, clearly an all-male lineage. Nonetheless, the "feminine" gave them definition through opposition; the *puta* was repudiated and annihilated; the long-suffering image of the Patria empowered and uplifted them to hero status. As Laura Mulvey notes in "Visual Pleasure and Narrative Cinema," "the paradox of phallocentrism in all its manifestations is that it depends on the image of the castrated woman to give order and meaning to its world." (T, 6).[5]

The military heralded its ascension to power as the "dawning of a fecund epoch" (T, 31), although the generative process was not, strictly speaking, "natural," as Videla, Massera, and Agosti recognized. Recuperation demanded Christian sacrifice and manly prowess, which they exhibited in word and spectacle. Opposed to the hidden, invisible interiority associated with subversion and femininity, the military represented itself as all surface, aggressively visible, identifiable in uniforms, ubiquitous, on parade for all the world to see. The spectacularity of their display of power indicates that the visual image was considered as important as the narrative in controlling their public's attention. Staging order was perceived as a way of making it happen. Photographs of the military leaders lined up next to the Catholic archbishops illustrate the degree to which visible military order simultaneously reenacted and constituted the new social order: male-dominated, Catholic, and strictly hierarchical even while seemingly egalitarian. Rows upon rows of erect figures stood with their shoulders back, heads high, stomachs held in and neutralized by broad leather belts. The high black-leather boots and the caps, or, at times, helmets, erased all traces of individuality or human vulnerability. The military body was a contained body, always ready for action, always under control. On parade it moved as one: one body, one will, an efficient, disciplined military machine.

As its leaders asserted in their first proclamation, the military would be an example for the population to emulate (T, 108). So, too, the truth it stood for was simple, straightforward, and self-evident, legitimated by Christian, national, and family values.[6] The struggle was not only against agents of the anti-Patria and the anti-Christ. It was also against "extremists," "terrorists," and anyone else, even foreign correspondents, who refused to cooperate or believe in the project. Everyone, as the junta had warned, had to be made to identify with the project and participate in the fantasy: "All sectors represented in this country must feel themselves clearly identified with these shared aspirations, and therefore, committed to the common enterprise that will lead to the greatness of the Patria" (T, 108). The struggle had to be waged in order to restore harmony. The chaos of the previous government, all those unruly, uncontrollable (feminine) elements, "threatened to submerge us in dissolution and anarchy" (T, 107).

Sacrifice and violence were at the very heart of the reorganizing enterprise: state terrorism was presented as only a natural, purifying antibody to an infested body. As such, violence was redemptive. Like a body's own antibodies, the struggle also had to be fought in the invisible, hidden cavities of the rotten social organism (in the interstices of the *puta*), all for the sake of the Patria. So while the military prided itself on its visibility and uprightness, it also claimed the right to possess those invisible interiors as well. The insidious, hidden dangers had to submit to military might; the hidden would be exposed, the invisible made visible. While the military's language and overt comportment seemed logical, upright, and positive, the text and public image hid the lethal underside, the dead, mutilated bodies of those who did not fit in or comply with the script. In spite of the aggressive visibility and uprightness, the military systematically conducted secret rituals of violence on their thirty thousand victims—rapes, torture, and exterminations were methodically carried out in dark, hidden places, the 340 concentration camps and detention centers that cropped up throughout Argentina.

The violence, whether inflicted on males or females, was an attempt to feminize the population in general, and the "subversives" in particular.

The violence was sexualized; females were routinely raped as, less often, males were. But both females and males were turned into penetrable bodies, their genitals and orifices poked and prodded by the elecric rod, or *picana*. The victims, and the population at large, were rendered passive, submissive, silent. Thus, the military men, the supreme organ of the nation, could maintain themselves to the degree that they could safely control or eliminate their feminine other. As if by magic, those dangerous, contaminated bodies were disembodied, disappearing into thin air.

The script or master narrative developed by the military leaders had a beginning and an end; it was full of plots and action; it involved undercover work, the discovery and investigation of the hidden enemy; it entailed heroism. It was a narrative that used females as raw material to be turned into the cause (*putas*) and justification (Patria) of violent politics. While male and female bodies were gendered feminine, passive, penetrable, disposable, the conflict itself was presented as universal (disembodied), "transcendent" (T, 108): good versus evil, life struggling to overcome death. The population was encouraged to participate in the quasi-cosmic war against evil, to identify with the military model of rectitude, morality, and efficiency.

.   .   .   .   .

Seven years after the downfall of the last junta, the military's representation and discourse of sexual potency, predicated on the hatred and annulment of actual women, continues to "penetrate" and reproduce itself in the cultural sphere. Here, I will suggest ways in which theatre, as one system of representations, both mirrors and constitutes another—society as a whole. I will focus on one play, Eduardo Pavlovsky's recent production, *Paso de dos* (Pas de deux, 1990), based on his 1989 script, *Voces* (Voices), precisely because it might seem an odd choice to illustrate an authoritarian discourse on violence and sexuality: Pavlovsky, a psychotherapist /playwright /actor is a prominent leftist and confirmed enemy of the military regime. He narrowly escaped abduction by military forces by jumping out of a window in 1978; he went into exile in Spain until 1980. Moreover, his plays are known to deal explicitly with Argentina's recent history of state violence and torture. The script *Voces*, a one-act piece with two characters ("He"/"She"), is the most recent of his many plays focusing on torturers and victims. *Paso de dos*, as usual in Pavlovsky pieces, stars Pavlovsky and, since his marriage, his wife, Susana Evans. Although the performance is based on the script, it has undergone considerable change due to the year and a half of rehearsal with director Laura Yusem and to the addition of another actor, Stella Galazzi, who plays She's voice. Still, as in all his scripts and performances, the spotlight continues on torture and the male torturer. Some Argentine critics go so far as to suggest that Pavlovsky is monomaniacal on the subject, that he insists on belaboring a period that is dead and buried. Dead, it may be, but not buried. The neofascist discourse, fantasies, and structures in Argentine society, unlike much else, have not "disappeared." The police and military men responsible for the torture and other human-rights violations still hold their jobs; the third serious uprising instigated by the military of the far Right took place in November 1990; the last of the nine junta generals convicted of ordering thousands of deaths was released (in December 1990, as a result of President Menem's infamous decision to grant them an *indulto*, or amnesty). As one commentator stated, "There's talk of monuments to these men, to their heroic war against subversion."[7] While one might expect the continuation of fascist fantasies from the Right, these traditional political categories, as *Paso de dos* illustrates, are clearly insufficient in analyzing the deep-seated and widespread appeal that this discourse holds for many on the Left as well as on the Right, for psychotherapists as well as military men, for women as well as men. I single out Pavlovsky not to suggest that he is *particularly* blind, sexist, or perverse but rather to indicate how active and unconscious the participation in the fantasy of masculinity actually is and to challenge the role assigned to women within it.

Voces ostensibly tries to illuminate Argentina's recent past. "He," the male protagonist, was a torturer during the *proceso* who becomes obsessed with one of his female victims. Even before meeting her, simply hearing about her from his fellow torturers, he confesses later, "I had already created an image of you" (V, 13). "I was obsessed with the thought of possessing you . . . claiming you as a trophy, I was always thinking about your body . . . Overpowering you forcefully . . . suddenly . . . like when an animal catches its prey" (V, 14). He needs her; she is his "NECESSITY. The necessity of our bodies . . . together" (V, 11). His dependency makes him feel vulnerable, violent, and insanely jealous: "Not being with you was like facing the void; the horror was knowing that my intensity could cease at any moment, that it depended entirely on you" (V, 12).[8] "She," the script tells us, becomes caught up in his search for intensity. They engage in a tortuous ceremony where he inflicts pain on her body—another secret ritual with violence against women at its core. She endures the ordeal stoically, but, then, he did not want "answers"; he wanted her to resist, to keep silent, so that the interrogations and sessions might continue and intensify his pleasure. "I wanted to possess your body, your cavities, your smells, each part of your body that I struck; I knew the color of every one of your bruises" (V, 28). He feels compelled to expose and control her interior, innermost parts. Now, after the *proceso* is over, he still needs her—not as a source of intensity but to give him his identity: "I don't understand you, now you could scream out my name and again you choose to keep quiet, you won't say a word, confess you bitch, scream out who I am, who I was. . . . Because I existed! Why? Why won't you name me?" (V, 28). Her final choice, at the end of the script, is again to keep silent—she will deny him the hero status of the generals who now walk freely down the streets of Buenos Aires. He demands, he interrogates, tortures, and possesses her "entirely" (V, 22), but she "wins." She, not he, the play wants us to believe, holds the ultimate power.

Reading the script of *Voces*, the reader might draw the conclusion that the play is about the torturer's perversity, a term Robert Stoller defines as "the erotic form of hatred."[9] After all, it has been well documented that the Argentine torturers routinely raped their victims. The play might also be read as an example of the military's version of masculinity. "He," one might argue, much like Theweleit's Freikorps soldier males, is acutely conscious of being trapped in a highly vulnerable body, a "feminized" body full of holes ("*huecos*," V, 9) which he tries desperately to fill and discipline: "I want every gesture to make sense, I mean, I want every gesture to have a feeling of spontaneity. I don't want any holes" (V, 9). Onstage, he is forever pushing out his shoulders, standing straight, flexing his muscles, sucking in his gut. The entire play could be interpreted as his struggle to constitute himself against his own weakness, his "femininity." Pavlovsky the psychoanalyst even gives us a little comic book Freudianism on castration anxiety to "explain" how the male killer got to be that way: as a child, a bully beat him up; he complained to his father; his father took him back to the group and promised to hold the other boys back while his son took on the bully one-on-one. The boy failed; he did not even take on his opponent; terrorized, he wanted to go home. His "cowardice" and "weakness" transformed him into a "shit" in his father's eyes. He has failed the young soldier's ritual of initiation designed to "transform rituals of bodily pain into 'intoxicated consciousness.' "[10] One moment has shaped his entire life. Now shunned permanently by the father, he himself must play out those rituals of intensity (intoxicated consciousness) one-on-one, on a safe body, on the body that will not fight back, the woman's body. Her body allows for his virility; her silence justifies his actions; she is passive, he is active, but he depends on her absolutely for his masculinity. Alone, he himself pursues the "fascist aesthetic" of turning his body into a well-functioning machine:[11] "I turn my head to the right, now to the left, now to the front again. Pause" (V, 9). Pavlovsky is conjuring up the military discourse, replicating in his play the cultural narrative that transforms females into the basis for the rejection and erection of male identity. The protagonist's identity depends on his being able to dominate her absolutely, just as military identity is predicated on its absolute ability to control and annul the feminine body and then appropriate her "natural" birthing capabilities. He is born again as a new man, a military man, by "imagining" and "possessing" her— another ethereal Patria; yet the physical woman must be devalued and destroyed in the process. Individuation becomes necessarily linked to violence, but, then, we are concerned only with his individuation, for the "subject of violence" in these narratives, as Teresa de Lauretis notes, "is always, by definition, masculine; 'man' is by definition the subject of culture and of any social act."[12] The violence onstage is both brutal and capricious, reflecting thus the two themes that run through the testimonies of the survivors of the "dirty war," the "ultimate brutality and absolute caprice" of their ordeal.[13] *Paso de dos* confirms Susanne Kappeler's observation that this gratuitous violence "is the form of his [the white male's] free expression of himself, an assertion of his subjectivity."[14]

It is when we consider the stage production of *Paso de dos* that we realize that this is not a play *about* perversity; it does not create or even permit the critical distancing between itself and its topic that might encourage the spectator to reflect on the structure and significance of this sexualized, militarized violence. It *is* perverse. Whether it intends to or not, it replicates and affirms the fascination with eroticized violence, the Patria/*puta* split, the phallocentrism and authoritarianism of the political order. Intensely beautiful, set to some mournful tango, this production presents the woman's destruction as somehow coherent, necessary, and, yes, aesthetically pleasurable and morally redemptive. Much like the military's representation of their actions, this play too tends to reduce the spectator's response to stunned silence.

The lack of distance is in part caused, in part epitomized, by the fact that Pavlovsky himself takes on the role of the torturer and his wife, Susana Evans, enacts the woman's body. The woman's voice—now separate from the body—is played by Stella Galazzi. Pavlovsky admits he envisioned himself playing the role; he threw himself totally into the character and throughout this performance encouraged the spectator to identify with him/He. His fascination with torturers and torture produces a riveting effect on the audience. A different actor, Argentine or non-Argentine, might have been able to achieve different results. This production of *Paso de dos* highlights problems already existing in the script and creates new ones: What happens when the voices telling a horror story become bodies, staging that horror right before our eyes? The ambiguous, timeless space in the script becomes a small, circular tub (about eight feet in diameter) full of mud in which He annihilates She. For fifty excruciating minutes he beats her, strips her, rapes her. While she is flung and splayed in the mud, he always remains in control. Literally and figuratively, he keeps his pants on throughout. Any nudity on his part is carefully measured and always to advantage; he shows his naked torso off to the public, flexing his muscles, puffing out his chest, posing and strutting while she lies facedown in the mud, naked. He talks incessantly while she grovels at his feet, moaning and groaning. The brutality he confesses to in the script materializes into an endless series of slaps, blows, tugs, and yanks to her naked body. Now, in the staging, however, she seems to enjoy and even crave the violence inflicted on her. At one point in the production, she begins to strip herself. In an orgiastic frenzy he kills her, but this too seems acceptable in the search for intensity, the outcome of mutual desire and consent. So is the play about sadomasochism? Or is it about torture and the *indulto* (the torturer goes free at the end of the play)? What does the closing scene suggest about power, choice, and victimization (already mythified in the script), when the final image has him putting on his quasi-military jacket and towering over her body, which is wrapped in a shroud, half-buried in the mud? True, her voice from the back of the theater rings on. Even though she could not help enjoying her annihilation, he is not going to get away with it. Her retribution? She is not going to tell, thereby renouncing the only outlet victims have historically had.

What are we watching, anyway? And what is the spectator's role in all this? One "reading" of the spectacle that reviewers seemed to reiterate was that *Paso de dos* was a *testimonio*, something along the lines of Peter Weiss's *Investigation*, here based on the testimonies of the victims televised during the generals' trials. As one commentator stated: the play stages Argentina's recent tragedy.[15] Another claimed that it was in the horror of the production that its redemption lay: "*Paso de dos* is horrible. There lies its triumph over a horrible part of our history."[16] How so? What would the victims and their families think of this representation of Argentine repression that not only focuses on the oppressor but that depicts the victims as longing for and participating in their own torture and annihilation? Since when do victims of torture hold the ultimate power over their torturers? Or is this a porn show? Does it mean to imply that fascism is no more than a sexual aberration? What happens when her *intimidades* and *intertiscios* (V, 22), repeatedly alluded to in the play, become bare breasts, buttocks, and vagina in the spectators' faces? The poster advertising the production, moreover, focuses specifically on a nude frontal of She in the process of being strangled. People paid money to watch this show; it was full every night. Was the sex and violence— indisputably theatre's two major selling points—the uplifting sight for those cramped in the tiny, sordid cubicle of a theatre? Pavlovsky, in an interview, posits another possibility. He calls the play a "love story" in which both partners enjoy themselves: "I imagine them enjoying themselves like dogs in this love story."[17] Love or fascism? Pornography or docudrama? Is this merely one more male fantasy of sadomasochism pro-

jected yet again onto a social "body," or a politically committed attempt
to demythify the violence of Argentina's "dirty war"? And how do we
decide?

·   ·   ·   ·   ·

One of the major critical problems posed by Pavlovsky's production
clearly centers on his use of the body, particularly the continual slippage
from the biological, sexual body, to the gendered body as a social and
theatrical construct (woman, military male), to the body as metaphor of
social identity and, finally, to the textual body, *Voces*, as an "autonomous" work of art, part of the corpus of Pavlovsky's work. Here I will
concentrate on the tension between the biological and gendered body (the
representation of which is a particular problem in theatre) and its relationship to social body—as we have seen, also represented in the military
discourse as gendered.

The slip between the sexual and gendered bodies, both female and
male, deserves attention more, I would argue, because of what it says
about a patriarchal, authoritarian society than what it says about the
play. She/He: the opposition between two characters is based fundamentally on gender, the great, the unbridgeable yet nonetheless artificial di-
vide. And because the two are reduced to gender differences, the play
seems to be about those seemingly irreducible differences. He (the oedipal
male) is socialized to prove his potency to his father by asserting his physical force, by fighting the bully. Having failed the test before the unforgiving parental spectator, the all-seeing Father, he must prove his potency in
his narcissistic search for *intensidades*. She, the essentialized woman, is
masochistic and powerless. Her masochism, moreover, is not depicted as
an idiosyncratic characteristic (some individuals do enjoy having pain
inflicted on them). Rather, masochism is depicted as the female's almost
"natural" role in this erotic pas de deux, much as Freud delineated in
Three Essays on the Theory of Sexuality.[18] Parental (military) authority,
this narrative reads, constantly hovers near, watching the process of maturation, ready to welcome the young warrior into the fold. Agency equals
aggressivity; dependency equals fatal weakness.

She, we recall, is split into two characters, the body played by Evans,
the voice by Galazzi. Pavlovsky insisted on casting his wife in the part
because he finds her body beautiful, that is, pleasurable to the paying
spectator, who, this casting suggests, is presumed to be male. Because of
the intense violence inflicted on her, combined with the fact that her training is in dance, not theatre, she was unable to say her lines. Laura Yusem
solved the problem by casting Galazzi as the voice that comes from the
bleachers offstage, where the audience sits. The lighting principally illu-

minates Galazzi's face, partially wet and muddy, and only a little of her rather demure dress. No matter how the split came about, however, here they are again—puta and Patria, one naked and disemboweled onstage, the other ethereal, long-suffering, and now physically positioned in the bleachers, somehow above it all. The first is killed, but no matter—her position is still victorious because the other prevails. Approximately ten thousand women were raped, brutalized, and murdered in Argentina during the "dirty war," but the Patria lived on.

Unlike the military's discourse using gendered bodies as metaphor, however, theatre's materiality reminds us that bodies are always physical, gendered bodies. Slapping and pushing a woman around the stage is an act of misogynist violence—not an act of male individuation; the suffering of the woman in the bleachers cannot merely be dismissed as national sorrow. In theatre, as in life, it is hard to make a body disappear, although not for that did the military stop trying. It takes a considerable imaginary leap on the part of the population to make those bodies "mean" something else—national unity or dissolution, for example. We have to be taught to deny the reality we see with our own eyes. And that is what both the military's representation of its exploits and Pavlovsky's production attempt to achieve. But when all is said and done, the dead bodies remind us that the triumphalist scripts are inseparable from the gruesome performance of power.

Nonetheless, even in theatre, or *especially* in theatre, the split could have been interesting in highlighting the discrepancy between script and performance. It could have functioned much like a Brechtian Gestus, an alienating effect that separates the act from the actor, thereby allowing the spectators some emotional distance on the action that would permit a critical response or attitude toward it. This, in *Paso*, would entail deconstructing the spectacle of potency and violence against women by contextualizing gendered violence and illustrating how and why the "feminine" in Argentina has become the site of political conflict. As Patrice Pavis notes, "the Gestus radically cleaves the performance into two blocks: the shown (the said) and the showing (the staging). Discourse no longer has the form of a homogeneous block. . . . Far from assuring the construction and the continuity of the action, it intervenes to stop the moment and to comment on what might have been acted on stage."[19] Feminist theatre scholars such as Sue-Ellen Case, Elin Diamond, Jill Dolan, and Deborah R. Geis have embarked on a reevaluation of Brechtian techniques to split the actor from the role. The last proposes that "to show the subject-in-process or the nonunified subject . . . is to begin breaking the 'rules' of what happens to the speaking body onstage. Traditional theatre uses the actor's immersion in a character, and the audience's resultant empathy, as a way of closing up the occasional gaps between the languages of the body (both explicit and implicit) and the spoken language of the character: costumes, voice modulations, even lighting and music work to create an illusion of coherence, which is sustained by the spectators' complicity. Brechtian theory often serves as a paradigm for challenging or displacing these conventional strategies of representation. In Brecht's 'A-effect' the ongoing refusal to permit audiences empathy—or the concomitant distinctions between actor/character and story/history—allows for a constructive disengagement (or, more accurately, a historicized 'reading') of the speaking body and its signifiers."[20]

Paso de dos allows for no such distancing: both female bodies are "characters," fully identified with the action. Galazzi, who reminded me of a Botticelli painting, delivered her lines from her seat. Her beautiful voice, coming from offstage, had little impact on the visual performance. The split did not disrupt the action or challenge the "rules" of what happens to the body onstage. If anything, it did the opposite; the split reproduced the displacement of female desire and perspective in patriarchy. Her body, as usual, was presented as passive and open; her objections and desires were, once again, pushed aside. Although Pavlovsky clearly meant to suggest that her words empower her, the fact that her voice is distanced to the very limits of the stage more accurately represents the position of most Argentine women. If they are heard at all, it is only from the margins—and their words, even objections, serve only to legitimate the violence and exclusion that is being inflicted on them. He, who controls the action from center stage, can use her words as proof of her equality and willingness to participate in the action. Yet her words, now lamenting, now conciliatory, now accusatory, functioned as little more than background noise in the spectacle. And, in the grand old tradition of theatre in a patriarchal economy, the female body is exposed for the (male) viewer's pleasure. She (voice) said her lines, but given what was going on onstage, who could listen? Nor did she say anything meaningful or important. She echoed his words, questioned him, asked him to explain himself. She declared at one point that there was little difference between them, supposedly because her desire was little more than the mirror image or, rather, echo of his. Any condemnation she might utter was effectively neutralized insofar as it supposedly existed in the dialogue itself, a part of the complicitous sparring. But then, there was no real dialogue in the performance, just his raving monologue that her words offset and highlighted. Much as with the military's appropriation of the speaking subject (their *we* supposedly represented everyone),[21] the audience is encouraged to suppose that a monologue is a dialogue. The voices of the military's victims, too, faded into the distant past, echoes falling on the deaf ears of a population caught up in the phallo-military display. After all, who was listening?

The implications of the voice/body separation are far-reaching for what they suggest about gender inequalities as well as what they say about victimization. The play, much like the discourse it reflects, functions only insofar as it can erase gender as a category to be reckoned with. We are not talking about women, the military might have argued, we are talking about nationhood and identity (played out through the image of Woman). Nor, would Pavlovsky admit, does *Paso* have much to do with women. By separating the voice from the body, Pavlovsky reaffirms two deadly stereotypes—the voiceless woman and the bodiless victim. Thus, the possibility of an embodied, vocal, victimized woman effectively "disappears."

The play tells two tales; one about erotic intensity, the other about criminal politics. It is the dangerous slippage between the two that makes it perverse. *Paso de dos* slides from the realm of military violence to that of pleasure.

In the first, the female body is apparently committed to the pursuit of erotic, deathly pleasure, which the play tries to convince us is hers, not just his. This is the world of seemingly mutual desire and consent. And few, with the exception of Jesse Helms perhaps, would argue against leaving consenting adults alone. Pavlovsky's "intensity" seems equivalent to Georges Batailles's eroticism, "the assenting to life to the point of death." True, it is the woman who dies, but as Bataille himself insists, that has always been the case: "I must emphasise that the female partner in eroticism" is "seen as the victim, the male as the sacrificer." Here, too, eroticism is tied into male individuation, it "is that within man which calls his being into question." But the annihilation of the female simultaneously serves a collective goal, for when "the victim dies . . . the spectator shares in what [the] death reveals."[22] Again, the split: the dead body/ the redemptive image. Much as in the military discourse, the *puta* dies but the Patria reunites a shattered population. So violence against women can miraculously do all at once—provide pleasure and identity for the male sacrificer-torturer and enlightenment for the spectator; the image of the bleeding Patria once more unites and uplifts the population, and, besides, the bitch is dead. Not only that, she likes it! The conquest is complete and empowers him beyond the actual rape. He has truly penetrated her deepest being. She now has no desire that is not merely the extension of his desire. The play does nothing to demythify the fatal linkage between male identity, male violence, and male pleasure. The female body (*puta/ women*) is simply the inert mass on which that violence and pleasure takes place; at the end of this production, her body was almost indistinguishable from the semiliquid, endlessly malleable mud of the pit. Furthermore, the play reproduces the violence it seemingly sets out to reflect because the spectator's pleasure in *Paso de dos* depends on and develops what Barbara Freedman calls the "coercive identification with a position of male antagonism toward women."[23] Yet, miraculously, violence against women/Woman does all—sadism and redemption for the price of one single ticket. The dead, naked body of Susana Evans lying in the mud fills the house; Galazzi's painful voice offstage allows spectators to share in what the death reveals.

The perversity of the depiction of female pleasure and desire, as illustrated in the first of these two tales, is even more noxious than the above suggests. It is not only that women are cast as victims to be exterminated for male pleasure, under the misnomer of *female* pleasure. The violence and repression inflicted on women is intrinsic in the very way we are forced to "be women," that is, pushed into a sex system in which, as Gayle Rubin points out, we "are robbed of libido and forced into masochistic eroticism" and obliged to act out obligatory sexuality and gender roles. "It is certainly plausible to argue," she maintains, "that the creation of 'femininity' in women in the course of socialization is an act of psychic brutality, and that it leaves in women an immense resentment of the suppression to which they were subjected."[24] The depiction of She's desire and erotic pleasure as masochistic reaffirms the notion that female sexuality develops from the experience of pain, envy, frustration, and humiliation. Hence, as the play suggests, women "like" brutal treatment, enjoy it, need it, respect the hand that beats us—the acceptance and even pleasure in pain affirms our femininity.

On the contrary, some might argue. I, not the play, am victimizing She by denying her pleasure, her delight in this mad tango, this pas de deux. Karen Newman has raised valid objections to Gayle Rubin's sex/gender paradigm that, by extension, might pose a relevant critique of my interpretation. The sex/gender paradigm, Newman states, considers only one of a whole network of power relations, which includes class, race, and sexuality. More pertinent to the issue here, however, is her argument that "[by] presuming that the object position is always undesirable, we overvalue a phallic model of sexual pleasure. . . . We foreclose for women and men the object position's potential for desire and pleasure."[25] In the context of *Paso de dos*, however, and against the explicit sociopolitical frame of the "dirty war," defending She's right to pleasure in pain only reiterates what the Argentine military, wife abusers and, ironically, Pavlovsky, are already saying: She likes it! It's all right to kill her because she enjoys the intensity.

The voice tells a different, but no less troubled, story.

The voice tells us that the play is about victimization, retribution, and the *indulto*. The junta leaders She accuses once more strut down the streets of Buenos Aires, proud of what they have done. "You want me to name you, don't you, that I tell everything, all the details. I know that would make you feel better, proud that everyone knows you touched me. You want to be a hero, like the rest, proud once again of what they've done, proud to be walking free, defiant, always on the look-out. Heroes once again" (V, 29). Yet while the play supposedly gives the woman a voice, it effectively silences her. There was no desire expressed or envisioned in the play that is not simply an extension, an echo, of his desire. He has the power to speak, to initiate language; she is condemned to repeat or take up what he had said. Insofar as the female voice in *Paso*, like the mythical Echo herself, cannot initiate dialogue, her only "power" comes from her refusal to speak, from her silence. But this is hardly *power*. Women have been refused *voz y voto* (voice and vote) throughout much of history. Although the play ostensibly grants her a voice and allows her a quasi-critical response to her predicament, in effect she is cast as an echo. The play thereby repeats the military's strategy of silencing its public. The population's responses, which censors make certain are insignificant, only serve to give the appearance of open dialogue. As Francine Masiello notes in a recent essay, the military dictatorship attempted "to reduce the interpretative activity of the population to an echo of the official word and abolish the contesting voices of those 'others' opposed to the government."[26] Under the political guise of denouncing victimization and the "dirty war," the play carries out a systematic assault on the feminine; the female body is destroyed through violence; the voice vanishes into a metaphor for victimization, hovering at the outer limits of the military discourse.

.   .   .   .   .

What does this silencing do to the critic, specifically the feminist critic, who is not content, as supposedly She is, to remain trapped in his fantasy? Clearly I was not the intended spectator, although Pavlovsky himself had generously allowed me into the packed house. I critiqued the play twice in Argentina; on August 6, 1990, at a public forum on authority and authoritarianism, in which Yusem was an invited speaker, and a couple of weeks later in a private interview with Pavlovsky. The "authority and authoritarianism" forum was designed to question the authoritarian structures still in place in Argentina and their effect on artists. Yusem was arguing that an artist could be conscious of those structures and could challenge them. She, an avowed leftist like Pavlovsky, cited *Paso de dos* as an illustration of this dismantling. When I suggested to Yusem that the performance reproduced rather than dismantled the military's authoritarian discourse, she immediately ordered me to be silent. She refused to speak to me, except to point out that I was not Argentine, I had not lived in Argentina during the "dirty war," I had not experienced torture and therefore knew nothing about it and should keep quiet. In short, I was dismissed as a "Yanqui (imperialist) feminist." The fact that my "identity" and alliances as a Canadian/Mexican woman living and working in the United States were more complicated than that was beside the point. Latin Americans have always been sensitive to others' lack of knowledge about what goes on in Latin America and, thus, their inability to approach and interpret Latin American "culture" in its broadest sense. Rightly so; the politics of interpretation are loaded. Here, however, the insider/outsider tension was being exploited in order to shut off debate and preclude the possibility of another kind of coalition politics. Alliances can be established between people with significant "differences" to achieve similar ends; those coalitions can work along the lines of race, class, gender, sexual orientation, and religion, to name only some possibilities. National identity is not the only basis for coalition—as Argentina's internal strife makes clear. So the problem was not only that I was not from Argentina; I did not participate in the fantasy of masculinity, and that was profoundly disturbing for the female director who did. She had to reject me on the basis of those things that differentiate us (national identity and location) in order to obscure our shared position as women in relation to repressive patriarchal societies. She did not seem aware of the irony, in her position as director, of telling an audience member that she could not understand the play because she had not personally lived through the experience represented. The implications of that idea to notions of mimesis, identification, empathy, "A-effect" (alienation effect) and all the other traditional theatrical concepts are irrelevant here (as they were there). What I did point out, however, was that her reaction was also authoritarian. Moreover, it echoed an utterance that an infamous military leader had made just the day before in a major newspaper, *Página 12*: Coronel Mohamed Seineldín, a *carapintada* (painted face) of the ultra-Right, had said on August 5: "What I can't tolerate is that some foreign general, loaded down with medals, comes here telling me what to do. If he's a foreigner, then he has to behave the way my father did when he first came to this country: keep silent, work and listen."[27]

Pavlovsky, having heard about the exchange, met me at his office with icy formality and a stack of newpaper clippings in which he had underlined references to the woman's victory. She wins! he kept reminding me. She likes it! Look, the papers themselves say so! Both Pavlovsky and Yusem (in the separate encounters) had insisted that the play is historically "true." It reflects reality. A *montonero* (left-wing opposition) woman had actually fallen in love with her torturer. What about the thirty thousand cases in which that wasn't true, I asked? Is this a true representation of a torturer/victim relationship? And why, out of thirty thousand stories, do you choose to represent that one? Isn't that already suspect? Pavlovsky insisted that, yes, the play is urgent and political insofar as it addresses the imminent *indulto*. However, he added, he doesn't write political pamphlets for the theatre; a work of art has its own laws and logic that don't necessarily constitute political statements. (There is a difference, he reminded me, between fiction and reality.) And besides, how could this play be offensive to women? She "wins."

The strategy to silence me in my capacity as spectator/critic was two-fold: one explicit, one far more subtle. Both Pavlovsky and Yusem were explicitly reproaching me because I was not content to echo the concerns as they had been presented to me; in both cases, I was initiating, not repeating, speech. I was reminded of Tania Modleski's warning to feminist critics who give up the struggle to acquire the power of interpretation, thereby "unwittingly echo[ing] Echo's words by cautioning us against the exercise of a critical will to power."[28] My role as critic, much like the audience's role as spectator, was to willingly suspend my disbelief. I, too, had to like it. And that, in a nutshell, is the role the military had assigned its population. More difficult to overcome, however, is what I perceive as the trap laid out for those who would critique such representations of violence. Am I not opening myself to the very charges I bring against Pavlovsky? Can I help but reproduce the violence against women by describing the performance? Is silence, as in the play, the truly heroic response? Again, I feel I have to speak back to the performance, even at the risk of falling into the trap. Rather than add to the violence, my intention is to illuminate that which must be suppressed or repressed—her pain and her extermination—in the performance/text/master narrative in order for the triumphalist reading to work.

Paso de dos, like the military's representation of its project, wants everyone to participate in the fantasy of reciprocal desire. It reproduces and eroticizes the annihilation of women under the guise of historical veracity, political urgency, and aesthetic necessity. Moreover, it limits the possibility of response. Insofar as Pavlovsky and Yusem are leftists, those who oppose the military in Argentina must, theoretically at least, feel aligned with their views to some extent. The problem, of course, is that the particular discourse of potency being enacted here transcends even extreme political differences. The contradiction between Pavlovsky's politics and his practice, in fact, blurs all distinctions between Left and Right. These authoritarian structures go far deeper than any such political pronouncements. The notions of masculinity that he reenacts result in the splitting of the feminine and have historically been proved fatal to women. While he is obviously antimilitary, he cannot help but repeat their moves. His great show of virility, onstage and off, is predicated on the silencing of the female. Evans, too, likes being battered around the stage, it "relaxes" her.[29] Women get killed because of these fantasies in which the male's search for identity, empowerment, and intensity are born out of her splitting and annihilation, and not just women in the hands of torturers during periods of civil strife. The leading cause of death for women of childbearing age today in Argentina is wife abuse, another example of *hombría a golpes* (virility by blows; see Graciela B. Ferreira's *La mujer maltratada* [The mistreated woman, 1989]). The violent husband too claims that she "likes" it. *Paso de dos* implicitly reaffirms the macho's position on rape through its depiction of the woman's body/voice as split—she may say no, but her body wants it, asks for it. Her body dies but her feminine spirit survives.

To conclude: The problem with this play is not (or not only) that it is "violent," not even necessarily that it represents violence against women. Given the social environment in which women live, it would be bizarre if theatre did not deal with violence directed at them. But there are playwrights in Argentina and elsewhere (Griselda Gambaro, for example) who provide an insight into misogyny without mystifying it. What is particularly troublesome about *Paso de dos* is that it reveals and reaffirms the gendered structure of representation itself—onstage and off. Representations are not innocent, transparent, or true; they do not simply "reflect" reality. They help constitute it. Theatre, as one system of representations, participates in the larger, cultural network—society as a complex system of representations. And Pavlovsky is only saying what the military have been saying all along: the military "man" creates himself through the annihilation of woman. This spectacle of brutalization, moreover, perpetuates the traditional power relation: the male agent (author/actor) exposes himself to his (male) audience. The woman's body is merely the object of exchange, the common ground that allows the males to position themselves—agents/clients, author/audience, military/population—all united by the bleeding woman. The phallus continues to command social respect by filling all those empty voids. So where is this fine line between fiction and reality, between author and authority? And how can I, even if I wanted to, obey the role assigned to me in this structure and keep silent?

NOTES

1. Videla, Massera, Agosti, "Proceso de reorganización nacional" and "Estatuto para el proceso de reorganización nacional," both of March 24, 1976, in Oscar Troncoso's collection of documents, *El proceso de reorganización*

nacional: Cronología y documentacíon, vol. 1 (henceforth T) (Buenos Aires: Centro Editor de América Latina, 1984), p. 112. Videla announced that the military takeover was a result not of "vocation" but of the necessity of "filling the void of power" ("vacío de poder"). Rodolfo H. Terragno (a reporter and military apologist), in *Revista Cuestionario* of June 1976, stated that "the men of arms were convinced that the working classes in the country were completely undisciplined and they proposed to put an end to this state of affairs" (T, 137). All translations from Spanish, unless otherwise noted, are my own.

2. Although there is no doubt that María Estela Martínez de Perón's government was corrupt, the description of her government as *diseased* is interesting; her rottenness has resulted in "the irreparable loss of the feeling of greatness and faith" (T, 107).

3. While I will focus only on the proclamations of March 24 here, the same images were constantly reiterated by the military and their representatives on other occasions. As Minister of Foreign Affairs César Augusto Guzzetti diagnosed, "the social body is contaminated by a disease that gnaws at its entrails" (T, 141). In January 1977, Jorge L. García Venturini described the enemy as hidden, hypocritical and subtle: "it holds on to the skirts of human rights all the while involved in the utmost negation of those rights. . . . With this pathetic baggage, the enemy advances toward the total conquest of the globe. . . . Weakness, lack of conviction, guilt-ridden and guilty complacency, a certain apathy or fatalism, these are some of the conditions that make it possible for the enemy to gain ground in this Third World War" (Andres Avellaneda, *Censura, autoritarismo y cultura: Argentina, 1960–1983* [Buenos Aires: Biblioteca Politica Argentina, 1986], 2:145).

4. This polarization of women into two extreme positions is interesting to note, especially in the light of Cooke and Woollacott's introductory remarks that some contributors "argue that war holds no lasting, and certainly no positive, changes for women," while others "contend that the fluidity of war allows for linguistic and social renegotiations." In Argentina, one can observe both the restrictive and liberating forces that war, here an undeclared civil war, brings forth. On the one hand, the situation for women during this period is even more restrictive than usual for Latin American women. The crisis collapses the semiotic quadrangle drawn up by Jean Franco in "Beyond Ethnocentrism: Gender, Power, and the Third World Intelligentsia," in *Marxism and the Interpretation of Culture*, ed. Cary Nelson and Lawrence Grossberg (Urbana: University of Illinois Press, 1988), p. 507. Women in Latin America, are seen as occupying four possible positions, all in relation to the phallus:

mother	virgin
	(nun, spinster)
phallus	
not virgin	mother
not mother (whore)	virgin (Mary)

In Argentina during the "dirty war," however, the woman is further limited, now to two, rather than four, possible positions. She is either the nonexistent, pure, sacred virgin mother (Patria) or the whore/mother (previously viewed as incompatible in Latin America, where the mother was considered almost sacred). The

Mothers of the Plaza de Mayo were discredited by the military as being mothers of subversives, bastards, "schizophrenic delinquents without a Motherland" (T, 59). The Patria, however, still represents the castrated woman, defined by Gayle Rubin as "the 'phallic mother,' e.g., she is believed to possess the phallus. The oedipal-inducing information is that the mother does not possess the phallus. In other words, the crisis is precipitated by the 'castration' of the mother, by the recognition that the phallus only passes through her, but does not settle on her. The 'phallus' must pass through her, since the relationship of a male to every other male is defined through a woman" (Gayle Rubin, "The Traffic in Women: Notes on the 'Political Economy' of Sex," in *Toward an Anthropology of Women*, ed. Rayna R. Reiter [New York: Monthly Review Press, 1975], p. 192n). The liberating possibility that came about through the "dirty war" was the politicization of the "Mothers" movement, previously held to be a private and social (rather than political) role. The Mothers, without a question, contributed to the downfall of the military. They succeeded because they were women, because they could mobilize in ways and in spaces that were closed, or too dangerous, for men. The men stayed home and had the women's dinners waiting for them after the rallies, demonstrations, and clandestine meetings; see Alejandro Diago, *Hebe Bonafini: Memoria y esperanza* (Buenos Aires: Ediciones Dialectica, 1988), p. 74. Still, it remains questionable to what degree these changes in gender relations produced lasting change in postmilitary Argentina. One could argue that by politicizing motherhood exclusively, the movement in fact shut off other positions of legitimacy to Latin American women.

5. Laura Mulvey, "Visual Pleasure and Narrative Cinema," *Screen* 16, no. 3 (Autumn 1975): 6–18.

6. This government, the junta proclaimed, "will be imbued with a profound national spirit and will only respond to the most sacred interests of the Nation and her inhabitants. . . . In this new stage there is room for everyone in the struggle. The task is arduous and urgent. It is not without sacrifices, but one embarks with the absolute knowledge that the examples will come from above downwards. . . . The process will be executed with absolute firmness and vocation" (T, 108). Evelyn Fox Keller's observations on visibility and power in "Making Gender Visible in the Pursuit of Nature's Secrets" (in de Lauretis's *Feminist Studies/ Critical Studies* [Bloomington: Indiana University Press, 1986]) are illuminating in regard to this gendered struggle for power and representation: "the invisibility of nature's interiority, like the invisibility of women's interiority, is threatening precisely because it threatens the balance of power between man and nature, and between men and women" (74). Military power in Argentina, much like the modern science she examines, claims to have the capability of making the invisible visible, the laws of nature "knowable, that is to say, visible to the mind's eye" (74). Military power, like scientific power, tries to promote the myth of openness and truth: "the authority of modern science is simultaneously everywhere and nowhere; on the one hand, it is manifest, self-evident, the arch-enemy of secrets and secrecy, and on the other, anonymous, uninterpretable, and unidentifiable" (74).

7. Marguerite Feitlowitz, "A Dance of Death: Pavlovsky's *Paso de dos*," *Drama Review* 35, no. 2 (Summer 1991): 60.

8. Eduardo Pavlovsky, *Voces* (hereafter V) (Buenos Aires, Ediciones Busqueda, 1989). All translations from the text are my own. Dependence on Woman, as in Pavlovsky's play, must be compensated for by absolute control of and brutality toward real women. I will differentiate between woman and women, following Teresa de Lauretis's distinction between the two: "woman, the other-from-man (nature and Mother, site of sexuality and masculine desire, sign and object of men's social exchange)" as opposed to women, "real historical beings who cannot yet be defined outside of those discursive formations, but whose material existence is nonetheless certain" (*Alice Doesn't: Feminism, Semiotics, Cinema* [Bloomington: Indiana University Press, 1984], p. 5). Dependence on Woman (Patria) is acceptable and even desirable, but that safe dependency on an ethereal image justifies the annihilation of her opposite—flesh-and-blood women. As Jessica Benjamin notes in "A Desire of One's Own," male autonomy in patriarchy is dependent on the subordination of women: "The intention is not to do without her but to make sure that her alien otherness is either assimilated or controlled, that her own subjectivity nowhere asserts itself in a way that could make his dependency upon her a conscious insult to his sense of freedom" (in de Lauretis, *Feminist Studies/Critical Studies*, p. 80).

9. Robert J. Stoller, *Perversion: The Erotic Form of Hatred* (New York: Pantheon Books, 1975), p. 4.

10. Klaus Theweleit, *Male Fantasies* (Minneapolis: University of Minnesota Press, 1989), 2:147.

11. Ibid., p. 197.

12. Teresa de Lauretis, *Technologies of Gender: Essays on Theory, Film and Fiction* (Bloomington: University of Indiana Press, 1987), p. 43.

13. *Nunca Más: The Report of the Argentine National Commission on the Disappeared*, intro. Ronald Dworkin (New York: Farrar Straus Giroux, 1986).

14. Susanne Kappeler, *The Pornography of Representation* (Minneapolis: University of Minnesota Press, 1986), p. 10.

15. Horacio Verbitsky, *Página 12*, April 29, 1990.

16. Roberto M. Herrscher, "The Never Never Land," *Buenos Aires Herald*, May 28, 1990.

17. In "Torturadores y heroes," interview with Pavlovsky by Adriana Bruno, *Página 12*, April 29, 1990.

18. For Freud sadism and masochism become perversions only in extreme cases, and they generally appear in males and females respectively: "The sexuality of most male human beings contains an element of *aggressiveness*—a desire to subjugate; the biological significance of it seems to lie in the need for overcoming the resistance of the sexual object by means other than the process of wooing. . . . The term masochism comprises any passive attitude towards sexual life and the sexual object." And although at this point Freud stressed that sadism and masochism usually appeared in the same individual, he later developed a theory of erotogenic masochism that included feminine and moral masochism (Sigmund Freud, *Three Essays on the Theory of Sexuality*, trans. and ed. James Strachey [New York: Avon, 1962], p. 48, Freud's emphasis, and n.).

19. Patrice Pavis, *Languages of the Stage: Essays in the Semiology of the Theatre* (New York: Performing Arts Journal Publications, 1982), p. 45.

20. Sue-Ellen Case, ed., *Performing Feminisms: Feminist Critical Theory and Theatre* (Baltimore: Johns Hopkins University Press, 1990); Elin Diamond, "Brechtian Theory/Feminist Theory: Toward a Gestic Feminist Criticism," *Drama Review* 32, no. 1 (Spring 1988): 82–94; Jill Dolan, *The Feminist Spectator as Critic*, vol. 52 of *Theatre and Dramatic Studies*, ed. Oscar G. Brockett (Ann Arbor, Mich.: UMI Research Press, 1988); and Deborah R. Geis, "Wordscapes of the Body: Performative Language as Gestus in Maria Irene Fornes' Plays," *Theatre Journal* 42, no. 3 (October 1990): 292.

21. See Francine Masiello's "Cuerpo/Presencia: Mujer y estado social en la narrativa argentina durante el proceso militar" in *Nuevo texto crítico* for further discussion of the military's "proyecto monolítico" (vol. 4, ed. Mary Louise Pratt and Marta Morello Frosch [Stanford, Calif.: Department of Spanish and Portuguese, Stanford University, 1989], p. 155).

22. Georges Bataille, *Eroticism: Death and Sensuality* (San Francisco: City Lights), pp. 11, 18, 29, 22.

23. Barbara Freedman, "Frame-Up: Feminism Psychoanalysis, Theatre," in Case, *Performing Feminisms*, p. 59.

24. Rubin, "Traffic in Women," pp. 197, 196.

25. Karen Newman, "Directing Traffic: Subjects, Objects, and the Politics of Exchange," *Differences* 2, no. 2 (Summer 1990): 51.

26. Francine Masiello, *Nuevo texto crítico*, p. 155.

27. *Página 12* (Buenos Aires), August 5, 1990, p. 7.

28. Tania Modleski, "Feminism and the Power of Interpretation" in de Lauretis, *Feminist Studies/Critical Studies*, p. 127.

29. See Marguerite Feitlowitz's interview with Pavlovsky and Evans in "A Dance of Death."

PART II
WAR MYTHOPOEIA

Chapter 3

THE THRESHOLD OF THRILL: LIFE STORIES

IN THE SKIES OVER SOUTHEAST ASIA

STANLEY D. ROSENBERG

TWO DECADES after the United States' air superiority in the Pacific brought World War II to a rapid close, we were once again involved in air combat in Asia. A similar period elapsed between the end of the last major air offensive in Vietnam in 1973 and the commencement of Operation Desert Storm in the Middle East. These four decades have seen enormous changes in both the technology and the psychology, individual and collective, of air warfare. In this chapter, I will present some results from an ongoing longitudinal study of Vietnam-era veterans. My particular focus will be on the oral histories of combat pilots, particularly their representations of their war experience. These "war stories" are a central part of the men's attempts to construct a narrative identity: a workable conception of self. While combat pilots are only a very small minority of all service veterans, their impact, in terms of the outcome of modern war, is extraordinarily disproportionate. Moreover, their experiences seem paradigmatic of how warfare has changed, especially in the second half of the twentieth century. Their construction of that experience, a process which is clearly part of a shared language game, is in turn paradigmatic of a particular concept of masculinity, one which these pilots continued to live even while being uneasy with its meaning and its costs. In recounting their experiences in Southeast Asia, the pilots tell us much about how they were, collectively and individually, enabled to do that which seems quite inconceivable.

To understand these life-story narratives, which reflect the pilots' struggles to live with and integrate the complex experiences of excitement, self-affirmation, fear, horror, guilt, avoidance, and denial during the war, I will juxtapose the war stories of the Vietnam pilots with parallel texts from World War II, and will allude to the evolution of this genre as manifest in Desert Storm. This comparison underlines not only the defensive distortions that permit the pilots to cope and to perform, but also the intimate relationship between the construction of a certain type of masculinity, which the pilots codify through their concept of the "warrior," and the conduct of high-technology air warfare. As the weapons systems' technology evolved from World War II to Vietnam, it facilitated the construction of this version of the self. Indeed a distinctive feature of the warrior identity, as evolved in the pilots' culture by the late 1960s, was a linguistic fusion between the self and the technology employed. Not only was the technology anthropomorphized in their discourse, but these men identified with and adopted the qualities of their aircraft and weaponry. At the same time, the application of this technology for purposes of mass destruction (including the destruction of noncombatants and their civilization) was dependent on the ideology and identity these pilots came to adopt and to teach one another.

These characteristics of the subculture of air warfare have continued, apparently, to escalate. The war against Iraq was, of course, primarily represented in the American media as an air war. As thousands of sorties per day were flown by allied pilots over Iraq and Kuwait, we were allowed to listen in to a specialized, privileged discourse: the restricted code utilized by the highly trained, highly skilled young air force, marine, and navy fighter pilots. *People* magazine, along with nightly network broadcasts and daily newspapers, permitted us to hear the metaphoric constructs these men employed to frame (or perhaps to obscure) the nature of their activity. *People* quotes a marine harrier pilot (call name "Disco") describing his experiences in dropping three thousand pounds of cluster bombs on a target near the Saudi-Kuwaiti border: "You're coming down the pike, hauling the mail . . . and you're staring at that bad boy, and you roll in and hit the pickle and get outta Dodge."[1] Much of this discourse was reminiscent of an earlier discourse, now almost two decades old. *Time* magazine spoke casually of the U.S. Air Force "Wild Weasel" F4 as if this endearing, plucky electronics weapons system were an old friend fondly remembered from Southeast Asia.[2] The same black humor, swagger, and sense of slightly reluctant, "aw shucks" heroism was once again associated with the pilots' dangerous efforts to evade, suppress, and destroy enemy surface-to-air missiles.

This animation and anthropomorphizing of high technology aircraft and weapons systems, the condensation of highly complex and destructive acts into acronyms which belie and sidestep their meaning, appear to be part of an evolving language game by which we manage the anxiety and guilt associated with the employment of modern air power. The black humor tone of such terms as "collateral damage," "incontinent ordinance" (bombs and artillery shells that fall off target and hit civilians), and "area denial weapons" (cluster bombs)[3] suggest collective psychological mechanisms for performing and accepting potentially horrifying acts, mechanisms of derealization, suppression, and reversal of affect and denial. While these mechanisms may be an inherent part of all warfare, they seem to have become a particularly prominent component of military lexicon since Vietnam, and to be especially associated with air warfare. Air war, only really a prominent part of mass war for the last fifty years, still seems to excite and strain our consciousness in many ways, including its singular man/machine (or, even more recently, woman/machine) relationship; that is, "a greater proportion of machinery to men than any other weapon of warfare"[4] and a more massive and more remote capacity for destruction of life. In Southeast Asia, where U.S. forces engaged in almost continual air war for over a decade, a rich lexicon for communicating about the fearful and the nearly unthinkable was created. Since capture was the most conscious fear of American pilots, Hoa Lo Prison became the "Hanoi Hilton," its receiving center the "Heartbreak Hotel." The most high technology weapons systems, such as television guided air-to-surface bombs, were given the most folksy names like "walleye."

Desert Storm can thus trace its linguistic roots to operations Flaming Dart, Rolling Thunder, Linebacker I, and Linebacker II. These were the names given to the major phases of the U.S. air campaign against North Vietnam. Each of these metaphors embodies a set of claims to a collective identity, implies a moral justification for collective action, and simultaneously obscures or transforms the nature of the actions being performed. Thus American football, which symbolizes and embodies classic hand-to-hand combat as a controlled "game," ironically becomes one root metaphor for understanding actual air combat, the linebacker being the most mobile and most ferocious defender. As we will see, this combat-as-game metaphor has profound implications for both the experiences and actions of the combat pilots. Flaming Dart evokes quite different connotations and justifications for problematic acts: connotations of righteous retribution, as if by an Old Testament deity. Indeed, this latter campaign was a plan for retaliatory air strikes against North Vietnam for what were defined as heinous acts of aggression by the Viet Cong (e.g., a Christmas Eve attack on U.S. officers' quarters in Saigon). Like Desert Storm, Rolling Thunder is evocative of magisterial power, of manly endeavor, and of righteous wrath. At the same time, these names avoid the implication of purposive killing as, for example, was contained in the names given some forty years ago to the air campaigns against North Korea: Strangle I and Strangle II. Such names as Rolling Thunder and Desert Storm also depersonalize war, as if it were conducted by forces of nature rather than by individual human beings.

The purpose of this chapter is to describe, and attempt to understand, the life-story narratives of a group of fliers who, two decades ago, participated in the air war in Southeast Asia. I am particularly interested in how the language which frames their experience reveals the conflicts, desires, and psychological defenses associated with being the human instruments of modern strategic and tactical air warfare. This experience appears to be inextricably bound up with the evolving technology of war—the capabilities of the aircraft itself, including the destructive capacity of its weapons systems—and the evolving culture of air combat in the American military. Although the helicopter played a very large and even unique role in Southeast Asia, my focus here will be on fixed-wing aircraft pilots who served both in the air force and navy. These men were part of a larger study of adult development and personal narrative being conducted at Dartmouth Medical School. This project is examining the life experiences of Dartmouth College graduates of 1967 and 1968. We have gathered approximately two hundred such oral histories over the last several years. Half of these represent stories of men who experienced combat in Southeast Asia, including a substantial number who served as naval or air force fighter or attack aircraft pilots, primarily in single-seat aircraft.

These men have filled out questionnaires about that period of their lives, and about their current situation. Extensive data on psychological adjustment, academic performance, and personal style of these men and some six hundred of their classmates prior to and during their college careers have also been collected. While this background data is useful in "objectively" locating those interviewed in the universe of their peers, the texts I will focus on in this chapter were elicited in lengthy (three to four hours), open-ended interviews conducted with these men in many parts of the country and the world. In each interview, the person is invited to engage in a narrative reconstruction of his life which is begun by focusing on "the sixties" as a historical moment of choice and emergence. These oral histories can be understood as "texts of identity,"[5] whereby the creation, justification, and maintenance of self is grounded in a discourse. Given the demand for narrative coherence in such texts, they typically move forward and backward in time, looking at family and childhood experiences, personal relationships, school, the social issues of the era, the Vietnam War and its aftermath as context and force in the forging of personal identity.

Understanding these narratives requires several types of comparison. That is, the unique quality of the pilots' life stories can be appreciated only by comparing them with the oral histories of other types of veterans (combat and noncombat) as well as with parallel texts from airmen from earlier conflicts, particularly World War II.

I will argue that the commonalities in their narratives reflect their shared participation in a very specialized subculture, which they allude to as a "fraternity," that is, a symbolic order. This system functioned as a "collective defense," by structuring their discourse and by establishing the terms by which texts of identity could be constructed. Both the group culture and the men's efforts at narrative self-construction can be seen as attempts to ward off unbearable anxiety, both instinctual and traumatic in origin. As with all neurotic structures, the collective defense involved such mechanisms as splitting, denial, projection, compartmentalization, and reversal of affect. These processes of distortion and self-alienation permitted the participants to live with death (their own potential death, their comrades' deaths, the deaths of the victims of their bombs, cannon, and napalm) as if death were not real. This lent their enterprise the quality of a dream, a ritual, or a game: as if it were time out of time. Their subsequent lives—as seen in their need to construct later chapters of autobiography—are thus often fraught with profound tensions. The life of being a warrior/god in Southeast Asia is the central defining moment in their construction of self, but is simultaneously a potentially shameful moment filled with meanings that must continue to be repressed and distorted if a viable self is to be maintained.

The concept of a collective defense was perhaps most fully explicated by Elliot Jaques. Studying the group culture of modern industrial enterprises, he argues that "one of the primary cohesive elements binding individuals into institutionalized human association is that of defense against psychotic anxiety. In this sense individuals may be thought of as externalizing those impulses and internal objects that would otherwise give rise to psychotic anxiety, and pooling them into the life of the social institutions in which they associate."[6]

Once anxiety has been thus collectivized, relationships between people are divided into their formal, consciously agreed upon components, such as chain of command; and a second, underground level, that of "the fantasy form and content, which are unconsciously avoided and denied."[7] At this second level, we find multiple distortions of meaning and desire such as denial, negation, projection, and derealization. These processes are made all the more potent because of their collective nature. Each person can draw support from the group culture in defensive efforts to relabel experience, efforts that are in fact anticipated and encouraged by collective tropes. Most particularly, I am interested in examining how the group culture enables combat pilots to cope with the extraordinary violence of their roles and how they come to incorporate the experience into their texts of identity. If much of the personal and moral framing of the combat pilot's experience derives from the military subculture in which he functions, it is important to understand the beliefs, goals, values, and ethical codes which characterize that subculture.

In Southeast Asia, as in the recent Middle East conflict, the United States–led forces almost immediately established air superiority. In both conflicts, the United States sought to exploit this advantage in order first to cripple and then to bludgeon the enemy into submission. This represents, of course, the strategic approach to utilizing air power that developed after World War I. Despite the innocuous role played by the airplane in that conflict, future World War II air commanders, such as generals Curtis Lemay, Frank Andrews, and Carl Spatz, were educated by proponents of strategic bombing in the interwar years. At the Air Corps Tactical School (ACTS) established at Maxwell Field, air power was advocated as a means to demolish the enemy's war-making potential, by obliterating not only its capability but its will to fight. From the very beginning of its articulation, this philosophy of air power was riddled with euphemisms and ambiguity in that it appeared to espouse, or at least accept, the terrorization and killing of civilian populations without making this fully explicit. Thus, at a lecture at ACTS in 1936, it was observed that "a nation's attacking air force would be at liberty to proceed directly to the ultimate aim of war: overthrow of the enemy's will to resist through the destruction of those vital elements upon which modern social life is dependent."[8] While this doctrine stressed disruption of transportation, steel, iron ore, and power facilities as the vital elements to be attacked, its first real use against Germany in World War II made clear that attacks on concentrated civilian populations were seen as quite worthwhile. Thus, at the Casablanca Conference it was announced that the Combined Bomber Offensive would not only attempt to destroy the German power sources and transportation and air defense systems, but that British night bombing air raids were "to have a maximum effect on the morale of industrial workers."[9] It would appear that even the architects of this strategy were initially uncertain of its limits, limits which seemed to expand as the conflict evolved. Thus, after first achieving clear air superiority and making the destruction of oil reserves the highest priority of the air war, a new directive was issued in late January 1945, selecting as targets cities in eastern Germany, "where heavy attack will cause great confusion in civilian evacuations from the east and hamper reinforcements." Prior to the February 3 attack on Berlin, Lieutenant General James Doolittle, Eighth Air Force commander, seemed somewhat uncertain of or incredulous about this mandate. He wired General Spatz asking, "Is Berlin still open to air attack? Do you want priority oil targets hit in preference to Berlin if they definitely become visual? Do you want center city in Berlin hit or definitely military targets such as Spandau on the western outskirts?"[10] Spatz's terse reply ameliorated the earlier ambiguity: "hit oil if visual assured; otherwise, Berlin—center of city."[11] Doolittle's pilots, hampered by cloud cover, attacked their secondary targets: downtown government buildings in close proximity to civilian populations. In this raid, twenty-five thousand people were killed. The air assault on Dresden ten days later killed at least thirty-five thousand civilians, indicating how far the aesthetics of air war had moved since 1943, when

General Eaker had declared, "We must never allow the record of this war to convict us of throwing the strategic bomber at the man in the street."[12]

If the use of massive air power was novel to the generals and Allied High Command, it was even more novel to the young pilots who executed their strategy. As the first group of men called upon to employ this technology of mass destruction, they could not be guided by a well-articulated language or culture in their efforts to cope with the experience. Only in 1941 were the Army Air Forces created in place of the more subservient Army Air Corps, and its identity and functions more fully articulated. Both the military and the public were clearly ambivalent about the use of air power, particularly strategic bombing. On the one hand, there was hope that massive bombing might represent the fastest, least costly way to end the conflict. On the other, there was a growing repugnance with the German blitz against England. Edward R. Murrow's radio broadcasts from England conveyed the message that "air war against England, like that waged earlier against Spain and China, had proved its futility as well as its barbarism."[13] Despite this ambivalence, *Life* magazine declared its satisfaction in August 1941 that the British bombing of Germany "was enough to lift the hearts of all free peoples," and indicated pleasure that the British "were dishing it out as well as taking it."[14]

Given the ethical, institutional, and personal novelty of this first great air war, the reactions of the men engaged in it may give us a rather undisguised view of its individual, human dimension. Both the medical and anecdotal literature on World War II suggests that airmen experienced a high degree of stress and fear, and that the morale of fliers was a continual problem throughout the war. For example, the high incidence of emotional casualties among fliers in the early years of the air campaign against Germany led to a specific study of the problem, and the institution, in the spring of 1943, of a definite tour of duty. This limited fliers to twenty-five combat missions,[15] despite an acute shortage of qualified aviators. Indeed, the general belief in the very unique stressors associated with air combat led to the "discovery" of a specific psychological reaction known as "flying fatigue" (to be contrasted with the more generic "combat fatigue" or "operational exhaustion").[16] While the boundaries of this new disorder remained somewhat vague, it was seen as remarkably limited to the combat situation itself, presenting symptomatically as a sort of circumscribed "cockpit phobia." In contrast to the combat fatigue seen in other services, it was noted that "many of these men had few bodily symptoms of anxiety and needed little in the way of treatment other than removal from flying."[17] Indeed, once removed from the cockpit, a number of these aviators performed well enough to receive rapid promotion. Such outcomes were seen as politically intolerable, and in late 1943 the air force command required a change in psychiatric nomenclature. Pilots afraid to fly could either be classified medically as cases of "operational exhaustion" (those thought to have become truly neurotically disabled) or administratively as cases of "lack of moral fiber." It is clear from these reports that American World War II aviators were very much afraid of the hazards of their mission, and suffered from symptoms of fear. It is much less clear to what degree they experienced, as a group, particular guilt over the mass damage caused by their bombs.

In a document rather parallel to the oral histories of the Vietnam-era pilots, Robert Heussler has written a personal history of his enlistment and experience in the "Dartmouth Squadron."[18] Inspired by a recent graduate's buzzing of the campus in a P40 fighter, forty-five students petitioned the Army Air Corps in 1942 for enlistment as aviators. The army responded positively, and they planned to report to Maxwell Field, Alabama, in January 1943. Of the original group, a number "washed out" for physical or other reasons, and twelve ultimately received their wings together as multiengine pilots. Several went on to become fighter pilots; more—including the author—were assigned to heavy bombers. Of this group, two were killed during the war and seven shot down; six of these became prisoners of war. Although Heussler attempted to elicit reminiscences from all surviving members of the group, he relies most heavily on recounting his own experiences as a bomber pilot in the 303d Heavy Bombardment Group of the Eighth Air Force, nicknamed "Hell's Angels." Heussler's narrative is striking in a number of ways, including its emphasis on the modes of titillation and release he recalls reluctantly engaging in as a nineteen-year-old boy. As we shall see, these standard World War II narratives of drinking and womanizing as male rites of passage all but disappear in the war stories of the Vietnam-era pilots. Male identity claims shift, in the more recent conflict, to the narrower domains of technical proficiency, a warrior disposition, and ability to bond with the male fraternity of fliers. On leave in Texas, en route to his first assignment as a B17 copilot, he detours with two of the other Dartmouth recruits to Juarez, Mexico.

> Mexican champagne was two dollars a bottle. With second lieutenant's pay burning holes in our pockets we started drinking right away and kicked back two bottles each in about an hour and a half. On the way back to the border the taxi driver had a good idea. Would we like to see a "cho." . . . The cho consisted of two overstuffed teenagers, naked as jay birds, one of them fitted out with appropriate male equipment, having at each other in a dingy motel room without benefit of music or theatrical lighting. Would we like to join them? Hain was vaguely interested, or anyhow thought he ought to say he was; Heape was marvelously drunk; and I was wondering if I could keep my breakfast down. We went back to town, drank more champagne and missed the train by an hour. The next morning we were in Pyote, humble and hungover, where we

were carpetted by a captain who seemed to be having trouble keeping his face straight. . . . So began our careers as officers and gentlemen.[19]

In a similar vein, Heussler seems every bit the rakish young daredevil aviator as he recounts flying his brand new B17 from Kearney, Nebraska, on his way to England.

We took off in the dark and were over East Aurora by late morning. The place lay under a thick blanket of snow, looking smaller than it should have, all of its streets embraceable in a single glance, though they had taken long hours to walk and bike through only a few years before. I got down to tree-top level in a series of slow, gliding sweeps around the edges of the village and then made a pass directly over my house, where I saw my mother struggling out through the snow on the roof of the porch off my older brother's bedroom. Buzzing the house once more I turned and flew down the main street from west to east, then wagged the wings in farewell and handed the controls over to our rather nervous first pilot, who climbed on course for his hometown two hundred miles farther on. My mother later wrote to tell me that the school superintendent had made an announcement on the PA system, identifying the pilot of the bomber that had just flown over. My youngest brother, ten years old at the time, was in the school and got his share of attention for an act that was against civil and military regulations. The crew seemed to enjoy it. As we left East Aurora our wise guy ball gunner, Paul Pesetsky, asked me on the intercom, "Who was that broad waving from the roof?"[20]

The narrative begins to shift in tone, however, after Heussler's assignment to his combat wing in Huntingdonshire. He comments on the airline pilots' lament that "their work is nine tenths boredom and one tenth terror" remarking that "1944 was like that for us, only I think most of us would have changed the percentages a good deal."[21] Heussler describes his time between missions as divided between omnivorous reading in his bed, some exercise, and efforts to trade his whiskey and cigarette coupons for candy (for which he apparently had an inordinate craving at this time.) One gets the impression that, confronting the reality of air combat, he quickly went from being that cocky pilot who buzzed East Aurora, New York, to a rather frightened, unhappy boy:

Most of the time when we were not flying we shivered in the barracks during a winter that was one of England's coldest. . . . The building was drafty, dirty and full of an unspoken tension that never relaxed and that got regular feeding when orderlies came to collect the belongings of men who had not returned from missions.[22]

Indeed, Heussler is quite candid in describing his fear during a bombing run over Lorraine. Encountering heavy flak, he observes other B17s blowing up all around him, a sight that "froze the blood." Heussler recalls that "my gut was in a knot, ice in my armpits."[23] While he is thus cognizant of the danger around him, and of his own fear, Heussler also exhibits a sort of motivated obliviousness that may reflect a broader shift in how strategic or massive bombing was rationalized. As Sherry has observed, "Piecemeal evolution of air war produced relief that reality was less terrifying than the nightmare and gave Americans time to absorb and accept this new descent into barbarism." At the same time, "American disapproval of Fascist bombings manifested itself in a desire for revenge, rather than a desire to abolish bombing."[24] For whatever combination of reasons, Heussler is able to remark offhandedly about "dumping bombs all over the place" over Berlin "in what was frankly a terror session aimed at civilian morale."[25] Not only is Heussler nonplussed, he also seems to have been able to dissociate his missions from any concrete repercussions to the "civilians" he sought to "terrorize." Describing a meeting long after the war with a former Luftwaffe pilot, Heussler learns what it was like being on the ground during one of the American raids. *I was surprised that the roar of our engines . . . was so loud and so terrifying to the people below, not to mention the effect when our bombs landed.*[26] It would appear, then, that this form of dissociation was one mechanism which facilitated the pilots' continued performance of bombing raids: a form of denial that was prescribed and supported by the hierarchy in which they functioned. Heussler clearly basks in the affection and approval implied when the major announces his promotion by tossing two silver bars on his bed, quipping, "Lieutenant, you're out of uniform," and several days later announcing, "You're too young to be in the war. . . . I'm sending you home to your mama."[27] By refusing to count his missions, acting unconcerned about how close he is to completing the required number of twenty-five, Heussler is able to win approval through suppressing his own concerns and identifying with the group mission. Only when so relieved of the weight of his combat role is he able to comment on the suppressed temptations to flee, which he may have been struggling against. He recalls Eisenhower's personal pleas to them for "extraordinary sacrifices," and describes the aviators' reactions to it:

> Most of us took it fatalistically, but some did not. A number of planes had landed in Sweden or Switzerland with little or no damage. A co-pilot in another squadron from ours shaved off all his body hair, put red stuff on his face like a girl and kissed his navigator right in front of the CO and the flight surgeon in the club bar. He went home under arrest and was dishonorably discharged, though we heard later that he was doing fine. There were other kinds of odd behavior. And some who went back to the States in straightjackets were not acting.[28]

Observations about the high level of anxiety, and the pilots' constant misgivings over remaining in combat roles, are also reported in numerous other narratives of World War II. Writing about the "Flying Tigers" in the early days of the war in the Pacific, for example, pilots openly speculated about an upcoming mission as being "the most dangerous undertaking [we] had done, going 120 miles into enemy territory where, if the Japs don't get you, the jungle will."[29] The sense of dread around these missions was so extreme that, cautioned about contaminated drinking water, one of the pilots rejoined, "Well, after tomorrow, I don't think it will make any difference."[30] Similarly, even the most successful fighter pilots in the Battle of Britain exhibited this sense of fear and strain. By 1941, this group of fighter pilots consisted of regular Royal Air Force, U.S. volunteers known as the Eagle Squadrons, and regular contingents of the U.S. Eighth and Ninth Army Air Forces. Roger Hall, recipient of the Distinguished Flying Cross, testifies to the felt uniqueness of his combat experiences: "There existed no counterpart to our mode of life in any other sphere of human experience on earth."[31] Although this statement can refer to many different components of Hall's reaction, he tells us that the "prolonged mental stresses of combat" led to his loss of flight rating in 1942, "another [psychological] casualty of the air war."[32] One of the differences between these fighter pilots and those who served in Vietnam was that the World War II veterans were exposed to very direct sensory experiences of the violence of their activity. Rather than suppressing this awareness, their narratives were characterized by graphic reconstructions of these events. For example, Hall, as a twenty-three-year-old fighter pilot, describes a dogfight early in the war. He observes an allied Hurricane pilot bail out of his burning plane. Hall just loses sight of the pilot as he engages with the German 109s, but then catches a glimpse of one of them "firing at the pilot at the end of the parachute. . . . I saw the tracers and the cannon shells pierce the center of his body, which folded like a jackknife closing, like a blade of grass that bends toward the scythe. . . . The red I could see was the pilot's blood as it gushed from all quarters of his body. I expected to see the entrails dangling in midair. . . . His whole body was limp also, like a man just hanged . . . bloody, scarlet with blood."[33] The diaries of the Flying Tigers similarly were filled with scenes of pilots on fire, of aviators with limbs torn off by large caliber bullets, of a comrade whose jaw "had been almost completely blown off."[34]

These experiences led to many types of reactions. Fear and crippling anxiety ("flight fatigue") were also interspersed with pride, relief at surviving, and pressured, swaggering, acts of release. The coda to Heussler's combat exposure almost appears to be a reprise of his precombat baptism in Juarez. In both instances, he regards himself as an almost passive participant, but one who is establishing some claim to manhood by engaging in a sexual encounter for which he experiences some distaste or disdain. Heussler once again teams up with another Dartmouth pilot, and they go off to a local church dance.

As we stood outside wondering if we wanted to go in and if we would be welcome, a pair of girls came up to us and started a conversation. They were twin sisters, dark, short, heavily painted and very friendly. . . . Though they had never met any Yank officers they had heard we were not so aloof as British ones. Here was a chance to find out.

We danced with them for a while and drank some orange squash. The one who had attached herself to me was called Polly.

"I thought all Yanks were meant to be fah-st," she confided. "You're not. You're shy, you are."

While I tried to think of an answer she went on.

"You're not keen on orange squash, are you? No, I thought not. I know where we can get something stronger, and I expect you'd like to buy me some cigarettes."

Polly was unquestionably in charge, not only of me but of her sister too. She piloted all of us out of the church. . . . She told us to wait on the corner and rejoined us a few minutes later carrying a parcel that turned out to have eight bottles of lager in it. . . . The sisters led us to a cemetery in the gathering darkness. . . . As we drank the beer, for which I had paid, it was made unmistakably clear that they expected a convincing display of American virility. This was to take place where we were on the grass among the headstones. Furthermore, Polly explained, the operation was to be performed side-by-side at close quarters.

"Me and my sister do everything together, love," she whispered in my ear. "We feel safer that way. You never know what kind of people you'll meet in wartime."

Polly also directed that there would be a change of partners half-way through. "Like at the dance, you know," she concluded.

It sounded all right. But with shoes on and our pants around our ankles Tony and I were not all that maneuverable. When the time for rearrangements came we ran into each other and I got the giggles. Polly did not take kindly to this at all. The proceedings were abruptly stopped and the ladies departed, muttering earthily. As we stumbled back to the base I asked Tony what they had been so upset about. He threw an arm around my shoulders and grinned. "You nitwit. You're not supposed to laugh at a time like that."[35]

In these marker experiences, alcohol, sex, and fraternity are fused in a ritual assertion of manhood, which itself seems rather devoid of pleasure. Rather, the actors seem almost driven by a compulsion to ward off the fear of isolation and death. Once again, these are stereotypical forms of defense, represented ad nauseam in almost every World War II–era novel and movie about men in combat. In the enactment—and most certainly in the narrative—Heussler constructs his experiences of highly personal events in a way largely prescribed by the military culture that mediates it.

Fear is acknowledged but must be controlled if he is to be an adequate man, warrior, and pilot. Guilt or moral qualms are arbitrated by a changed aesthetic of warfare, one that now allows what was, only a few years earlier, condemned as barbaric. Sexuality becomes a fraternal act for asserting aliveness and potency.

Keeping in mind this nascent culture of air combat—this initial attempt to construct a collective defense—I will try to sketch some of the strains and conflicts encountered by the Vietnam-era pilots. I would like to examine some of the major themes in their oral histories, and to understand these commonalities as their particular subculture's attempt to deal with the particular forms of anxiety inherent in their experience. It may be helpful at this point to synopsize the chronology of the U.S. air war in Southeast Asia in the period immediately preceding the arrival of the pilots we will be discussing. The U.S. Air Force was first invited in 1961 to train the South Vietnamese Air Force in Bien Hoa. This initial deployment consisted of a detachment from 4420th Combat Training Crew Squadron ("Jungle Jim") and a group of pilots "prepared to fight guerilla wars . . . [and] qualified to conduct sub rosa air command operations."[36] While covert operations against North Vietnam, including U2 and electronic intelligence collection flights, began in this period,[37] overt air operations against North Vietnam began in August 1964, ostensibly in retaliation for North Vietnamese PT boat attacks on U.S. ships in the Gulf of Tonkin. The next major phase of the air war—Operation Flaming Dart— began in February 1965 and was, once again, represented as a retaliation for a series of attacks on naval vessels and, also, for Viet Cong aggression in South Vietnam. This campaign quickly evolved into "Rolling Thunder," a program of sustained bombing against North Vietnam that continued until November 1968.

In this period of escalation, fliers from both the air force and navy were involved not only in "deep interdiction" (strategic attacks in both North and South Vietnam, as well as in other parts of Southeast Asia) but also missions in pursuit of "air superiority" (attempts to disable enemy air capabilities and air defense systems), "armed reconnaissance" (sorties in search of "targets of opportunity"), defoliation, and "close air support" (in close proximity to friendly forces engaged in ground combat).[38] This was the recognized context of the air war that was already established when the young pilots from Dartmouth began arriving in Southeast Asia. Less well known to the public was a series of covert operations against other targets, such as the air campaign against the Plain of Jars in Laos. From May 1964 through September 1969, "over 75,000 tons of bombs were dropped on it, over 50,000 airmen were involved . . . thousands were killed and wounded . . . and the entire society leveled."[39] The new arrivals thus joined a seasoned group of combat pilots, men who had already become quite accustomed to daily missions against military, tactical, and civilian targets both declared and secret.

From the beginning of covert air operations in Southeast Asia, a certain attitude was characteristic of the pilots' discourse. I will cite several of their published war narratives to provide a sense of how the lexicon and affective tone of these representations was well established before our Dartmouth pilots arrived in Southeast Asia. While individual variation occurred at the level of detail, it is clear that it was a quite stylized genre. Daniel White, a naval aviator who would serve five tours in Vietnam, flew missions that ranged from dropping mercenaries procured by the CIA into North Vietnam in 1964 to making bombing runs over North Vietnam at the war's end. His recollection of the early years of covert operations seem representative:

> The 123s took a lot of hits, and that made the job interesting. We had ECM [electronic countermeasure] gear in the airplane, a commercial brand that was just exceptional. You could tell what was coming, pinpoint it, and also zap it. We were fired at by AAA [antiaircraft artillery], and sometimes even SAMs [surface-to-air missiles]. Low and slow and still getting SAMs, all very colorful at night. Our routes were planned to stay away from the known sites, and were well protected: [flying at a] low level; down below the mountain tops; in the valleys; and all of this was at night, so there usually was moonlight to see by. Really sort of exciting . . .
>
> The people dropped up North weren't of the best quality. They were a cutthroat bunch. Basically thugs, but the best thugs money could buy. They liked watches and radios, that was a big incentive. Sometimes we needed armed guards on the airplane to get them to even jump out. One flight (and I wasn't on it, Lou was), a shootout took place in the back of the airplane. The thugs just didn't want to jump.
>
> On the ground, we were never sure when coming in for a drop, who was down there. The thugs were getting caught, probably even giving up, although I don't know that. In a couple of incidents, all the signals were right but planes were shot down. . . . 34A had the air ops and a mar [maritime] ops—little swift boats and nastys that ran up North and which really caused the war, in my estimation. The PTs had to be back across the DMZ [demilitarized zone] before daylight, and if [they were] chased, we'd pounce on the chase boats in the A-1s. The A-1 flights were intermingled with the C-123 missions and the A-1 was more fun because I got to shoot back. Sometimes we'd also have regular strikes in the A-1; really neat work, fun work.[40]

We already observe a rather different tone to this oral history as compared to those of World War II. There is considerably more identification and cathexis, even some fusion of pleasure and pride, associated with the technology itself. Acronyms and restricted code are used whenever possible, and the sensual pleasures of the experience are emphasized. We also see an amoral cynicism displayed in sardonic humor, and a dramatic shift in the overall affective evaluation of the experience. Air combat is no longer a terrifying experience from which one can barely wait to escape, it has become redefined as "neat work, fun work."

By 1967, in the heart of Rolling Thunder, this ethos, the concept of the true warrior, had become the more articulated image of combat pilot. T. R. Swartz, a highly experienced pilot with Attack Squadron Seventy-Six aboard the USS *Bon Homme Richard*, exemplifies this discourse in his account of his action in Vietnam in 1967.

> A warrior just wanted to get in the airplane, and do as good a job as he could. He was as good as he could get in that airplane, he tried to get everybody else around him to be as good as possible, and he didn't hesitate to go and take on the enemy and make them burn, bleed, and blow up because that's what the hell he was getting paid for. . . .
>
> ". . . When you're in a no-shit dogfight with somebody else—who can put a weapon on you and blow you out of the sky—it's kind of like just before you go out on the ballfield or get in the ring with somebody. . . ."
>
> I would feel more comfortable once the guns started up and the SAMs came up because you knew they were worried and awake and you knew where they were. I was always worried when nothing happened, and was always waiting for something to happen because then it was time for action, the adrenaline ran, and you were ready and working.[41]

The reliance on sports metaphors, the quest for action, the pursuit of technical mastery, the sense of invincibility, and the intense feeling of connection to an elite fraternity all saturate Swartz's autobiographic text.

> In VA-76 we had some real warriors, guys like John Waples, Les Jackson, and Paul Hollingsworth. We lost the CO—Guy Fuller—to a SAM and the XO, Ken Cameron, went down early; and as far as I was concerned, the squadron was Hollingsworth as operations officer, Jackson as maintenance, myself as admin, Waples, and four or five other pretty God damn good bombers and airplane fliers. We were calling the shots, leading the alpha strikes, the maintenance was getting done. We believed we could go out and beat the hell out of the North Vietnamese on the ground with the airplanes, take on the SAMs, dig them out, and dig out the guns if we had to. Our sister squadron, VA-212, had some good people—Homer Smith was the CO—and Jack Monger was one of the best CAGs around, an old attack pilot.
>
> It was kind of fun over the beach, like pro football, where you take the ball, get on the field, kick everybody's ass, and come home. We weren't concerned with what the hell the war was all about; we were more concerned with getting it done right, getting everybody back, and doing some good damage to the enemy.[42]

This sense of bravado and intense enjoyment, this feeling of being in a privileged, magical time and place, of doing extraordinary things, must be juxtaposed with an inescapable reality. For example, in this same period that so stimulates Swartz, there are hazards to be dealt with. From June to October 1967, the North Vietnamese were well prepared for the U.S. sorties. Flying over Hanoi, "you could get everything—missiles, MiGs, guns," notes Siegel. "The next little town down the road was Hai Duong, which had no missiles, but an incredible amount of bullets. And Haiphong had everything."[43] This weaponry was often effective: during the month of August, sixteen Navy aircraft were shot down over Haiphong alone.[44] From 1962, when action was quite light, through August 1973, a period that included Linebacker II, the last major air offensive against the North, U.S. Air Force losses included 2,257 aircraft, 2,118 fliers dead, 3,470 wounded, 599 missing, and 368 returned after being held prisoners of war. As our subjects testify, it was this last possibility which often was the most frightening for combat pilots in Southeast Asia, to the extent that fear was recognized at all. The dangers of capture, injury, and death were part of a larger array of realities that made the fliers' experience, by all accounts, rather surreal. At points in the war, for example, the air campaign was so intense that "the skies were clogged with bombers, fighters, helicopters and other airplanes," to a point where "South Vietnam's airports became the world's busiest."[45] Despite intermittent intensity of combat, even for those at remote posts, "the menu at Thanksgiving and Christmas featured turkey, cranberry sauce and candied yams."[46] Deprivation of various sorts was juxtaposed to all the comforts and affluence of home. The main PX near Saigon "was only slightly smaller than the New York Bloomingdale's, its counters laden with everything from sports clothes, cameras, tape recorders, and radios. . . . A GI might even be solicited by representatives from Wall Street brokerage firms that had set up offices in Saigon"[47] To add another dimension to these contrasts in the pilots' lives, there was also the reality of how their weapons were drastically reshaping a country, and decimating populations. A Vietnamese describes the experience from the ground: "The Americans had denuded the jungles with their napalm and there was no place to hide. They would drop bombs everywhere. . . . Some of the wounded had lost arms or legs, or their bellies had been ripped open by bomb fragments, and their intestines were spilling out. Others were horribly burned by napalm."[48] It is estimated that the U.S. air campaign against the North alone killed one hundred thousand civilians. Cluster bombs, exploding with hundreds of lethal, high-velocity pellets, were dropped by U.S. aircraft on populated regions in the South as well, "killing or maiming thousands of civilians." General H. K. Johnson, army chief of staff, boasted that "we act with ruthlessness, like a steamroller."[49]

Despite this array of "facts," air combat is primarily remembered by our subjects as a unique thrill. A naval aviator, the pilot of a carrier-based attack aircraft, reminisces: "There were days when you'd get shot off the front of the ship, a beautiful day at sea. And I'd get to do something fun, maybe a low level or something like that. It was such a kick in the pants to do this that you couldn't believe they'd be paying you to fly around in this multimillion dollar high performance machine and do all this stuff." This testimony is paradigmatic of another shift in the narratives of the Vietnam pilots in comparison to their World War II counterparts. In the reconstructing of their experiences in Southeast Asia, there is no longer a bifurcation between combat per se and the erotic; air combat has itself become eroticized, even to the point of an acknowledgment of the arousal associated with risking death. Women fade entirely into the background in these oral histories. This is not to argue that Vietnam era pilots did not spend as much time with prostitutes between missions or that World War II pilots didn't derive stimulation from flying. However, it is immediately apparent that the pilots' culture encourages and allows a much more erot- icized identification with, and immersion in, the male fraternity of fliers, a culture dominated by high-tech machines, danger, and death as its cen- tral icons.

An air force fighter pilot describes the atmosphere that prevailed in the pilots' quarters when he arrived in Vietnam in 1969: "A lot of guys were on their second, third, fourth tour. They loved being there. 'This is real. This is fun. It's good flying. I'm with friends.'" His enjoyment is even more specifically focused on the stimulation of combat flying. He de- scribes a sortie in which one of his primary targets is deemed inaccessible, and he calls in for alternative uses for the two bombs still on board. The air controller responds: "'We've got something you'll really love: a bridge.' When you hear something like that, your incisors come down. They loved A7s because our bombing systems were so accurate and the pilots so good."

The pride and pleasure are thus fused, each sortie experienced as an- other opportunity to prove competence and self-worth. A fighter pilot who flew over three hundred combat missions in Southeast Asia recalls: "Flying an airplane in combat is a very stimulating situation. It's a chal- lenging environment because it's so transparent. You can't hide. You have an objective and you get daily assessment of your professional skills. . . . The work is very exciting." A naval aviator declares simply: "The combat was exciting and exhilarating."

This challenge and excitement is represented as magnetic, addictive. The pilots describe an enormous eagerness to fly above all else. A naval aviator recalls the boredom and restlessness of the period between mis- sions and comments: "Flying was a way to get off the ship, to break the monotony of shipboard life." Rather than welcoming the end of their fixed tour, as did the World War II aviators, our subjects frequently described a powerful desire to return to the combat situation after they had been rotated out. "I pulled two tours of direct combat. I had to lobby in front of my wing commander to go the second time, even though my wife didn't want me to go. I had to get back, loved being there." An air force pilot states: "Everyone wanted to fly. Holidays were a great opportunity [because some of the pilots were off on leave.] I remember going up on Christmas Day 1969; flying close support for the troops on the ground. 'We don't want the bombs, just the nape.' I dropped four cans of nape, but they don't go off. 'No problem,' I think, I'll just strafe and set them off, I know just where I dropped them. I swung back and 'biirp,' the guns jammed. I said 'Uh oh, I'm getting out of here and going home.' " This story is recounted with great relish and amusement, underlining the absence of anxiety in the narrative reconstructions of these seemingly harrowing combat experiences. This absence or suppression of anxiety is clearly tied to the construction of beliefs about invulnerability commonly found in the pilots' discourse. The fliers repeatedly tell us, "There was a real bravado thing. It couldn't happen to you, only the other guy." There were a number of beliefs used to buttress these assumptions. For example, there was a sense that veteran pilots, who had proved their mettle, were too experienced and too wily to be shot down. "We found out that a man was more likely to get killed in his first ten missions. If he made it through that, he was okay." This formula of skill leading to immunity was also represented at a group level: "I was in an air wing that did exceptionally well in terms of losses. We were lucky [chuckles] or a very good air wing."

The pilots' narratives emphasized a powerful, shared belief in their own and each other's special qualities of superiority, intellect, talent, and emotional control that made it possible for them to do extraordinary things. Virtually all of them emphasized the extensive weeding-out process at every level in training and assignment, which meant that fighter and attack aircraft pilots were by their own definition, the "crème de la crème." "By the time you got to an operational squadron, these were exceptional people." Another flier observes: "These were smart people. You can't do it if you aren't . . . to use a trite phrase, they've been through the crucible of war. You wouldn't believe the ego a fighter pilot has. 'Hey, I'm a better man.' " A career officer, asked to account for the lack of fear he observed in himself and other squadron members, echoes the same belief in a more understated way: "A college trained person can deal with those kinds of stresses."

This subcultural formula—competence → invulnerability—is enormously functional for the pilots when under extreme stress. When in the most acute danger, they describe themselves as being able to perform with enormous speed and awareness, and to make instinctively correct decisions by substituting this belief for fearful anticipation of disaster. The phrase used to encode this response is, "in a situation like that, you get real busy." Another pilot elaborates: "While I was actually in combat I didn't think of anything but combat. I was all business." When this formula fails, however, the pilot can feel startled and betrayed: "I was on an attack mission, dropping cluster bombs in Laos. We were attacking a gun site. I took a hit in the belly of the airplane and was on fire, but could still fly it. The engine quit and I got real busy trying to see if I could get out over water, not North Vietnam. I went into the water and the helicopters picked me up. It was as benign as an incident like that can be." He remembers no fear associated with the incident, except "when I was in the parachute coming down. The top kit opened, then it fell away and everything sank. Then I tried to inflate my LPV, but it wouldn't inflate. I thought, 'Oh shit, I did everything right and I was still going to drown.' "

Part of the pilots' sense of specialness is found in their repeated emphasis on how their experience was radically different from that of "grunts." This distinction both reflects their belief in their superiority and the compartmentalization of experience that allows for the pilots' denial of danger and negation of their own fear. "Flying off an aircraft carrier was somewhat unique. On the ground there was danger twenty-four hours a day, seven days a week. I only flew for one and a half or two hours once or twice a day." As he hears himself speak some years after the fact, he begins to question the logic of his own proposition and muses: "At times, the relative risk was higher for me. Certainly for the time I was over North Vietnam. . . . Probably the most dangerous time for me was landing back on the ship at night." After another moment's pause, he adds, "Of course, when Nixon called for unrestricted bombing [Linebacker II], then it was a more dangerous couple of weeks." Another pilot recalls meeting a Dartmouth classmate in Saigon who was serving in the marines. Despite flying daily missions over North Vietnam, Laos, and Cambodia, despite being hit by ground fire, he is impressed by his old friend's description of his duty near the DMZ: "Ground combat is scary." He remembers exclaiming, "How do you do that day after day?" He seems almost puzzled by his friend's response: "Hey, it's not that big a deal. You couldn't get me to fly that plane of yours for anything." The pilots' feelings of superiority (sometimes implied, sometimes explicit) do not seem based on a sense of greater physical courage than that possessed by ground soldiers. Indeed, their proclivity to compartmentalize their universe (bullets are scary but SAMs are a technical challenge) and deny personal danger leads them to experience ground combat as more frightening than flying. The pilots surely regard themselves and each other as brave; but their self-defined uniqueness lies more in combining this courage with intelligence, extraordinary cerebral control under stress, physical capacities, and the ability for concentration and organization.

The pilots also exhibit consistency in their explanation about why air combat is less frightening. "We don't see dead bodies, wounded people, guys shot up. If you don't come back, you don't come back. You just have burnt metal on the side of a mountain, a distant flame. No broken bodies." Once again, the distance from the physical reality is used to shore up the defensive denial of violence and danger, which appears only as an absence. "I didn't think about danger in the cockpit. I never looked an individual in the eye and tried to kill him. . . . It's a very distant thing, like, 'My roommate didn't come home today.'" This seemed almost a hypothetical way of describing the encounter with death, until some minutes later in the oral history. This pilot reveals some retrospective sense of being afraid, expressed in concern over potential capture and about cockpit fires. He attempts to dismiss these fears by stating, "Of course, you can jump out of an airplane." He tries to further reassure himself: "I've never seen an airplane blow up in four hundred combat missions. I've even been shot down." He then ends the string by what seems a tangential association: "I lost a roommate, but we never knew what happened to him. He was MIA."

Another salient aspect of the experience which is represented as a source of comfort, was the camaraderie with fellow pilots. A former member of Sigma Nu while at Dartmouth recalls his arrival at the pilots' quarters at Bien Hoa: "I never left the fraternity. It was like I had a reunion with my buddies from the Sig House. I went from the Sig House to the pilots' house. We flew together, partied together, got shot at together." A second pilot offers the same analogy: "You went everywhere together. You fought together, went to bars together. Flying combat is a very stimulating situation. You want to be able to talk to someone who understands what you're doing." One corollary of this fraternity-like experience is a sense of mutual support; another is a sense of group obligation and potential shame should one exhibit weakness: "I would never have allowed myself to be perceived by any member of the group as not wanting to step forward and take part." Even (maybe especially) those most enthusiastic about the experience are able to observe its protracted adolescent quality, and its removal from time and history: "The social concern was nonexistent. I was totally wrapped up in the technical aspects of flying an airplane. At the end of my tour, I was not much more mature than when I left. When I got home, I became painfully aware of how much the world was passing me by. So I went back to Southeast Asia."

The addiction to that life was best described in a story which was told by one of the air force pilots. Early in his tour, he received a sardonic warning from a group of air force academy graduates who had been in Vietnam from the beginning. He narrates their description of the natural evolution of the combat pilot, an evolution based on the escalating "threshold of thrill": "First, just flying the airplane is a thrill. Then, you need to be dropping bombs. Then, you have to see what you're dropping bombs on. Then, to feel the thrill, you have to see that you've hit what you're dropping bombs on. Then, you need to be getting shot at while you see what you've blown up. Then, you have to be getting hit to feel the thrill, and the last thing is, to get dead." It seemed almost a slogan among air force fliers that "it isn't fun unless you're getting shot at." While this might be seen as the veteran's use of hyperbole to haze the rookie flier, it appears to capture trends in the narratives of many of the survivors. After telling of this encounter, for example, the same respondent describes taking a reporter with him on a mission over Laos. After a bomb run on a bridge, he circles back to show his passenger the results of his efforts. He laughs: "This time they knew we were in the neighborhood and were ready. We were getting shot at. . . . It was real exhilaration." He adds parenthetically, "That was really dumb, you're never supposed to go back like that. It's against every rule."

Along with the fantasy of immortality, and the flirtation with the thrill of death, these men speak of a sense of timelessness to their experience in Southeast Asia. When asked about his thoughts in 1969–70 about his own future, one respondent replied: "I was kind of in neutral. This is fun. The war is going to go on forever. We'll be here in '78, in '88." But time, like the repressed, returned to the narratives. Somehow, temporality punctured the collective and individual defenses to a degree that allowed these men to stop volunteering for more tours. The pilots are much less articulate about this shift, which most still regard with ambivalence. One man recalls, "I kiddingly say I got tired of getting shot at. The flying stayed the same. I really did just about everything I could do with the airplane, being in the war and so on. That part of the challenge was gone." Another is even more opaque: "You get to think when you're about twenty-eight, it's time to get out."

In attempting to understand these men's conflict between personal survival and pursuit of the "threshold of thrill," it may be illuminating to turn back again to the observations made in the relatively innocent air war of the 1940s. Psychiatrists who worked intimately with the air combat groups observed that the pilots had become fixated on death: both its enactment and its denial.

The inference was inescapable, and this was borne out by evidence, that the unconscious impulse to suicide in flying personnel was prominent. A careful study of survivors of aircraft accidents, for example, would at times demonstrate that the accident was unconsciously determined and, thus, was really no accident at all. At times, this tendency led to horrifying disasters, as, for example, in the case of the pilots of two heavy bombers. They played tag or follow the leader soon after arrival in the overseas theater, flying at water level into the mouth of a river which emerged from a ravine, and then were unable to climb out of the steep ravine, with a resulting double crash, killing 20 men. Were such accidents rare, they might be explained on the basis of pure chance. However, they were not rare. Many losses in combat were, in fact, due to taking suicidal chances, as any combat pilot knows.

This suicidal tendency was covered up by the defense of denial so that it was easily missed. Another factor contributed to the difficulty in the perception of this tendency; namely, the unconscious belief in immortality, spoken of by Freud as the unconscious belief that death is impossible, that the ego can not actually die. In the South Pacific, dangerous missions were always generously volunteered for; a discussion of this fact with the volunteers demonstrated that these men actually believed that while others might die, they could not do so. Thus, by denying the probability of death, they were able to undertake missions in which there was small chance for survival.[50]

This linkage between aggression, suicide, fantasies of immortality, and depression seems somewhat arbitrary, and yet it accounts for much of the text under examination. As in the psychoanalytic formulation, the pilots' "acting out" (risk taking, rule breaking, implicit violence) can be seen as a way of managing the depression engendered by these very same activities. That is, if depression represents a turning against the ego of aggressive drives,[51] there will be a tendency to find relief of depression through external aggression, and a parallel process of aggression once stimulated to be turned against the self. A vignette from the Pacific theater in World War II helps to illustrate this process and perhaps underline the meaning of the repeated incidents of blasé risk taking the Vietnam-era pilots narrate:

A pilot had expressed resentment, as had many other American officers, at the policy of an Australian officers' club located in a grass hut in a nearby Australian encampment, in excluding all but Australian officers while the United States officers' clubs were not thus exclusive. He had become increasingly morose and withdrawn. This pilot had taken off for a practice flight, shortly after which a fighter plane was seen flying low over the Australian encampment. It was assumed that he was doing so to gain the attention of nurses at a nearby hospital as not infrequently occurred, although this low flying over an encampment was forbidden. However, shortly thereafter, the plane apparently stalled at a low altitude and fell directly into the Australian officers' club in question, where it exploded and burned to death 12 officers in addition to the pilot. It is, of course, impossible to ascertain whether or not, as seems likely, this represented a successful suicidal attempt together with a homicidal protest against fancied discrimination.[52]

This may represent part of the underside of the collective defense constructed by and for the pilots. In permitting them to fold death under, to live with it while being its agents, the defense may, to some degree, habituate them to it. This may leave them either with the need to continually pursue danger and violence—without which they feel less than alive—or to experience the emergence of a disguised depressive substrate that may be very difficult to tolerate. Anecdotal evidence from the men's life stories suggests that both such reactions occur, although with varying degrees of intensity.

Notes

The author wishes to express thanks to Matthew Friedman, Delia Kostner, Nathan Smith, Peter Tannenbaum, and Sheila Vowinkle for help in gathering the interviews discussed, and to Harriet Rosenberg for help in analyzing the interview material and critiques of earlier versions of this manuscript.

1. *People*, March 4, 1991.
2. *Time*, February 11, 1991.
3. *Time*, February 25, 1991.
4. M. S. Sherry, *The Rise of American Air Power: The Creation of Armageddon* (New Haven: Yale University Press, 1987), p. 95.
5. J. Shotter and K. J. Gergen, *Texts of Identity: Inquiries in Social Construction* (Newberry Park, Calif.: Sage Publications, 1989).
6. E. Jaques, "Social Systems as a Defense against Persecutory and Depressive Anxiety," in Melanie Klein, Paula Heimann, and R. E. Money-Kyrle, eds., *New Directions in Psychoanalysis* (New York: Basic Books, 1955), p. 479.
7. Ibid., p. 497.
8. M. Clodfelter, *The Limits of Air Power: The American Bombing of North Vietnam* (New York: Free Press, 1989), p. 2.
9. Ibid., p. 5.
10. Ibid., p. 6.
11. Ibid.
12. Ibid.
13. Sherry, *Rise of American Air Power*, p. 95.
14. Ibid.
15. H. B. Jennings, *Neuropsychiatry in World War II* (Washington, D.C.: Medical Department, United States Army, 1973), pp. 861–79.
16. Ibid., p. 881.
17. Ibid., p. 865.
18. R. Heussler, *Interlude in the Forties: Memories of Dartmouth and the War* (Lunenburg, Vt.: Stinehour Press, 1980).
19. Ibid., pp. 30, 26–27.
20. Ibid., pp. 28–29.
21. Ibid., p. 30.
22. Ibid., p. 31.
23. Ibid., pp. 34–35.
24. Sherry, *Rise of American Air Power*, p. 96.
25. Heussler, *Interlude in the Forties*, p. 34.

26. Ibid., p. 37, italics mine.

27. Ibid., pp. 39–40.

28. Ibid., p. 40.

29. D. Schultz, *The Maverick War: Chennault and the Flying Tigers* (New York: St. Martin's Press, 1987), p. 222.

30. Ibid.

31. P. Kaplan and A. Saunders, *Little Friends: The Fighter Pilot Experience in World War II England* (New York: Random House, 1991).

32. Ibid., p. 71.

33. Kaplan and Saunders, *Little Friends*, p. 68.

34. Schultz, *Maverick War*, p. 219.

35. Heussler, *Interlude in the Forties*, pp. 42–43.

36. J. S. Ballard, *The United States Air Force in Southeast Asia: Development and Employment of Fixed-Wing Gunships, 1962–1972* (Washington, D.C.: United States Air Force, 1982), p. 11.

37. J. C. Thompson, *Rolling Thunder: Understanding Policy and Program Failure* (Chapel Hill: University of North Carolina Press, 1980), pp. 15–17.

38. Ibid., p. 39.

39. F. Branfman, *Voices from the Plain of Jars: Life under an Air War* (New York: Harper and Row, 1972), p. 4.

40. J. L. Levinson, *Alpha Strike Vietnam: The Navy's Air War, 1964 to 1973* (Novato, Calif.; Presidio Press, 1989), p. 8.

41. Ibid., pp. 168–69.

42. Ibid., p. 169.

43. Ibid., p.18.

44. Ibid., p. 82.

45. S. Karnow, *Vietnam: A History. The First Complete Accout of Vietnam at War* (New York: Viking Press, 1983), p. 437.

46. Ibid., p. 438.

47. Ibid.

48. Ibid., pp. 455–56.

49. Ibid., p. 437.

50. Jennings, *Neuropsychiatry in World War II*, p. 922.

51. S. Freud, *The Ego and the Id*, std. ed., vol. 20 (London: Hogarth, 1959).

52. Jennings, *Neuropsychiatry in World War II*, p. 924.

Chapter 4

TECHNO-MUSCULARITY

AND THE "BOY ETERNAL":

FROM THE QUAGMIRE TO THE GULF

LYNDA E. BOOSE

IN A 1989 COMPARISON of his own presidency to that of the legendary Abraham Lincoln, President George Bush emphasized that while Lincoln had been "tested by fire" in a war of "brother . . . killing brother," he himself had not yet had the opportunity for such a test. Within his rhetoric of war, something on the scale of the 1991 Gulf War was almost predictable. For while invading Panama to bust Manuel Noriega may have bettered the scale of any of the "tests by fire" that had been staged by Bush's immediate predecessor, for Lincolnesque historical stakes, nothing so paltry would suffice.

Nor was George Bush alone in his preoccupation with an epic return to male-conquest mythology: even before the bombing of Iraq began on January 16, 1991, there were signs that American culture was literally saturated with such desire. The writer of an October 1990 *Newsweek* article, "The Civil War and Modern Memory," for instance, becomes so enthralled by the model of such "tests by fire" that, after briefly mentioning "nationhood . . . [and] the wounds of race and class," he goes on to find, as the core significance of the Civil War for modern Americans, that "it's to that moment of testing that Americans, especially American men, so often respond when they think of the Civil War: Would I fight? Would I die? Would I measure up?"[1]

So—forget about the fact that not all "Americans, especially American men" are white. Forget about slavery, the nation divided, and even the issue of union. For by October 1990, with the first American troops already in Saudi Arabia, American history was getting shoved aside by a refurbished mythology of manhood being tested. And what that test of manhood signified was, quite explicitly, the space in which sons confirm their authority with the fathers. For, as *Newsweek* goes on to say, "While Saudi Arabia is not Shiloh—at least not yet—the threads that connect them may be one reason so many people were drawn to the PBS series.

Those ties that bind us to the Civil War are astonishingly short. . . . Former Secretary of State Dean Rusk recalls in his recently published memoirs that both of his grandfathers fought for the Confederacy. Rusk, a World War II veteran, went on to help plan the Korean War and the Vietnam War, the line unbroken."

And so the American parade is back in line: the war that was fought to define the nation's moral geography collapsed together with—as if it could impart heroic meaning to—America's imperialist intervention in Vietnam's civil war. Beneath the glibness of such ideological condensations,[2] history is pounded to oblivion under the hoofbeats of an imagined cavalry charge from the past, a father to son relay transmitted through the "line unbroken" and "threads that connect." Presumably, blest be such "ties that bind."

In *Newsweek*'s blithe transformation of the reproduction of sons into the reproduction of war, what has been conveniently elided is the glaring contradiction that the story itself invokes by its use of the Rusk family as a synoptic illustration of war's unbroken patrilineage. For while former Secretary of State Dean Rusk may have fought in World War II and had grandfathers who did so in the Civil War, Dean Rusk's son did *not* fight in Vietnam. The line was broken. Richard Rusk (as were, likewise, both the son and daughter of former Defense Secretary Robert McNamara)[3] was—and still is—deeply opposed to both the war in Vietnam and his father's role as "the architect of that murderous human tragedy." The Rusk memoirs that *Newsweek* glosses over are ones that Richard Rusk recorded in a series of painful, unresolving interviews that attempted to come to terms with the father whose authority he had twenty years ago rejected. Richard Rusk was intent, says his father, on trying "to find any ties that might still bind us together."[4] What had severed those ties was the war in Vietnam.

What *Newsweek* has elided in its narrative of war and sonship is the gap, the break, the halt to the parade that the Vietnam War threatened to insert in the nation's repetitive pattern of war every twenty to twenty-five years, one to allow each generation of sons its opportunity to be tested. In each of the miniwars staged in the decade before the Persian Gulf crisis, America's primary goal was not, as had earlier been suspected, merely to undo defeat in Vietnam: It was to put to rest the legacy of resistant sons bequeathed by that conflict. January 1991 offered a unique opportunity. With Soviet power in collapse, a war in Iraq allowed America to demonstrate that it was the only big man around. There was now no one to impede American military muscle, block American control of the United Nations, or provide an alternative power base around which to rally any opposition. Simultaneously, through round-the-clock saturation bombing, subnuclear weaponry, tactics that flouted the Geneva conventions, overt censorship of media information, intransigence in all negotiations, and the rejection of all third party ceasefire proposals—in short, through the repeated choice of high violence options gratuitously disproportionate to the level of threat, an unfettered U.S. militarism was internally staging its own rebirth. Freed by history from external check, it was simultaneously demonstrating its freedom from and throwing off the inhibitions that had been imposed by antiwar sentiment residual from Vietnam. When in January 1991, the United States turned the full power of its conventional arsenal on several hundred thousand Iraqi soldiers trapped underground, George Bush did have a domestic priority: to bury in the desert the antiwar discourse signified by "Vietnam."

A key observation that the feminist perspective has contributed to the critique of culture is the recognition that every public power arrangement depends on the control of femininity and masculinity as concepts, from which notions the control of individual, sexed subjects becomes possible.[5] The road from the Quagmire to the Gulf was built upon the manipulation of just such concepts. It was, furthermore, built out of an antiwar discourse that was itself always composed of two incompatible, strongly gender-marked narratives. Within the undifferentiated, widespread antiwar sentiment that compelled the 1973 withdrawal of American troops lay a range of potential contradictions that had managed to coexist not only within the loose antiwar coalition of the early 1970s but even within the attitudes of single individuals. By the end of the 1980s, most Americans from the social class whose desires and memories define the nation's dominant discourse probably still remembered Vietnam as a "bad war" that "we didn't win and probably shouldn't have gotten into." But the key ideological issues that had constructed that opposition—just *why* Vietnam was a "bad war" that the majority wanted out of—had receded into oblivion, along with much of the rest of the era's history.[6] It was a public consciousness ripe for a surgically swift memory implant. And behind the official rhetoric connecting massive U.S. intervention in the Gulf with "overcoming the Vietnam syndrome" was a discernible effort to segregate remembered opposition to the Vietnam War into competing narratives so that one could be reclaimed from its antiwar affiliations and the other one anathematized. Behind the propaganda campaigns that had accompanied the various U.S. post-Vietnam mini-invasions of the 1980s lay a strategic objective to generate what the Gulf War finally produced on a large scale: the parades, the cheers, the public excitement over military hardware, and the popular sloganeering about a "new pride in America" that such cheap, easy victories progressively enabled—in short, a revivified militarism that could once again become self-reproducing.

As historian Marilyn Young eloquently illustrates and as U.S. government documents make explicit, the security establishment that the cold war entrenched in American government maintains a profound distrust of and determination to root out the pacifism that remained, even after World War II, a sizable factor in American attitudes.[7] Displacing that ethic in post-Vietnam culture depended on segregating the residual antiwar discourse along often unconscious but deeply culturated associations of gender. In the recuperable one of these two narratives, issues about Vietnam were dealt with by strict containment: the war was restricted to a focus on the individual American soldier; discussion of U.S. involvement was isolated to issues concerned only with winning and losing; and geography was even relocated from the actual war to the one on the home front where revisionist history has staked its loudest claims. In this scenario, if Vietnam was a bad war, it was bad because we lost; and what we should not have gotten into was a war that was doomed to failure by the refusal of the American people to support their troops.

In the other, more global narrative that the Gulf War was targeted to excise, the focus was on the morality of America's foreign policy and military conduct and its impact on both the Vietnamese people and American soldiers. The two narratives had been politically held together by consideration of the American soldier(s). But in the second narration, the importance of the individual American soldier was implicitly leveled and the question of whether America "won" became almost inconsequential, since U.S. intervention in Vietnam was itself viewed as an unjustified act of political imperialism. At the core of this second narrative lay an ethic outside of the claims of patriotic nationalism—the claims for which the American soldier is signifier. Labeled during the Vietnam era as issuing from "bleeding hearts" and "sob sisters," it was a set of ethics that, by the very nature of its self-reflexivity, its internalization of guilt, and its antimilitarist, antiviolence ethos, had asserted—and for a time successfully promoted—an identifiably "feminized" structure of values against the distinctively "masculine" priorities of the other.

Teresa de Lauretis has argued that narrative is by definition masculine and oedipal in structure.[8] And indeed, while the Vietnam counternarrative may have been "femin*ized*," it stayed resolutely centered on the creation of male subjects, never deviating into anything that might be imagined as a "femin*ine*" story. Nonetheless, it effectively challenged the hegemony of American culture's traditional self-presentation. And while the long hair, flowers, and flowing robes disappeared from post-Vietnam male popular culture, what did not so readily disappear was the potential for an ethically reconstituted masculinity that those semiotics of resistance signified. What the debacle of America's masculinized, militarized policies on both fronts of the Vietnam War had opened up was the sudden space in American culture for an alternative to the mythology of a national self born in and valorized by a history of conquest and dominance.

Even given the problems of retroactively measuring cultural weight, it seems accurate to say that the 1970s were not spent in a national agony over having "lost the Vietnam War." As was then widely recognized, the putative "loser" had lost mostly pride, while the uncompensated "winner" was left with millions of dead, missing, and homeless, cratered by bombs, saturated in chemicals, and was then punished for its victory by being cut off from all Western assistance for decades to come.[9] So long as repugnance was attached to the violence that had rendered the distinctions of "winner" and "loser" meaningless, America's so-called loss in Vietnam could not become a political rallying point—but culpability for the vast, continuing tragedy in Southeast Asia and for the anguish of the men who had been sent there still decidedly could. In the late 1960s to the 1970s the American people perhaps came as close as they ever have to considering America's global guilt in the promotion of war. But by the relentlessly underlying binary of gender, that psychic space is already constellated as a "feminized" site and one that the nation apparently could occupy only so long as repugnance remained at bay, associated with the opposite. In a progression that fits the classic Freudian model of delayed traumatic experience, the newly aggressive, antispeculative American self that emerged as the driving force of 1980s American politics did so in convulsive reaction to the 1979 takeover of the American embassy in Teheran—the event that was to define Jimmy Carter as a "wimp" and guarantee Ronald Reagan's presidency.[10] In that triggering recall of the humiliation and capture of an American embassy, in those pictures of U.S. hostages again held captive by jeering Third World males, in the too-familiar nightly voice of Walter Cronkite spelling out the latest national debacle, and even in the image of the crippled American helicopters abandoned this time in the desert rather than in the South China Sea—all the old, repressed humiliations came flooding back. And repugnance switched sides.

Throughout most of the 1970s, an antimilitarist discourse and the latent conditions for extending its impact did exist. Its influence in the culture at large is evident in such barometers as the 1970s market demise of military toys and G.I. Joe dolls—items that returned again in the mid-1980s and soared to market records in the wake of the Gulf War.[11] But while the Vietnam War had precipitated a crisis of gender that had opened up the myth of the so-called national character, and since that persona both produces and is produced by the nation's understanding of masculinity, the attempt to change it was, finally, experienced very differently by women and men. American women emerged from the 1960s and

1970s with an optimistic sense of social/self liberation born in the streets along with the women's movement during the era of civil rights and anti-war protest.[12] For men, however, the pressure to reinvent manhood unavoidably threatened the destruction of a masculine selfhood tenuously acquired in negative differentiation from the feminine and socially constructed by a valorization of dominance. Given the profound personal and sociohistorical investments involved, such change was thus always susceptible to recuperation. Faced with fundamentally rethinking an ideology of power, the masculine values instead retrenched. And from such trenches, the "problem" of Vietnam was reformulated. Thus reconceived at a safe distance from images of either napalmed Vietnamese children or returning American body bags, the problem was no longer the excessive deployment of militarized values but the failure to deploy them strongly enough. The problem became "fighting the war with one hand tied behind our backs," "kowtowing to the lily-livered liberals, peaceniks, and doves in the Congress who curtailed American bombing," and being too tolerant and not tough enough on protesters. And the language of the 1980s became an echo-box for reconfirming the ethics of "getting tough," "playing hardball," "being a winner," and not "flinching" or "wimping out."

This return to patriarchal values would be politically comprehensible were it limited only to a response from the Right. To find it likewise as chosen ideological solution for liberal/progressive men like Robert Bly, premier antiwar poet of the Vietnam era and now founder of the "men's movement" in America, may suggest the profound extent to which a perceived threat to masculinity lies behind the revalorized aggressiveness of the national character. The men's movement is an odd political polyglot. Having apparently recognized the need for masculinity to reconceive itself, Bly's philosophy begins with values culturally identified with the feminine—the need for men to connect to their fathers and to acquire a greater openness, intimacy, and so forth. But the path into Bly's Jungian woods veers suddenly to the right, away from recognizing the inherent imperialism of patriarchal systems and toward an affirmed return to male privilege. As "Iron John" and Bly's newly masculinized "wild man" are celebrated in a reaffirmed hierarchy, the meaning of patriarchy for women goes wholly ignored. At least nominally, the abandoning father is held to blame for incoherent male identity. But any system that reflects as much fear of gender blurring as does Bly's inevitably ends up finding the real culprit in the mother, whose maternal affection he defines as a "baptism into shame" that undermines the father-son bond.[13] Bly directly associates the problems of masculinity with the Vietnam War. He also associates them with that universal explanation for contemporary male angst, the feminist movement. And while I would argue that the pressure to reinvent manhood was not so much an effect of the women's movement as it was a synchronous event, when debate over U.S. aims and methods in Vietnam surfaced again in the 1980s, that very synchronicity, recycled as evidence of feminist castration designs, helped fuel the recuperation of a cultural ethic uncontaminated by values that might "feminize" it.[14]

The Hollywood movie has long been the popular culture site where America constructs and fine tunes its self-mythologies to fit the libidinal exigencies of its foreign and defense policies. As America's military interventionism resurged in the 1980s, filmgoers concurrently began witnessing the reascendancy—with a vengeance—of a masculine ethos so narcissistic in its need for self-display that it progressively eroded most of the space hitherto even available for female representation. So considerable was the shrinkage in women's roles between 1980s films and those from the 1930s to the 1970s, in fact, that in 1989, 1990, and 1991 the Academy Award industry actually had difficulty even coming up with five women in substantial enough roles to nominate for best actress. According to actress/writer Carrie Fisher's survey of Hollywood films produced between 1988 and 1990, only 28 percent of the speaking parts were written for women, fewer than 5 percent for women over forty.[15]

The films of the late 1980s and early 1990s—an oeuvre dominated by male buddy/cop films, boys' rite-of-passage films, sons' quest-for-father films, and so-called adventure films populated by lone "terminators"— spell out a metanarrative of violent masculine reassertion and feminine erasure that many of the films quite literally enact. Such a cultural metascript is, furthermore, being written by dominant trends in the representation of the sexualized body. As women's roles have shrunk, their bodies have progressively become subjected to a chillingly literal evisceration: "slasher" films with their inevitably female victims have proliferated, and films featuring women raped or women assaulted included, by 1990, one out of every eight movies Hollywood made.[16] Meanwhile, while female embodiment and female bodies were being whittled down, the screen has filled up with inflated male torsos of the sort that, before the 1980s, had been relegated to Tarzan movies. What dominated the 1980s screen iconography of gender was a determination to move male representation away from the new explorations of male sensitivity that had rather tentatively emerged in the first post-Vietnam decade. From Dustin Hoffman, Al Pacino, and the small, dark, vulnerable, often ethnically identified bodies that Hollywood foregrounded in the 1970s, the cultural ethic visually embodied in the lead male figure had by 1990 done a 180-degree reversal.

What defines a newly dominant American film genre is the "techno-muscularity" packaged into films featuring incredible hulk stars such as

Sylvester Stallone, Chuck Norris, their numerous grade-B video clones, and Arnold Schwarzenegger—the virtual apotheosis of the male mega-body and the highest paid actor in 1991 America. Yet as the masculine icon has undergone such literal inflation, the representation of maleness and the narrative in which it is imagined—which together constitute a set of culture-specific dreams, desires, and fears—has become progressively less adult as a projection and more and more the cartoon image of a little boy's fantasy of manhood. Inhabiting narratives that frequently belong to an identifiably post-Vietnam genre that imagines reshaping the future by changing the past, the fortresslike body image of the masculine hero who arose in post-Vietnam America reassures its audience of a masculine dominance made invulnerable by the arsenal of high-tech killing devices that this genre obsessively imagines as necessary extensions of male body power. Movies starring the Hollywood hulks are narcissistic and ho-moerotic. They are focused on a male body image that signifies not heter-osexual virility but potency over other male contenders played out within a graphics that writes female desire as a cipher and offers male bodies up to the gaze of other men. Such films are cultural isomorphs of the football game—an aggressive enactment of male bonding and competition played by males, for males, with women authorized only as cheering admirers of male prowess.

It is Arnold Schwarzenegger who plumbs the deepest subtending fanta-sies of techno-muscularity. Both on screen and off, he inculcates the most unacknowledged (and unacknowledgeable) fantasy of domination em-bedded in the myth not just of German but U.S. history. Like the unspo-ken signified that lies behind the myriad U.S. interventions in Third World countries, the meaning of the fantasy is unavoidably present in everything an audience hears and sees in Arnold Schwarzenegger's phe-nomenally popular militarism. For American viewers weaned on Holly-wood Nazis, the Schwarzenegger accent, physique, and even the mechani-zation of the characters he plays are undissociable from the Nazi dream of Aryan domination that U.S. wars in the Third World covertly play out. It seems equally impossible to miss the Third Reich allusion in the phrase "Desert Storm Troopers." And while associations between Schwarze-negger and Nazism are factually unfounded, they derive reinforcement from Schwarzenegger's widely publicized advocacy of right-wing politics.

The crossover in film from "sensitive male" to impervious behemoth is as much as recorded in the chronology of Sylvester Stallone's 1976–88 Rocky/Rambo sequence. The attempt in Rocky (1976) to construct a masculine hero in opposition to the macho ethic marks the film as a definable product of the 1970s. In it, the male fighter does not triumph in the ring but—with help from the woman in his life—achieves a moral victory by supplanting the "win" ethic with one that involves simply having the will to "go the distance." But in subsequent *Rocky* films the woman's role is crowded out of significance and the moral ethic disappears as the narrative of masculinity and the need to prove physical dominance nullify the ethic of 1976. By the time of *Rocky IV* (1985), the male hero's struggle had been enlarged to the international arena. There, morally impelled to avenge his fallen buddy, the American fighter is transformed into America's Fighter, embodied signifier of American valor who must single-fistedly stage America's comeback and show the world that an underrated America can defeat even the superhuman Russian(s).

In the counterpart Rambo film of that same year (*Rambo: First Blood, Part II*), the militarized physique appeared inside the fantasy that gave rise to it in the first place: the Vietnam War and the by-now obsessive concern over losing it that the Rocky/Rambo figure reinforces, even as his all-powerful body promises to undo its loss. And in *Rambo*—the most popular of all Vietnam War films made up until 1991, when their production was abruptly suppressed by the arrival of a "good" war—the nearly naked Stallone, visual signifier for the erect phallus and embodiment of American techno-muscularity, strides in dominion through the jungles of Southeast Asia and is made invulnerable by the infallibility of his high-tech American weaponry. But the feature of this movie that invigorated a whole subgenre of Vietnam War films is its fantasy of repetition, return, and redoing. In this film, the unjustly rejected Vietnam vet goes back to the scene of America's loss to rescue the figural representation of a "missing" American masculinity embodied on-screen as the emaciated and emasculated versions of maleness who are imagined as having been left behind, the "missing in action" that yet continue, even at this date, to haunt the filmic and the literal fantasies of the American public.[17] And Stallone's most famous line in the film—"Do we get to win it this time?"—helped to produce the angst it reflected over the issue that by 1985 had come to traumatize the national psyche. Given the retroactive emergence of that trauma and the concomitant obsession with a manhood imagined as having been abandoned by U.S. "withdrawal" (a term that itself connotes masculine shame), the way Stallone's question plays out in the movie does something more. By giving narrative reality to the fantasy that forces located somewhere in American culture had not only deprived men like John Rambo of their entitlement to heroism back in the Vietnam era but had afterward worked to perpetuate the imprisonment of American manhood, Stallone's resentful line effectively rationalized the amorphous male resentment that was increasingly adrift in American culture by 1985.

Throughout the 1970s and early 1980s, the Vietnam War had been shrouded in a silence born out of national shame. When it reemerged as a topic in American society, it did so via film—surfacing at a site outside of argumentation or rebuttal and carried by the symbol-laden depiction of the male body. Through *Rambo*, Stallone's gleaming physique became the virtual equivalent of an ideological stake onto which American masculinity became firmly lashed to a political stance on the Vietnam War. After *Rambo*, the body of the hero in successive Vietnam films became a signpost for political perspective. Those films that construed their position as "anti" war represented the Vietnam experience through male bodies filmed to seem small, vulnerable, and implicitly destructible—bodies like those of Chris Sheehan, Michael J. Fox, Willem Dafoe, and Tom Cruise. Meanwhile, the right-wing films of Norris, Stallone, Hackman, and Schwarzenegger, to which *Rambo* gave life, used the megabodied male to articulate the vision of an invincible America that did not "lose" the war so much as it was prevented from winning it.

These highly popular MIA narratives served the recuperation of militarism extensively, supplying a format for fictitious projection into Central America during the years when U.S. invasion of El Salvador and Nicaragua seemed likely and even suggesting equivalencies between the plight of military Americans putatively held in Vietnam and civilians taken hostage in Lebanon from 1985 onward. The ante of American pride thus upped considerably, a pugnacious subtext bridging Vietnam and the Middle East was slowly becoming part of the popular baggage that American culture was inexorably acquiring. At its center was the image of the newly beefed-up American male, his right to dominate the world inseparable from his dramatization of the heroic will to redo.

. . . . .

If the widespread narrative of threatened masculinity helps explain why American men were lured back to the fold of militarism so shortly after the Vietnam debacle, women's response to the Gulf War (listed by Harris polls at 73 percent in favor on January 21, 1991) is less readily explainable. The most intriguing sign to consider is the pervasive phenomenon of "yellow-ribbonism" and the belligerant demand to "love our boys" that the ribbons and the American flag displays encoded. Around those symbols, the nation's women as well as men were eventually mobilized, moving with alarming rapidity in less than six weeks from a widespread disinclination to fight a war for which not even the White House could articulate a compelling cause to a cheering reaffirmation of U.S. militarism, its essential causelessness swallowed up in a media-orchestrated roar of national self-confirmation.

The yellow ribbons served as a coalescent sign that both subsumed and offered to placate the peculiar anxieties that America had carried into the 1990s.[18] Used in the 1980s as a sign of remembering the hostages held in

Lebanon, they were already correlated with unexpressed hostility toward the Middle East. But they served the nation's desires in an even more important way. Through the capacity of the ribbons to signify the feminine, they enabled the construction of a rigid binary of gender; and through that binary, all potential responses to the war could be contained. Noting the way that the gender gap measuring support for the war had shrunk from a substantial twenty-four-point differential five days before U.S. bombing of Iraq began to a mere ten points four days after it started, Cynthia Enloe commented that

> in tying a yellow ribbon 'round an old oak tree—or car antenna, porch pillar, or shop sign—most women probably do not see themselves as endorsing something so grandiose as a new world order. They probably see themselves as providing moral support to particular sons, daughters, neighbors, and friends. But, for the U.S. national security elite, they are voluntarily constructing a feminized "homefront" to complement—28,000 American women soldiers notwithstanding—a masculinized battlefront.[19]

By being positioned as the virtuously beribboned feminine, the civilian home front not only invoked the binary that reemphasized the exclusively masculine position of the military but effectively delegitimated resistance to the war from either men or women. The yellow ribbons helped to undo two alternative versions of gender that had first been imagined on a broad scale in the 1960s and 1970s: the masculinity that had been oppositionally constituted around resistance and militant pacifism, and the alternative femininity that had imagined divorcing itself from playing dutiful spouse/maternal producer for the needs of the masculine, military state. During the Gulf War, with women soldiers for the first time at the combat front, conditions at least theoretically existed for a blurring of the strictly gendered binary through which war has traditionally been spatialized. But through a tightly policed feminization of the home front, masculinity was contained solely on the battlefront and femininity at home as a gold star mommy. As George Bush's target date for the display of American dominance came progressively closer, increasing pressures inside the culture began strictly dichotomizing all available civilian responses within the feminine options of the good mommy/bad mommy, loyal nurturer or unfaithful betrayer. Civilians could, in short, choose between playing Penelope or Clytemnestra, the archetypal good girl/bad girl models of Western culture's Ur–war narrative.

America's entrance into the Gulf War abounded in ironies of gender that the media carefully avoided placing into juxtaposition before the American reader/viewer. The public was not invited to consider, for instance, that while America—chivalric knight arrogant—was preparing to send its military to avenge the widely reported rape of Kuwaiti women by

Iraqi soldiers,[20] probably more American women recruits were concurrently being raped on military bases by their fellow soldiers than Kuwaiti women had been by the Iraqi military. In fact, the instance of reported rape and sexual assault at U.S. military training installations escalated so dramatically in the months leading up to the war that finally the Pentagon and the chairman of the Senate Armed Services Committee were embarrassed into ordering investigations.[21] Besides savior of women, the image of the U.S. military that the press helped craft was that of special savior of children. Yet while the propaganda machine was busy bruiting forth stories (later proven wholly false) of Kuwaiti infants ripped out of incubators by Iraqi soldiers,[22] the American war machine was at that very moment mapping out air strikes that would wipe out the majority of urban sanitation capabilities and would consequently eventuate—according to postwar United Nations estimates—in the 1992 death of some 170,000 Iraqi infants.[23] At stake in the media's avoidance of such enlightening ironies was the positive male persona that George Bush and Company had so diligently crafted—the good-father image that seemed consciously designed to suppress the identity of rapist and baby killer that had emerged as the defining signifiers of U.S. troop actions in Vietnam. Such media willingness to reproduce the official Gulf War narrative unchallenged was in itself eloquent testimony to the impact that the revisionist narrative of the Vietnam War had made. Determined not to be again held accountable for the United States' having lost a war,[24] the press and the public tacitly collaborated in a hear-no-evil/see-no-evil policy about Gulf War information. The mainstream press never really fought the imposition of government censorship and, as surveys showed, under the aegis of "protecting our boys," the majority of Americans would have approved of censorship that was even more stringent than that which was put in place. The American media and the public they play to may love violence, but the violence they love is only that which supports certain myths. As the press had discovered two decades earlier from the outrage it provoked from approximately 80 percent of Americans by airing stories of the My Lai massacre,[25] American viewers make a critical distinction between "good violence" and "bad violence": bad violence is that which works to undermine or expose contradictions in the cultural myth for which good violence is the paradigmatic structure. And the sacrosanct story around which this nation's understanding of itself has been built and then adumbrated into millions of mediated narratives is the story of American masculine heroism. At the center of the story, within a semiotics defined by the male symbolic, lies the constructed image of the innocent American soldier. And American militarist ideology has been built on top of a public investment in protecting that image. As protesters of the Gulf War discovered, the threat to destroy the signified—the rectitude of U.S. military action—is tantamount to·attacking the boy himself. For while "supporting the troops" is recognized as a public sign of support for the war they signify, to withhold such affirmation goes beyond merely the negation of that meaning. It situates the protester at the juncture where the society's two most negative figures are condensed: the national enemy and the withholding mommy.

With the media and the government acting as complicit mythographers of the scenario the public wanted to hear, the "bad violence" stories that were incompatible with the vision of America's innocent soldier boys were judiciously delayed in their release and/or soft-pedaled in mainstream media coverage. Quite unlike the obsession with quantifying the enemy "body count" that drove the Vietnam War, statistics on Iraqi troop deaths were left unreported and ultimately unknowable, registered only as perhaps several hundred thousand uncounted bodies, unmarked and unceremoniously bulldozed beneath the sand. By such action, the United States was flagrantly guilty of doing precisely what it had for twenty years accused the Vietnamese of having done: violating the Geneva convention mandating the identification, interment, marking, and transmission of information about enemy soldiers' graves. With the September publication of previously concealed information about U.S. tactics in the Gulf, the irony of U.S. accusations over Vietnamese treatment of America's putative MIAs reached cosmic proportions. The U.S. Army, as it crossed into Iraq, had conquered the enemy with specially designed plows that had buried alive some thousands of Iraqi soldiers dug into seventy miles of trenches. In the vocabulary of one of the American officers, the operation was "cost-effective."[26] In terms of the Biblical discourse that defines Western culture's most powerful vision of peace, however, the incident literalized the most grotesque parody possible of the turning of swords into plowshares.[27]

In spite of how thoroughly the technologized annihilation of a country with a GNP the size of Kentucky's flew in the face of all mythology that defines the heroic, up until the more sobering facts of the economic recession began to be felt, post–Gulf War America seemed determined to celebrate its returning troops as exemplary American heroes. Nevertheless, such celebrations themselves were dominated by a distinctly hostile festivity. Instead of with parades made up of the usual high-school bands and bicycle brigades, the Gulf War victory was celebrated by a display of technologized, phallic aggression distinctly reminiscent of the old Soviet May Day shows or the fist flexing of some Argentine junta, as massive tank formations, guns, armored personnel carriers, and missile launchers rolled across Memorial Bridge into the nation's capital.[28] But perhaps Washington, D.C., site of so many Vietnam War protests, was the appropriate space for playing out the veiled threat that is encoded in parading such military violence. The enemy that those tanks and guns were implicitly leveled at was the antiwar consciousness of twenty years ago—a consciousness that had been progressively demonized through the 1980s by association with all that is outside the masculine.

As the yellow ribbons began sprouting on front doors, in supermarkets, and on used car lots across America, there was a particular underlying impetus, beneath all the excessive and anxious patriotism, that invested this sign of "homecoming" with its talismanic power. The ribbons, the parades, and the "welcome home" celebrations that went on throughout the summer of 1991 were not really even about the Gulf troops. Displaced responses to the 1980s revisionist narration of Vietnam, they were half-conscious, guilt-ridden attempts to placate the by-now mythologized figure of the rejected and betrayed Vietnam veteran.

For the 1991 Gulf War, the Vietnam veterans once again got drafted. This time, however, their commander in chief ideologically evoked them to serve on the home front as accusatory signifiers of the son betrayed. Over the course of the 1980s, the Vietnam veteran had slowly been transformed from dangerous embodiment of ideological subversion into the sympathetic symbol of a war that had emasculated a generation of American men by stigmatizing them as losers. Inside this narrative, the figure responsible for all of the veteran's pain is the war protester. And simultaneously, the position of all those who had not "loved our boys in Vietnam" came to be anathematized as feminine. In story after story that began in the mid-1980s to pour forth from Vietnam veterans,[29] any and all rejection that some of them may have experienced upon return—together with guilt for actions in Vietnam that such stories disguise beneath the figure of a rejecting external accuser—was remembered in the person of a woman: a wife, a sister, a girlfriend, an airline stewardess, or even, in the 1988 film *Hamburger Hill*, an invented account of soldiers being greeted upon return by Berkeley coeds throwing dog shit. The connection is most vividly dramatized through Jane Fonda, the condensed figure of antiwar activism who selectively bore the weight of a vilification that escalated even as the war itself receded in time. Even in 1990, Fonda was still the object of considerable negative media attention; at the Vietnam War Memorial, "Frag Jane Fonda" patches continued to be popular items of sale. But once Fonda had been romantically linked with conservative capitalist and sportsman Ted Turner, the image of her on Turner's arm apparently signaled her return to respectable femininity. Having been harassed for years over Vietnam, Jane Fonda was suddenly exempt from query: her views on the Gulf War were never even questioned.

By contrast, men who had opposed the Vietnam War seemed by the mid-1980s to be suddenly at a premium. What had faded out of the public narrative were men who acknowledged having been part of the large group of college-attending males whose resistance to the war combined with their political importance as a status group had been the single most important factor in giving the antiwar movement its national impact. Unlike their fathers, who had signed up the day after Pearl Harbor, this was a generation that resisted, whether tacitly or overtly. Yet because males of this status were for the most part able to use the system to resist the war from behind a draft exemption, they were left twenty years later still exempt from the necessity even to take responsibility for that resistance—exempt, in other words, from the major issue of their generation and all its ideological consequences. Men in positions of authority who had once been part of the massive white flight into protected statuses—men like J. Danforth Quayle—had by the late 1980s adopted a handy "prowar" retropatriotism, behind which their decisions to avoid Vietnam were conveniently hid. As the antiwar position lost respectability, it began retroactively to lose the now-middle-aged men who had once made it respectable. And as the public's sympathy for the rejected veteran grew, no one seemed to remember—or even notice the absence of any narrative about—the unsung heroism of those who had gone to prison or left their country in opposition to the war. Retroactively, the only hero-victims of the era were those who had gone to Vietnam, and this group was itself being remembered through 1980s distortions that eradicated the narrative of resistance that distinguishes these veterans in American history. Vietnam Veterans Against the War remained active as a postwar organization trying to keep a history of that opposition alive. But the public at large no longer seemed aware of how powerful the antiwar movement within the active duty military had been, or just how many veterans had returned to become a part of the civilian antiwar movement. The history of male war resistance had been under such suppression that when uniformed veterans gathered in protest outside of a Boston opening of *Rambo* in the mid-1980s, they were attacked by a horde of outraged teenagers. According to the teenagers screaming at the vets to go home, it was Sylvester Stallone—a real man—who was also "a real veteran."[30]

By 1991, not many of the veterans who had become part of the resistance nor men who had maneuvered to keep themselves out of Vietnam wanted to be identified with the newly negative and feminized position of war protest. While history was being rewritten and the Vietnam War brought back into the fold of masculine sacrifice, what was also getting conveniently forgotten was that the *real* mechanism that had enabled this return to a heroically militarized masculinity was a revised military recruitment system that no longer placed middle class sons in harm's way. No longer threatened by a draft, the dominant class lost all memory of its role in the 1960s opposition and embraced the 1991 war enthusiastically, subsuming terms like "U.S. imperialism" under hypocritical euphemisms about all good men being willing to come to the aid of their country. The "all" no longer involved them.

The Vietnam veteran who had returned as emblematic antiwar spokesman and who was still in evidence in 1983 when the wall in Washington was dedicated had, like Yossarian's friend Dunbar in *Catch-22*, "been disappeared." As Harry W. Haines comments, what still baffles many veterans is "the extent to which cultural forms now produce a vision of the Vietnam War that obliterates the[ir] lived social experience of ideological crisis . . ., coopting the very experience that makes Vietnam veterans, for better or worse, unique in the national story." By 1991, the Vietnam veteran's once-volatile political opposition had been reconstituted into an "ideological certainty" used to justify the very policy of imperialist intervention that the war had so thoroughly discredited. The "rehabilitated veteran," Haines observes, now "serves the interests of patriarchy, antifeminism, *and* imperialism."[31]

As part of that "rehabilitation," any way of thinking that connected the widely publicized adjustment problems of the Vietnam vets to the real sources and agencies responsible for them was erased from public memory. No one seemed to remember anymore that it had been the government, not the peace movement, that had for years blocked treatment of posttraumatic stress disorder, impeded research into and denied responsibility for Agent Orange–related problems, welcomed the wounded home into shockingly understaffed and ill-equipped Veterans Administration hospitals, failed to set up employment and loan provisions comparable to those given veterans of other wars, problematized Vietnam disability claims, and sharply cut services from the VA budget that were still needed by many of the returnees. These stories and the story of the greater catastrophe of the Vietnam War that inevitably surfaced in veterans' statistics on alcoholism, drug addiction, homelessness, cancer-related deaths, suicides, and birth-defective children became such anathema to the Reagan administration that they were finally just elided by a directive to cease recording Vietnam veterans' statistics separately and amalgamate them into the happier records of the returnees from World War II and Korea. By 1991, the American public remembered that the Vietnam veterans had had special problems, but they no longer connected such trauma to its basis in the memory of things seen and done in Vietnam.[32] All that anyone seemed to remember by January 1991 was that the Vietnam veterans, increasingly imagined as victims, had, upon return, been "spat on by war protesters" and "never got a parade."

The Gulf War marks a particularly disturbing conjunction of interests. It marks the moment when the media, having suddenly recognized the boundless commercial potential of war, began, in columnist Sydney Schanberg's words, to look "more and more like an arm of the government's executive branch."[33] Thus it would be easy enough to locate the source of America's militant new "pride in itself" strictly in the government and the media. But consumers as well as producers participate in national myth making. As Richard Slotkin points out, the consumers of an ideology are "respondents capable of either dismissing a given mythic formulation, or affiliating with it."[34] Popular desires were complicit with governmental policies, each one acting to reproduce the other, in what Claude Lévi-Strauss calls the "will to myth."

In an analysis of the "will to myth" published prior to the Gulf War, Gaylyn Studlar and David Desser identify the key displacement and anticipate the model that would be used to fan the Gulf War into being:

> the question "Were we right to fight in Vietnam?" has been replaced (displaced) by the question "What is our obligation to the veterans of the war?" Responsibility to and validation of the veterans is not the same as validating our participation in the conflict in the first place. Yet answering the second question mythically rewrites the answer to the first. [And] one of the key strategies in this displacement of the crucial question of America's Vietnam involvement is that of victimization.[35]

What carried over so effectively to the Gulf War was the public's attempt to atone for the accusation implicit in that second question. The nation atoned for having been "unsupportive" of the Vietnam vets by aggressively wearing yellow ribbons for the Gulf troops, and the veterans laid claim to a place within rather than outside the tradition by reconstituting themselves as national victims. No longer in focus were the angry questions about U.S. policy that the veterans themselves brought back from their experience of napalmed villages and dismembered Vietnamese civilians, of field units that gave three-day passes to squads with the highest enemy body count and no passes to those with the highest number of enemy prisoners.[36] Instead, in newspapers across the country, in a raft of letters and "my turn" editorials from Vietnam veterans that began to appear by the late 1980s, the war of twenty years ago was now selectively remembered, with resurgent bitterness, through a script that eliminated everything that happened in Vietnam itself and rewrote the war as the individual soldier's return home. The story of resistance eradicated, the tale of the victimized and unsung veteran's return had, by 1991, become the emblematic narrative of the entire Vietnam War. By the time U.S. troops returned from the Persian Gulf, the grossly inflated model of the vet who had acquired posttraumatic stress disorder apparently from the venom of a war protester's saliva was firmly fixed in the nation's retroactively constructed memory.

The narrative of the unsung Norman Schwarzkopf, victimized by the ingratitude of the American public that did not give him a parade, is merely one of many more like it. However, Schwarzkopf's Vietnam story—much publicized during the Gulf War—contained just the patriarchal resolution to appeal to the anxieties of 1991 America: faced with a sister expressing reservations about the war in Vietnam, Schwarzkopf threw her out of the house. Yet when this story was first told to me, the figures were reversed and it became Schwarzkopf who, upon return from the war, was thrown out of the house by his hippie, war-protester sister. So familiar with the female-assigned rejection of Vietnam veterans had the public become that the story had been unconsciously rearranged into the pattern that told it "right."

In all of these revisionary narratives, the most remarkable transposition lies in the way that the American soldier who fought in Vietnam—not the hapless two million Vietnamese who by choice or accident got in his way—has become the victim. The physical violence routinely directed against war protesters—evidence of which the nation had been forced to witness via televised broadcasts of the 1968 Chicago Democratic Convention—had been displaced by stories of veterans who had been victimized by words and gestures. And photographic images as vividly definitive of the Vietnam era as the killings at Kent State, the Vietnam Veterans Against the War hurling down their medals on the steps of the Capitol, the napalmed Vietnamese girl running screaming toward the viewer, or the young Viet Cong soldier being shot in the head by the Saigon police chief—images that had once visually formed a seemingly indelible counternarrative to the thoroughly discredited official one—had been all but evacuated from the remembered story. Perhaps they faded because they were not finally "about" nor did they enhance the all-important national story of American male heroism that unconciously conditions how Americans rank the importance of the narratives they take in. The only "event" in the revised story that the nation seemed to remember in 1991 was a narrative of American male subjectivity constructed by an act of collaborative imagination: as the nation reacted against the national guilt that it had tentatively begun to confront in the 1970s, the only image that America "saw" by the late 1980s was the convincing picture of itself as the proverbially innocent U.S. soldier, returning from the war and being victimized by the insults of "spitting and jeering throngs."[37]

A *Los Angeles Times* editorial entitled "Vietnam Vets Weren't Feted by Parades," by Robert McKelvey, is in many ways a paradigmatic 1991 account. In its opening comparison, former Marine Captain McKelvey bitterly measures the Marine Corps commandant's idealized tribute to "our wives and loved ones supporting us at home" against the irony of his own wife's having "joined tens of thousands of others marching on the nation's capital to protest U.S. involvement in Vietnam." Two distinct narratives are at work here. In one, the veteran registers an uneasy awareness of the moral issues that prompted opposition to the war: "It was a divisive, unhappy time. Few people believed the war could be won or that we had any right to interfere in Vietnam's internal affairs." Nor does McKelvey himself ever argue that the war was morally—or even strategically—valid. We learn, in fact, that after returning home and living with the Quakers, he "felt almost ashamed of the uniform I was still wearing . . . [and] began to feel as if I had done something terribly wrong in serving my country in Vietnam." But that narrative is continually at odds with another, decidedly more pugnacious, eventually determining story. In this other narrative, his wife's failure to play out Penelope in a prescripted story that was always about not her but her husband, comes to stand for everyone who was not "supporting us at home." Eventually, this becomes the site where all of the latent, internalized blame in his first narrative gets displaced.

> Even though our family and friends meant us no harm by protesting our efforts, and probably believed they were speeding our return, their actions had a very demoralizing effect. Couldn't they at least wait until we were safely home before expressing their distaste for what we were doing? But by then, the military had become scapegoats for the nation's loathing of its war, a war in which draft dodgers were cast as heroes and soldiers as villains. . . . I recalled stories of comrades who had been spat upon in airports and called "baby killers." . . . Watching the Desert Storm victory parades on television, I was struck by the contrast between this grand and glorious homecoming and the sad, silent and shameful return of so many of us 20-odd years ago. . . . [For us] there were no family, friends, well-wishers, representatives of the Veterans of Foreign Wars or children waving American flags. . . . The feelings aroused in me by the sight of our victorious toops marching across the television screen are mixed and unsettling. Certainly they deserve their victory parade. But there is also envy. Were we so much different from them? . . . Seeing my fellow Vietnam veterans marching with the Desert Storm troops, watching them try, at last, to be recognized and applauded for their now-distant sacrifices, is poignant and sad. . . . A sense of hurt still lingers on and, with it, a touch of anger. Anger that the country we loved, and continue to love, could use us, abuse us, discard and then try to forget us. . . . It was our curious, sad fate to be blamed for the war we had not chosen to fight when in reality we were among its victims.[38]

The issues that defined the first narrative—whether "we had any right to interfere in Vietnam's internal affairs" (or, for that matter, in the Middle East's)—pale to inconsequentiality beside the all-consuming desire that not only motivates this memoir and determines the writer's affirmation of U.S. militarism in the Gulf but ultimately convinces him that he and his brother veterans were really the war's "used, abused, and discarded victims." To McKelvey, he and his brothers are victims because they did not get the applause that he imagines as every soldier's basic entitlement, irrespective of the morality of the war in which he served.

Former Captain McKelvey's letter is written from the world of boyhood—the boyhood of a white American male growing up in the glorious aftermath of World War II, imbued with the unconditional promises life seems to have made to all such little boys. Gone from adult consciousness is any historical recall of just how grotesquely inappropriate it really would have been to applaud a show of U.S. military strength in 1973 or in any way assist the Nixon government's attempt to displace the sober national mood with symbolic practices affirming U.S. actions in Vietnam. In McKelvey's reconstruction, the political is overwhelmed by the personal and adulthood by regressive desire: all that matters is that he and his comrades went to war and came back—for which they are entitled to be heroes who get a parade. Even his insistence that he/they should not be "blamed for the war we had not chosen to fight" seems especially telling, for as an officer in the U.S. Marine Corps, McKelvey cannot wholly be exculpated from "choosing to fight." What he did not choose—and what seems grossly unfair to him—was to be born to a generation that did not get offered any good wars but that got instead the war that may have bequeathed American males the opportunity for agonized moral wisdom but refused them the hero's glory they had from boyhood grown to expect.

Because heroism must be conferred by a woman—without whose cheers it cannot be constituted—this perceived injustice ends up being peculiarly the fault of his wife/women. Angrily, McKelvey envisions the war as a rewards system "in which draft dodgers were cast as heroes and soldiers as villains." To situate the draft dodgers as "heroes" loses sight of the father's approval essential to the cultural definition of "hero" and suppresses the price paid by those who left the country or went to prison. Nonetheless, the affiliation between draft resistance and the feminine—in this case, his wife's literal alignment with war protest—compels the victimized-veteran script into such a polarity. The draft dodgers, like the unworthy suitors whom it was Penelope's job to deny as she dutifully awaited the return of Ulysses, are traditional figures in this myth. They appear in the U.S. Army marching song "Sound Off" condensed into the figure of "Jodie," the imagined feminized male who stayed behind and has now "got" the soldier's wife, his sister, and his Cadillac,[39] all of which are signifiers of the real object of social desire, which is male heroism.

This male-constructed myth of heroic destiny—along with several other cherished American self-conceptions—failed catastrophically in Vietnam. But McKelvey's story unwittingly demonstrates how such unconsciously held mythic models, reinvoked for the Gulf War, served to polarize the Vietnam veteran against the antiwar movement with which he actually shared a crucial history.[40] By degrading the deeds of the collective and hence the individual soldier, the antiwar position that refused to praise the slaughter in Vietnam and defined it instead as a large-scale atrocity became the agent that deprived the Vietnam soldier of what, within the myth, is construed as his entitlement. And that negative position, imagined back to the scene of its origin, is the space of the withholding mommy.

Such entitlement to heroism is an assumption in which the American public at large participates vicariously, as was made abundantly clear in the angry public reaction evoked by the Iran-Contra charges against Oliver North, who may have been no more than a face on television to the American public but whose image instantly fused with some subconscious picture of boyishly heroic, beleaguered American innocence. Nonetheless, despite being presumed across genders, American heroism originates in a logic accessible only to American males. It is, problematically, the same logic that informs Oliver Stone's antiwar film, *Born on the Fourth of July*. From its opening shot, the film makes quite clear that little Ronnie Kovic and millions of boys just like him grew up in the years between World War II and Vietnam playing war stories and participating in a Hollywood-inspired mythic history of self and nation that was understood as a rehearsal for manhood. Within that context, America's little boys—Oliver Stone included—apprehended the promise of heroic glory and its public confirmation of manhood imagined through the cheering applause and ticker-tape parades that Robert McKelvey enviously laments.

What this suggests is that for post–World War II American males, war is far less a matter of cause than of half-conscious expectation fueled by desire: George Bush's anticipated "test by fire." Director Stone's conscious intent, quite clearly, was to denounce (the) war by exposing the problematic connection between war and masculinity. But if the film does anything, it tells us only how tenacious that association is, for *Born on the Fourth of July* can no more reach a satisfactory conclusion without fulfilling the young male's presumed entitlement than can Robert McKelvey's scenario. In Stone's film, his Vietnam veteran gets a parade. Kovic's newly claimed masculinity—confirmed in the film's third and final parade sequence when he triumphantly wheels himself past the cheering throngs onto the speaker's platform—remains thus implicated in the same problematic source of desire from which warriors, and war, are constructed. Within a year of the film's release and inside of a discourse paving the way from Quagmire to Gulf, that same issue of "getting a parade" would surface as the site of a national angst that, by any terms other than gender, might border on the ludicrous. Yet despite being based largely on Hollywood fictions (in reality, not many returning World War

II troops were personally fêted with parades) and regressive as such a desire may be, within it lies a crucial motivater for the impulse to re-write—and ultimately restage—the Vietnam War.

In the new narration that has been under labored construction for the past decade, the patriarchal military state has been returned to its pre-Vietnam status of wise father. Its executive branch and military brother-hood have disappeared from the list of the culpable, and blame for Viet-nam is associated almost exclusively with everything outside of those two masculine locations: the unsupportive home front, the congressional cur-tailment of U.S. military potency, the peacenik press, and an effeminate Pentagon leadership that General Norman Schwarzkopf describes as "a cottage industry [that] developed in Washington, D.C., consisting of a bunch of military fairies that had never been shot at in anger."[41] The general's uninhibited invocation of the homophobic lexicon in itself says a great deal about how, in the wake of the Gulf War and its affirmation of masculine ideology, the categories of gender and sexuality had, in ef-fect, been retooled into social bludgeons.

.   .   .   .   .

By all outward appearances, the American public in 1991 had come full circle back to a militarism built upon the reinvestment of a national/ personal selfhood in the image of the American soldier. But playing out the prodigal son's return to the fold has proved complex for the genera-tion of American sons caught up in that compulsion, for what the Viet-nam War set in motion was the radical truncation of the oedipal journey: a narrative, ultimately, of hollowed-out paternity and perpetuated son-ship. Besides meaning a war that was lost and an era of committed and bitter political division in the country, what "Vietnam" signifies is the site of a traumatic break between the men of one generation and those of another—between the fathers and the sons. Something dimly understood to be occurring even at the time and termed "the generation gap" proved to be a systemic rupture on the scale of mass culture. America emerged from the Vietnam War still a patriarchal system—but a patriarchy with an unoccupied and no longer occupiable center. Chronologically brack-eted by the assassination of the national father at one end, marked by the forced retirement of his successor at the middle, and culminating in the disgraced resignation, a few steps ahead of impeachment, of the final fa-ther figure of the era, the battles that America's sons waged in and over the Vietnam War were played out against a history repeatedly defined by a both literal and symbolic evacuation of authority.

The expulsion of the father has not served to liberate the sons, how-ever, for America's post-Vietnam narrative is stamped with the intensity of a generation stuck in its own boyhood and now playing out, with increasing violence, an unconscious cultural myth that attempts to recover the father. Within the drama of manhood being staged across the psyche of American popular culture, the Vietnam veteran functions as proleptic historical signifier of the moment when the father was lost, the moment of refusing the father's dictates, and the moment of failing them. And the veteran's story of striving and rejection has come to be weighted with such significance not because it particularly reflects the actual experience of most veterans, but because it captures the shared, symbolic truth of what happened to American males of the whole Vietnam generation, veteran and nonveteran. Inside the oedipal framework of the only narrative through which the culture has been able to imagine itself, this whole generation of men shared the same fate, regardless of which side of the war they were on: none of them got a parade, none got heroized, none earned the father's approval, and all were stranded in a never-completed transition to manhood, left poised in one gap en route to inheritance of the gap now signified by the father's vacated space. Twenty years later in the wake of the Gulf War, while the president spoke affirmingly about the nation having at last "gotten past the Vietnam War," the central issue that had come to dominate the sociopolitical discourse was the dawning recognition that, within the span of a single generation, the American family had devolved into a predominantly fatherless unit.

The Vietnam War brought into being a historical collision of values that collectively compelled the nation's young men into severance from the fathers. Many severed themselves by rejecting their fathers' World War II reading of the Vietnam conflict, and many such sons were quite literally banished from their paternal houses. For defying the draft, some were forced into exile and others into federal prisons. But while back then, the culture imagined the war protester versus the Vietnam soldier in terms of the classic Huck Finn/Tom Sawyer, bad son/good son binary, the conditions of the Vietnam War made even the space of good son impossible. The young men of the Vietnam draft were forced by the dictates of the father-text to "choose," as a condition of masculinity, among a sadistically constructed series of virtually self-annihilating options: to fight a war for which no plausible ethical justification existed; to refuse induction and, as criminals, serve hard time in prison; or to banish themselves from the father's house and flee hunted in exile from their country. And if the second and third choices more obviously signify the father-son rupture, the choice to fight in Vietnam proved incapable of preventing it. Ultimately, not even those men who sequestered themselves in draft exemptions could escape the culturewide severence from paternal authority.

The father is synonymous with the law that dictates patriarchal society and sets out its inflexible requirements for masculinity. He is unforgiving.

Thus, despite even the readiness of the dutiful sons to prove themselves heirs to the patrilineal "line unbroken," even the sons who went to Vietnam failed. They did not return winners, as had their fathers from World War II, but left an unforgivable blot on the unblemished war record they inherited. And the fact that some 120,000 of those who returned have by now committed suicide—twice over the number that even the war managed to kill[42]—strongly suggests that some far more powerful source of rejection was at work in American society than any braless hippie shouting "baby killers" could account for. It suggests that the sons of patriarchy unconsciously hear and obey a silent but omnipresent dictum written out in ancient Sparta as the edict to return from a war with one's shield or on it.

It was not, however, merely a matter of failing the father. The Vietnam generation was compelled into the revelation that patriarchy disallows: that they had been lied to and used by the fathers. They, the youth, had been used by the old men who either did not go to Vietnam or who, if they went, betrayed their task of leadership;[43] the young men had been asked in the name of a tradition that bound them to personal, national, and historical fathers to kill, to die, and to taint their souls for mystified ideals they later discovered were shrouded in political lies. Some, while yet in Vietnam, took aim with grenades or rifles and tried killing the father. But even those who tried not to see the lies returned to America to stony rejection for failing to keep the fathers' myths intact. The popular, politically useful story would have it that it was the antipatriot who met and reviled the returning soldiers; but the unspeakable truth is that returning veterans were treated as pariahs by the Veterans Administration and were probably more scorned by groups like the American Legion and the Veterans of Foreign Wars than they were by war protesters.[44] Moreover, the whole generation of men was scarred by the war, including even those lucky enough to be outside the reach of the draft. Having been given the opportunity to undergo patriarchy's "test by fire," they had failed, for Vietnam was the war of their generation, the heroic moment they had grown up to anticipate, and the only war they had. And it is not in the least uncommon today for men who happily avoided the war to look back on Vietnam and find themselves with "the distinct feeling that they had missed a critical 'rite of passage' in coming to terms with their manhood."[45]

As the example of Richard Rusk's fruitless reunion with his father should suggest, it is not just the men who fought in Vietnam who find themselves inexplicably caught up twenty years later in the rhythms of repetition and return that mark out the psychic landscape of the son's always impossible quest for the father. It is all the men caught in the ten-year long war—the generation that has now moved into power in this country and the one whose psychic needs are now dictating everywhere the shape of a deeply regressive national master plot. The quest for the father—which might seem to be a reparative ideal—is dangerously regressive and invariably futile because what was required at the time of transition to adulthood cannot, by very definition, be incorporated twenty years later. For a short space in the 1960s–70s, American culture set out on the difficult and uncharted quest for new masculine narratives that might move beyond the equation of masculinity with the figure of the cultural father and the patriarchal world he defines; but such a progression was always in contention with the seductive impulse toward repetition and return. The Gulf War gave the clearest possible evidence that America had turned back, with compulsive desperation, regressing into boyhood deeds that demonstrate masculine loyalties and contempt for the feminine—the conditions for earning the oedipal validation that time has already rendered moot. In the four "tests by fire" that the United States has staged since its defeat in Vietnam, the pattern has been one of a progressively escalating use of force and an increasing reliance on weapons of mass destruction demonstrably disproportionate to any imputed threat. For the rest of the world, America's bildungsroman is dangerous, for the pattern strongly suggests a psychic quest that becomes compulsively more urgent with each successive proof of its impossibility.

Judging from such signs as America's heroized mythology of baby-faced gunfighters like Billy the Kid or from its traditional representation of its national historical self as the "young," "new," and "innocent" nation, one could say that this country has always valorized male adolescence. The choice of Audie Murphy as the national embodiment of the World War II American soldier reflects the attraction; and certainly for Henry James, adolescent selfhood was a definitively American trait, producing a brashly honest, stubbornly innocent American character that James finally found culpable for his refusal to grow up. But the positioning of the father strongly differentiates the film models of American boyishness clustered around World War II from those made in the post-Vietnam era.

In the fictions of the filmmakers of the Vietnam generation, the father-son rupture gets repeatedly narrated, always from the consciousness of the son. Figures of authoritative, compassionate leadership like John Wayne's Sergeant Stryker of *The Sands of Iwo Jima* are simply gone, their absence narrated into post-Vietnam movies as either the father's betrayal of the son or the son's quest to revalidate the father, or both. Films about World War II were generally organized as love stories and included girls/wives back home, but films about the Vietnam War—caught up in the regressions of the oedipal compulsion—are never love stories, and their narratives are often violently inhospitable to even the presence of women.

In these films the unresolvability of the father is frequently represented through an implicit accusation of him that is simultaneous with attempted exoneration, sometimes further complicated—as in *Apocalypse Now* and *Platoon*—by competition between several sites of vacated paternal authority within a narrative that impels the son to kill the father. In both these films the immediate position of the father is malevolently occupied and the good father displaced. But even when a benevolent father is put into the fantasy, as are the hero's mentor figure in the two Rambo films and Ron Kovic's father in *Born on the Fourth of July*, domestication has feminized him, and his weakness and ineffectuality lead to a direct betrayal of the son anyway, leaving the father's position once again vacant. In the second Rambo film, blame is deflected away from the father by locating it with the pudgy, effeminate Pentagon civilian; in Stone's film, it is shunted onto the castrating mother, who is blamed both for sending her son off to war and rejecting him when he returns.

Most of the footage of combat units in Vietnam films suggests a total vacuum of authority. In films like *Casualties of War*, or *Apocalypse Now*, or *Full Metal Jacket*, the war is a chaotic moral landscape with no fathers on hand, a war fought by boys led by boys, a space abandoned to the rule of frightened and lethally armed adolescents. *The Deer Hunter*—one of the few to include a focus on the hometown—lacks fathers in even that space. There are only brothers. But while the law of the (absent) father—represented by the "one shot" model of male ethics—is offered on the one hand as the highest ethical code available and as that which saves the oldest/strongest son (Robert de Niro), it proves lethal to the sensitive son (Christopher Walken). Furthermore, the older son's attempt to move into and redeem the space of the father by going back to rescue the other sons proves bitterly insufficient to save or return them whole. The film's one literal father/son pair offers a bleak comment on the transition of the Vietnam sons into any paternity of their own: in this pair, the paraplegic veteran cut off at his manhood and returned from the war to a state of near-infantile dependency is symbolically situated as the putative father of a son who is not his. And though much in this film seeks resolution in regression to the myths of frontier individualism in which American imperialism was born, the film is nonetheless radical in its understanding of "Vietnam" as signifying the end of the idealized nuclear family. *The Deer Hunter* and *Apocalypse Now* were among the first Vietnam War films that emerged belatedly at the end of the 1970s; and the bleak integrity of their father-son representations reflects something of the attempt to confront and get beyond the father—the response that could still be imagined in that first decade. By the time of *Uncommon Valor* (1983), the need to recuperate the father and resecure patriarchal authority had become so pressing that this film, which features a military father (Gene Hackman) going back to Vietnam to rescue the son, even tries to situate the Vietnam War and the sense of abandonment and exile it bequeathed to American sons inside of a good-father narrative. But even this fantasy of paternal affirmation stops short of staging the father and child reunion, tacitly conceding its impossibility through a narration in which the son dies in captivity before the father arrives.

Of all the father-obsessed films of the era, the most obsessive was a blockbuster that was Hollywood's first overt attempt in years to valorize militarism and affirm its positive connection to masculinity. The George Lucas *Star Wars* trilogy attempts to construct a legitimating oedipal narrative out of the father-son schism by creating an epic model of the son who, after a journey toward an Eastern/New Age sort of wisdom, can confront the abandoning force of the Dark Father and succeed in the oedipal redemption of male subjectivity anyway—all of which necessitates replacement by a second, fairy godfather of sorts who mystically appears to endow the son with the emblem of warriorhood/phallic authority, to which the originating father has lost moral entitlement. A story that predicates the son's recovery of masculine authority on the militarism of joining the force to go fight for your galaxy, *Star Wars* reached through the screen in 1977 to offer an allegorized resolution to a silently building cultural crisis that was subconsciously being carried into every theater by every American audience. In the Lucas allegory, Luke Skywalker's education into manhood can begin only when, directed by the surrogate good father, he turns away from the antiwar position in which he was raised and seizes his destiny to be a national warrior hero. The film that carried the most overt such fusion of father and military state was *Top Gun* (1989), which locates its narrative impetus squarely in the losses of the Vietnam War. This film proved to be literally the best recruitment device the U.S. Navy has ever helped to produce. In it, the Vietnam War exists as a memory through which to enact, both on- and off-screen, the seduction of sons necessary for any militarist state. On-screen, in shots of high-tech military aircraft and jet pilot maneuvers that packed in young males across the country, the son (Tom Cruise) becomes a warrior in order to recuperate the honor of a father whose death in Vietnam was enmeshed in obscure charges that have left his name (and, thus, his son's) falsely dishonored. What was simultaneously under recuperation was the reputation of the U.S. military, likewise sullied in Vietnam. Through the logic that only by going to war and redeeming their fathers can the sons of the Vietnam generation lay claim to their own honor among men, an unconscious script was being valorized for a nation to do likewise.

Neither *Top Gun* nor *The Great Santini* (1979) is usually categorized as a Vietnam War film, but both should be. In their representation of the peacetime military playing out a model of war as game and flight squadron as fraternity, these two offer especially acute visions of the ethos that traveled from the high-tech warrior cadres of Vietnam to define the wholly technologized U.S. military operation in the Gulf. In Vietnam films as well as World War II films, the paradigmatic soldier is characteristically remembered as an enlisted army or marine corps GRUNT embodying a certain moral seriousness associated with his proximity to killing and dying. *Top Gun* and *The Great Santini* explore a radically different ethos, that of the elite technicians of war, the studied *sprezzatura* and gamesmanship of the high-flying macho men of the air who are almost always officers and who experience war from the detachment of button-pushing technology, firing rounds at the enemy by squeezing the "joy stick" conveniently located between the pilot's legs. It is the ethos behind the sports-heavy metaphors through which interviewed American pilots reexperienced their aerial devastation of Iraqi ground troops as the scoring of points in some competitive contest; ultimately, it became the moral and linguistic visor through which the American public—who experienced the war as a military talk show—likewise conceptualized it.

Robert Duvall's Lieutenant Colonel Bull Mechum, alias the Great Santini, is a type of the well-loved hero particularly valued within the conformity of the military—a hero whose leadership fuses with the kind of little-boy risk-taking, nonconformist contempt for the rules that made legends out of Patton and MacArthur. For air groups, the code also involves a Rabelaisian mockery of moral seriousness and a studied disregard for regulations and bureaucracies. A rigid family disciplinarian who reveres the marine corps, Bull Mechum is also a forty-plus-year-old adolescent whose boyish pranks perform the highly important American fiction of nonconformist individualism through rebellions that never seriously question or attempt to overthrow the status quo. No one belongs more completely to the established national norms than does Bull Mechum, whose pranks and rebellions merely play out the time-honored drama of son against father/authority; and Mechum is himself driven by obsessions about masculinity that not only compel his son to play sports and be a winner but also dictate the father's compulsive need to compete against and defeat his own son in order to hold on to the position of boy eternal.

Masculine game mentality is hardly unique to this country, but the manic level of it that Bull Mechum represents may be. No matter how old the male or how inappropriate it may be for him to constellate his sense of selfhood around athletic prowess, his ability to defeat other males in various sports contests has become so overly invested a national feat that it quite openly affects even international interactions on the presidential level. Not only does George Bush thrive on setting up sports competitions as tests with which to challenge visiting foreign leaders but the mentality extends to even the new parlance his administration has coined for the device that launches nuclear war—a device inside of a black box that, with eloquent simplicity, is now just called "the football." For the president whose public fidgeting at world news conferences has been compared to that of an "elementary school student when [he gets] bored . . . a child inhabiting the body of an adult,"[46] the term presumably creates a nuclear sports joke about the nation's "quarterback" deciding to "throw the bomb."

It was through such a sports/game discourse, with its underlying dictum of "win," that the American public was connected to the Gulf War. While the rest of the world may have been puzzled or even offended at hearing U.S. pilots on CNN return from bombing runs and jubilantly relate the slaughter of Iraqi soldiers in terms of football and baseball metaphors, Americans understood the connections because they, too, had grown up in the uniquely American school system where sports take priority over academics, high schools produce sports heroes and colleges professional athletes, and the *real* curriculum that the system is tacitly organized to teach and test is one that could be called Comparative (Competitive) Masculinity. No one but Americans probably recognized the dedication of Superbowl 1991 to America's boys in the Gulf as a genuine tribute of high seriousness in the culture. Quite obviously, the Italian player on Seton Hall College's basketball squad who returned to Italy under physical threat from the fans did not understand what sacred premise he had violated in declining to participate in the team gesture of sewing an American flag on his uniform to signify support for America's Gulf troops. But Americans understood: the drive to make sports a part of the public educational curriculum had originated in the United States at the end of the Civil War as a substitute to provide "the moral equivalent of war."[47] And if Americans who did not grow up male did not wholly grasp the sacred connections that link a team of players and their playing field to the nation's warriors out on a battlefield, they had the opportunity to learn a critical lesson from the public outrage and presidential denunciation that Roseanne Barr provoked after a San Diego Padres baseball game, where her rendition of the national anthem seemed, wittingly or not, to mock the nation's sacred masculine investments in baseball. At least in President Bush's eyes, her gesture had mocked all of America.[48]

In films like *Big, Back to the Future, The Sure Thing, Dead Poets Society, Bull Durham, Home Alone,* and myriad others, filmmakers of the 1980s and 1990s have been writing out a culture's regressive desires into big-screen fictions of the boy eternal. The opening programs of the 1990 fall television season were so marked by a childish "elevation of behavior that can only be described as irresponsible" that the *Baltimore Evening Sun*'s television critic insightfully assessed the season as "a clumsy attempt by baby-boomer-aged producers to translate the generation gap that formed one of the main conflicts in their lives into a contemporary setting."[49] The world imagined by this television sitcom fare is one in which male adolescents, evermore in subject position, move through misogynist narratives marked by domineering mommies and either ineffectual or absent fathers: *Get a Life*, where a thirty-year-old paperboy who still lives with his parents persuades his best friend to play hooky from work and spend the day in the park eluding the friend's killjoy wife, illustrates a representative plot. Nor did the victory in the Gulf allay the need for such regressive fictions. Post-Gulf male fantasies could still be read through their projection onto big-screen narratives of men's boyhood heroes, a repertoire that included 1991's *Dick Tracy* and *Batman* and expanded in 1992 to produce *Hook*, the ultimate fantasy of suspended boyhood, produced for a target audience of middle-aged Peter Pans. Writing in the *Washington Post*, Andrew Ward recognizes the film's mirroring of cultural production, seeing it as "of a piece with what my entire generation has done to childhood itself. We have ruined it by refusing to let it go."[50]

But the media fiction that best captured the accumulated masculine desire that post-Vietnam America carried with it into the final decade of "the American Century" was a narrative where a cornfield transformed into a baseball field becomes the sacred space of rescue for "all America's" oedipal dreams. *Field of Dreams*—set in the mythic space of heartland America and so much a favorite of male audiences that it was a 1988 nominee for best picture—offered a mythologized history of the 1980s looking back on the 1960s. It also offered an epic of middle-class, white-male dreams, universalized to presume that they represent those of "all" America.

Before the motion picture of Ray Kinsella's (Kevin Costner) new life as a farmer in Iowa can begin, it is literally brought to a stop by still photographs from the past and the accompanying narrative of his father's disappointments. The film thus opens in medias regression with the doughboy image of a father who returned from World War I to put on a baseball uniform, try unsuccessfully to make it in the minor leagues, and raise his son on stories of baseball heroes. Two events left Ray's father permanently disappointed: the 1919 disgrace of the Chicago White Sox and his son's going off to Berkeley and joining with "the hippies and protesters . . . majoring in the sixties."[51] The father died in 1974 with the ruptured relationship to his son unhealed; and although Ray married Annie a few months later and thus set out on a life of his own, in 1987, Ray, age thirty-eight, is haled by an omnipotent male voice saying, "If you build it, he will come," and thereupon sets out on a mythic journey backward to fulfill the father's dreams and undo the rebellion against him that is locked up in resistance to the Vietnam War signaled by Berkeley in the late 1960s.

Field of Dreams inscribes a masculine consciousness caught between two systems of desire. In many ways the movie wants to critique the 1980s rule of material greed and renegotiate the values of the 1960s into viable play; simultaneously, it wants to bring back the father, although the father is himself the signifier that is incompatible with the 1960s. So the narrative sets out on its circuitous quest: first, before the father can be recuperated, the band of defamed warriors who, like the Vietnam soldiers, were denied their entitlement to heroism, must be brought back and authorized as genuine American heroes. It does not really matter to the film that the Chicago White Sox did, in fact, accept bribery money in the 1919 World Series and were thus guilty of the behavior that led to their disgrace—the only thing that does matter is that they were American baseball players, and they are therefore presumed entitled to the space of glory promised to America's (white) males. With the baseball field in place and the legendary 1919 Chicago team out practicing on it, the film next turns its energies to recovering a 1960s transformed enough to ac-commodate the return of the father.

The central signifier of the 1960s who Ray sets out to find is Terence Mann, black Pulitzer Prize-winning novelist, former war protester and civil rights leader, whose ideas inspired the sixties generation and have by 1987 become subject to PTA book bans. It was, we learn, when Ray read Terence Mann's novel *The Boat Rocker* that he started "refusing to have a catch with his father . . . [and] never played catch with him again."[52] But Terence Mann, it turns out, is a model of 1980s reform who now rejects the notion of political causes and is no longer into rocking boats. What will "ease his pain" and substitute for the relinquished passion of his political past will be that which will likewise recuperate the space of the father and reinstate his uniformed heroes—*baseball!* And so James Earl Jones (looking a bit embarrassed for affirming racial privileges that his role demands he seem oblivious to) leaps down off the bleachers and, speaking as Man(n), pleads for Ray not to sell the field because it and its players represent the space that allows "all" Americans to return to the dreams of their childhood—dreams that are embodied, of course, in an all-white, all-male baseball team on which no black players (let alone women) would have been allowed to play. But Mann passionately insists that this team is emblematic of American heroism and that America needs to partake vicariously of that experience once again:

> People will come. . . . They'll come to Iowa for reasons they can't even fathom, . . . innocent as children, longing for the past. . . . They'll find they have re-served seats . . . wherever they sat when they were children and cheered their

heroes. They'll watch the game, and it will be as if they'd dipped themselves in magic waters. America has rolled by like an army of steamrollers. It's been erased . . . rebuilt, and erased again. But baseball has marked the time. This field, this game . . . it's a piece of our past. It reminds us of all that once was good. And that could be again. People will come. People will most definitely come.[53]

It is not only the racial gap that gets falsely foreclosed in the film. The wife is restricted to a thoroughly unrealistic, 1960s version of Donna Reed—the ultrasupportive spouse who appears only in scenes about her husband and is utterly unfazed by his decision to risk the mortgage money on a voice that tells him to build a baseball field. Annie is the model Penelope—the good wife of the male-constructed narrative who has dutifully remained fixed in time at the point of his regression, never progressing forward but remaining a memorial image of the 1960s, a leftover hippie whose vocabulary is still punctuated by "far out." As Annie goes indoors to make coffee while the men enact their rituals of bonding out on the male playing field, it is the benevolent gaze of the woman that in fact affirms and makes possible the little-boy heroism of the fantasy. As women, Annie and the daughter, Karin, are crucial inclusions in this story: they are the creatures in culture who intuitively Know but who, being women, lack agency and cannot Do. It was Annie who insisted on buying the farm to begin with, Annie who identified Terence Mann for Ray; and it is Karin who, Sybil-like, prophesies the film's final fantasy of what Terence Mann articulates as an America reunifying around a vision of its own innocence. The film even seems conscious that in a world defined by competitive male bonding, women are subject to the kind of annihilation that almost happens when little Karin, caught between two angry men, gets jarred off the bleachers and falls into a coma. *Field of Dreams* does recognize that, for women to survive in a world wholly dictated by male fantasies, it is necessary for some men (Burt Lancaster) to step back across the line, give up the game, and take their place on the sidelines as healers of all that gets broken beneath the obsessive weight of male plots such as this one. But nonetheless, for all its awareness of the threat faced by women who are co-opted into mediating male bonds, the film goes right on compulsively playing out that fantasy. The narrative finally integrates the black male at the margins of its white-male bond, but since women disrupt the father-son totality, it cannot integrate gender. The field of dreams it creates is one that first controls the problem of the father by bringing him back at age nineteen in the structure of son and then offers narrative closure in a scene of reunited father and son playing catch into the night while Annie goes in to make their dinner and the headlights of "all America" stream toward this vision.

Ultimately, the field constructed within this fantasy is a field on which women and blacks must relinquish the dreams of liberation they acquired in the sixties in order that America can once again participate in the "all-American" game—in order that a patriarchal world with its uniformed heroes may be resurrected and American men reconfirm their innocence in the figural space of boy eternal.

For the past decade, Americans have been devouring movie after movie about reclaimed sonships and perpetuated boys' rites of passage. But however enamored of the adolescent his own countrymen may be, all this boyishness in American behavior has costly consequences for the rest of the world. In Graham Greene's Vietnam novel, *The Quiet American*, the culpability of the boy-man version of American diplomacy is depicted through the fifty-five-year-old American of the title who is out planting bombs on bicycles in order to save the Vietnamese from communism, yet whose "young and unused face . . . gangly legs and his crew-cut and his wide campus gaze . . . seemed incapable of harm, . . . impregnably armoured by his good intentions and his ignorance . . . as incapable of imagining pain or danger to himself as he was incapable of conceiving the pain he might cause others."[54] As Greene's novel about the Vietnam of the 1950s prophetically recognized, America's "crew-cut" version of itself as the righteously innocent adolescent is a mythic self-image that allows the nation to behave in just such massively irresponsible ways as its foreign policies reflect. No more than the nation really holds its adolescent males accountable for their excesses does this country seem to imagine, for instance, that it should be held responsible for the political, economic, and human wreckage it has caused in the last decade as it has bullied its way across the yards of its Latin American neighbors, determined to keep proving itself a "winner," even when there has been nothing at issue that could logically be imagined as a competition. As for the some thousand-plus civilians who got in the way of America's little 1989 military Christmas show in Panama and were apparently then dumped in unmarked mass graves, the U.S. Army clearly felt annoyed by any imputation of moral responsibility. Leaving it up to the Panamanians to sort out the aftermath, America picked up its planes and trucks and went home to have a parade.

To the American boys on the sports field/battlefield and to Boy George, the overaged preppie in the white house whose film tastes run to the cartoon heroics of Stallone, Schwarzenegger, and Norris,[55] being a bully is apparently fun—as much fun, for instance, as the international American prank that was staged in Panama under direction from Washington with U.S. soldiers bombarding the papal nuncio and his staff inside the Vatican consulate with ear-splitting, round-the-clock rock music until Manuel Noriega was handed over from sanctuary. Yet even though such

1980s American "victories" were transparently the ego-driven posturings of an overgrown bully beating up the smaller kids, Americans in the late 1980s seemed incapable of registering anything but glee over actions that, in the mid-1970s, would more likely have provoked a challenge to the government that ordered them. Outside of remnant peace organizations that the press came increasingly to ignore, by 1990 the American public registered neither a sense of moral responsibility nor even curiosity about the price that civilian populations routinely pay for the United States' enjoyment of watching its own deadly technology go bang in the night. To be concerned for the plight of the many hundred civilians killed by a laser-guided hit on an Iraqi bomb shelter or to question the orders that selected that target would introduce exactly the kind of potentially emasculating ambiguity that war films educate their male viewers to discard. Ambiguities and doubts belong to the feminine; and American heroes from the Western movie onward have always been heroes precisely because their masculinity depends on having the fortitude to stand firm against all such compromising complexities as those with which the "Vietnam Syndrome" had threatened permanently to mar America's discourse of war.

The annihilation of the Iraqi army and the "Willie Horton" tactics of the 1988 U.S. presidential election together attested that winning—whenever and by whatever means possible—had clearly replaced all other possible ethics in America's reassertion of manhood. But the compulsions that drove the "win" mentality signified anything but achieved adult status. The short-lived adulthood that had once visited the Vietnam generation and, through their experience, had offered the nation a chance to grow up had come in the form of sobering loss and painful self-knowledge, not as the movie ending of a cheering parade. The Gulf War provided the counteroffer of the parade. But in turning back to that option and enacting its regressive desires into full-scale war, what America produced and televised for the world to admire was, ironically, an all-too-appropriate depiction of the culture of American masculinity that the latter half of the twentieth century had shaped: an image of wanton boys, killing for their sport.

NOTES

1. Jonathan Alter with Lucille Beachy, "The Civil War and Modern Memory," *Newsweek*, October 8, 1990, 64.

2. The Chrysler Corporation's advertisement that appears on the HBO videocassette preceding *Platoon* employs the same strategy. As Lee Iacocca comes upon a World War II army jeep, he tells us: "This jeep is a museum piece, a relic of war. Normandy, Anzio, Guadalcanal, Korea, Vietnam . . . it was the same from the

first musket fired at Concord to the rice paddies of the Mekong Delta: they were called and they went. That in the truest sense is the spirit of America. The more we understand it, the more we honor those who kept it alive. I'm Lee Iacocca." See Harry W. Haines, "'They Were Called and They Went': The Political Rehabilitation of the Vietnam Veteran," in *From Hanoi to Hollywood: The Vietnam War in American Film*, ed. Linda Dittmar and Gene Michaud (New Brunswick, N.J.: Rutgers University Press, 1990), pp. 81–97, 81.

3. See James Reston, Jr., *Sherman's March and the Vietnam War* (New York: Macmillan, 1984).

4. Dean Rusk, *As I Saw It*, as told to Richard Rusk, ed. Daniel S. Papp (New York: Norton, 1990).

5. Susan Jeffords has written widely and richly on connections between post-Vietnam America and anxieties about masculinity. See esp. her book *The Remasculinization of America: Gender and the Vietnam War* (Bloomington: Indiana University Press, 1990).

6. My paraphrasing condenses the typical responses my Dartmouth College students received when they quizzed their parents about their attitudes toward the Vietnam War. A similar point about the antiwar coalition is made by David W. Levy, *The Debate over Vietnam* (Baltimore: Johns Hopkins University Press, 1991), p. 172.

7. See Marilyn Young, *The Vietnam Wars, 1945–1990* (New York: Harper Collins, 1991).

8. Teresa de Lauretis, *Alice Doesn't: Feminism, Semiotics, Cinema* (Bloomington: Indiana University Press, 1984), p. 108; see also Michael Selig's use of this model in "Boys Will Be Men," in Dittmar and Michaud, *From Hanoi to Hollywood*, pp. 189–202, as a tool for analyzing Jane Fonda's role in one of the earliest of the (1978) Vietnam War films, *Coming Home*. Selig notes the displacement, midfilm, of Fonda's narrative by Voight's. It needs also be noted, however, that *Coming Home* is one of the few Vietnam films to allow women so substantial a place in the story at all.

9. Philip H. Melling, in *Vietnam in American Literature* (Boston: Twayne, 1990), documents the vindictiveness with which the U.S. government throughout the 1970s and 1980s not only refused help to Vietnam but refused to allow any other nation to give it. A representative incident: "When India [in 1977] tried to send a hundred buffalo to Vietnam to replenish the herds destroyed by the war, the United States threatened to cancel 'food for peace' aid to India." The sympathies of the American people in the late 1970s, however, ran in direct opposition to those of their government. According to a *New York Times* poll of July 1977, two-thirds of Americans supported sending food and medicine to Vietnam and a majority favored economic assistance to help the country rebuild (p. 87).

10. In light of the evidence presented in 1991 by historian Gary Sick implicating the Reagan-Bush campaign in a secret deal to ensure that the hostages not be released until after their continued captivity had guaranteed Jimmy Carter's election loss to Ronald Reagan, the event has a complexly ironic history in America as a signifying event in the circulation of masculine power.

11. James William Gibson, "Paramilitary Culture," *Critical Studies in Mass Communication* (March 1989): 90–94, offers insightful comments on the connections between consumerism and paramilitary culture in the circulation of "a pow-

erful myth [of] warrior heroes operating at the various margins of large-scale bureaucracy" (93). See also Susan Spillman, "Rambomania: Action Dolls, Other Tie-ins Spark Toy War," *Advertising Age* 5 (1985): 3–63. In June 1991, the Associated Press reported on the boom in Gulf War toys and games that had continued unabated, even three months after the shooting stopped, the most popular item being the Patriot missile model. See David Disheau, "War's Over, Let the Games Begin," for the Associated Press; rpt., *Valley News* (Lebanon, N.H.) June 1, 1991, 7.

12. See Sandra M. Gilbert and Susan Gubar, *No Man's Land: The Place of the Woman Writer in the Twentieth Century* (New Haven: Yale University Press, 1988) on women's liberation in the wake of male wars.

13. Bly's book *Iron John: A Book about Men* (Reading, Mass.: Addison-Wesley, 1990) became a national best-seller in the fall of 1990 and his "wild-man movement" received the media attention of a cover story in *Newsweek*. One of the first places Bly aired his "Iron John" story and the place I initially encountered it was at the first national retrospective on the Vietnam War held at Salado, Texas, in October 1982. For Bly's presentation and my summary of the conference, see *Vietnam in Remission*, ed. James F. Veninga and Harry A. Wilmer (College Station: Texas A & M University Press, for the Texas Committee for the Humanities and the Institute for the Humanities at Salado, 1985). See also Suzanne Gordon's *Los Angeles Times* editorial, "Patriarchy, in Any Form, Is Anti-Woman," rpt., *Valley News* (Lebanon, N.H.) September 7, 1991, 14, from which I have in part drawn my summation of Bly's book.

14. Again, see esp. Susan Jeffords's ground-breaking book, *Remasculinization of America*.

15. Carrie Fisher, interview, "Fresh Air," National Public Radio. According to an October 1991 report by Women in Communications, only 13 percent of the people referred to in *Time*, *Newsweek*, and *U.S. News and World Report* during 1991 were women (quoted in the *Progressive*, January 1992, 17).

16. "U.S.A. Number One" was certainly accurate as far as international preeminence in rape statistics: four times higher than Germany, thirteen times higher than in England, and 20 times greater than in Japan. See *Newsweek*, July 23, 1990, 52.

17. Although *Rambo* chronologically followed the MIA fantasies of *Uncommon Valor* and *Missing in Action*, it was the popularity of Stallone's film that retroactively invested its predecessors with increased public credit. On the whole issue of the Vietnam MIA/POWs see especially H. Bruce Franklin's essay, "The POW/MIA Myth," *Atlantic Monthly*, December 1991, 45–81. According to a *Wall Street Journal*/NBC News poll cited by Franklin, 69 percent of Americans believed even as late as 1991 that U.S. prisoners of war were still being held in Southeast Asia.

18. At the conference on "Cultures of U.S. Imperialism" (Dartmouth College, November 1991), Michael Rogin connected the yellow ribbons to the U.S. Army's campaign against the American Indian, thus defining their origins within a racist military policy.

19. Cynthia Enloe, "Tie a Yellow Ribbon 'Round the New World Order" *Village Voice*, February 19, 1991, 370.

20. Any concern over the literally raped Kuwaiti women often became displaced by its translation into the metaphoric "rape of Kuwait." On the use of the rape discourse in the Gulf War, see Susan Jeffords, "Protection Racket," *Women's Review of Books* (July 1991): 10. As Jeffords points out, "the rape-and-rescue scenario metaphor is hardly new in American thought" and can be traced back as far as the captivity narratives about the abduction of American women by Indians.

21. The ensuing U.S. Navy study showed reported sexual assaults and rapes had risen by 55 percent between 1989 and late 1990. Furthermore, three-quarters of the women and half of the men surveyed acknowledged sexual harrassment within their commands, with junior enlisted women being the most frequently targeted recipients. The report implies that overt sexism seemed to have been more widespread in the navy because women's assignments were more restricted in that military service than in any other branch (Molly Moore for the *Washington Post*; rpt., *Valley News* [Lebanon, N.H.] April 4, 1991, 10). A year after the war was over, as revelations about the rape of American service women continued to surface, the army acknowledged that it had confirmed some thirty-five instances. This statistic is more probably just the tip of the iceberg.

22. The stolen incubators story, which George Bush cited repeatedly and which apparently had a major impact on rallying both popular and congressional support for a war, had originated in testimony at a congressional hearing and, before being proven false by Kuwaiti hospital officials, was circulated by Amnesty International as fact. The mysterious witness who had provided the testimony then turned out to be the Kuwaiti ambassador's own daughter, who had been coached in advance by Hill and Knowlton, the Washington, D.C., public relations firm that not only enjoyed a close connection to the Bush White House but had been hired for $10 million of Kuwaiti royal family money to sell the war to the American people (CBS-TV, "60 Minutes," January 20, 1992).

23. See Alexander Cockburn's "Beat the Devil," *Nation*, November 25, 1991, 658–59, and May 5, 1991, 1–22. See also "Report Criticizes Bush for Post-War Actions," by Robin Wright for the *Los Angeles Times*; rpt., *Valley News* (Lebanon, N.H.), May 5, 1991, 1.

24. This line of the revisionist scenario focuses especially on media coverage of the Tet offensive of February 1968, the moment from which a decline of public support for the war can be dated. See especially Peter Braestrup, *Big Story: How the American Press and Television Reported and Interpreted the Crisis of Tet 1968 in Vietnam and Washington* (Garden City, N.Y.; Doubleday, Anchor Press, 1978). Most mainline Vietnam war historians reject the revisionist model of an "antiwar press" and point to the way that the mainstream press advocated U.S. participation and blocked stories that might undermine support. Neil Sheehan's experience as Saigon United Press International chief supplies evidence for this in *A Bright Shining Lie: John Paul Vann and America in Vietnam* (New York: Random House, 1988). See also Charles Mohr, "Once Again—Did the Press Lose Vietnam?" *Columbia Journalism Review* (November/December 1983).

25. The 1968 massacre at My Lai of some 350–500 civilians and the attempted military cover-up first entered the news via the print media, breaking into the *New York Times* in the final months of 1969. After a serious editorial debate about

whether or not to do so, *Life* magazine did publish the photographic evidence. Charges were originally brought against fourteen army officers, including two generals and two colonels, but only Lieutenant William Calley was convicted. He was given a life sentence that was subsequently commuted by Richard Nixon. The most diligent investigative reporter of the massacre was Seymour M. Hersch, in *My Lai 4: A Report on the Massacre and Its Aftermath* (New York: Random House, 1970), and two years later, *Cover-Up: The Army's Secret Investigation of the Massacre at My Lai 4* (New York: Random House, 1972).

26. Patrick J. Sloyan, "Iraqis Were Buried Alive," for *Newsday*; rpt., *Valley News* (Lebanon, N.H.), September 12, 1991, 1; and Patrick J. Sloyan, "U.S. Annihilated Iraqi Division after Cease-Fire," for *Newsday*; rpt., *Valley News* (Lebanon, N.H.) May 8, 1991, 1.

27. "They shall beat their swords into plowshares"—probably the best-known model of peace in Western heritage—appears in both Isaiah 2:4 and Micah 4:3.

28. In a coincidence that seems less than coincidental, the Washington, D.C., homecoming parade was suddenly scheduled on the same day as—and thereby thoroughly displaced—the scheduled lesbian and gay pride day celebrations.

29. See esp. the returning vet narratives collected in Bob Greene's *Homecoming: When the Soldiers Returned from Vietnam* (New York: Putnam, 1989). The accounts were themselves solicited by Greene's asking, in a weekly *Chicago Tribune* column, for any veteran who had been spat upon by a war protester to send him his story.

30. The incident is cited in Kevin Bowen, " 'Strange Hells': Hollywood in Search of America's Lost War," in Dittmar and Michaud, *From Hanoi to Hollywood*, pp. 226–35, 230.

31. Haines, "They Were Called," pp. 82, 84, 87.

32. Peter Marin's "Living in Moral Pain," *Psychology Today*, November 1981, 68–80, the best psychological analysis I have read of the Vietnam veterans, discusses why traditional psychology has dealt so poorly with this group.

33. Sydney H. Schanberg's editorial for *Newsday*, "Another View of the Gulf War 'Victory' "; rpt., *Valley News* (Lebanon, N.H.) July 10, 1991, 16. The documentaries that Bill Moyers has produced since the mid-1980s—including "After the War," his June 1991 report on Gulf War television coverage and the film footage that none of the major channels would air—likewise indicate Moyers's growing concern over the increasing chumminess between the White House and the media.

34. Richard Slotkin, "Gunfighters and Green Berets: The Magnificent Seven and the Myth of Counter-Insurgency," *Radical History Review* 44 (1989): 65. Of the various cultural assessments of Vietnam and its aftermath, *The Vietnam War and American Culture*, ed. John Carlos Rowe and Richard Berg (New York: Columbia University Press, 1991), offers a particularly rich collection.

35. Gaylyn Studlar and David Desser, "Never Having to Say You're Sorry: *Rambo*'s Rewriting of the Vietnam War," in Dittmar and Michaud, *From Hanoi to Hollywood*, 101–13, 104.

36. Barry Romo, National Coordinator of Vietnam Veterans Against the War, lecture at Drake University, Des Moines, Iowa, October 24, 1990.

37. The phrase comes from an otherwise unquoted letter to a local newspaper.

38. Robert McKelvey, editorial for the *Los Angeles Times*, "Vietnam Vets Weren't Feted by Parades"; rpt., *Valley News* (Lebanon, N.H.) June 20, 1991, 22.

39. David Rabe invokes these lyrics in the first play of his Vietnam War trilogy, *The Education of Pavlo Hummel*. "Jodie" is likewise the name given to the Jon Voight figure—the war protester who in the 1978 Vietnam film *Coming Home* does in fact "get" the wife of the soldier (Bruce Dern).

40. Here and elsewhere, my use of the term "the Vietnam veteran" refers to the public perception of such a figure that has emerged from dominant representation and whose image works to subsume the multiplicity of political perspectives that are, of course, actually held by the many different men and the women (never included in the public image of the veteran) who served at different times, places and in widely different circumstances in Vietnam. As Cynthia Enloe points out, the model of "the Vietnam vet" has taken "15 years and a lot of celluloid and paper to create, but today he is a potent figure inspiring complex emotions . . . [and] it is the unappreciated, alienated male Vietnam vet whose image looms over the present war" ("Tie a Yellow Ribbon," p. 370).

41. *Newsweek*, May 27, 1991, 17.

42. Barry Romo, lecture at Drake University.

43. The failure of any military leadership in Vietnam and the widespread careerism among senior officers is well documented. See esp. Loren Baritz's description in *Backfire: A History of How American Culture Led Us into Vietnam and Made Us Fight the Way We Did* (New York: Ballentine, 1985), pp. 276–318.

44. See esp. D. Michael Shafer, "The Vietnam Combat Experience: The Human Legacy," in *The Legacy: The Vietnam War in the American Imagination*, ed. D. Michael Shafer (Boston: Beacon Press, 1990), pp. 80–103. In discussing Vietnam veterans' "cruel . . . often callous treatment by the VA hospital system," Shafer points out how the acute-care needs of the several hundred thousand young, seriously wounded Vietnam combatants were essentially ignored in favor of the chronic-care needs of aging World War II veterans, the constituency that had numerical and political clout (96). The Legion and the VFW—veterans in the father position to the Vietnam returnees and also men who "strongly supported the American cause in Vietnam and often blame Vietnam veterans for defeat"— further protected such interests by aggressively lobbying to block funding of outreach, drug rehabilitation, and psychological counseling programs for Vietnam veterans (97).

45. Sam Brown, "The Legacy of Choices," *The Wounded Generation*, ed. A. D. Horne (Englewood Cliffs, N.J.: Prentice-Hall, 1981); rpt. in *The American Experience in Vietnam: A Reader*, ed. Grace Sevy (Norman: University of Oklahoma Press, 1989), pp. 195–203, 201.

46. Maureen Dowd, "Tame Latins and No Eggs Greeted Bush," *New York Times*, December 9, 1990, international ed., A3.

47. *Newsweek*, October 8, 1990, 64. Much has been written on the Gulf War and its sports metaphors. See, for instance, Molly Ivins, "Super Bowl in the Sand," *Progressive*, March 1991, 46.

48. See "Chronicle," *New York Times*, July 27, 1990, B4; "Roseanne Strikes Out! The Whole Crazy Story of How She Turned into a National Disgrace,"

National Enquirer, August 14, 1990, 28–29, 36; and Carolyn Marvin, "Theorizing the Flagbody: Symbolic Dimensions of the Flag Desecration Debate, or, Why the Bill of Rights Does Not Fly in the Ballpark," *Critical Studies in Mass Communication* 8 (1991): 119–138.

49. Michael Hill, "New Fall Season Glamorizing a Lot of Irresponsibility," *Baltimore Evening Sun*; rpt., *Valley News* (Lebanon, N.H.) September 11, 1990.

50. Andrew Ward, "Paunchy Peter Pans," editorial for *Washington Post*; rpt., *Valley News* (Lebanon, N.H.) December 31, 1991, 16.

51. Quoted from the final draft of the filmscript *Field of Dreams*, based on the novel *Shoeless Joe*, by W. P. Kinsella; screenplay by Phil Alden Robinson, September 9, 1987, p. 2. My reading of this film is particularly indebted to Janice Haney-Peritz.

52. Ibid., p. 86. Given the strong Canadian opposition to U.S. actions in Vietnam and given also the compulsions of this script, it seems incongruous to realize that W. P. Kinsella is a Canadian, not an American, writer. In a letter commenting on this essay, Ric Knowles at the University of Guelph perceptively suggests that the politics defining Canadian government during the 1980s and Canada's cheering enthusiasm for the American-instigated Gulf War may themselves be comprehensible by considering U.S.-Canadian relations inside of this same father-son model of recuperation.

53. *Field of Dreams*, pp. 101, 102.

54. Graham Greene, *The Quiet American* (London: Penguin Books, 1973), pp. 17, 179, 62.

55. *Newsweek*, April 16, 1990, 25.

PART III
HOME/FRONT?

Chapter 5

NOTES TOWARD A FEMINIST PEACE POLITICS

SARA RUDDICK

IN THIS PAPER, I outline one version of a feminist peace politics. The
peace politics I imagine is not preoccupied with the question, When,
if ever, is it right to kill? Nor is it committed to the absolute renuncia-
tion of violence often associated with pacifism. Rather, this politics expresses a sturdy suspicion of organized violence even in the best of causes.
Accordingly, it seeks to expose the multiple costs of violence and to disrupt the plans of those who organize it. This politics also ferrets out hidden or less organized violence wherever it appears—in boardroom or
bedroom, government council or factory. Finally, this politics is committed to inventing myriad forms of nonviolent disruption, cooperation, respect, restraint, and resistance that would replace violence and would
constitute "peace." Speaking generally, a feminist peace politics contrib-
utes in distinctively feminist ways to the threefold aim of fomenting
sturdy suspicion of organized violence, disclosing hidden violences, and
inventing the strategies and ideals of nonviolence.

Both within the United States and throughout the world there are
many feminisms, some explicitly militarist, some suspicious of any
"larger" cause that might dilute feminist energies. In these remarks I develop one variant of antimilitarist feminism in which feminist and antimilitarist commitments are interwoven from the start.[1] Someone—a
woman or man—becomes, simultaneously, feminist and antimilitarist at
least partly because she or he sees war making as an extension of "masculine" domination and "masculine" domination as a reflection of and
preparation for war. In a letter she wrote during the First World War,
Virginia Woolf expressed colloquially one version of this feminist/antim-
ilitarist weave.

> I become steadily more feminist, owing to the Times, which I read at breakfast
> and wonder how this preposterous masculine fiction [the war] keeps going a
> day longer—without some vigorous woman pulling us together and marching
> through it.[2]

In order to outline three aspects of an emerging feminist peace politics,
I will take far more seriously than she could have intended the rhetoric of

Virginia Woolf's letter: War is masculine, war is a fiction, and a vigorous woman—or womanliness—might march us through it.

WAR'S MASCULINITY

Nearly everyone agrees that war is in some sense "masculine." Throughout history and across the globe, whatever the "race" or history of particular cultures, men have greatly predominated among the generals, chiefs of staff, and heads of cadre, tribe, nation, or state who direct wars. In technologically developed states, men predominate among the business entrepeneurs who fund wars and among the defense intellectuals and philosophers who justify them. Still today, men predominate among the soldiers who execute war strategies. But there is no ready conclusion to draw from war's masculinity. Many militarists celebrate and many civilians accept the conjunction of war and manliness as a "natural" or necessary component of war. By contrast, many feminists who clearly perceive and heartily resent war's masculinity challenge military practices in the hope of securing for women a citizen's right to fight and to command fighters.

Antimilitarist feminists address war's masculinity in a double voice. They aim to *challenge* the connection between war and masculinity which, along with the belief that masculinity is biologically determined, renders men "naturally" warlike and war a "natural" male and, therefore, legitimate human activity. Therefore, speaking in one register, they recognize many "masculinities," all of which, whatever their connection to biology, are socially constructed and subject to change. Yet despite their skeptical and pluralistic stance toward gender categories, antimilitarist feminists also underscore the masculinity of war. Their aim is to make a familiar masculinity freshly evident and also evidently objectionable in ways that demean both war and one norm of warlike masculinity.

To this end, antimilitarist feminists attend relentlessly to a "male"-defining, women-excluding misogyny and homophobia[3] that threads through military speech and practice. The "monstrous male, loud of voice, hard of fist" who goes off to war singing of the "Persian pukes" he is ready to "nape," the faggot assholes he is ready to sodomize, the dead and diseased whore he is ready to rape, expresses even as he caricatures this common military attitude.[4] This conception of masculinity is expressed in a lower register in boot camp training rituals, soldiers' chants and songs, graffiti on bombs and guns, tough talk by generals, metaphors of strategists, and the gestures, bonding, and "boyish" boasts of soldiers returning from battles and bombing raids. Criminally, this "masculinity" is expressed in actual acts of rape, sexual assault, and torture.

Certain feminists go beyond merely reporting on soldiers' attitudes and offer a psychoanalytic account of the acquisition of a "normal" masculinity which is expressed under pressure in defensive, aggressive misogyny. According to these psychoanalytic feminists, in social groups where men hold the principal governing posts and are responsible for hunting, war, or other "legitimate" forms of aggression, and where women are responsible for child tending, masculinity is highly valued, potentially aggressive, and fragile.[5] Men must ward off their envy of female birth giving and their longing to be cared for by mothering women, and at the same time affirm their male privilege and assuage their misgivings (if any) about male dominance and aggression. To this end they learn, as boys becoming "men," to define themselves as not-female and better than female. Accordingly, they tend to devalue bodilyness and emotionality, both of which are evoked by physical vulnerability and associated with the bodies and emotions of females, whose care they need, fear, and long for.

If this story is to be believed, men's culturally prized masculinity may never be so vaunted, fragile, and incipiently misogynist as in war. Women are metaphorically and psychologically "behind the lines," resented for their safety, scorned for their ignorance of the "real" and really masculine experience.[6] Yet images of women—one's own at home, the enemy's at hand—are ever present, representing, as they often do in civilian life, vulnerability and emotionality. In extraordinary circumstances, soldiers must control ordinary emotions of fear, rage, and desire. Understandably, many rage against absent women and the emotionality they represent. They may also blame women for their own longings for women that allegedly divert them from soldierly duty, thereby endangering them and their comrades.[7] In this strained emotional ambience of danger and separation, commanders often encourage "masculine" aggressive impulses. Given this encouragement and the pressures to which their "normal masculine" defenses are subject, it is not surprising if many soldiers imaginatively elaborate or actually engage in rapes and assaults on women.

Assaultive misogynist masculinity is not even the only model of military masculinity. The just warrior, restrained and self-sacrificing, protective of women and vulnerable people, is also marked as masculine. So too is the conquering hero, dashing and well mounted (previously on horseback, now in tank or plane), who enacts the national interest/glory. The models of swaggering assaultiveness, restrained warrior, and conquering hero combine with other conceptions of masculinity ranging from the eternal boyishness of competitive jousters to the comradely victory lust of team players. Together they create an ideal of soldierly brotherhood that unites men against women, who cannot share the bond of battle, and often, also, against civilian/government/fathers who "slay their sons."[8]

[margin handwriting: Just war Objectifies the Enemy]

Different militaries, different wars invoke for their soldiers and project onto the enemy models of masculinity that spur fighting. Especially among racially assimilable enemies, both sides have heroes, while a too easy surrender is contemptible and feminine, and spoils a good fight. Typically, masculinities are also divided between the enemy and "our troops." "We" are the just warrior-protectors. By contrast, a particularly malignant form of swaggering masculinity—a criminal, sexualized aggression—is attributed to the enemy. When enemy males are racialized as predators from whom innocent countries or women-and-children need protection, they become killable killers ready to be burned and buried in their trenches.

In highlighting swaggering, assaultive masculinity, feminists do not simplify the motives of individual soldiers. In war, as in civilian life, the ideal of assaultive masculinity is oppressive to many men who struggle with and against a gender identity that would immerse them by "nature" in violence. It does seem that in the best of causes, there are men who love war and take excited, sometimes explicitly sexual pleasure in assaulting bodies. Yet many of the soldiers who are excited by, and act upon, the sexual and aggressive lusts of battle are also often ashamed of their emotions and deeds later in the day, or in later years. Whatever the cause, war stories reveal men on all sides of battle lines who are running, surrendering, or hiding. There are also courageous but constrained and reluctant fighters as well as men with equal courage who refuse to kill. And in the worst of causes, there are soldiers who believe that they are fighting justly and protecting others.[9] By highlighting—and deploring—soldiers' arrogant, homophobic, assaultive misogyny, antimilitarist feminists have at least three aims. First, they want to make one variant of masculinity evident and repellent whenever it appears, whether in political, domestic, or military battle. Second, they want to block the split between our masculinity and theirs, revealing instead *war*'s ugliness. And, finally, by stressing the social construction of assaultive masculinity while also revealing its repellent character, they want to make it easier for men to reject this particular gender norm.

In highlighting assaultive, misogynist masculinity, antimilitarist feminists also address themselves to women. In most cultures, war's masculinity is constructed in tandem with a distinctly military femininity. As Virginia Woolf lamented in the midst of the Second World War, "No, I don't see what's [to] be done about war. Its manliness; and manliness breeds womanliness—both so hateful."[10] "Womanly" militarists acknowledge the exclusionary male bonding of battle. They take up *distinctive* war work that is either feminine, such as nursing the wounded, or is seen as only a temporary substitute for the work that men will return to when they come home from war. Less prosaically, they express, within the confines of loyalty, the losses and sexual dangers of war. Bereaved women weep for war's victims; endangered women cry out for protection from the enemy's rapacious, cruel marauders.

The loyal military female, in contrast to misogynist soldier, is androphiliac. In the midst of battle excitement, she eroticizes "our" heroes, memorializes "our" just warriors, and matronizingly cheers "our" boyish adventurers. Masking or denying the sexual assaultiveness of "our troops," she ascribes to enemy men "the naked, hideous male gratification" of assaultive masculinity.[11] After battle, she can repair military enmity by mourning *all* casualties and, if the war has not been too bitter or self-righteous, she can honor all heroic fighters.

In highlighting assaultive masculinity, antimilitarist feminists aim to destabilize military femininity. Their hope is that a woman who sees *wars* as eliciting assaultive masculinity will be disarmed of the racist and military split between "their" marauding males and "our troops." Then her military hero may look like an abuser, not an unfamiliar figure in civilian life; conversely, the civilian abuser will be deprived of any militarist glamour. While the military woman's generalized, romantic androphilia is disrupted, she will still love particular men; only now war's mores of abusiveness threaten to transform the beloved lover/mate/brother/son/father into "a boisterous male . . . hard of fist."[12] Fearing the effect of war's manliness on men she loves as well as the effect in her own life of abusive, war-made men, the loyal lady of sorrows may well begin to weep disloyally, to politicize her fears.

The misogynist domination that pervades military life and lore fosters brutality and domination both on and off official battlefields. While an ethos of assaultive masculinity legitimates abusive war and warlike abuse, a myth of manly protection, sustained by military androphilia, prevents men and women from seeing what they already know: wars almost always leave everyone in their vicinity radically *un*protected. By looking through myths of manliness, women and men should be better able to see the cruel realities of war engraved on bodies of all ages and both sexes.

PREPOSTEROUS FICTION

Many women and men would continue to support war for moral reasons even if they deplored its psychosexual character. "Warism," "the belief that war is morally justified in principle and often justified in fact,"[13] is a dominant and a majority ideology in most past and present societies and states. To arouse sturdy suspicion of war, it is necessary to undermine the kinds of *thinking* that legitimate war making as an institution and, within that institution, sanction particular wars. ＞113-14

In many wars, and notably in the recent Persian Gulf War, warism is influentially and attractively expressed in just-war theory. Just-war theorists are cognizant of war's horrors and begin by condemning war in general, though allowing it in principle. Their task, then, is to judge particular causes and particular ways of fighting according to standards of "justice." Briefly, one can go to war only as a last resort, only if the fight is justly conducted, and only if the cause is just: one's own or another state is attacked; innocent people are being slaughtered; or, more controversially, the balance of peacekeeping power is threatened.

In judging wars, just war theorists take seriously several realities. Men are transformed by uniform and recruitment procedures into "soldiers," who are legitimate killers and targets of killers. Boundaries, often initially established by military conquest or imperial negotiation, become the real, legitimate markers of states. Wars are spatially and temporally bounded events. They are fought on or above "battlefields,"[14] begin with the detonation of weapons or the "exchange of fire," and end with victory or surrender. These and other realities—for example, innocent civilians, military targets, clean, smart weapons selectively aimed—are the primitive terms, the basic referents, for the abstract language through which wars are judged to be just or unjust. (114)

In late-twentieth-century high-technology wars, it becomes increasingly difficult for anyone to believe in the bounded realities to which just-war theorists refer.[15] By way of contributing to an increasing skepticism of the realities just-war theory assumes, antimilitarists can bring into play recent feminist critiques of prevailing ideals of rationality. According to these feminist critiques, prevailing ideals of reason reflect compulsive tendencies to defend, dissociate, and abstract.[16] To the extent that "men of reason" are governed by these dominant Western ideals, they thrive on boundaries and definition, eschew ambiguity, suspect particular attachments, and separate thought from feeling, mind from body. On the other hand, men of reason seem almost compulsively attached to detachment. To adapt a phrase from Klaus Theweleit, they thrive on a fantasy of transcendence based on a "tradition of freeing the thinking brain from the depths of the most pressing situations and sending it off to some (fictive) summit for a panoramic overview."[17] Yet the discourses of reason barely conceal the emotions that permeate them—anxiety, defensiveness, addictive sexual assertion or fear of sexuality, distaste for and envy of female sexual and birth-giving bodies, and competitive aggression.

These ideals, I suggest, are exemplified in just-war languages and the "realities" to which they refer. In Western philosophy, ideals of reason have sometimes been created in explicit connection with the ideals of war. As Plato put the point boldly, an education in reason "must not be useless to warlike men [or women]"; rulers must prove themselves "best in philosophy and with respect to war."[18] Whatever the historical connections between reason and war, contemporary war theorists, like other men of reason, resort to abstraction, binary oppositions, and sharply bounded concepts. Most notably, "defense intellectuals," who "create the theory that informs and legitimates American nuclear [and high-technology] strategic practices" conceal, even from themselves, the bodily mutilation their policies require.[19] Also, like their philosophical counterparts, these defense intellectuals reveal the anxieties, aggression, and even the sexual and procreative envies and desires, that are familiar from soldiers' stories.

Superficially, the languages of justice and strategy seem quite unlike. Just-war theorists do not deny war's sufferings; if war weren't so damaging, one would not require a *moral* theory first to justify and then to control the damage. Unlike technostrategists who explicitly eschew moral questions, just-war theorists insist upon the interdependence of ethics and politics, thereby providing the moral (soft and feminine) counterpart to realistic (hard and masculine) instrumentality.

Yet despite these differences, the justificatory languages of morality and strategy are intertwined. The success of just warriors is dependent on the strategies that defense intellectuals legitimate. Just conduct of a war (*jus in bello*) depends upon the "smartness" and "cleanliness" of weapons, who acquire these virtues within the strategic discourse that brackets pain and suffering as "collateral damage." To be sure, there is a frightening disconnection between morality and strategy: might does not make right, but it does make victories. The capacity to defeat and demoralize depends far more upon economic and technological than on moral resources. But the high moral tone and abstract moral puzzles of just-war theory tend to divert attention from this fundamental, often heartbreaking indifference of war to virtue.

Taken on its own terms, just-war theory is far more like its technostrategic counterpart than its moral concern would suggest. Like their strategist counterparts, just-war theorists resort to abstraction, dichotomy, and bounded definition. Like their counterparts, just-war theorists employ abstraction to take a distance from unreasoned emotionality. Partly because the language of just-war theory is less evidently sexual/aggressive itself, it is even more able than strategic discourse to occlude the sexual aggressivity of war. The moral emotions just-war theorists do invoke—righteousness, indignation, and (perhaps) shame and guilt[20]—conceal as well as license the cruelty and delight in destruction that war provides. Most seriously, like its technostrategic counterpart, the language of morality too easily obscures the realities of terrorizing and injuring, the defining activities of war. To repeat: Just-war theory does *not* deny, and indeed insists on, the pain of victims. But as one learns to speak within the theory, to unravel the puzzles the theory sets for itself, to assess "causes" and strategies by criteria the theory establishes, it becomes increasingly difficult to give *weight* to the varieties of loss and pain suffered by individual victims and conquerors, their communities, and their lands.[21]

Confronted with the apparent irrationality, the "craziness," of war, many people are compelled to be, to feel, and to appear "reasonable"— deliberative, coherent, and controlled. Although, and partly because, they obscure war's messy realities, both technostrategic and just-war discourse provide the illusion of rationality. In order to combat just-war thinking, it is necessary to offer alternative modes of reasoning that can provide the comforts of reason but that do not obscure emotion and pain. To this end, I would invoke ideals of reason that are central to the "different voices" of a feminist "ethics of care."[22] Very briefly, these alternative modes of reasoning arise out of attention to concrete particulars, develop insights within ongoing, changing relationships, test these insights in the context of collective and often passionate and conflictual enterprises, and convey them in open-ended narration.[23]

It seems likely that women or men who reason predominantly in these alternative modes will be less apt to accept the realities of just-war theory. Although as aware as any just-war theorist of the blessings of nonviolent stability, they might not take so seriously extant boundaries established by diplomacy and war. They might be less apt to appreciate the moral significance of burning soldiers up as opposed to burying them in their trenches or of bombing a water supply rather than a market. Indeed, because they are generally skeptical of moral discourse governed by abstract distinctions and procedural rules, they might reject the fundamental premise of just-war theory: young men (and women) can be transformed by policy, weapon, and uniform into legitimate killers and targets.

As I have learned from the frustrations of teaching just-war theory, people who reason in these "different voices" can appear disturbingly uninterested in just causes and rules of war that are meant to constrain battle and whose violation is often an anguished focus of war memoirs. It is not that these skeptics are unable to distinguish between the pain and destructiveness of rifle shot and napalm, smart bomb and random missile. Nor do they confuse killing armed, fighting soldiers with bombing those same soldiers in retreat or dealing with them cruelly when they have surrendered. They appreciate the particularity of horrors—rape or torture of individuals, undiscriminating slaughter of people, burning of whole villages or cities. But they see all the horror—the lesser and greater—as predictable ingredients of high-technology wars. Hence they refuse to believe in the categories and conventions through which just wars are presented, refuse to be drawn into a fiction of good-enough combat that is used to sanitize and legitimate violence. >16-17

Those who reason in a concrete, contextual, narrative mode would also be slow to accept the fundamental fiction that war is a discrete phenomenon that is arranged by diplomats and takes place on battlefields. There is, of course, a sense in which wars are temporally bounded events whose beginnings and endings have clear consequences. Few see so differently that they deny the terror of a bombing raid or the relief of "peace." But wars rarely have the neat endings their planners envision. Moreover, the rewards even of neat victory are often compromised or reversed in decades, if not in months. In women's "postwar" stories, there is a thematic, recurrent underlining of the unboundedness of war.[24] Physical disabilities, psychic injuries, social disruptions, and socioecological destructions of battle last long after surrender. > 117

Nor does war begin only on the day of invasion. As the (then) East German writer Christa Wolf enjoined: "You can tell when a war starts, but when does the pre-war start? If there are rules about that we should hand them on. Hand them down inscribed in clay, in stone. Do not let your own people deceive you."[25] Discrete episodes of legitimate violence are predictable consequences of daily warlike ways of living. Speaking in a voice she explicitly attributes to her experience as a woman, Virginia Woolf envisioned a system of violences in which "the public and private worlds are inseparably connected; the tyrannies and servilities of the one are the tyrannies and servilities of the other."[26] Looking at the patriarchal (her word) family, and particularly at education and professional life in England, Woolf saw an ethos of male dominion and military domination in the making. People are taught "not to hate force but to use it" in order to keep their possessions, defend their grandeur and power, through varieties of economic, racial, and sexual violences.[27] >117

A contemporary feminist, Cynthia Enloe, has looked with equal suspicion at the connection, particularly as wrought by the United States, of militarism, international corporate capitalism, racism, sexism, and assaults against the poor. In *Bananas, Beaches and Bases*, Enloe reveals an economic and military war *system* that allows the United States to initiate, fund, fight, or avoid discrete "wars." In this system a military ethos, sustained by military spending, prepares for and exploits racial and masculine domination despite, and partly because of, the fact that armed service appears to provide minority and female citizens, especially those who are poor, material advantages and symbolic status otherwise unavailable to them. To further the system, war planners manipulate allegedly private and sharply genderized relationships, playing upon class interests, racial fears, and sexual norms in order to recruit women's bodies, services, and labor for military affairs.[28] >117

Just War kills feminism ⌐In rejecting the realities of just-war theory, feminist antimilitarists do not deny the existence of conquest, massacre, tyranny, enslavement, exploitation, and economic injustice. The issue is *how*, not whether, to resist these evils. A feminist peace politics, like peace politics generally, searches for alternatives to exploding, cutting, bombing, and starving. The abstract, bounded, justificatory concepts of just-war theory short circuit this search by allowing the morally troubled to accept good-enough wars in place of the many kinds of cooperation, compromise, and resistance required for peace. ⌐118

A "VIGOROUS WOMANLINESS": TOWARD A POLITICS OF CARE

⌐The most thorough unraveling of the concepts and fantasies that legitimate violence will only lead to despair without viable conceptions of peace making, or new ways of cooperating and fighting. Conversely, if people cannot imagine peace, they will be unable to see war wholly or to reject it steadily, especially when war's cause is dear to them. ⌐118

As there is no sharp division between the violences of domestic, civic, and military life, there is also no sharp division between the practices and thinking of private and public peace. Even in the midst of war, people cooperate, and care for each other. In their ordinary lives, most women and men, including many who are frequently violent, sometimes express anger and resolve conflict without injuring. One of the tasks of peace making is to transform this ordinary peacefulness that surrounds us into a public commitment to, and capacity for, making peace.

As war is associated with men, peace is associated with women and the "womanly." These dual associations are expressed most succinctly in the clichéd opposition of mother and soldier, and, more generally and prosaically, of caregiving and war. Although most mothers and the majority of caregivers may be women, neither mothering nor caregiving generally are intrinsically female or feminine. Some men fully engage in mothering and most are, at some time in their lives, active caregivers. Many women are uninterested in mothering and reject the caregiving that is expected of them. Yet, historically, the obligations of care thread through women's lives, creating, in specific social conditions, distinctively feminine patterns, as well as burdens, of knowledge and of love. It is understandable, then, that some feminists, already partisans of women, would look to "womanly" practices of caregiving for intimations of ordinary peacefulness.

Caregiving *appears* to depend upon peace and to be peacelike. War, like other less attractive violences, always disrupts and often ruins the caring labors of feeding, clothing, sheltering, nursing, tending children and the elderly, maintaining kind and neighborhood ties. The contradiction between caregiving and organized violence may be most poignantly expressed in the laments of mothers who are unable to protect their children amid war, who may even kill their children rather than let them continue to suffer violence.[29] Yet despite the opposition between war making and caregiving, most caregivers have complied with, and often enough have devoted their energies to, war. To set militarism and care at political odds, to give their opposition emotional and political weight, it will be necessary to contrast in detail caregiving and military enterprises.

In the spirit of detailed comparison, I have contrasted maternal with military battle. Mothers fight with children and on their behalf. They "make peace" between children in their household, neighborhood, and extended family. Often, they also fight in the same household, family, or neighborhood in which they make peace. The mothers I have known are often overcome with a sense of failure—with memories of their abuse or neglect of their children or of their collusion with those who hurt them. Nonetheless, I have come to believe that there are enough maternal practices that are sufficiently governed by nonviolent principles to provide one model of nonviolent action. These maternal principles of reconciliation, resistance, and refusal to injure are analogous to, although also different from, principles developed by Gandhi and King.[30]

In a similar spirit, I would like to contrast military and caregiving concepts of control. Like militarists, caregivers often set out to control the wills of others—to get children to stop fighting, turn out their lights, go to school; to get patients to cooperate with painful testing; to get an elderly person to eat. Like militarists, caregivers control within a particular conjunction of power and powerlessness.

Typically, militarists strive for a position of superior strength from which they can dominate people and resources by threatened or actual assault. Only an enemy's efforts to achieve "equal strength" lead militarists to settle for a "balance" of power or terror. By contrast, caregivers are already powerful; they attempt to control people who are, by dint of the caregiving relationship, vulnerable to threats of damage or neglect. For many years, mothers can injure, terrify, or humiliate their children. In other caring relations such as nursing, aiding the disabled, or tending the frail elderly, caregivers often seem able to neglect at will, or to subtly threaten or hurt the bodies and psyches of people dependent upon them. Unlike militarists, caregivers are unable to rely upon balances of power or equal strength to control their own or others' aggression. Unequal strength is a structural feature of caring labor. Vulnerability, as we like to remember, often elicits protection. But vulnerability also allows for, and sometimes excites, domination, abuse, or neglect. Powerful caregivers may be more than usually tempted by sadism, self-indulgent aggression, self-interested exploitation, and self-protective indifference to the real needs of people whose demands seem overwhelming.

∠Both militarists and caregivers often feel and are powerless. Militarists who feel powerless attempt to arm themselves. Initially their efforts may be defensive, but strategies, weapons, social policies and group motivation conspire to turn defense into offensive threat and action. Militarists then can display the power that caregivers take for granted. Despite undeniable power, caregivers also often feel powerless in the face of the willful, resentful impatience of those they care for. But powerless caregivers cannot arm themselves; they are already armed. The simplest implements at hand—a toy block, a kitchen knife—can be put to deadly use; bribes and punishments can be backed up by threatened or real physical force. Armed yet powerless caregivers can, and sometimes do, resort to violence. But violent display of power only increases powerlessness. A beaten child beats her brother, a patient whose arm is twisted behind her back still spits her medicine in her nurse's face. Some strong and armed caregivers nonetheless become entrapped in patterns of escalating violence that excite and relieve even as they fail in their purpose. But often enough, and ideally, caregivers, despite their strength and the "arms" at their disposal, see through the promise of violence and discipline themselves to nonviolent strategies. ＞120

∠The resulting contrast between powerful/powerless nonviolent caregivers' and violent militarists' control reflects fundamentally contrasting attitudes toward embodied willfulness. By "embodied willfulness" I refer to two facts. For humans the capacity to will is rooted and expressed in bodily life; and human bodies are subject to pain, fear, and memory. It follows from these facts that people are able, in general, though certainly not in every case, to dominate the will of others if they can credibly threaten to injure or can actually damage their bodies. ＞120

< Militarism and militarized diplomacy involve, by definition, a readiness to exploit embodied willfulness, that is, to impose one's will upon others by threatening or actually injuring them. That militarists often injure for the sake of causes that are, or appear to be, just does not alter their *willingness* to injure. Probably most militarists would prefer to threaten rather than injure, bomb empty factories rather than air-raid shelters, destroy launchers rather than water supplies, provoke bloodness surrender rather than burn men up or bury them in the sand. Nonetheless, the willingness to burn, bury, cut, blow apart, and starve bodies is essential to militarist enterprises; forms of coercion that rule out in advance deliberate damage to bodies are not militarist. ＞120

By contrast, caregiving involves a *commitment* to refrain from neglecting or assaulting bodies. Someone who claims to be caring but who, over time, willingly abuses the bodies in her charge and is neither remorseful nor ready to change is not engaged in caring labor. Ordinary "good enough" caregivers often fail to fulfill their commitments, and their failure often is no fault of their own but rather of policies and communities that have denied them the resources of care. But to be committed to caregiving work, to be engaged in caregiving labor, means, among other things, to count assault or neglect as "failure." However often a caregiver fails, her refusal to exploit embodied willfulness through injury and threat of injury is a requirement of "success."

This nonviolent stance to bodily life is not simply given to caregivers. A violent stance toward embodied willfulness also arises plausibly from daily work under pressure amid disturbingly willful, uncontrollable, vulnerable bodies. In the most malignant form of caregiving, resentful or cruel mothers exploit their children's bodies as the site and opportunity of sadism, sexual exploitation, and domination. Less dramatically, many ordinary "good enough" caregivers struggle against a compulsion for order and effectiveness that could lead them to dominate their "unruly" subjects through bodily shame, neglect, or threat. Even the most benign caregivers are sometimes likely to take their child's "nature," or their elderly parent's or patient's willful embodied being, as an enemy to be conquered. Caregivers are not, predictably, better people than are militarists. Rather, they are engaged in a different project. Militarists aim to dominate by creating the structural vulnerabilities that caregivers take for granted. They arm and train so that they can, if other means of domination fail, terrify and injure their opponents. By contrast, in situations where domination through bodily pain, and the fear of pain, is a structural possibility, caregivers try to resist temptations to assault and neglect, even though they work among smaller, frailer, vulnerable people who may excite domination.

Positively, caregivers, at their best, foster the embodied willfulness and desires of those they care for. Mothers learn to accept, even treasure, the messy, unpredictable, willful bodies of children. Those who work with failing, faltering, soiling bodies resist their own impatience, fear, and disgust in order to foster, against the odds, a sense of effective willfulness amid bodily disarray. Even the smallest infant, the sickest patients, and the feeblest elderly thrive upon a caregiver's ability to identify and respond to their self-generated, willful acts. Recognizing, as militarists do, that for anyone, at any age, in any stage of health, the capacity to will is enacted in a bodily subject vulnerable to intrusion and pain, caregivers set themselves to respect bodily integrity. They thereby protect the willfulness of a person they are *unwilling* to dominate, a person lively with her or his own desires and projects.

There are many ways of contrasting caring labor with war making. As I mentioned earlier, some people are looking at conflicting norms of rationality in the two enterprises. My remarks about war's masculinity begin to contrast two attitudes toward the manipulation of sexual desire and affectionate attachment. I would like to see studies of the two practices that compared for each of them the place of passion and the meaning of particular emotions such as bitterness and anger or the weight of attitudes such as trust and forgiveness. I would like to explore self-realization and self-loss in the two practices, and the stances of each toward change, or their respective identifications of evil. To reveal the peacefulness of care it will be necessary to compare, in detail, and over a wide range of characteristics, militarist and caregiving enterprises. In the act of comparing, it is crucial to highlight militaristic or, more generally, domineering and oppressive aspects or liabilities of caregiving. It is certain *struggles within* the caregiving enterprise that will illuminate struggles for peace.

Even when all the comparisons are in, it will not be easy, conceptually or politically, to extend the values of domestic battle to public wars. One cannot simply *apply* rationalities and moral orientations that arise in particular relationships between a few people to more public, impersonal domains. Caregiving depends upon caregivers—upon people with real power who are committed to self-restraint. Most evidently, maternal nonviolence depends upon a mother whose power is limited but real and upon children who are subject to that mother's power. State governments and their leaders are not bad mothers—they are not mothers at all. Adult citizens are not "children," nor can adult citizenship be described in terms of the illness or frailty of citizens, though some citizens are of course ill and frail. Most adult citizens may retain fantasies of politicized parental or healing power; leaders may imagine themselves as good parents or as physicians to a sick populace. But social democracy depends upon renouncing, or at least checking, familial or medical fantasies and creating in their stead robust images of responsible participation in states and communities. Social democrats can draw upon *ideals* of mutuality and reciprocity that govern the actions of many caregivers. But social democrats would have to express these borrowed ideals in a language that did not presume anything like maternal will or childlike compliance.

People can learn from the moral orientations of care whether or not they are caregivers. It is more ambitious to imagine caregivers themselves creating a new, antimilitarist political identity. Of the many difficulties attending this creation, two seem preeminent.

Given the pervasiveness of militarism, obedience is the handmaid of war, resistance the prerequisite of peace. Socially, caregivers tend to be powerless; often they expect, and expect themselves, to delegate "political" decisions to others. Even in a just world where caregivers were empowered, caregivers—mothers in particular—are responsible for insuring their charges' respect for authorities, including for the caregivers themselves. Minimal obedience is a requirement of safety and, for children especially, of education and moral development.

Many caretakers do "resist," even within the context of obedience, simply by continuing to care under appalling conditions of tyranny, poverty, and neglect. There are also many examples of mothers and other caregivers—especially physicians and nurses—who resist collectively and *politically*, in the name of care. These women and men bequeath a history of resistance for feminist peacemakers and caregivers to extend and transform. Without denying the proper place of obedience within the work of care, feminist antimilitarists can strive to represent, in speech and act, a political identity that includes within the requirements of care a reflective readiness to disobey.

Caregivers' disobedience is far more likely when authorities threaten their "own" work, their "own" people. Caregivers are notoriously "partial." Mothering especially is rightly seen to be embedded in passionate loyalty to one's own children and the people they live among. Ordinary partiality of good-enough mothers is magnified by warlike circumstances in which violence is legitimated and fueled by racism and one people's children are set against another's.

Despite maternal partiality, there is a literary and historical record of maternal identification with "other" mothers and their children—including those of the enemy. To cite only one example, many mothers (Madres) in Argentina who suffered quite particular and brutal assault against their own children came in the course of protest to identify with anyone who had disappeared in their country, and then with children across the globe who had suffered direct violent or abuses of neglect.[31] This is not transcendent impartiality but a sympathetic apprehension of another grounded in one's own particular suffering.

Such a groundedness may prove sturdier than transcendance. The partiality of caregiving, most often seen as a liability, is also a strength. *People* are partial, passionate, local. What looks like the ability to transcend particular attachment is often defensive, self-deceived, or a luxury of the strong and safe. Political relationships of mutuality and respect will have to be created in the midst of passionate particularity, not outside of it.

But I do not want to deny the real and inevitable tension between caring for one's own and caring for others. Those of us who are trying to translate caregiving commitment into public action begin with different metaphysical orientations. Many of us are able to draw upon and modify religious accounts of each person's inclusion in divine care. Others of us require a secular and agnostic grounding for a translation from one's own to the world's (as to God's) children.

The work of extending care is in its beginnings; it is a work worth doing. Nonviolent caregiving offers one construction of power which refuses domination, respects embodied willfulness, but does not let abuse go unchallenged. The morality of care originates in everyday life amid fantasies and experiences of violence and love. Most men and women are caregivers, to varying degrees, at different times in their lives. Everyone is sometimes subject to practices of care whose mix of violence and non-violence is enacted on their bodily spirit at its most vulnerable. Anyone who is willing to remember honestly and listen attentively can learn care's lessons. Caregiving is only one of many ordinary practices that offers hints of peace and of the price of its violation. Given the pervasiveness of warism and the multiple costs of war, peacemakers can ill afford a competition among themselves to decide who is the best peacemaker. It is enough to identify a practice whose ubiquity and emotional potency makes it one distinctly valuable resource for peace.

NOTES

I have delivered versions of this paper to various feminist and peace studies audiences. I am grateful to the many people who listened and offered correction, insight, and amplfication and would like to mention especially Berenice Fisher and E. Ann Kaplan. A different version of this paper was published under the title "A Fierce and Human Peace" in a volume produced by Concerned Philosophers for Peace entitled *Just War, Non-violence and Nuclear Deterrence*, edited by Duane Cady and Richard Werner. I am grateful to Duane Cady for a careful, useful reading of that earlier version. Throughout the preparation of this final version, I have profited from informative, entertaining, and critical conversations with Miriam Cooke about this paper and, more generally, about issues of war and peace.

1. I develop one version (my own) of one variant of feminist peace politics. I draw upon a larger literature in ways its authors might not have intended. For brevity, I speak generally of feminist peace politics—e.g., "feminist antimilitarists hope, believe . . ." I hope to represent fairly widely held tendencies in some versions of feminist peace politics but I am finally imagining a prospectus that I invent.

2. Virginia Woolf, *Collected Letters* vol. 2. ed. Nigel Nicolson and Joanne Trautman (New York: Harcourt Brace and Javonovich, 1976), letter 748, p. 76. Woolf remained suspicious of violence even in the best of causes. In her life, these best causes were armed resistance to Franco's forces in the Spanish Civil War and the war against Nazi Germany. Currently, many critics are assessing the origins, strengths, and limitations of Woolf's feminist antimilitarism. For an overview with references, see Mark Hussey, ed., *Virginia Woolf and War* (Syracuse, N.Y.: Syracuse University Press, 1991).

3. While militarist misogyny seems culturally pervasive, it is not always intertwined with homophobia, as it is in the United States. Plato, for example, imagined an army of gay men.

4. For methodologically and politically distinct accounts of assaultive masculinity, see Klaus Theweleit, *Male Fantasies*, vols. 1 and 2 (Minneapolis: University of Minnesota Press, 1987, 1990); Robin Morgan, *Demon Lover* (New York: Random House, 1988); Christa Wolf, *Cassandra* (New York: Farrar, Strauss and Giroux, 1984). In this passage I am drawing especially upon Joan Smith, "Crawling from the Wreckage," in her *Misogynies* (New York: Ballantine Books, 1990), and Virginia Woolf, *Three Guineas* (New York: Harcourt Brace/HBJ, 1966). The literature is vast and, I assume, familiar. I do not mean to be reporting on this literature; rather I am reflecting upon its feminist or antimilitarist purposes.

5. Both Klaus Theweleit and Joan Smith explicitly invoke an object relations variant of psychoanalytic theory. See also Nancy Hartsock, "The Feminist Standpoint," concluding chapter of *Money, Sex and Power* (New York: Longman, 1983). For a more generally Freudian and influential account, see Dorothy Dinnerstein, *The Mermaid and the Minotaur* (New York: Harper and Row, 1976).

6. In addition to the writers cited in note 4, see William Broyles, "Why Men Love War," in Walter Capps, ed., *The Vietnam Reader* (New York: Routledge, 1991); Tania Modelski, "A Father Is Being Beaten: Male Feminism and the War Film," in *Feminism without Women* (New York: Routledge, 1991); and Susan Jeffords, *The Remasculinization of America* (Bloomington: Indiana University Press, 1988).

7. For an example of "good" war stories by a "good" soldier who nonetheless uses women in this way, see Tim O'Brien, *The Things They Carried* (Boston: Houghton Mifflin, 1990). In O'Brien's stories death is embodied in the death of a nine-year-old girl; thoughts of a sweetheart lead a man (as he sees it) to neglect his men; women won't answer letters or respond to men's wars; a dumb Cooze (middle-aged woman of liberal sentiments) does not understand O'Brien's stories.

8. Wilfred Owen, "The Parable of the Old Man and the Young," *Collected Poems* (London: Chatto and Windus, 1963). On the genderization of war experience, including governments, see especially Jeffords, *Remasculinization of America*.

9. Indeed, if the *New York Times* of May 1, 1991, reporting on the military's aid to Kurdish refugees is to be believed, soldiers would rather comfort than create the victims of war.

10. Virginia Woolf to Shena, Lady Simon, January 1941, in *Collected Letters* 6:464.

11. Wolf, *Cassandra*, p. 74.

12. Woolf, *Three Guineas*, p. 105.

13. I take this definition from Duane Cady, *From Warism to Pacifism* (Philadelphia: Temple University Press, 1989).

14. Any city, village, or "territory" can, of course, be marked as a battlefield.

15. See, for example, Miriam Cooke, "Postmodern Wars: Phallomilitary Spectacles in the DTO," *Journal of Urban and Cultural Studies* 2, no. 1:27–40.

16. Many feminists have contributed to these critiques. In addition to Theweleit see, especially, Evelyn Fox Keller, *Reflections on Gender and Science* (New Haven: Yale University Press, 1985), and Carol Cohn "Sex and Death in the

Rational World of Defense Intellectuals," *Signs* 12, no. 4 (Summer 1987): 687–718.

17. Theweleit, *Male Fantasies* 1:364.

18. Plato, *Republic*, 543a, 521d. See also Genevieve Lloyd, "Selfhood, War and Masculinity," in Carole Pateman and Elisabeth Grosz, eds., *Feminist Challenges* (Boston: Northeastern University Press, 1987).

19. Cohn, "Sex and Death," p. 688. Cohn coined the term *technostrategic rationality*.

20. Michael Walzer in *Just and Unjust Wars* (New York: Harper Collins, 1992) is somewhat sardonic about J. Glenn Gray's discussion of guilt in *The Warriors* (New York: Harper and Row, 1970). For the connection between abstract thought and abstract emotions see, Gray, *Warriors*, and Hannah Arendt's foreword to the 1970 edition.

21. Many feminists have argued that dominant ideals of reason, in both their civilian philosophical and military forms, reflect a subjectivity that is both "masculine" and reflective of social privilege. They point out that these ideals have been articulated mostly by economically advantaged men of dominant "races" or ethnicities (though similarly advantaged men have also articulated alternative ideals); that many male philosophers explicitly have stated that ideals of rationality were inaccessible to women of any social group, to men of laboring classes, and to anyone of "inferior" "race" or ethnicity; and that these ideals legitimate and serve male-dominated and culturally dominating institutions such as war, academia, or the law. In diagnosing "masculinity" within a system of privilege, some feminists refer only to texts, while others explain the acquisition of philosophical masculinity by the same social constellation of female caregiving, "legitimate" male aggression, and masculine privilege that allegedly gives rise to military misogyny. This literature and comment upon it is vast. For sample specimens of feminist critique see Keller, *Reflections on Gender and Science*; and Christina Di Stefano, *Configurations of Masculinity* (Ithaca: Cornell University Press, 1991).

22. It has been claimed, notoriously, that this "different" voice is heard more frequently in women than in men, that it pervades African and African-American women's thinking, and that its values arise from a strong identification and engagement with mothering and other forms of caregiving and with community survival and resistance to oppression. (As Margaret Urban Walker pointed out, many people have been so preoccupied with deciding who speaks in a different voice and why that they have barely attended to what the different voice is saying.) I claim here that whoever speaks in the "different voice" will find it difficult to speak just-war theory.

23. I am drawing here, especially, on Margaret Urban Walker, "Alternative Epistemologies for Feminist Ethics," in Eve Browning Cole and Susan Coltrap McQuinn, eds., *Explorations in Feminist Ethics* (Bloomington: Indiana University Press, 1992). Walker gives a perspicuous overview of various feminist writers, including Carol Gilligan and Nel Noddings. Walker's account seems to me substantiated in Patricia Hill Collins, *Black Feminist Thought: Knowledge, Consciousness and the Politics of Empowerment* (Boston: Unwin Hyman, 1990).

24. Many men's war stories also talk about the postwar fate of the soldier—giving special prominence to his fate, and his transformation as an individual. Ron Kovic's story as told in the movie *Born of the Fourth of July* offers a splendid and moving example. The women's stories I think of first highlight the effect of the soldier's return or loss on his family and community. Rebecca West's post–First World War novel *Return of the Soldier* (reprint, New York: Dial Press, 1982) names and typifies the genre. Two classics that also recall the First World War, Toni Morrison's *Sula* (New York: Knopf, 1973) and Virginia Woolf's *Mrs. Dalloway* (London: Hogarth Press, 1925), inextricably entwine the violences of war and postwar as they are played out in family, community, and—behind the scene—official policies of state.

25. Wolf, *Cassandra*, p. 66.

26. Woolf, *Three Guineas*, p. 18.

27. Ibid., p. 142. "Do they [the facts of history] not prove that education . . . does not teach people to hate force but to use it? Do they not prove that education makes [the educated] . . . so anxious to keep their possessions, that 'grandeur and power' of which the poet speaks, that they will use not force but much subtler methods than force when they are asked to share them? And are not force and possessiveness very closely connected with war? (p. 29). "The Facts . . . seem to prove that the professions have an undeniable effect upon the professors. They make the people who practice them possessive, jealous of any infringements of their rights, and highly combative if anyone dares dispute them. . . . And do not such qualities lead to war?" (p. 66).

28. Cynthia Enloe, *Bananas, Beaches and Bases* (Berkeley: University of California Press, 1990). In this connection, Duane Cady called to my attention George Bush's celebration, during black history month, of the military as an equal opportunity employer.

29. See, for example, Linda Johnson, "No Words Can Describe: Japanese Women's World War II Narratives" (unpublished manuscript) on Japanese mothers who killed their children rather than let them starve or—in one case—insisted on saving them only to watch them die painfully. In Toni Morrison's *Beloved*, the heroine, Sethe, attempts to kill her children to prevent them from returning to slavery and succeeds in killing one.

30. *Maternal Thinking*, (Boston: Beacon Press, 1989) chap. 7.

31. I wrote about the Madres in *Maternal Thinking*, chap. 8.

Chapter 6

SISTERS AND BROTHERS IN ARMS:

FAMILY, CLASS, AND GENDERING

IN WORLD WAR I BRITAIN

ANGELA WOOLLACOTT

> I went for a walk—it was November, grey, sad-looking as autumn is when the trees are bare and the sky overcast. I told myself, "It is nearly all over and Oliver has come through it," and then, from some awful inner voice, came the foreboding, "There is still time for something to go wrong."[1]

A solitary walk during wartime, a woman's thoughts exclusively focused on a man at war, and a sense of dread: familiar elements, but what is significant about these lines from Peggy Hamilton's memoir of World War I is that it is her brother, rather than a husband or lover, on whom she is so focused. Hamilton's foreboding, perhaps vitiated over the years by mental replaying before she recorded it in the 1970s, was proven correct: her brother Oliver was indeed killed in an air accident on November 10, 1918, the day before the Armistice.

This essay examines World War I brother-sister relationships, specifically British women's representations of their relationships with combatant brothers.[2] The powerful images of male-female relationships distorted by World War I, drawn by middle-class women writers in their memoirs and novels, help us to consider the ways in which the war affected the close familial relationships of working-class women. Vera Brittain complained that "like so many women in 1914," she was suffering "from an inferiority complex," and later she lamented that the war had put "a barrier of indescribable experience between men and the women whom they loved."[3] Irene Rathbone described her life and those of her women friends after the war as the hollow, rudderless existence of survivors, suggesting that they may as well have died as their men had.[4] Despite their own active participation in the war effort, for these women writers the guilt, anger, and adoration that their brothers and fiancés evoked in their role as warriors subsumed their own novel freedoms, including the partial granting of suffrage in 1918.

It is difficult to find similar accounts of emotional devastation by working-class women. For many working-class women in Britain, World War I proffered employment opportunities in "men's work" at three times their prewar wages. Higher wages made possible a degree of autonomy that meant independence from their family, including husbands, fathers, and brothers. Munition factories and other areas of employment desperate for women's labor encouraged working-class women to move around the country to an unprecedented extent. For many women, their health improved because their wages allowed them to eat better than they ever had. They bought new clothes, went to the cinema, and played sports.[5] At home, with the patriarch of the family absent, they could exercise choices over the newly adequate family income. When the men finally did return from war, they found a domestic world that had functioned in their absence. "Older men came back to homes which had been running perfectly well without them," Irene Rathbone observed of families less affluent than her own, "to children whom they didn't know; to wives who had been free and well-off on separation allowances, and who resented having to submit once more to male interference, and to perpetual male presence. . . . There were men whom the war made. There were a far greater number whom it ruined."[6]

One important factor of difference is that many middle-class women, certainly as represented by those who became writers, were turned into pacifists by the war. They were thereby torn between a conviction that their brothers' and lovers' sacrifices had been pointless and the desire to empathize with and valorize those sacrifices. Tension created by the prevailing view that patriotism and pacifism were irreconcilable fraught their own lives. That tension was underscored by the sense, shared by many of them, of their exclusion from the real events of the war. As the parson in Rose Macaulay's *Non-Combatants and Others* puts it: "To have one's friends in danger, and not to be in danger oneself—it fills one with futile rage. Combatants are to be pitied; but non-combatants are of all men and women the most miserable. Older men, crocks, parsons, women—God help them."[7]

For the million working-class women in munition factories around Britain, in contrast, their own roles in the war effort were in accord with those of their men. Peggy Hamilton was one of a small number of middle-class women who worked in munition factories during the war. The majority of women munition workers, by far, were from the working class; their production of the munitions of war implicated them in the making of war as much as their brothers, fiancés, husbands, or fathers in the armed services. Mostly not pacifists, they experienced no comparable deep conflict. It is evident that women workers were torn by a mixture of emotions on seeing their men in uniform: pride at their manliness, anxiety at their vulnerability. Yet there is no evidence that they too felt their lives were emptied of meaning by the loss of brothers or fiancés in the postwar world.

Feminist scholars have been concerned to recuperate the female voice in war narratives, to demonstrate the fallacy of assuming that war narratives have been exclusively male.[8] Miriam Cooke's essay in this volume epitomizes that project. In theorizing the female war narrative, however, it is equally fallacious to assume that there is only one female experience of war as of any other lived reality. Female experience varies by race, by culture, and by class. Irene Matthews's essay in this section shows how war tore even further apart the familial world of sisters and the public stage occupied by brothers: the Mexican sister's indictment of her brothers' selfish lack of concern about their mother reflected just one part of how the military broke "family bonds" along with "regional bonds of attachment to a parish." English middle-class sisters did not, however, see brothers as remote or uncaring, but rather as heroic and glamorous warriors who often retained these hues of chivalry even when the woman/sister had long since become a pacifist.

Women of different classes not only experienced their brothers' participation in the Great War differently, but their memorialization of their brothers records and illuminates those differences. Debate amongst historians and literary critics has, at times, reduced issues of women's experience of the war to a binarism: on the one hand, some argue that liberation was the dominant female experience, while on the other, the critics of that view propose instead a view of devastation or disempowerment. This reduction has polarized debate; worse, it has in its impulse toward simplification obscured the complexity of female experience. Part of my purpose here is to hint at this complexity by exposing the discrepancies between middle-class and working-class women's memorialization of their brothers. It is also my purpose to show the impossibility of essentializing gender, or any relationship or social position, in war. Class differences lead to different experiences of war, even for those engaged in the same war activity.

One problem this essay confronts is the diarchic nature of the texts on which it is based. In contrast to middle-class women's memoirs and novels, texts that lend themselves readily to the expression of sentiment, women workers' accounts of their lives are through oral history interviews and shorter autobiographies that emphasize action and circumstantial detail more than emotions. As Margaret Higonnet notes in this volume, "a recognition of the slippages between diary, testimony, autobiographical fiction, and novel has made it possible to reassess the 'life/lines' women have drawn from war." It is possible that the apparent difference in affective bonding is, at least partially, only one of expressive style. It would seem that women workers were more phlegmatic in their attitude to their brothers than were middle-class women novelists and memoirists; yet this too could be a factor of the texts.

．　．　．　．　．

Brothers occupy a central space in middle-class women's accounts of the war. They loom as the dominant planets in their emotional universes. The death of a brother, to some, is even more devastating than the loss of a fiancé or sweetheart.

A middle-class woman's relationship to her brother comprised the most secure, and often the most affective, bond she shared with a man. In their study of the English middle class from 1780 to 1850, Leonore Davidoff and Catherine Hall explicate the multiple reciprocal bonds between brothers and sisters:

> Brothers who were older by many years acted as mentors to younger sisters left at home. They were trustees and business advisers for their sisters and sisters sought refuge in the homes of brothers when widowed (or abandoned), even if several brothers had to club together to make up an income. In return, sisters were expected to give personal service to brothers; a service which was regarded as good in itself but also as the best preparation for learning wifely duties. The literature stressed a sister's religious and moral influence on more worldly brothers.[9]

Of Victorian society as represented in its literature, Marianne Hirsch demonstrates "the conflict between paternal authority and fraternal nurturance that is central to the female family romance plot."[10] A Victorian daughter sought emotional connectedness through her brother, an unthreatening, supportive presence in her life. Ideally, Hirsch shows, the "brother tongue is nurturing, sympathetic, accepting, and undemanding," yet it simultaneously asserts control.[11]

In the early twentieth century, middle-class women's dependence on their brothers stemmed from social conventions that limited their movement and made their brothers an important source of social contacts, particularly for meeting men of their own age group. Brothers were often away at school from an early age, making them remote and idealized figures. They provided a source of intellectual stimulation and information, as well as the embodiment of the future of the family name, family property, and their sisters' guarantees of economic survival in adverse circumstances. For a young, unmarried middle-class woman, a brother remained her best contact with the public world, the masculine domain of educational institutions, politics, finance, and culture. Although women were themselves establishing their presence in all these arenas, their marginality meant that their associations with the centers of power were mediated. A brother offered an intimately connected masculine ally who could perform such services of mediation. As Sara Ruddick has so aptly put it:

> Because he is male, a brother is a sister's guide to the male world, the "real" adult world. Having learned to control his superior physical strength and multiple aggressions in the context of familial love and hate, he may protect his sister in a world where he is strong and routinely "aggressive", she vulnerable and innocent. Just because he is a tamed animal, neither lover nor father, he may be his sister's guide and "conrade-twin", free from the corruption of sex and power.[12]

The importance of a "comrade-twin" to a middle-class sister was exacerbated in the late nineteenth and early twentieth centuries by a demographic imbalance of more women than men and, therefore, fewer marriage partners.[13]

In Sonia Keppel's memoir of her youth in the Edwardian years and during the war, she explains the extraordinary strength of the bond she shared with her cousin Edward, who was both a brother figure and an object of romantic devotion in her life. More importantly, Edward was a gender-changing mirror, showing her herself as she would have been as a male. "This was my own contemporary, almost interchangeable with myself, and with a shared present and future. . . . Where I had first loved Edward because he had so resembled Papa, now it seemed to me that I had grown to love him partly because, in some idealized way, he stood as an embodiment of myself, as I would have been had I been Papa's son." At the moment of Edward's departure for the war, she later claimed to have "realised that there was a terribly selfish element about my distress at his going. I would miss him with all my heart, not only because I was losing a loved companion, but because, without his strength, I would lapse back into weakness." Although she corresponded weekly with many men at war, "Best of all," she recalled, "I loved getting Edward's letters which, whatever his mood, continued to give me that sense of duality, of simultaneous flowering on the same branch." To her great grief, Edward died in combat in mid-1917.[14]

Middle-class girls grew up with the discrepancy in social evaluation of their own public worth and that of their brothers. It was abundantly clear to them, for example, that their brothers received a superior education. This was so deeply ingrained, Carol Dyhouse shows, that autobiographer Molly Hughes "lived vicariously through her brothers' school experiences, and she clearly regarded her own education—at the North London Collegiate School under Frances Buss—as a very inferior product to theirs."[15] Virginia Woolf eloquently indicted this injustice perpetrated by families in her formulation of Arthur's Education Fund, the ancient English familial institution into which money was poured for the education of sons but not daughters, which she saw as being at the heart of women's intellectual and professional disfranchisement.[16] Inured to the two-tiered system in education, middle-class women simply translated it into the assumption that their brothers would play the vital, heroic roles of war while they themselves would perform supportive services. The Edwardian school system itself had prepared them for this assumption. As Deborah Gorham shows of Vera Brittain and her brother Edward, at the same time as the public school system inculcated the values of patriotic, militaristic manliness in boys, girls' schools had echoed the same ethos.[17]

In the supportive roles many women offered and many men gratefully accepted during the war, as correspondents, senders of packages, and as objective reasons to return home on leave, women became metaphorical sisters to soldiers at the front. The heroines of the literature of the war commonly spend their spare moments in replying to multifarious letters from the front. To Joan in H. G. Wells's *Joan and Peter: The Story of an Education*, men at the front "wrote to her at first upon neat notepaper adorned with regimental crests, but their later letters as they worked their slow passages towards the place of death were pencilled on thin paper. She kept them all. She felt she could have been a good sister to many brothers."[18]

Jane Marcus has named the dominance of the brother-sister relationship in women's literature of World War I "the brother/sister incestuous 'we' of the narrative of the generational war," seeing in women's identification with their brothers their desire "to be soldiers themselves and fight alongside their brothers." As their generation lost its manhood in the war deaths of their brothers, she contends, women lost and mourned those parts of themselves which were militant, the selves who engaged in the political struggles of the prewar period and in work as nurses during the war.[19] Because it was, mostly, young people who were caught up in the active service of war, their unique generational identity was forged by war experience. Thus the women of this cohort who were bereft of their brothers and lovers lost not only companions of a prewar normalcy, but also the men who shared the knowledge of this war and its horrors.[20]

In Irene Rathbone's novel-memoir of World War I, *We That Were Young*, Joan defines the war in retrospect as coterminous with her own generation. Speaking to a woman only nine years her junior, she exclaims, "Betty and me, and all our generation—all our brothers and our friends. No other generation ever was so young or ever will be. We were the youth of the world, we were on the crest of life, and we were the war. No one above us counted, and no one below. Youth and the war were the same thing—youth and the war were us."[21] To Joan, the loss of her brother Jimmy was a far greater devastation than that of her fiancé Colin. Jimmy had always been her closest partner, and the future with him had seemed far more real than any future life with Colin she had ever been able to imagine. Despite Joan's hectic life in the 1920s, including active involvement with the peacekeeping League of Nations, Rathbone depicted her life and those of her women friends who had been through the war as without meaning or direction—their desires had gone during the war, along with the lives of their brothers and lovers.

In Vera Brittain's *Testament of Youth*, also an elegy for the generation who fought the war and were decimated and paralyzed by it, the claims of brother and lover-fiancé are equally if serially powerful. Brittain was devastated by grief over her fiancé Roland's death at the end of 1915, and came to replace him with her brother Edward as the central object of her love and thoughts. Yet her feelings about Edward as a combatant were conflicting. In the face of her growing pacifist conviction of the futility of the war, Brittain is overwhelmed with pride when Edward receives the Military Cross for bravery, deeming it "unspeakably splendid."[22] When he is killed in battle in Italy, her single-minded concern amidst her grief is to know the details of his death and specifically just how heroic it had been.[23]

Vera Brittain and Rathbone's heroines were all directly engaged in the war effort, particularly in nursing, the quintessential feminine task of healing and nurturing that did so much to turn these protagonists into pacifists. In Rebecca West's *Return of the Soldier*, in contrast, the male/female binarism is not that of battlefront/hospital ward but that of violent war/peaceful domesticity. The female narrator of the story, Jenny, is cousin rather than sister to the hero-soldier, Chris, a sufficient dilution of the family tie to allow the romantic and sexual dimensions to the relationship to become overt. When Chris's shell shock causes him to reject both Jenny and his wife in favor of a past love, Jenny is sustained by touching him vicariously through his lover: "Then as our hands touched he was with us, invoked by our common adoration; I felt his rough male texture and saw the clear warmth of his brown and gold colouring. I thought of him with the passion of exile. . . . She moved past me to the garden. . . . My moment, my small sole subsistence, ended in a feeling of jealousy as ugly and unmental as sickness. This was the saddest spring."[24] Later, another vicarious physical contact: "We kissed, not as women, but as lovers do; I think we each embraced that part of Chris the other had absorbed by her love."[25] Young Edwardian middle-class women had limited access to men outside the family as possible objects of erotic desire. With few other choices, brothers (or cousins) became the proximate but hidden locus of young women's erotic and romantic fantasies.[26] Ellen Moers has noted that in intellectual middle-class families of the Victorian period, "the rough-and-tumble sexuality of the nursery loomed large for sisters: it was the *only* heterosexual world that Victorian literary spinsters were ever freely and physically to explore. Thus the brothers of their childhood retained in their fantasy life a prominent place somewhat different in kind from that of the father figures who dominated them all."[27] Brothers' friends easily provided a legitimate object of transferred desire.[28]

In comparing the brother-sister relationship of the middle class with that of the working class, one critical point of difference is the fact of financial dependence for many middle-class women. After their parents, brothers, as the primary inheritors of family wealth, were their main sources of support. In *Return of the Soldier*, for example, the narrator has no plan or prospects for her own existence other than serving and pleasing her cousin and his wife in exchange for her keep. Jenny defines the purpose of her existence during the war as being to help her cousin's wife maintain the household in a state of tranquil grace, a fitting home for the adored warrior to return to. Yet, when he comes back as an amnesiac, she is torn between her desire to keep him happy, alive, and away from the war and her own need for him to become once again his traditional masculine self, the soldier, and therefore return to the front and a likely death in battle. Her whole life is designed in contradistinction to him as man and patriarch, but in regaining him in this form, she will probably lose him entirely.

For Rose Macaulay's protagonist Alix, the loss of her brother through his suicide at the front combines with her alienation from her lover, due to his changed psychological and emotional needs, to make her question her own most basic values. An atheist, she turns to Christianity; a woman who is infuriated by the exclusion of women from the action of the war at the battlefront, she decides to become a pacifist activist. Her own internal quest is propelled by the image of her dead brother: "Paul was driving her to find things out; his desperation and pain, her own, all the world's, must somehow break a way through, out and beyond, fling open a gate on to new worlds."[29] No matter what the material circumstances of Alix's postwar life, her intellectual landscape has been radically altered by the knowledge of her brother's agony.

The reaction of Cicely Hamilton to her brother's death during the war suggests that we must look beyond factors of financial and emotional dependency to understand the power of the sister-brother tie. A leading suffrage activist, a feminist writer and actress who lived quite independently of family money, Hamilton participated in the war effort in France in several capacities: she worked as an administrator at a Scottish Women's Hospital close to the front from November 1914 to May 1917, when she briefly joined the Women's Auxiliary Army Corps, and from there went to the Concerts at the Front organization that entertained troops under the auspices of the YMCA. When Hamilton learned of her brother Raymond's death in battle in September 1918, she herself had spent the entire war close to the front and was all too familiar with its reality. A lesbian, she had kept men at the periphery of her adult life; moreover, she had not seen Raymond for over twenty years, due to his migration to Australia, until 1916. All the more significant, therefore, that when in 1919 she was contemplating visiting his grave for a second time, she felt his presence.

> She did not see Raymond but knew for certain that it was his presence which she was experiencing so intensely. The importance of this event for Cicely lay not in what she saw but in what she felt and she always insisted that words were totally inadequate to express it:
>
> > "I know that I was in an atmosphere I had never breathed before; I know that it throbbed so swiftly and strongly that it was impossible to breathe in it; I suppose I should have died if the ecstasy—for ecstasy it was—had continued. . . . The fact remains that his apparition—call it what you will—has left me with a conception of love that is beyond the human, of love that it is impossible for me, in the flesh, to attain."[30]

It is relevant to note that Hamilton was a Christian who believed in the immortal soul, yet that in itself does not explain the power of the emotion evoked by this brother whom she had known as an adult only remotely.

In many middle-class women's accounts of the war, unlike Hamilton's, brothers mediate the experience of combat and battlefront, as they had always mediated the male, public world of events and power for their sisters. Their accounts reveal to us the ambivalence of their authors about their brothers' participation in the war: pride and physical admiration mixed with fear and anguish. The presumed-irreconcilable principles of patriotism and pacifism are in fact intertwined for them. Even though Brittain and Rathbone/Joan were themselves active in the war effort, their own lives were little endangered and their jobs were by definition for the duration: their prospects for the postwar world were a return to a semblance of their prewar normalcy, quite probably without the brothers, lovers, and male friends, the masculine half of the generation whose identity was so critical to their own. For middle-class women, the death of a brother became not just a personal loss, but a loss of their own person.

Middle-class sisters were accustomed to waving their brothers farewell as they departed on forays into the world of public events. When a brother went off to school, to university, to the City, or to India, the sister's life was enhanced through vicarious access to and knowledge of the public world. But waving them off to war was entirely different; their emotional and practical dependence on their brothers charged that departure with the fear of possible loss and suffering which would impact themselves in immediate ways. War threatened not only the loss of a brother but the loss of mediated access to public events and, therefore, a reduced world.

. . . . .

Working-class women acquired an unprecedented degree of financial autonomy during the war. They were less dependent on husbands and fathers than they had ever been. Few working-class women had relied directly upon their brothers' income, although brothers' contributions toward the joint family income had helped sustain them. Education was less obviously discriminatory for the working class: while boys received practical training intended to help them find a trade and girls were taught domestic skills thought to be of benefit whether they became domestic servants or wives, education for both sexes was merely elementary. Prior to the war, the school-leaving age, at which a child was legally permitted to leave school and take full-time employment, was fourteen. During the war, people were less likely to look closely when even younger children sought employment. The law applied equally to boys and girls, and, except in the minority of households where girls were more needed at home to help with the household than they were to bring in a wage, girls and boys both entered the adult world of the weekly wage earner at fourteen or before. Both sexes were immersed in the world of the hierarchy of skilled versus unskilled labor, long hours, and tough working conditions. The psychological and emotional enormity of this step into adulthood is clearly shown in Kathleen Woodward's account of having to start work at a premature thirteen in 1909:

> When I consider how my days were spent before I went out . . . to work, it seems odd that the change should have assumed the tragic proportions it did assume, filling my days with a haunting fear, conjuring up in my imagination the most menacing prospects. I shuddered at the very thought of it, while resigning myself to the inevitable; for I was nearly thirteen, and as long as I could remember I had been disciplined to the prospect of earning my living in the world outside. . . . Moreover, what was obvious to me, though utterly without comfort, was the fact that all the other girls and boys . . . did, in the order of things, go out to work at the earliest possible moment. They took on a new way of looking at life, and put away childish things.[31]

There was very much less sense, then, in which brothers mediated the outside world for their sisters. True, brothers were given a social autonomy that sisters lacked, and enjoyed eligibility to vote and other legal rights, but otherwise both sexes had to fend for themselves, and both were only roughly equipped to do so. Because of this greater parity, it might be argued, brothers' experience of going off overseas to fight during the war was a factor of greater discrepancy between working-class brothers and sisters than it was in the middle class, where sisters were familiar with brothers' departures. For working-class women, brothers, prior to the war, had not usually gone so far. Brothers and sisters were separated, such as when one or both went into service, the brother enlisted or found employment at some remove from the home neighbourhood, or one or both emigrated, but that separation affected both equally. Even when they lived in the same locality, both knew that in the course of earning their way in the world, such family separation had to be expected. Working-class brothers' departure for war was, geographically, a more radical change from sisters' expectations, yet the threat of loss of their brothers was not so immediate to their own lives. Working-class women did not count on their brothers to support them emotionally or financially, or to augment their access to public events, even when they remained in geographical proximity.

There is evidence that government authorities, at least, believed that women workers' affections were focused on the well-being of their brothers at war. At Woolwich Arsenal, when women workers went on strike over what they believed were extortionate prices at the canteen, the welfare supervisor harangued them on their selfishness and "talked about their poor brothers in France, at war, waiting on the ammunition so they could continue their work protecting their country and all the rest of it. So the girls all burst into tears and went back to work. That was the end of the strike."[32] Demographically, such an emotional ploy stood to reason because women munition workers were predominantly in their late teens and twenties and therefore far more likely to have at least one brother in the armed services than to have a son or even a husband at war.

Like the middle-class women who corresponded with many soldiers at the front, in order to be sisters to many brothers in need of succor, working-class women also did what they could to support unknown soldiers who were to benefit from their work. Anonymously, women in factories making helmets, gas masks, and other items which they knew would be opened by a soldier at the front would write notes expressing support, even giving their names and addresses in order to initiate a correspondence. Women also, of course, corresponded with soldiers they knew, sometimes many at a time. Caroline Rennles, who worked at Woolwich Arsenal, later recalled how much of her wages she spent sending parcels to men at war:

> I used to send ever such a lot of parcels out to different boys I knew, know what I mean? And each parcel more or less used to cost me a pound. I'll tell you what,

we used to get a big block of chocolate for five shillings, and then there used to be a tin of cigarettes for five shillings, and then a big packet of Wrigley's spearmints for five shillings. . . . Most of my parcels cost me a pound.

So I remember my dad saying to me one day, he said, "When all those boys come back", he said, "they'll cut your throat". I said, "Look, dad, I'm not sending them out because they're all boyfriends of mine." It was just because, you know, I was so patriotic, if you understand my meaning. Because they had a terrible time in the First War . . . A terrible time.[33]

In their own accounts of the war, some women workers held their brothers as the lens through which to achieve an emotional focus on the war and its import, in a way not dissimilar to the pivotal role that brothers played for middle-class writers. Lottie Barker, who worked as an overhead crane driver in the Chilwell shell-filling factory, later recalled that during the war

my mind once more returned to the reason for death, so many young men were being killed in France and there seemed to be no end to the dreary days of war, and although I was only in my teens I realised the misery and anxiety this brought to families with men and boys of military age, and although my dear brother, was too young for service, I could sympathise with the parents and young wives whose sons and husbands had answered the call of Kitchener for volunteers.[34]

Despite her sadness at the waste of male youth, she forgot the casualty list sufficiently to enjoy weekly dances. "Nothing could be more entrancing than to dance to the strains of the two piece orchestra piano and violin in the arms of a smart young civilian or maybe a darling soldier home from the front," she recalled.[35] Neither such an account of unencumbered enjoyment nor the unimportance of the distinction between civilian and soldier occurs in the texts written by middle-class women.

It was significant that Barker's brother was central to the anguish she felt for the families of soldiers. When he enlisted, immediately after the end of the war, she and her sisters were all thrown into a frenzy of anxiety.

It was in 1919, the war had been over about 2 months and we were thanking God that as a family the war had not come too near us, inasmuch as Tom was not of age, and, then out of the blue, when he was only just seventeen he decided, and did join the army.

What horror, what heartache, the apple of Sarah Ann and Emilies [sic] eye, they [her older sisters] were both horror struck.

It was a cold Tuesday evening in January when I went to see dad, but he would not listen to my plea, We that us [sic] Emily, Sarah Ann and myself only asked for support, no money we would raise that ourselves in an attempt to free our dearest of brothers from his own foolhardy, [*sic*] but dad would have none of it, he could only say, "He had made his bed he must lie on it, will make a man of him". [*sic*] Despite lack of cooperation from dad and the delight of young sister Lizzie who said, "he has given me many a hard punch I am glad he had [*sic*] gone", we decided to write to his commanding officer.

This job fell to me, and subscribing a very pathetic letter informing him that our brother was only just seventeen years of age and if this could not be classed as a reason for him not being accepted, then we were prepared to buy him out.

Of course we were ignored, but my father received a letter informing him that to all intents and purposes his son was 18 years of age and because it was his desire personally to make the army his career there was nothing more to be said. You can never immagine [*sic*] the awful despondency caused by this abrupt dismissal.

After this every Friday evening was spent in making jam tarts, swiss puddings and mince pies which were dispatched in a tin box to be received at Catterick Camp on Monday morning. Sarah Ann would run up to the post office with her parcel every Saturday morning.[36]

Yet despite this deep anxiety on the part of Tom's older sisters, when he first returned home on leave, they were all utterly spellbound by his new-born manliness.

It was weeks before we saw him and then joy of joys the letter arrived to say he was coming home on furlough. No one was prouder than the Martin family that day, dad shed a few surreptious [*sic*] tears! poor old man, and Sarah Ann as usual ridiculed him for so doing. My brother made a perfect figure of a man, or shall I say boy, for there he stood, 17 years of age, 6 foot 4 inches in stocking feet and every inch a soldier.[37]

This account suggests that working-class women felt torn between their soldier-brothers' vulnerability, on the one hand, and manliness, on the other, in a way comparable to that expressed in middle-class women's writing.

For working-class and country-bred Australian Mary Brennan, who spent three years of World War I in Britain first as a munition worker and then as a member of the Women's Land Army, the participation of three of her brothers in combat produced a gamut of reactions. She was deeply saddened by the 1915 death in the Dardenelles of her brother Jack. After the war she felt great pity for her brother Martin when his life was ruined by shell shock; he suffered recurrent bouts of insanity, became dependent upon her and her mother, and finally died young. Her attitude toward brother Bob, whom she saw several times in London when he was on leave, was supportive and pragmatic.

> The first time I met him was just by chance, walking along a London Street [*sic*], with a typical Picadilly [*sic*] lady on his arm—fur coat and no drawers. I was very pleased to see him again but he was different altogether—a real wreck. He'd look at everything: flowers, scenery or food.
>
> "This is enough to make a man weep," he'd say.
>
> He said even the bread in France was black.
>
> He was very crook after being in the trenches all those months. He was on the guns all the time you know. He was in a terrible state. You could see the horror in his eyes. . . . He look[ed] like an old man, though he was still only young.[38]

Brennan's own life during and after the war was unaltered by her brothers' experiences at war. Her anxiety and grief for her brothers did not detract from the fact that it was the war which occasioned her trip to Britain, privileging her with travels and exposure a working-class woman from the dominions could not normally expect. Although she found factory work stifling, she enjoyed London and took to land-army work with alacrity.

In Kathleen Dayus's autobiography of working-class life in Birmingham, which has achieved popular renown in Britain, the chapters on the war open on a dramatic note: "When war broke out in 1914, life changed for us all. My brothers Jack and Charlie joined up at once, without waiting for their call-up papers."[39] Yet after this foregrounding, Jack and Charlie all but disappear from her chronicle of wartime life. Instead, the first years of war are skipped over as insignificant other than for her ardent anticipation of leaving school; her own entrance into the adult world of work in 1917 subsumes all else. With no reference to any kind of concern for Charlie and Jack, her account of wartime revolves around her attempts to learn the facts of life from older women at work; her own misadventures in the realm of dating and sexual encounter, as well as those of her ill-fated friend Winnie; her growing self-confidence in social freedom as she dresses as a woman in satin blouses, hobble skirts, and makeup; and her aspiration to learn to speak as the middle class does.[40]

Of brother Charlie's fate at war we learn nothing. When Jack finally re-enters the story, it is through the perspective of the excited disruption his week's furlough creates in the family routine. First of all, there is the extraordinary procedure of delousing him. Second, there is the family pride in showing off their strapping soldier-son to neighbors and in local pubs. Third, there is the marring of the family's pride and excitement by tension over Jack's courting a young widow of whom his mother disapproves. Only cursorily does Dayus mention the family's sadness at seeing Jack back off to the front at the train station, a momentary acknowledgment of their awareness of his reality at war as opposed to his temporary impact on their lives, otherwise complete and seemingly impervious to the facts of war at the front.[41]

. . . . .

The middle-class women's novels and memoirs on which I have drawn here were nearly all written within fifteen years of the war,[42] whereas the interviews and autobiographies of working-class women were recorded in the subjects' old age and are therefore likely to reflect the acceptance of a long-distance, retrospective view. Importantly, the novels and memoirs were written while there was still only the Great War to take into account. For the working-class subjects of the interviews and autobiographies, another war had intervened, adding a whole other set of war memories that could become entangled. However, the very difference in nature of the texts represents the differences in the circumstances of their lives. Middle-class women used the introspective analysis of writing (for the many who kept diaries as well as the few who became novelists and memoirists) to help them come to terms with their anguish. Working-class women lacked leisure time and were not in the habit of assessing their lives in writing. For the few who ever had the opportunity to record their lives, it mostly came toward the end of them, usually through the agency of an interviewer or otherwise at someone else's urging.[43]

The elapse of time and the question of agency are not the only issues of difference in the structure, style, and affective nature of these texts. There are also the question of the cultural construction of subjectivity and assumptions about the role of narrative. Regenia Gagnier's study of autobiography led her to the view that " 'the self' is not an autonomous introspectible state—. . . a unique point of view—but is instead dependent upon intersubjectivity, or the intersubjective nature of language and culture. . . . One of the most interesting contrasts . . . is, I believe, that between writers who do claim an autonomous introspective 'self' and those who do not—a distinction that appears strongly class-based."[44] If workers do not place their "selves" at the center of their life stories in the same way that middle-class writers do, then they must also be less likely to depict the intimacies or passions of their personal relationships. If their narratives are built from more material and circumstantial detail, and less reflection, this may be a mirror of the pressures of their daily lives. It may also, however, be merely a tradition of narrative that keeps the most personal matters veiled. The apparent marginality of their brothers in most working-class women's accounts, therefore, cannot be taken to indicate lack of caring.

Nevertheless, we can identify differences that are other than textual, that are in fact the products of the exigencies of their lives. Mrs. Walters, who worked in a tetryl factory at Chaul End, Luton, recalled when interviewed in later life how sad she had been over the death of her brother. He had joined the Grenadier Guards, was wounded twice, and came home both times. He told them he knew he would not come back, and in fact he was killed. She recalled having worried about her brother until he was killed, and her sadness at the time of the Armistice about her brother. But her brother's death made no practical impact on her own life: she continued to work as she would have done, and otherwise pursued her own life.[45] While working-class women expressed grief and sadness at the loss of a brother, they did not experience his loss as a devastation, or as the end of their own lives in any sense. Their lives continued in much the same tenor as before, though, when the soldiers returned, they were hit hard through the loss of jobs and livelihood.

The gendering effects of World War I were class differentiated, as prewar brother-sister relationships had been. This essay offers one case in which gender construction within war can be seen to be a complex process tied to other factors, factors of difference in prewar patriarchal expectations, familial relationships, engagement in the public sphere, and wartime experiences. The greater significance of brothers in the lives of middle-class sisters is apparent in their representations of their brothers' involvement in the war and their own reactions to the loss of a brother. I am not arguing that these class differences were in any way inherent or fixed: gender roles in all classes were subject to transformation by women's inclusion in citizenship in 1918 and 1928, their legal right to enter professions obtained in 1919, and more gradually their greater access to education, among other changes. But to understand the interrelationship between gender and war in World War I, we must take the evidence offered by women. The different memorialization of brothers at war in working-class women's accounts suggest that masculine/feminine, brother/sister, combatant/noncombatant binary pairings are inadequate interpretive strategies. Women's conception of their own roles at war depended on whether they were actively involved, and whether their active work was that of healer and nurturer or that of propagator of warfare. Moreover, for the vast majority of women who were on the home front rather than in the battle zone, their understanding of the fighting came largely through the involvement of brothers. Their degree of affective bonding with, and practical dependence upon, brothers thus shaped the potential impact that the war could wreak on their own lives. The less that potential, the less likely women were to construct themselves as the passive feminine observers on the sidelines of warfare. Class differences must be included in any analysis of the construction and operation of gender; perhaps most particularly at moments of social crisis, such as war, factors of difference disrupt the commonalities of gender.

NOTES

1. Peggy Hamilton, *Three Years or the Duration: The Memoirs of a Munition Worker, 1914–1918* (London: Peter Owen, 1978), p. 122.

2. The brother-sister relationship, despite its ubiquity, is shaped by culture and by class. The analytical utility of the brother-sister relationship consists of its preclusion of change (particularly the impossibility of marriage), its balance of class and social status, and its relative lack of hierarchical distinctions. Especially when close in age, brothers and sisters offer each other a lifelong benchmark of experience and achievement differentiated only by factors of sex and gender. In Margaret Atwood's *Cat's Eye* (New York: Bantam, 1989), Elaine's brother Stephen is her benchmark of boys' greater niceness to each other than girls', as well as boys' greater ease of success and happiness. More significantly, he is also her "space twin," her counterpart whose life diverges from her own and enters a different time dimension in his death, such that she will get older and he will not (p. 414). Curiously, for my purposes here, his death is a gratuitously violent and shocking event in the comparative mundanity of the rest of the text, a death in the prime of life through arbitrary and meaningless (to her) international terrorism, thus equivalent to a death in war. Like the women writers of World War I, she is left by his death bereft of the masculine counterpart she had believed essential to her own identity.

3. Vera Brittain, *Testament of Youth* (1933; reprint, Wideview Books, U.S.A., 1980), pp. 104, 143.

4. Irene Rathbone, *We That Were Young* (1932; reprint, New York: Feminist Press at City University of New York, 1989), p. 449.

5. See Angela Woollacott, *On Her Their Lives Depend: Munitions Workers in the Great War* (forthcoming); J. M. Winter, *The Great War and the British People* (Cambridge: Harvard University Press, 1986); and Gail Braybon and Penny Summerfield, *Out of the Cage: Women's Experiences in Two World Wars* (London: Pandora, 1987).

6. Rathbone, *We That Were Young*, pp. 431–32.

7. Rose Macaulay, *Non-Combatants and Others* (1916; reprint, London: Methuen, 1986), p. 144.

8. Claire Tylee has pointed out that Paul Fussell's thesis in *The Great War and Modern Memory* (London: Oxford University Press, 1975), that the First World War has shaped culture and understanding ever since, erases women from culture and understanding in the twentieth century. Tylee's project is to document and interpret how women's writing on the war has shaped women's culture and un-

derstanding. *The Great War and Women's Consciousness: Images of Militarism and Womanhood in Women's Writings, 1914–64* (Iowa City: University of Iowa Press, 1990), pp. 6–8.

9. Leonore Davidoff and Catherine Hall, *Family Fortunes: Men and Women of the English Middle Class, 1780–1850* (Chicago: University of Chicago Press, 1987), p. 349.

10. Marianne Hirsch, *The Mother/Daughter Plot: Narrative, Psychoanalysis, Feminism* (Bloomington: Indiana University Press, 1989), p. 80.

11. Ibid., p. 81.

12. Sara Ruddick, "Private Brother, Public World," in Jane Marcus, ed., *New Feminist Essays on Virginia Woolf* (Lincoln: University of Nebraska Press, 1981), p. 186.

13. This imbalance was widely perceived and testified to, for example, by Clara E. Collet, *Educated Working Women: Essays on the Economic Position of Women Workers in the Middle Classes* (London: P. S. King and Son, 1902), esp. pp. 29–37.

14. Sonia Keppel, *Edwardian Daughter* (London: Hamish Hamilton, 1958), pp. 147, 151–52.

15. Carol Dyhouse, *Feminism and the Family in England*, 1880–1939 (Oxford: Basil Blackwell, 1989), p. 19.

16. Virginia Woolf, *Three Guineas* (1938; reprint, San Diego: Harcourt Brace Jovanovich, 1966), pp. 4–5.

17. Deborah Gorham, "The Education of Vera and Edward Brittain: Class and Gender in an Upper-Middle Class Family in Late Victorian and Edwardian England," *History of Education Review*. (Journal of Australian and New Zealand History of Education Society) 20, no. 1 (1991): 34.

18. H. G. Wells, *Joan and Peter: The Story of an Education* (New York: Macmillan, 1919), p. 468.

19. Jane Marcus, Afterword to Rathbone, *We That Were Young*, pp. 490–91.

20. The importance of this generational self-consciousness is searingly evoked in Helen Zenna Smith, *Not So Quiet . . .* (1930; reprint, New York: Feminist Press, 1989). The siblinglike relationship of the protagonist with "the boy next-door" is temporarily transformed into one of passion due to their mutual experience of the battle zone; what draws them together is their knowledge of each other's war aversion in opposition to their parents' uncaring jingoism. It is perhaps significant, though, that Evadne Price, for whom Helen Zenna Smith is a pseudonym, did not write from her own experience but based the book on another woman's diaries, and years after the war at that.

21. Rathbone, *We That Were Young*, p. 464.

22. Brittain, *Testament of Youth*, p. 287.

23. Ibid., pp. 440–44. It may be significant, however, that at the time of writing Brittain may have believed him to have purposely let himself be killed in battle to avoid a court-martial for homosexuality. See Deborah Gorham, "The Education of Vera and Edward Brittain," p. 29.

24. Rebecca West, *The Return of the Soldier* (1918; reprint, New York: Carroll and Graf Publishers, 1990), pp. 131–32.

25. Ibid., p. 184.

26. In Klaus Theweleit's view, women's affective focus on their brothers during the battles waged by the Freikorps in Germany in the early 1920s was due in good part to the brothers' insistence on their own primacy in their sisters' lives. *Male Fantasies* (Minneapolis: University of Minnesota Press, 1987), 1:112–13.

27. Ellen Moers, *Literary Women* (Garden City, N.Y.: Doubleday and Co., 1976), p. 105. I am grateful to Marianne Hirsch for this reference.

28. In *Testament of Youth*, Brittain's fiancé Roland is her brother's closest friend; in *We That Were Young*, Joan's eventual fiancé Colin is brother to one of her close friends. Such patterns did not only obtain for the middle class, however. For women workers, too, brothers' friends and brothers of friends were accessible prospects for romance. Among women munition workers interviewed by the Imperial War Museum's Department of Sound Records, London, for instance, Lily Truphet met her future husband because he was a friend of her brother (000693/07).

29. Macaulay, *Non-Combatants and Others*, p. 107. Macaulay dedicated this novel "to my brother and other combatants."

30. Lis Whitelaw, *The Life and Rebellious Times of Cicely Hamilton: Actress, Writer, Suffragist* (Columbus: Ohio State University Press, 1991), pp. 165–66.

31. Kathleen Woodward, *Jipping Street* (1928; reprint, London: Virago, 1983), p. 67.

32. Elaine McKenna, ed., *Better Than Dancing: The Wandering Years of a Young Australian, Mary Brennan* (Melbourne: Greenhouse Publications, 1987), p. 187.

33. Imperial War Museum, Department of Sound Records, 000566/07, p. 25. It has been pointed out to me that the monetary sums in this excerpt are inflated, probably reflecting values at the time of interview, in the 1970s or 1980s.

34. Lottie Barker, "My Life as I Remember It, 1899–1920" (typescript, Brunel University Library, Oxbridge), pp. 56–58.

35. Ibid., p. 58.

36. Ibid., pp. 69–70.

37. Ibid., p. 70.

38. McKenna, *Better Than Dancing*, p. 178.

39. Kathleen Dayus, *All My Days* (London: Virago, 1988), p. 40.

40. Ibid., chaps. 4–7. Dayus's autobiography is in three volumes, and in each of these she covers the span of her life while emphasizing different parts. In the second volume, *Where There's Life* (London: Virago, 1985), she again dwells on her wartime experience of learning the adult world of work and sex, although this time her promiscuous friend is called Nelly. Again, Charlie and Jack are mentioned only in passing as having volunteered early in the war, as well as Jack's concern that "his widow" should be faithful.

41. Dayus, *All My Days*, pp. 69–71.

42. Again Peggy Hamilton, whose memoir was published in 1978, is an anomaly here.

43. Kathleen Dayus wrote her multivolume autobiography of her own accord, but she too only did so in the relative freedom of older age. Mary Brennan wrote

hers at the urging of her great-niece Elaine McKenna, who edited it. Lottie Barker recorded her youth in typescript because of a working-class autobiography project conducted at Brunel University.

44. Regenia Gagnier, *Subjectivities: A History of Self-Representation in Britain, 1832–1920* (New York and Oxford: Oxford University Press, 1991), pp. 11–13.

45. Imperial War Museum, Department of Sound Records, 9289/2.

Chapter 7

DAUGHTERING IN WAR: TWO "CASE STUDIES"
FROM MEXICO AND GUATEMALA

IRENE MATTHEWS

"MOTHERING" AND "WAR" have often been twinned in a sort of lethal symbiosis: whether collusive or oppositional, conceptual or practical, life giving and death dealing are seen to be connected. In her approach to alternatives to violence, Sara Ruddick deals with maternal practice as an expansive mode of *resolving* conflict, a mode—and an objective—not restricted to "natural mothers." My own essay here reverts, perhaps reactively, to "organic" motherhood as it is portrayed in active warfare. I ask: What does official violence mean and do to mothers, and to their *children*? What do two daughters make of their mothers' roles in wartime?

REVOLUTION AND CHILDHOOD: "NELLIE"

> Childhood is Paradise?
> "Yes, . . . it is Eden, but it harbors a serpent: called death."[1]

Mexico's northern plains and sierras saw some of the fiercest confrontations of the Revolution, produced some of the most notable and notorious of the warrior caciques, and inspired a great deal of the literature of the period. Nellie Campobello was born at the turn of the century into a family whose interests and income were scattered across the north of Mexico and into the south of the United States. The armed phase of the Mexican Revolution, however, fought between 1910 and 1920, reinforced for Nellie Campobello the importance of her smaller "motherland" and her local heroes. In her words, General Francisco Villa is "the only warrior genius of his time, one of the greatest in history; the best in America, and after Ghengis Khan, the greatest warrior that has ever existed."[2] As it asserts Nellie Campobello's personal admiration for Villa, this eulogy also assumes the rectitude of the Revolution and a positive (and uncritical) appreciation of the figure of the warrior throughout history. Nellie Campobello's childhood experience extended into a lifelong—idealized and partisan—fascination for military tactics and revolutionary strategies, for weaponry and the men who wield it. And she offers her testimonies of the Mexican Revolution—*Cartucho* (Tales of the struggle in northern Mexico) and *Las manos de mamá* (My Mother's Hands)—as personal and truthful memorials to heroism.[3]

Nellie Campobello's telling of others' lives and, above all, their deaths, is imprinted with both the immanence of childhood to the events, and with the effect—simultaneously distancing yet implicating—of self-reference to the adult narrator dwelling in the metropolis and recalling and reliving her childhood experiences. In both *Cartucho* and *My Mother's Hands* the narrative focus belongs to a young girl living out her urban childhood in the very thick of the fighting. The battle frame is correspondingly child sized: not the slope of a distant hilltop but the square of a window, the canyon of a small-town street, the angle of vision around the ample, discreet slope of a mother's skirts. From this "safe" spatial perspective, war and play are dangerously meshed with childish insouciance. *Cartucho*, for example, introduces the "Men of the North"—the heroic mounted warriors of the Flying Brigades—in diversions that combine a perilous paternalism, pride, spurious sentiment, and cruelty. They carry the narrator's baby sister Gloriecita into battle, make handkerchief slippers for her, lie about their "kills," boisterously shoot the head off the children's pet dove (which is then unremorsefully plucked and roasted to provide wartime protein). The brief portrayals of the men collapse the "normal" activities of girlhood into war through certain common connectors—the sweethearts and sisters and mothers of the soldiers, the domestic details that lend an air of familiarity and dailiness to a *guerrillero* class, and to the combat taking place on the very doorsteps and street corners. The setting for most of the sketches in *Cartucho* is Hidalgo del Parral, a strategic center on the main northern railway line very close to Villa's main stronghold and a constant target for government and guerrilla forces alike. This scenario of much of Nellie Campobello's childhood is also "Mamá's" hometown: when Villa's occupying army finally moves on, it is Mamá who organizes the removal of their wounded. When the Villa men die, it is Mamá who weeps for them: "She said it was the end of a real man" (*C*, 14).

The dedication of *Cartucho* to "Mamá, who gave me the gift of true stories in a country where legends are manufactured and where people live lulled from pain as they listen to them" (4) underlines from the beginning the political poetics of oral history and the maternal ethic of "truth" that brought Nellie Campobello to demythify the negative stories about her regional warriors circulating in Mexico in the post-Revolutionary years. But the most striking characteristic of Nellie Campobello's unusual version of the brutalities of war lies in the way her narrator's cool scrutiny subsumes a fiercely egocentric possessiveness: "My gunshot bodies,

sleeping in my green notebook . . . my dead men . . . my childhood toys"
(C iv). The dead men that "sleep" in the notebook are compressed like
rose petals as sentimental markers in an often ironic or even amused commentary that betrays no evidence of infantile trauma. Indeed, as she
moves into describing "The Executed," the narrator implies that for a
child the everyday occurrence of violence and death is intriguing rather
than disturbing; often exotic: "Guts, how pretty!" (35); or intimate: "It
seemed to me that dead body was mine" (37); or grandly quotidian:
"More than three hundred men shot at the same time, inside a barracks
is really very extraordinary, people said; but our young eyes found it quite
normal" (32).

Unlike most other narrators of the Revolution, Nellie Campobello's
narrator usually introduces her protagonists through selective but minute
physical description. Her vividly pictorial style reminds the reader of
the deadly photographs in Gustavo Casasola's famous *Historia gráfica*:
a selection of dreadful scenes exquisitely subtitled by an epitaphic cynic.[4]
A little girl's eye and ear replace Casasola's camera lens, and focus,
as the lens does, onto auspicious detail soon to rigidify in horrible death.
In *Cartucho*, the men are identified by a synecdochal gaze that empha-
sises their height, the way they walk, the color and slant of their
mustaches or sombreros, their eyes and hair and skin and jewelry—all
from the perspective of a girl child's own level eye and eye level. Elías,
for example, was "tall, [with] cinnamon skin, chestnut hair, green
eyes, two gold eyeteeth . . . a handsome man" (7). The colorful simplicity of these descriptions of the living heightens the visual impact of
the moment of death: "a scarecrow . . . wearing a dead man's trousers"
(16); "with red, red eyes, that seemed like he was weeping blood"
(23); "black, black blood . . . because he had died in a rage" (24). And
the face earlier described as a "ripe peach" reappears all too briefly: "it
was too bad they killed Elías so fast" (88). As Dennis Parle reminds us,
and as almost any phrase from the text proves, "*Cartucho* is paradoxically both the most poetic and the most violent novel of the Revolution."[5] We learn how death in war is usually accompanied by the invasion of dirt into the body, a naturalistic allusion to biblical ashes and
dust; how the coup de grace can be effected with and without mutilation
(by shooting through a dying man's shoe placed against the temple to
avoid powder burns on his face, for example). We learn, too, of the numerous terminal alternatives to the expenditure of valuable bullets: running victims literally into the ground or burning them alive or hanging
them from a telegraph post. "His *macuchi* cigarette had fallen from his
ear, and now the hanged man looked as if he was searching for it with
his tongue" (36).

As the reader shudders at *Cartucho*'s precise and unremittingly graphic
toll of violence, she is forced to seek solace—just as the child-narrator

did—in the resolute, preoccupied figure of Mamá. The apparent indifference in the narrative voice may reflect its gestation in an environment where the mother's personal hopes and ethics are engrossed by the need to (have her) relate history:

> When she was telling about something, suddenly she'd be unable to continue. . . . I liked to listen to those tragic stories, it seemed to me I could see and hear everything myself. I needed to have those terrifying pictures in my child's soul, the only thing I regretted was that telling them made Mama's eyes fill with tears. She suffered a lot when she witnessed those horrors. The only thing she had left was telling about the end of her people. (39–40)

When the town of Parral comes under fire, however, Mamá steps out from the group of choric women, the mere "witnesses of tragedies." Her agency becomes active and vital as she participates in the scenes of battle—she nurses, confronts enemy generals to protect "her" wounded men, saves her son from execution, survives the terror of facing an invading army with helpless children at her feet. Here, the narrative introduces details of creative, rather than merely reactive, feminine resourcefulness. The mother figure, the epitome of nurturance, is shown also to be astute, persuasive, even cunning, as well as physically and morally strong. In armed combat, power is mobilized through physical strength; weaponless women should also, therefore, be powerless. But even in, or perhaps especially in, "civil" war, other forces come into play. To be less powerful does not mean losing all battles, and Mamá's power goes beyond the simple strength of resistance: she takes the initiative and she takes risks, like a proper hero. Her daughter is very proud of her, "deep down inside, because Mamá had saved those men" (60).

We learn in a later sketch, however, that Mamá did not save Villa's wounded men, besieged in the hospital when the town changed hands again—they were carted off to die. The "facts" in *Cartucho*, as in wartime reportage, are revised as new information filters through the restructured immediacy. Throughout *Cartucho*, memory—the mother's "truths" and observations—is combined with fantasy, the child's imaginative and ideological projections: an artifice of narrative psychology whose slippages ironize the association between the mother's history and the child's desire. *Cartucho* is structured as a projection of infantile desire—represented in the difference between the demand for love and the appetite for satisfaction.[6] In controlling iteration (the mother's stories) through a written narrative that both intensifies and poeticizes others' deaths, the author also symbolically situates the child-narrator in the phallic-maternal role—powerful, meaningful, and expressive.[7] By emulating her Mamá, she—the child-narrator and the adult author—seeks both to disavow "manufactured legends" and to conjure the deaths of the Men of the North. The chronology of action is shuffled within the text to fit Mamá's (projected) desires, also.[8] In "Samuel's Cigarette" we learned how Pancho Villa, with his bodyguards Samuel Tamayo and General Trillo, "*went to sleep forever* there: felled by bullets" (66, my emphasis)—dreaming their eternal dream also within the pages of a young girl's notebook. Yet *Cartucho* ends on a retrospective note of optimism, upheld by the continuing Revolution under Villa's leadership. A great victory for the Villistas is retold by one of the soldiers and reflected by a child's interpretation of her mother's gaze as the ragged remnants of the enemy drag their way through the streets:

> Mamá's eyes had a lovely light in them, I think she was pleased. The people of our land had beaten the savages. . . . Our street would be joyful once more, and Mamá would take me by the hand to church, where the Virgin was waiting for her. (89)

REVOLUTION AND MOTHERHOOD: "MAMÁ"

> I know I came from a clarity.
> (*"Yo," por Francisca*)[9]

The childlike optimism that closes *Cartucho* seems also to close off Nellie Campobello's texts to sophisticated criticism. In his discussion of Nellie Campobello's first work, John Brushwood was doubly dismissive: "*Cartucho* is held together, if it can be said to have any unity at all, by the idea of the child's reaction. The view of the Revolution is, of course, limited by this device . . . [but] the author contributed nothing else to the theme of the Revolution."[10] This "limited" point of view reconstructs, however, the final vision of a vast number of the victims of civil warfare. And the critical comment that "the author contributed nothing else" ignored—among many other items—Nellie Campobello's poetic biography *My Mother's Hands*, published six years after the first edition of *Cartucho*. *My Mother's Hands* is also set in Mexico's northern plains, where the family tribe follows its menfolk around the battlefields but where, as I have already commented, Mamá is also at home: not merely an observer of the fighting but a participant in the domestic front, a peace-loving "collaborator." The "limited" perspective on the battles in *My Mother's Hands*—intimate, domesticated, child size, and often grimy—might be seen to parallel, or prescribe, Mamá's own life. The accidents of war are often a corollary to the perennial maternal alarms of supervising childhood:

> It was midday . . . the houses trembled. My little brother's arm, in shreds, appeared dragged by a blackened body; his face and clothes destroyed,

black. He was encrusted all over with lead. He ran to bring his broken flesh to Mamá. (112)

This little brother is not a casualty of battle, a hero; he has almost blown himself up—blown one hand off—while playing around with buckshot. The accident serves to connect the reader both with earlier accounts, in *Cartucho*, of the mother's activities in the Hospital of Jesus and with the context of children growing up in warfare. In *Cartucho* the descriptions of this hospital—conscripted by Mamá for the worst wounded of the Villistas after the battle of Torreón—were the direct, pragmatic recollections of a "nurse's aide," involving pus, sweat, blood, bullets, and buttocks.[11] *My Mother's Hands* offers an almost pastoral variant on the earlier naturalism of *Cartucho*; both the child-observer and her brother are infantilized again, and "returned to Nature"; the little boy is seen not inside the hospital but in its garden, where "he really did have the face of an apprentice saint. . . . The sun lingered, gleaming, on his shiny shaven head. But he now only had one hand and saints always have two" (*MMH*, 112). The "saintliness" of childhood innocence (where muteness seems to indicate the touch of God) is also infinitely susceptible to mutilation through boyish error. In the same scene, the narration shifts from the familiar small-town hospital tended by nuns, mothers, and sisters—all exemplars of feminine nurturance and reparation in and out of wartime—to the hospital in Chihuahua, where another brother, "the oldest of all," lies wounded. As if the narrator had never visited a hospital before, or perhaps to emphasize the difference between the provincial tending place and city modernity, we are told that this Chihuahua hospital "smelled very strong; later I learned that that was the smell of all hospitals" (112). The focus, and the scenario, however, shift rapidly away from the hospital beds and the wounded brother—"calm, and without the slightest remorse for Mama's suffering" (113)—onto baby sister Gloriecita's "savage" blue eyes and behavior (and a premonition, in a shattered watch, of another baby's "time" being shattered), then onto the return journey and the convulsive derailment of their train between Conchos and Chihuahua. Once again, innocent civilians are the principal victims:

> They laid out one woman in her own petticoat and tied her up like a bundle of laundry. One young man was placed carefully beside the track. You couldn't see a single mark on him, he was pale, and his eyes were open. I wondered why he should stare like that; he seemed to be alive. Someone threw a handful of earth on him and blotted out his stare. (113)

Literary descriptions of untimely death—particularly in war narratives—are easily susceptible to hyperbole or romanticism. In *My Mother's*

Hands, however, civilian and soldierly casualties are equated in terms that are discreet, almost lyrical, yet persistently unsentimental. The arbitrariness of wartime violence often builds a poetical bridge, but also excavates a psychological gap, between "reality" and "sensibility": "What an awful thing! My eyes were accustomed to seeing death by hot lead, shattering into little pieces inside the body" (*MMH*, 113). It would seem that the childlike view of wartime as a "natural spectacle . . . neither surprising nor moving"[12] that critics noted in *Cartucho* remained unfiltered by ethics or remorse in *My Mother's Hands*. In the report of the train incident, however, the major focus is not the cause or the scale of the disaster itself, nor its effect—or lack of it—on the child-witness, but the mother's reaction to the tragedy: she gathers her daughters to her and with the help of a guard picks her way across the sleepers of the high, dangerous river bridge to safety and comfort on the other side. The discourse shifts from narration of the child's memory to interpretation of the mother's mind—the mother's eyes look back at the track "where they have conquered life" and window her thoughts flying past the scenes of carnage they have just left, to her wounded son in hospital. Hot coffee and her mother's sensible words combine to allay a little girl's fears: "You have to do things quickly. That way you don't feel frightened" (114). The daughter's admiration for her mother is here embodied not in sentiment or uncritical idealization, but in respect for a pragmatic lesson learned in crisis.

Despite this exemplary framework for maternal heroism, both texts underline the senseless wastage of a "revolution" witnessed and sustained by women and children as the countryside is ravaged. In counterpoint to the mother's recommendation to fearlessness, the child-narrator constantly takes toll of the final shamefulness of pointless death, sliding neatly from impersonal quantification of carrion—How many kilos of meat, all told? How many eyes? How many thoughts?—to a relational qualification of the effects of death on the survivors:

> If men knew how much pity they arouse in their final pose, they would not let themselves be killed. . . . Strong men scattered there as a gift for my eyes, clutching between their fingers the hems that their mamas sewed onto the edges of their bleached clothing . . . and the gunfire would return and I would see dead young men with rigid arms outstretched and with open mouths where flies sang. (*MMH*, 118)

These words close one of the most significant passages dealing with the collision of two worlds in wartime, "*She* and Her Machine," when the noise of the cannon, booming as if "the sky gaped open over the graveyard," drowns out the "poor little noise" of the mother's sewing machine. Doris Meyer draws on Carol Gilligan's theories of gendered moral development to suggest that "Mamá's hands" represent, above all, an ethic of care in a world that privileged an ethic of rights[13]—a world, I would add, that subsumed all "rights" under the singular right to destroy and kill: the childlike perspective on that world emphasizes the frailty of the feminine ethic—the mother's hands serve and protect her own children, but are useless to prevent the death of the children of other *mamás*.

Also at play are the curious psychology of feminine intuition and the ominous cruelty of an objective (that is, uninvolved) observer. Soldiering is supposedly the profession of killing other soldiers; and the Mexican Revolution has often been viewed historically as a principal protagonist in the "macabre mythology" of fatalism intrinsic to Mexican manhood. As Edmundo Valadés comments: "It was your turn! That seems to be the litany whereby the revolutionaries marched 'indifferent to their fate.' A formula that explains the mystery and the inevitability of death: a fatality etched in advance and accepted as an imponderable truth, turning itself into a characteristic of the Mexican."[14] Valadés (and every other commentator) points out that the literature of the Revolution is "saturated" with the idea of someone's "number coming up" (or not). But Nellie Campobello deconstructs the conventionality and universality of this concept of fatalism. When her narrator hypothesizes above, "If men knew . . . ," she implies that violent death in warfare is the product not of "indifference to fate" but of its opposite, ignorance: of not knowing one's fate, far less accepting it. In both texts, the youthfulness of the dead soldiers, their unpreparedness, is reiterated again and again: "One little eight-year-old kid, dressed like a soldier . . . also died there. . . . His legs bent at the knees seemed to be taking a step—*his first step as a man*" (C, 31, my emphasis). Elsewhere, in descriptions of other boys co-opted into service with little military training and fewer military ideals, the narrator implies that these young men's "turn" is forced onto them, and unwillingly ratified in the rictus of death:

> Julio told his companions: "I don't want to fight up there where you're looking. Not out of fear. I'm not afraid. It's the war between us that makes me feel sad. For the love of God, I'd rather be little again. . . ." Julio was the last one. . . . He was burned all over. His body shriveled up. Now he was a child again. . . . They buried him in a tiny little casket. (C, 68)

"Julio" wanted to be little again so he could return from the masculine world of war to the feminine world of protection and avoid the grown-up version of children's squabbles: a grown-up world where the "enemy" was still "their cousins, their brothers, their friends" (C, 68). This regressive desire is underlined in references to other child-victims of warfare such as the eight year old, the twelve year old, or Mamá's "oldest son of all," at thirteen years old a wounded veteran in the hospital. These examples particularly reflect the failure of a "care-taking" ethic, a poignant *maternal* perspective: Why should women rear children only to give them to war? How young does a boy have to be to escape? How old to be allowed to choose?

Both *Cartucho* and *My Mother's Hands*, however, set up an ambivalent dialectic of responsibility for some aspects of warrioring. Among the adult victims, some are marked out by the narrator with a different weakness that flaws their battle armor—not inexperience or reluctance but romanticism, "another enemy, the most dangerous. Generally those who favored the perfume of flowers and songs of love died faster than the others, because they were already poisoned" (*MMH*, 121). These men, we are told, had two sides to their nature, one a "delicately contour[ed] 'self' . . . that was made for women and which they did not use to fire bullets" (*MMH*, 115). If, we wonder, Mamá did not "send Rafael Galán off with an embrace," or the "girls of the Segundo del Rayo" found the soldiers less appealing, would these in turn find warring less appealing?[15] Did the men fight *because* they loved women? Or did they fight *carelessly* because they loved women? Despite her incursions into this different sort of poetic fatalism, however, the daughter-narrator of *My Mother's Hands* leaves it to the reader to adjudicate the erotics of belligerence and herself categorizes heroes and villains not by the way they fight or die but by their treatment of Mamá. *My Mother's Hands* is, above all, the story of a mother who would die young, but who had survived—one might almost say, who flourished—in the direst moments of combat, when her maternal dedication to "life" was at its most costly and most valuable. Bearing and raising children in wartime is a social as well as an individual event: Mamá dares to expose her private persona publicly and question the demands that Revolutionary society makes on her children: "I've come to get my son. He's still a child. I do not want him to be killed so young. Wait till he is a man" (*MMH*, 122).

It seems that the Mexican Revolution, and Mamá's function within it, perfectly exemplify the oppressive context that theorists of "maternal thinking" expose:

> Almost everywhere, the practices of mothering take place in societies in which women of all classes are less powerful than men of their class to determine the conditions under which their children grow . . . : military and social violence and often extreme poverty.[16]

Unlike some (mainly earlier) interpreters of women's psychosocial condition and conditioning, Sara Ruddick sees women's alternative ethic not merely in terms of "caretaking," of gentle and unconditional love or *abnegación*, however. Instead, she suggests, although care is a "primary virtue of the morality of love . . . maternal love . . . , in fact, . . . is erotic, inseparable from anger, fierce and fraught with ambivalence."[17] The same emotion a mother feels toward her children, energizing yet controlled, can inspire her to action rather than reaction, to pacifism rather than passivity; the battling and the outrages against Mamá's family and her self make her stronger: "Mamá's eyes, grown large with revolt, did not weep. They had hardened, reloaded in the rifle barrel of her memory" (C, 33).

The "hardening" effect of war emends not only misplaced sentiment or romance but also the "natural" process of mothering children: many scenes in My Mother's Hands recall Mamá as an isolated figure looking into the distance or watching her children from outside, from a doorway. Despite her aloofness, however, the children "adore" their mother: it is no accident that she embodies the purity and the mystery of the Virgin, who in the end also lost her precious son. The Tarahumara poem with which My Mother's Hands is prefaced already points to that connotation—it addresses a mother whose "face of light" contains the luminosity of nature and the ethereality of sainthood.[18] The Virgin of Guadalupe, Mexico's own sweet, dark patron saint, crystallizes the purity, innocence, and maternal devotion of the Catholic Queen of the heavens. But the indigenous Virgin is also a defender-protector, as was Tonantzín ("little mother"), the benign Indian goddess she replaced.[19] The Mexican matriarch who embodies these strengths may rule with a particular power on her own terrain. Wartime, however, implies the violent invasion of that terrain, the enceinte (Julia Kristeva's term) of women's space and women's bodies. In her particular situation, which is compounded by the fatherlessness of her children, Mamá re-establishes and protects her enceinte by "reading" and subverting the most familiar evidence of penetration: she tears her blouse to "explain" her new baby in a legal courtroom by representing herself as a victim of men's violence, of rape. Mamá consciously and provocatively symbolizes a commonplace aspect of machismo[20] to show how the (masculine) ethic of protection has failed to preserve her female propriety. The (masculine) arbiter of rights (the legal bench) is forced—perhaps self-reflectively—to weigh the failure of assumed protection against violence and adjust the balance of the "contractual conception of justice" in favor of the feminine.[21]

The transferral and reincorporation in the mother of the patriarchal claim (reinforcing an earlier scenario where Mamá successfully fought to maintain her children as hers alone against the paternalistic interest of a military chief) also symbolically recognizes the phallic center of the family. In wartime, especially, many women are obliged to take over the "real"—as well as the symbolic—role of Father as well as mother; the mother in this book utilizes her empowerment (the public recognition of her private role) as a special shield against the destructiveness of the outside world, a shield broad enough to shelter liberty and even play.[22] This assumption of power by the mother, however, is not always celebrated by all its beneficiaries. Hidden under the daughter's revelation of the mother's courage and concern lies a sister's complaint that is repeated a number of times in both *Cartucho* and *My Mother's Hands*: the narrator's criticism of her brothers' lack of sensibility, in particular, their lack of response to and regret for Mamá. Military training, and the experience of war itself, capitalize on the "natural" psychological separation of male adolescence.[23] Purely psychological—"familial"—explanations of gendering are a minefield of proscripted essentialisms: in her essay "Sisters and Brothers in Arms," Angela Woollacott uses sibling relationships to warn against simplistic generalizations and to suggest how "gender construction within [overseas] war" is a complex process tied to many different social and relational factors, inside and outside war. But in both of Nellie Campobello's works, the narrator underlines and criticizes the selfishness in her brothers' "separate sense of self" by overtly comparing it to the love and concern that characterize "mothering" (and, more circumspectly, daughtering). In *My Mother's Hands*, the narrator tells us that her "thirteen-year-old brother, the oldest of all . . . was calm and without the slightest remorse for Mamá's suffering" (113). And the first (1931) version of *Cartucho* closes on an indictment of another brother, "el Siete" (saved from execution by Mamá and sent off across the northern border out of harm's way). He returns to Mexico once, "in 1924," so the reader knows that the mother is dead, yet her son

> didn't say a thing about mama, didn't mention her nor ask after her. He'd been doing a lot of studying and just came back to show us the quantity and quality of bad habits he had learned up there. If he had stayed under Villa's care he'd have been a bandit, too. But a Mexican bandit. (C [1931], 143)

Such ironic-nostalgic "nationalism" (which also "localizes" external influences on male adolescence), deconstructs another of the processes of the male world of war. If one of the effects and the goals of military training was to break or transpose the family bonds that have to do with the link of mother to son and encourage instead bonding between men, it sought also to break the regional bonds of attachment to a parish and privilege and instead encourage a sort of defensive and aggressive attachment to a *patria*. In civil war, however, the battlefront may also be the home front of either or both armies simultaneously: brother confronts brother, and guerrilla incursions surge and rupture around alliances of familiarity and friendship as often as around common social goals or projects of political gain. All these factors complicate the issue of military bonding and the idea of "home" and, above all, the place of the "noncombatant" in the strategies of the leaders and the mind of the soldier.

Throughout *My Mother's Hands*, the ungrateful dependency of Mamá's own sons is contrasted with her web of unconditional mother love that operates both within the "nuclear" family and spreads over all the "boys" on Villa's side and also to all the soldiers from the town and the region, no matter whose side they are on (for, as both texts show, there is a great deal of shifting of allegiances as the Revolution wears on). When her own allegiances are challenged, Mamá responds: "To me they are not even men. . . . They are like children who needed me and I gave them my help. If you were in the same condition, I would be with you" (*MMH*, 111). This generous infantilization—the inclusion of all men-in-need within Mamá's fold—while it perfectly exemplifies the total, mythic *abnegación* of the ideal Mexican woman, might also be read as both a self-conscious ethic and a protective strategy. *Civil* war (and Nellie Campobello's interpretation of it) mitigates the "glories of selfhood, citizenship and truly . . . universal concerns" that are a part of the "formidable" masculinity of (interstate) war.[24] Universal attentive love, the ability to understand and respond to others' suffering, cuts across the lines of aggressive partisanship. And because, perhaps, Mexico *is* a society structured on conventional and complementary gender roles, mother love transcends the private sphere and is "recognized" by all sides. We have already seen how Mamá is capable of reading "the symbolic" and appropriating "men's law." Once again, Mamá capitalizes on the seductive universality as well as the ambivalence in mother love (the angry energy and the solicitude) and transposes a concern for individual nurturance into a competitive ethic of rights: competitive not with the right to wage war but with the right to destroy bodies. In this conflation, even the "enemy"—however hypothetical and shifting—may be *individually* encompassed within her careful gaze. Although she seems to risk herself to epitomize the feminine—the ethic of care, the defense of the weak—Mamá is also defending her Self.[25]

MOTHERHOOD AND TORTURE: THE EXAMPLE OF GUATEMALA

> No persuasion would suffice to prevent her from taking her own life to avoid being defiled by another man, so they had her thrown to the dogs.[26]

> We had to accept that anyway my mother was going to die.[27]

Nellie Campobello's heavily gendered representations of war are not aberrational in their context. In many respects, although the 1910 Revolution was the marker for modernity in Mexico, and although its twin goals of restricted (re-)elective power and socialized land distribution are modern political concepts, the way the Mexican Revolution was fought and written about betrays it as a product of nineteenth-century, and "Latin," ideology and custom. There were certain codes of behavior—such as distinguishing between belligerents and non-combatants—that, although often breached, were equally often upheld. While huge numbers of the general population were involved in the war, for example, civilian deaths were nonetheless generally reported as accidental or as murder. And men and women were treated differently (although not necessarily "better" or "worse" than each other). In the second half of the twentieth century, however, civil war in Latin America takes on a different perspective, no longer of "socially sanctioned" open conflict but of a diffuse and generalized violence pitting unequal forces against each other: "overarmed militaries" on the one side and, on the other, traditionally unarmed civilian institutions—oppositional political parties, workers' unions, the Indian community, the Church, and the family.[28]

In wartime Guatemala,[29] women's familial power and men's indulgent protectiveness (as these were reported by Nellie Campobello in Mexico) are complicated by patterns of violent class control that operate through an ethnic as well as a gender hierarchy. In Central America, the *moza india*, the "Indian maiden" of my epigraph to this section, has re-enacted her scenario of violence in an interminable cycle over four hundred years of "conquest." In 1566, Diego de Landa depicted a classic torture scene where the male aggressor demands that the female victim pollute her store of truth and "reveal" her "secret"—her monogamous chastity—to him. Submission might have brought classic exculpation; but since the Indian resists submitting to ordeal by seduction, she brings upon herself the punishment of death. Rigoberta Menchú replays an almost identical scene of thwarted persuasion in her testimony of modern Guatemala. Doña Petrona Chona, a young married woman who resists the tortuous seduction of the landowner's son, is dismembered—not torn apart by dogs but chopped to pieces by machetes—as a punishment for her chasteness (*RM*, chap. 19). Doña Chona was aware of her danger and had planned to escape, but was caught unprotected at home instead of at work one day when "mothering" a sick child.

Like *Cartucho*, *I, Rigoberta Menchú* deemphasizes the singularity of women's experience: countless men, too, are the victims of the violence that oppresses women and children. Both the Guatemalan and the Mexican texts, however, point to men exclusively as the *perpetrators* of that violence. Additionally, the Guatemalan text's exposure of the most perverse treatment of "the feminine"—military men's torture of the narrator's mother—reveals a new level of official military cruelty[30] very different from the arbitrary brutalities of Nellie Campobello's civil war.

Rigoberta Menchú is the daughter of Vicente Menchú, the Guatemalan indigenous leader burned to death in the Spanish embassy massacre of 1980. Rigoberta's overt "filiation" with her father forged the first link in her chain of social consciousness. For his daughter, the father represents the most noble, the most social (and, subsequently, the most revolutionary) aspects of community life and traditions. Rigoberta Menchú's narrative notes—regretfully—that she has always been less cognizant of her mother's social role, despite the fact that, as a village leader and healer who traveled throughout the highland area to attend the sick and childbirths, her mother developed close ties early on with "the *compañeros* in the mountains, the *guerrilleros*, [and] loved them like her own children" (*RM*, 218). This mother had already lost two baby sons to the "everyday" conditions in which the Indian families have to live and work. She would lose another son when state terrorists publicly tortured and assassinated a group of "subversives," an incredible act of political obtuseness and sadistic impunity that certainly serves to instill fear in the local populace (a major military goal), but also, contrarily, unites the people in their outrage and their will to organize. The revolutionary militant bears a twin soul: revenge for the ills of the people and the conviction that by acting, he or she has nothing to lose. In the case of Rigoberta's mother, her son's death incites the anger necessary for overt action:

> She went straight to the women and said that when a woman sees her son tortured and burned to death, she is incapable of forgiving anyone or ridding herself of that hatred, that bitterness: "I can't forgive my enemies." (196)

As Rigoberta Menchú reconstructs her mother's thoughts and aspirations, she underlines the special combination of mother love and hatred for the enemies of one's children that gave her mother the courage to face overwhelming odds, and to strengthen others in resistance. Rigoberta's mother proves to be as much a social revolutionary as her father: her life is a "living testimony" to the other women to show them how they "had to participate as women so that when the repression came and it was time to suffer, it wouldn't be only the men who suffered. . . . Any evolution, any change, without women's participation would not be a change and would not be a victory" (196). Women's spirit of responsible belligerence in Guatemala is developing still out of this sense of personal and political community, whose principal ethic is that in order worthily to share a better future, the women must also directly share the cost. So in Guatemala's civil war, the classic structure of interstate warfare—where men are recruited to protect the women and children who are left behind to weep—is radically inverted, as it has been in so many contemporary confrontations, such as those in Argentina or Lebanon, into direct confrontation of the weak and the civil against the strong and the militarized. In *I, Rigoberta Menchú*, the women's willingness to confront the army is born of a deliberate attempt to read the rules of men's war:

> The women and children seemed to have a bit more respect from the army
> because they mostly kidnapped the men, the older men, precisely our commu-
> nity leaders. Because of this, our men would fall back first and the women
> would stay behind to face the blows. (127)

But this nostalgic co-option of the rules of "civilized" war is quite misplaced in "low-intensity warfare"; violence is everywhere, "immune"
space—the space of the domestic and of the feminine—completely
eroded. The militarizing of civilization has also had a regressive effect on
the popular body: the forces of "conquest" (or control) now often comprise young men co-opted from the indigenous population itself. And the
outraged body in *I, Rigoberta Menchú* is not that of just "any" Indian
woman (although it might be *every* Indian woman). Nor does it "simply"
represent the common commodity exchange of women's marital fidelity
for the military ethic of rewarding the conqueror. In a country where
colonial identity is still self-perceived through sexual and ethnic superiority, women are now punished not (only) because of their chasteness, nor
(only) to intimidate or humiliate their menfolk, but for the public nature
of their own actions: for their assumption of a voice—unprecedented and
unwelcome and insistent "noise" from a normally "discreet" source. The
mother's body is punished for daring to stray away from her silent subaltern identity and her home.

She is also tortured to give evidence as to where her "children" can be
found. We remember that all the *guerrilleros* were her *hijos*; additionally,
her daughter's text re-presents a still living, breathing, maternal body that
is inflicted with pain and humiliation and done to death as it is used to call
her own biological children (recognized as leaders and subversives) to
present themselves morally and actually to the event. The torture scenario
is reported as a timeless scene of sacrifice. The mother's clothes are put on
display as a proof of her capture and of her helplessness, her nakedness.
Her children are invited to expose *themselves* in order to cover up their
mother's "shame." In turn, her daughters ("deferring" to an absent
brother's opinion) must agree not to submit themselves to a certain death
just like their mother's:

> We had to keep that grief to ourselves as a testimony . . . because they never
> exposed their lives even when their grief was great, too. . . . And so we had to
> accept that my mother was going to die, anyway. . . . The only thing left for us
> to hope was that they would kill her quickly, that she should no longer be alive.
> (199–200).

Feminist commentators on the Mexican Revolution have criticized
"sentimental" representations of women's wartime roles. They have been
particularly hard on the *soldaderas* who, they claim, were not romantic

but "sick-minded" to follow their menfolk into battle and therefore expose their children to the dangers of war.[31] Mothers who remained at "home" like Nellie Campobello's Mamá also had to choose between dividing their family or risking the battle "front" with their children. In *I, Rigoberta Menchú*, however, the terrible dilemma of maternal "responsibility"—which will never be resolved in psychological abstractions or in feminist theory alone—is inverted into the equally acute distress of a *daughter's* sacrifice of her *mother* in wartime. The particular scene that is announced as the account of a mother's courageous struggle against violence is also, perhaps particularly, the story of the daughter's encounter with futility: "I never thought my mother would meet a death worse than my father's" (210). The daughter's denial of a normally attentive response, her refusal to comply with the torturers' demands that she present herself, may be the *only* way to break the cycle that is destroying her family—her father, brother and now her mother—and her people. And yet, if the daughter had only *consented* (to her own death) might her mother have been spared? This daughter will never know the truth but lives on in "panic" of emulating her mother: "I don't want to be a widow woman, and I don't want to be a tortured mother, either" (225).

Throughout *I, Rigoberta Menchú* runs a series of guilty subtexts that situate the daughter's conflictive desires and ideals. At the same time as the testimonial narrator cannot contemplate her own death (as a mother) under torture, a "cowardly" wish to die erupts from her other fear of being the last survivor of her family: "I couldn't bear it, it wasn't possible that I'd be the only one left. I actually wanted to die" (185–86). The daughter's instinct is to escape into insentience (as her father did when he sought solace in alcohol). The narrator's inexplicable love for her father is proferred against his relative weakness when faced with family problems, and against her mother's "greater suffering," which the daughter "never could have believed possible." In this text, torture—and the threat of torture—is a fate worse than death. Because of the dangers of witnessing military actions, none of the immediate family can be present at any point of their mother's torment. The enormity of her mother's agony must be recounted to Rigoberta Menchú through an (unnamed) informant: a *compañero* who can risk the perilous intimacy that the victim's daughter must forego. Finally, in order to convert the personal meaningfulness of suffering into a significant social experience, the testimony must then be filtered by the daughter through a third, alien appropriation that has no connection with the mother's own cultural experience—in a professional script emanating from "Paris . . . where whatever happens has repercussions throughout the world, even in Latin America" (xvii).[32] The irony of this geographical dislocation compounds a second "betrayal" in the daughter's testament to her mother: transliteration into the other *medium* of colonialism, the Spanish language, a translation that positions the daughter's voice when she "wills" her mother's death. But, according to the narration of *I, Rigoberta Menchú*, the mother has herself already "betrayed" her own family in breaking another cycle of conformity; she is a powerful, politicized woman who leaves her biological sons and daughters to become a beneficent social guerrilla. Her daughter admires this, but also notes how the family—"especially [Rigoberta's] brothers"—resent it: "they wanted my mother to stay home" (216).[33] In her own route to sociopolitical identity, Rigoberta Menchú finally—again—emulates her father, and rejects another "maternal" norm: of marrying, and giving birth to and being responsible for, children in jeopardy.

DAUGHTERING AND WAR: AUTO-GRAPHY

> I didn't have a childhood, I didn't have any schooling, I didn't have enough to eat, I didn't have anything. . . .
> How can it be possible?
> (*RM*)

> Mama, turn your head . . . Mama, Mama, Mama.
> (*MMH*)

It would seem that the shared experience of life under war informed Nellie Campobello's relationship with her mother and her relating of her mother's life very positively, very differently from that of Rigoberta Menchú. The title of *My Mother's Hands* is a key motif in both the structure of "mothering" and the genesis of the biography. Years later, Nellie Campobello recalls, "For me it was easy to find the title because of everything we receive from our mothers, her hands are, throughout our lives, what is in permanent contact with her children" (*Mis libros*, 32). The image of these hands, strong and gentle, rough and smooth, sunburned and pale, is reiterated throughout the text; they exemplify the multiple facets of Mexican femininity inherited from both Indian and European traditions—delicate yet practical, capable, creative, protective, and healing.

A web of myth and legend and nostalgic alienation colors the author's relationship with her mother and with the place and the time of her childhood. In her prologue to *Mis libros* (My books), an anthology of her writings published in 1960, Nellie Campobello tells us, "I love my land with the living love of someone who has forever renounced living there. Someone who, looking at the land, the color of a Comanche's skin, cannot kiss the grains of corn that burgeon from its entrails" (*ML*, 11). In

Nellie Campobello's reconstruction of "home," her feminized nature—separate, indigenous, and fecund—is itself transient, identified with and related metonymically to descriptions of the narrator's mother, of her mother's hands that worked the long stalks of corn to make tortillas wherever she might be. Feminized childhood was also a philosophical space, of liberty and of "the art of knowing where the straight line goes to" (11–12), once again personified in the little girl's experience as her mother's daughter. So, when Nellie Campobello's love of truth and justice bursts forth, the only voice "that could give the tone, the only one authorized: was the voice of childhood. Using its apparent lack of consciousness to expose what [she] knew" (12–13).

The deliberate resumption of a child's voice—the only one "authorized" (by her mother?)—neatly exemplifies Judith Kegan Gardiner's literary assessment of women's writing:

> The author may define herself through the text while creating her female hero. This can be a positive, therapeutic relationship, like learning to be a mother, that is, learning to experience oneself as one's own cared-for child and as one's own caring mother while simultaneously learning to experience one's creation as other, as separate from the self.[34]

Cartucho and My Mother's Hands are proofs of the process of maturation, in which the texts and the mother (the signifier and the signified) imply intense moments of both identification and separation in the mother-daughter dyad. In her prologue to Mis libros, however, Nellie Campobello is assessing her earlier works with the retrospective of another twenty years' experience. By "escaping to her refuge, her mother's skirt," the author finds the space to think honestly, but may also be deliberately infantilizing her responsibility for her words when she tells us "my little girl's mind said" or "my eyes blurred with childhood told me so." This amorphous yet conscious dependency complicates dyadic psychology and the "intention" of the texts it structures: in My Mother's Hands, the girl-child fully knows herself in the mother at the moment of "breaching" the boundaries of the semiotic, that is, in publishing her most intimate memories, yet she continues to envelop herself, to submit: "I hear Her calling me and I came towards you with the gesture of respect of someone faced with her idol" (97).

Like the continual conflation of "you" and "she" and past and present tenses in My Mother's Hands, the term idol is also fraught with ambiguity; an "apparent lack of consciousness" (Nellie Campobello's words in her prologue to Mis libros, cited above) exposes gaps and absences not only in others' references to their "truth" but also within the narrative structure of Nellie Campobello's Revolutionary texts themselves. While the central motifs of My Mother's Hands sustain the heroic identifications that I have suggested throughout my discussion, the narrative frame, the adult daughter's plea to her dead mother, indicates the inherent ambivalences. The epigraph that entreats "wake and weep . . . as you did then" recalls not only the luminosity of Mamá's face but also her tears; the originary image here is of a *mater dolorosa*, a painful revival—not only mythical—of a mother's eyes grown hard "when recharged in the barrel of a rifle" in *Cartucho*. Maternal vitality diminishes later into frequent absences and solitary walks. And at the same time as the mother's hands are inscribed as a unifying metaphor, the text constantly reminds the reader that this mother almost never *touched* her children, her daughter: "She did not cuddle us, didn't kiss us" (*MMH*, 102). The only time "Mamá would take me by the hand" occurs in the final phrase of *Cartucho*, and this is not a caress, but a directive—in the conditional tense—to the statue of the Virgin. We recall that the Virgin too has more than one face: she graciously celebrates victory but also *figures* complicitly in moments of sorrow and death. In *Cartucho*, "A Miracle for Julio" relates a gruesome inversion of the "miraculous" power of prayer and of the Virgin's robe: "She sent [Julio] a star from her robe. The star incinerated him" (*C*, 68). And in *My Mother's Hands*, the *virgen de la Soledad*, the Virgin of Solitude, "despite her infinite power could not halt the pneumonia that split the strong shoulders of the child" (125). The Virgin has many strengths, not all of them vital enough to counter the power of man and of nature. And so, as well as (instead of?) being a metonym for the intimacy and connectiveness of mother and child, in the daughter's narrative recollection, the hands of Mamá like the tears of the Virgin forever remain within the realm of the symbolic,[35] as a metaphor for absence and an index of lack.

And yet Mamá's heroic portrait remains undimmed, like those of the other heroes of Nellie Campobello's Revolution. It may be a biographer's good fortune that her subject die young.[36] This mother dies just at the (literary) moment when a natural distancing—that of a girl's "normal" physical maturity at puberty—might detach her from her daughter's emotional center. In many ways, the regressive artifice of *My Mother's Hands*—its historical (biographical-chronological) structure, and its pastoral context that feminizes the landscape of war and permits a return to a nurturant, womblike irreality—recomposes therapeutically the eclectic, impressionistic, and above all, destructive nature of *Cartucho*.

Rigoberta Menchú's text, on the other hand, leaves no space for escape into the nurturing communion of feminine continuity. Feminist critics' approval of the transferential relationship that may develop as the woman writer creates her female hero takes on a different, ominous cast when the "hero" is the narrated self and the representative remnant of a martyred tribe; when "thinking back through one's mother" invokes scenes of torture and terror and remorse. Nor does nature itself in Guatemala offer the sentimental succor of the idealized plains of northern Mexico. In *I, Rigoberta Menchú*, the narrative contrasts the tribal mystique, the political and the aesthetic importance to the Quiché community of the Highlands they till and love and share with the wild beasts, with the harsh fact that the groups so often have to leave their own land behind as they toil in other climes for other masters. Even though "there is something important about women in Guatemala, and that something is her relationship with the earth—between the earth and the mother" (*RM*, 220); even though Rigoberta's "mother loved the natural world very much" (213), that same nature, like the mother, can be (seen to be) hostile when it is a constant reminder of poverty. Nellie Campobello's biography recalled how "the earth was our companion—red like the palms of our hands and the heels of our feet—[it] opened its arms to us and protected us" (*MMH*, 103). Rigoberta Menchú remembers, "My mother could tell the days it was going to rain"; she also remembers, "when it rained . . . the mud split [my feet] and it went septic between my toes. . . . Sometimes I couldn't walk because the soles of my feet split" (*RM*, 213).

These are perhaps subconscious or accidental juxtapositions in Rigoberta Menchú's narrative. Like the narrator of the Mexican works, Rigoberta Menchú learned a great deal from her mother; but the text of *I, Rigoberta Menchú* makes clear that much of what Rigoberta learned were lessons in hardship, including the lesson that she must share her mother with others who demanded her time. In her continual struggle to evaluate her own position as she recounts both parents' influence and example, the adult Rigoberta Menchú vacillates between appreciation and irrational, preferential, individual love, the same sort of love her father showed for her but which her mother denied her: "my mother shared herself with all of us and said that if she loved one she had to love all. Or she'd have to reject all of us!" (218). In her radically social review of the history of her people and her family, Rigoberta Menchú establishes right from the start the dual, and not always congenial, responsibilities of mothering in an environment where "every child will not only belong to [the biological parents] but to the whole community, and must follow as far as he can our ancestors' traditions" (7). The apparently idoneous nature of this material and philosophical godparenting is contradicted by the other obligations of this particular society's maternality: "She [the mother] talks to the child continuously from the first moment he's in her stomach, telling him how hard his life will be" (8). The intelligent mother must prepare her child for the worst; the pleasures, rewards and small sensualities of mothering are seconded to the priorities of sheer survival. Any "personal identification" of the daughter with her admirable mother, whose own worth is wrung out of pain and despair, is overwhelmed by the "positional identification" with the mother as victim.[37] Rigoberta Menchú bravely searches her own soul as she assesses the incompatible demands that a society in peril makes on its most sensitive children:

> My mother was very brave but, nonetheless I learned more from my father. . . . There were many estimable things in my father. . . . And my mother too. . . . So I love them both the same. I love them both but I have to say that I grew up more at my father's side. My mother taught many people many things, but I didn't learn as much from her as I should have learned. (219)

Wherever war is fought, those who come late to resistance and retaliation, the mothers and widows and daughters of the early victims of warfare, are forced to learn how to utilize the subversive strengths of convention and discretion, how to seek succor in the group when the nuclear family "fails" them. Unlike Rigoberta Menchú's family, and unlike so many of the men and boys who peopled the Mexican Revolution and Nellie Campobello's notebooks, all the children of Nellie's Mamá survived the Revolution. But the mother did not work that miracle in isolation. Although her children "no longer had a father," they were cradled by the fraternalism and the paternalism of the men of the region, the Northern Brigades, whose excesses (and there is plenty of documentary evidence that were many)[38] were held in check by local history, by a child's-eye view of heroism, and by the strength of a mother's domestic integrity. Mamá is not herself a warrior, but the wife, then the widow, of a fellow officer; the soldiers treat her "as a gentleman would."

Mexican Revolutionary ethics did not (at least not officially) threaten those long-standing cultural formulas. In Guatemala, however, traditional paternal *and* group protection has been eroded by economic demands from outside and—increasingly in the past twenty years—usurped literally by the penetration of the army. Women's submission to capitalist production and patriarchal reproduction is essential, and "conquest" is reaffirmed through continued violence and seduction. In this exacerbated "social system," independent women and, especially, women *leaders* are a particular anathema to the military and a particular example to the people. In the history of almost five hundred years of "occupation," Guatemalan women have learned many techniques of both resistance and assimilation. Rigoberta Menchú lifts a curtain that hides women's defensive mechanisms: the revival of ancient abortion techniques for young women impregnated during rape, efforts to educate and arm themselves and to propagate female power through training women and children. Throughout her text, Rigoberta Menchú talks of how the Guatemalan army "tortures men and rapes women." That may be the army's biggest "intelligence" error: rape *alone* seems not enough to discourage women's empowerment.

Or is it? Rigoberta Menchú finally fetishizes rape—the one thing she says she is personally unable to confront, and "can say nothing about," perhaps because it does represent for her the worst outrage against women's "essence" and, above all, her mother's worst sufferings. Her mother's horrible rape and death presage the final and irreversible castration of the daughter's already hesitant identification with maternal, female power. Through their female narrators, both Nellie Campobello and Rigoberta Menchú recount their mothers' death in "sacrificial" circumstances. But Mamá "rejected life" and "chose to die,"[39] whereas in Guatemala it was the children—the daughter—who "rejected death" and "chose to live." The additional implication of Rigoberta Menchú in her mother's torment in some ways mirrors the fearsome and genocidal intent of Guatemala's war: categorized from outside as "low intensity," yet irretrievably traumatic to the generations that live on at the expense of the blood they share.

NOTES

I have revised the English translations where necessary to make clearer sense of the extracts.

1. Fernando Benítez imagines a response from José Emilio Pacheco in *Sábado* (the weekly review of *Uno más uno*, Mexico), April 16, 1978.

2. *Apuntes sobre la vida militar de Francisco Villa* (Notes on the military life of Francisco Villa) (1940), included in *Mis libros* (My books) (Mexico: Compañía General de Ediciones, 1960), here, p. 377 my translation). Further references to *Apuntes* and to other works cited after their first occurrences will be made parenthetically in the text.

3. *Cartucho* was first published by Ediciones Integrales (Jalapa, 1931); *Las manos de mamá* in 1937. *Mis libros* is based on the second editions of both texts. English citations are from *Cartucho* and *My Mother's Hands*, introduced by Elena Poniatowska, translated by Doris Meyer and Irene Matthews (Austin: University of Texas Press, 1988).

4. Gustavo Casasola's *Historia gráfica de la Revolución mexicana, 1900–1960* (Mexico City: F. Trillas, 1960, 1971) is the most celebrated, detailed, and often macabre photographic record of the events of the civil war.

5. In "Narrative Style and Technique in Nellie Campobello's *Cartucho*," *Kentucky Romance Quarterly* 32, no. 2 (1985): 202.

6. I am using Jacques Lacan's logocentric (and phallocentric) "definition" of desire in "The Signification of the Phallus," from *Ecrits: A Selection* (New York: Norton, 1977), p. 287.

7. Again I am using Lacan's comprehension of the phallus, as not an organ but a *signifier* (and phallogocentrism therefore not as a focus for domination but as a source of expression).

8. In her timely revision of psychoanalytical convention in favor of the mother, Marianne Hirsch suggests that "within a psychoanalytic framework, the mother's

desire can never be voiced because her desire exists only in the fantasy of the child as something the child can never satisfy. . . . The child, coming to language . . . accept[s] the exigencies of symbolizing desire in language and thereby transcend[s] the mother's silence" (*The Mother/Daughter Plot: Narrative, Psychoanalysis, Feminism.* [Bloomington: Indiana University Press, 1989]), here, p. 168.

9. An early self-portrait by Nellie Campobello ("Francisca," [Mexico City: Ediciones L.I.D.A.N., 1929]).

10. John Brushwood, *Mexico in Its Novel: A Nation's Search for Identity* (Austin: University of Texas Press, 1966), p. 208. So, Nellie Campobello's ballet scenarios and poems of the Revolution, *Apuntes sobre la vida militar de Francisco Villa* (her modern chronicle of conquest expounding military strategy, battle plans, goals, and personalities), as well as *Las manos de Mamá* are all demoted into a category that apparently plays no "role in society"; these texts become literarily "invisible."

11. "Pancho Villa's Wounded Men," in *Cartucho*, p. 59.

12. Antonio Castro Leal in *La novela de la revolución mexicana* (Mexico City: Aguilar, 1960), p. 924.

13. Doris Meyer, "Campobello's *Las manos de Mamá*: A Rereading," *Hispania* 68 (December 1985).

14. In Edmundo Valadés and Luís Leal, *La Revolución y las letras* (Mexico City: Instituto Nacional de Bellas Artes, 1960), pp. 34–35.

15. As Sara Ruddick puts it, "If women found soldiers disgusting, would the pleasure in fighting be significantly diminished?" In *Mothering: Essays in Feminist Theory*, ed. Joyce Trebilcot (Totowa, N.J.: Rowan and Allanheld, 1983), p. 254.

16. Sara Ruddick expounds on "Maternal Thinking," ibid. p. 220.

17. In "Remarks on the Sexual Politics of Reason," in *Women and Moral Theory*, ed. Eva Feder Kittay et al. (Totowa, N.J.: Rowan and Littlefield, 1987), pp. 257, 246.

18. The epigraph to *My Mother's Hands* reads: "Mu-Bana-ci ra Mací Reyé /Busá Nará Mapu Be-Cabe / Jipi Cureko Neje Sináa"— a 'Hai-kai' of the Tarahumara Indians: 'Your face of light, mother, wakes and weeps, as before, today when I call out to you.' "

19. There is an interesting discussion of the origins and effects in Mexico of the myth of the "maternal" Virgin, by Ena Campbell, "The Virgin of Guadalupe and the Female Self-Image," in *Mother Worship*, ed. James J. Preston (Chapel Hill: University of North Carolina Press, 1982).

20. I borrow Evelyn P. Stevens's definition to understand machismo as a "cult of virility [whose] chief characteristics . . . are exaggerated aggressiveness and intransigence in male-to-male interpersonal relationships and arrogance and sexual aggression in male-to-female relationships." Evelyn Stevens, "*Marianismo*: The Other Face of *Machismo*," in *Female and Male in Latin America*, ed. Anne Pescatello et al. (Pittsburgh: University of Pittsburgh Press, 1973), p. 90.

21. Doris Meyer also interprets the courtroom scene in *My Mother's Hands* (and whose words are reiterated in the final phrase in the text) as a successful attempt by the mother to reclaim her children from their father's family by feigning rape to account for a new, illegitimate baby ("Rereading," pp. 750–51). Al-

though we are both guessing from the veiled clues in the text, this explanation is not contradicted by the older Nellie's remembrance that "my mamá was very pretty, she always had lots of boyfriends" (in a personal interview with me, 1981). In the parish records at Villa Ocampo, several children, including "María Francisca," are registered as *hijos naturales* (and with no father's name specified) of Rafaela Luna, "Mamá."

Carol Gilligan writes on justice and gender "contracts" in *In a Different Voice: Psychological Theory and Women's Development* (Cambridge: Harvard University Press, 1982), p. 105.

22. Sara Ruddick "capitalizes" Fatherhood to indicate "more a role determined by cultural demands [material support and defense] than a kind of work determined by children's needs" ("Women and Moral Theory," in Trebilcot, *Mothering*, p. 258, fn. 15). Mamá again "exemplifies" Sara Ruddick's other point, that "mothering" children who are often simultaneously aggressive but fragile involves developing techniques of control that are not in themselves (reciprocally) harmful or violent—the perfect alternative to militarized force (ibid., esp. pp. 248–50).

23. Many studies of the roots of gendering illuminate this "masculine" tendency in psychological and sociological terms, among them Nancy Chodorow's revisionist examination of the Freudian developmental model. From her hypotheses in her article "Post-Oedipal Gender Personality," Nancy Chodorow concludes that "from the retention of preoedipal attachments to their mother, growing girls come to define and experience themselves as continuous with others; their experience of self contains more flexible or permeable ego boundaries. Boys come to define themselves as more separate and distinct, with a greater sense of rigid ego boundaries and differentiation. The basic feminine sense of self is connected to the world, the basic masculine sense of self is separate." (*The Reproduction of Mothering: Psychoanalysis and the Sociology of Gendering* [Berkeley: University of California Press, 1978], p. 169.)

In her essay in this volume, Sara Ruddick recapitulates some of the "separating" effects of military misogyny.

24. Genevieve Lloyd rereads Hegel in her article "Selfhood, War and Masculinity," in *Feminist Challenges: Social and Political Theory*, ed. Carol Pateman and Elizabeth Gross (Boston: Northeastern University Press, 1986). Here, p. 73.

25. In her examination of women's writings on the Lebanese Civil War (which have a lot in common with Latin American women's war texts), Miriam Cooke also uses Carol Gilligan's theories of gendered development to assess the Beirut Decentrists' "discursive activism [that] draws on feminine resources." She concludes that "for men . . . responsibility, [that is, requiring] that others are not hurt . . . is achieved by . . . deferring aggressive response, for [women] it is achieved by . . . initiating response to the needs of others" (*War's Other Voices: Women Writers on the Lebanese Civil War* [Cambridge: Cambridge University Press, 1988], pp. 170, 88–89.) Miriam Cooke's definition beautifully encompasses my reading of Mamá's feminine and self-reflexive strengths.

26. Diego de Landa's 1566 report on the Yucatan, *Relación de las cosas de Yucatán* (A narrative about Yucatan) (Mexico City: Truay, 1938) is cited in the

epigraph to Tsvetan Todorov's *Conquest of America* (New York: Harper and Row, 1989). I have revised the translation slightly.

27. Rigoberta Menchú, *Me llamo Rigoberta Menchú y así me nació la conciencia*, narrated to and edited by Elizabeth Burgos-Debray (Mexico: Siglo XXI, 1985), is translated into English by Ann Wright as *I, Rigoberta Menchú: An Indian Woman in Guatemala* (London: Verso, 1984). Quote from p. 199. Hereafter cited as *RM*.

28. I am using Margaret Mead's criteria for warfare as the "organization for the purpose of combat involving the intention to kill and the willingness to die, social sanction for this behavior, and the agreement between the groups involved on the legitimacy of the fighting with intent to kill" ("Alternatives to War," in *War: The Anthropology of Armed Conflict and Aggression* ed. Morton Fried et al. [Garden City, N.Y.: Natural History Press, 1967]), pp. 215–16.

Jean Franco emphasizes the "diffuse" nature of modern war in Latin America in "Killing Priests, Nuns, Women, Children," in *On Signs*, ed. Marshall Blonsky (Baltimore: Johns Hopkins University Press, 1985), pp. 414–20.

29. After a brief civilian interregnum of ten years, a coup in 1954 returned Guatemala to military rule and to "death squad," "counterinsurgency" activities, accounting for some 100,000 civilian deaths, 38,000 "disappearances," and a million refugees (internal and external) since then (figures supplied in 1989 by GAM, the Grupo de Apoyo Mutuo [a Guatemalan coalition of pacifist resistance groups], to various journals). The violence, directed principally against the Mayan population, escalated in the 1970s, peaked in the early 1980s, when Rigoberta Menchú was writing, and has continued under the civilian governments returned in 1986.

30. I borrow here from Georges Bataille's distinction (echoing Carl von Clausewitz) that cruelty is (one of the forms of) *organized* violence. This military "ethic" was recently benignly reconfirmed by Colonel Anthony E. Hartle of the U.S. Military Academy at West Point. His enumeration of the "exigencies of the profession" terminated on the "capability of inflicting great cruelties" (although Hartle allowed that this was "on the negative side"). "The Superstructure of Professional Military Ethics" (talk given at Dartmouth College, April 23, 1990).

31. Psychologist Juana Armanda Alegría is particularly critical of the *soldadera*: "The fact of taking their children to war and exposing them to death implies a serious lack of responsibility and an unprecedented irrationality" (*Sicología de las mexicanas* [Mexico City: Samo, 1975], p. 133).

32. *Me llamo Rigoberta Menchú y así me nació la conciencia* was edited by Elizabeth Burgos-Debray from Rigoberta Menchú's dictated narrative in a series of interviews in Paris. In the most widely available edition in Spanish (Siglo XXI), Elizabeth Burgos's name appears as *author* on the front cover and title page.

33. In each of the texts I examine here, "daughtering" is complicated by sisterly ambivalence: esteem for mothers evokes veiled "resentment" toward the mothers' sons. In her essay in this volume, Angela Woollacott examines in greater detail how literary wartime "sistering" reflects not only the gendered difference in the experience of (overseas) war, but also the multiple other factors that affect different levels of familial identification and affection.

34. Judith Kegan Gardiner, "On Female Identity and Writing by Women," *Critical Inquiry* 8 (Winter 1981): 357. Doris Meyer's useful essay on "*Las manos de Mamá*" first brought this association to my attention.

35. We recall that in the courtroom scene, Mamá's hands "tore her blouse to find her god" (*MMH*, 128), thus pitting not the Virgin's but the Father's symbolic strength against the Law of man.

36. Phyllis Rose considers this wry truth in "Fact and Fiction in Biography," her edited volume *Writing of Women* (Middletown, Conn.: Wesleyan University Press, 1985), p. 69.

37. Cf. the distinction Philip Elliott Slater makes between different forms of "identification" in *Footholds*, ed. Wendy Slater Palmer (Boston: Beacon Press, 1977), pp. 20–27.

Marianne Hirsch looks at "'disidentification' from the fate of other women, especially mothers" as a controlling fantasy in nineteenth-century female family romances (*The Mother/Daughter Plot*, p. 10). While the texts I look at here are very different from those earlier romances, much of what Marianne Hirsch concludes about "collusion" with or rejection of patriarchal models might usefully apply to the Latin American works. (But that's another essay.)

38. Elizabeth Salas's *Soldaderas in the Mexican Military* gives many examples of Revolutionary fighters' arbitrary violences against women and children as well as against other soldiers (Austin: University of Texas Press, 1990).

39. Mamá died of a "broken heart" when, several years after the end of the armed phase of the Revolution, her infant son died of pneumonia.

PART IV
ENGENDERING LANGUAGE

Chapter 8

̶W̶O̶-MAN, RETELLING THE WAR MYTH

M I R I A M C O O K E

N O, READER, you cannot read my title out loud. You can see it, but you cannot speak it. It is like women at the front—you can see them but until recently you could not speak them. Feminists are beginning to recognize even more clearly than ever before that praxis and theory, or, more simply put, activism and its interpretation, function interdependently. In other words, it is not enough for women to have been there; they have to write and interpret what it means to have been there. Such an activist discourse may become an agent of change beyond discourse.

Postmodern wars reveal the negotiability of war and of gender as one of its defining characteristics. This negotiation is conducted at the level of language, and it has the effect of blurring heretofore rigid boundaries between fact and fiction, between activism and writing, between experience and its recording. Recording women's presence and engagement at the front is crucial in order to counteract some of the distortions that have always been necessary to construct the age-old story of war as men's business. The challenge that gender studies present to the analysis of war is to narrow the gap between reality and myth. We must learn how to remember and hear and then speak the WO- in woman so as to avoid repeating the lies of the Homeric war myth. It is only thus that the myth can begin to approximate reality and that changes can begin to be acknowledged.

War is an activity and an event of such cataclysmic, existential significance that it has always been "above" questions of gender identity. Can gender be relevant when life and death are in the balance? YES. Gender analysis reveals that the prosecution of mass, legitimized, psychotic violence depends on a particular way of constructing and maintaining gender identities. After all, what could be more profoundly gendered than a space said to contain nothing but men, than an activity described as performed by men only? These male spaces and activities have been defined as gender neutral so as not to disturb the abstracted and universalized paradigm of men at the front dying to protect women back home. Is a soldier a soldier if he is afraid, weak, and vulnerable? Is a mother a mother if she is fearless, strong, and politically effective? These are the kinds of questions feminists ask, insisting that most cultures' war myths—of men in arms and of women at home—are a fiction. Many add that dispelling gender ambiguities and maintaining clear distinctions between masculinity and femininity during combat, when each is most threatened by the other, is a strategy necessary for the perpetuation of a particular way of constructing the memory of war.

How can war myths be broken? I submit that the solution lies in the hands of those who have experienced war as other than prescribed and who choose to describe and interpret their experiences. Outsiders must be made privy to those "atypical" war experiences. In the latter half of the twentieth century, creative writers, war analysts, photographers, and, above all, the media are increasingly recording war stories at variance with a supposed archetype. A remarkable outcome of this new recording enterprise is to complicate the instinctive erasure of women's presence in war. The Gulf War of 1991 is a vivid example. Throughout the air and then brief land offensive, the American media continued to refer to the servicemen *and* -women, even as they emphasized that included among the prisoners of war were women. It was only three months later that this inclusive language caused some trouble. The women combatants, for that is what they were, who were vying for a permanent spot in the War Story and a resultant change in combat rules ran up against the diehards. Most of the grunts as well as the crusty old officers demurred, even though none could come up with a rational reason for their reluctance to accept as equals the women who had often outshone the men in the desert theater of operation.

By placing gender at the center of an analysis of war, we begin to question the myth: the mystique of the unquestionable masculinity of soldiering, of the essential femininity of peace advocacy. We unlock a closed system in order to reveal the dynamic of gender constructions. The postmodernist challenges to discursive hegemony and binary thinking opens up new space in which previously unheard voices are valorized; today we pay attention to the warriors without uniforms, to the women and the children we had before ignored.

. . . . .

An area that has seen much sustained conflict and violence in the twentieth century, and whose wars are only beginning to be analyzed through the lens of gender, is the Arab world. Since World War II, most of the Arab countries that had remained under some form of foreign rule confronted and then shook off colonial rule—for example, Syria in 1946; Egypt and Sudan in 1952; Tunisia, Morocco, and Libya in 1956; Algeria in 1962; Yemen in 1967. Wars of national liberation spawned other wars. I shall examine the literary representations of wars in three Arab countries in which women have played unprecedented roles. Algeria, Lebanon and Palestine each experienced different degrees of colonial control and different kinds of war in the post–World War II era. The analysis of these wars does not begin to exhaust an understanding of postmodern wars, but rather provides a partial insight into how the postmodern condition has affected the waging and writing of war in one part of the world.

The war in Algeria was anticolonial and culminated in the expulsion of the French in 1962. The success of the Algerian Front de Libération Nationale against their European oppressor of 132 years signaled to others in similar situations the viability of what Fanon termed "sacred violence."[1] Until recently this revolution has been interpreted by the major, that is, male, players; women and others who had participated but who had had little or no political power acquiesced to their silencing. They seemed unaware that activism is nothing until it is recorded and then interpreted by the actors. The war in Lebanon has been named civil, despite its increasingly international profile, and it, too, finds its roots in colonial division and the apportioning of land, rights, and power. Unlike the Algerian Revolution, the Lebanese Civil War opened discourse to all; even the most potentially subversive writings were tolerated. The forty-five-year-old war in Palestine, of which the Intifada, or popular uprising, forms the latest stage, began as a colonizing war with European Jews fighting for hegemony over a piece of the eastern Mediterranean coast. After the 1967 Israeli victory and occupation of the West Bank and Gaza in a neoimperialistic drive to expand territory now assumed to be theirs, the nature of the conflict changed to assume the characteristics of a postmodern war. Many have written of Palestine, but it is only recently that previously excluded groups, such as women, have begun to question in fiction and nonfiction the means and goals of the revolution. Only recently has this questioning been taken seriously. These wars span and represent the transition from modern to postmodern forms of warfare: the Algerian Revolution was modern, the Lebanese Civil War was starkly postmodern, and the Palestinian-Israeli war illustrates the cutoff dating of postmodern warfare.

What do I mean by the term *postmodern* when I use it in conjunction with war? I am referring at once to a periodization and to a cluster of defining characteristics. Although the precise dating of postmodern wars may vary from one country to another, their relative dating does not. They fall into the post–World War II nuclear period and may be individually situated in a postcolonial context. However, by postcoloniality, I am referring not to a cultural but to a chronological marker.[2] Postmodern wars are the products as well as the consumers of the technological revolution.

Such wars provide multiple discursive spaces in which individuals can find, retain, and interpret agency. In postmodern wars women, who have always been part of war, can more easily articulate and therefore hold on to their participation. Women writers can and do formulate for themselves a role in the waging of postmodern war. Their writings threaten to undermine their cultures' war myths, yet they are themselves always threatened by the entrenchedness of such archetypes. The disenfranchised, who had submitted to the power of dominant discourse, which tended to distort their experiences, are making their voices heard and their faces seen. They thus expose the mechanisms of power consolidation. Their counterdiscourses disrupt the order of the body politic in such a way that they decenter and fragment hegemonic discourse.

Individual empowerment as a moral paradox is critical to postmodern wars. New individuals are empowered, and their empowerment and centering decenters others. Who are these newly emergent individuals in late-twentieth-century warfare? The question is difficult to answer because the postmodern combatant cannot be neatly defined and compartmentalized. Ever changing, she yet remains on a trajectory that passes through and across the following stages: terrorist/freedom fighter—guerrilla—liberation army activist—soldier in national army. Written thus, this chain is progressive. However, the mutations may happen between any two or more of these stages and in any order. What is critical to an understanding of postmodern wars is the fluidity of this model; individuals who have moved up may just as easily move back. The postmodern combatant may at some point seem to have been eliminated. Yet, this disappearance may in fact be part of a rallying and regrouping. Like a virus, combatants are learning to mutate so as not to be eradicated. How can the state eliminate the guerrilla when she is once again a terrorist and may tomorrow be the loyal soldier of the new state's military apparatus? Individual mobility and empowerment create anarchy but also order, not as paradoxes but as simultaneously potential presences.

These postmodern combatants are finding a space to commit, or even only to talk about committing, violent acts. The Latin American political scientist Juan Corradi describes such anomie as being a late-twentieth-century phenomenon. Today, violence is different, he writes, "not necessarily because it is more cruel or brutal, but because it is continuous, total and undifferentiated. . . . (Violence) is a narrative of deconstruction . . . (that breeds) a culture of fear. . . . Terror and terrorism can be seen as the accelerated and generalized appearance of violence in political and social relations . . . a terrifying impasse, horror, a catastrophe of meaning."[3] The centrality of violence for its own sake does not imply that its practice must continue indefinitely. Although the anomie of postmodern wars complicates outcomes, however "decisive," it does ensure some end through exhaustion. Then negotiations start about the victory and spot in history's limelight. These victories and historical spots remain open to infinite renegotiations; judgments once fixed can be reversed later. It seemed logical, even self-evident, to many that, almost twenty years later, America won the war against Vietnam through the victory over Iraq. But this "victory" then came under scrutiny. Already in the early aftermath of the war, Americans who had frantically celebrated in March 1991 were in the summer of the same year asking hard questions about the value of a victory against a weak enemy. National Public Radio acquired temporary financing from a group calling itself "The Gulf War. Triumph without Victory." And then in the theater of operation, the weak enemy was proving himself not so thoroughly defeated, as he quickly reestablished centralized control over rebel areas and resumed nuclear production. On June 27, 1991, George Bush returned to his golf cart in Kennebunkport, Maine, to reproduce images of the previous year's preparations for war. Hussein's nuclear activities, he sternly announced, might force the United States into another war—or, into a continuation of a war that had seemed to end but that apparently had not. And then in mid-January, Saddam Hussein celebrated the anniversary of his victorious war!

The foregoing argument about postmodern wars does not claim so much a substantive as a representational difference from earlier wars. It is not that other wars were more conclusive, but that they seemed to be so. Postmodern wars are presented as inconclusive and as though their outcomes were dependent on their representation, particularly through the popular press and the media. Postmodern wars are fought by the media but also, in a very important way, *for* the media. Although wars of national independence have many of the characteristics of the postmodern war, they lack a critical ingredient: hyperrepresentation. In the anticolonial war, like the Algerian Revolution, representation is carefully monitored for it is the monopoly of the colonizer. In the postmodern battlefield, all strive for representation. Even countries with little technological sophistication have learned to transform the media into sites for inserting their own, usually subversive, representations. Hostage taking and hijackings succeed because of the consistency of world media attention. Postmodern wars have become media events whose self-conscious manipulation of discourse is transparent. Violence has been theatricalized, so that its dramaturgical quality has come to supersede while, of course, not eliminating its injuring quality.

The media-tion of violence has collapsed apparent distinctions between various kinds of war: the Lebanese Civil War compares with Vietnam compares with the Intifada or Palestinian uprising compare with inner-city gang wars compares with the Gulf War. This homogeneity is due to the fact that war is increasingly presented as negotiable. Rules that used to govern how wars were to begin and end, how peace was to be defined as distinct from not-war, who was to participate, who was the enemy, how the fighting was to be conducted, what roles men and women were to play in war as opposed to in peacetime are being systematically broken. The media are instrumental in projecting this new reality of war, even though often behind a facade of compliance. They reveal the instability of war myths and their heroes, so that it is possible to perceive a shift in the articulation of war texts. War has become a simulacrum whose language derives from or is lent to both theater and sports. The interchangeability of the languages from these three domains blurs the distinctions so that participation in war loses its own reality to be replaced by the glory of the spectacle or the competition.[4]

Whereas wars previously codified the binary structure of the world by designating gender-specific tasks and gender-specific areas where these tasks might be executed, today's wars are represented as doing the opposite. Postmodern wars highlight and then parody those very binaries—war/peace, good/evil, front/home front, combatant/noncombatant, friend/foe, victory/defeat, patriotism/pacifism—which war had originally inspired. This challenge to binary modes of discourse and epistemology entails semiotic transformations. It reveals that both gender and war are highly fluid and negotiable structures within which meanings are constantly constructed and deconstructed. Postmodern wars participate in undermining a system of meanings that had been in place until the outbreak of the nuclear revolution.

Thus far, any references to postmodern wars have been restricted to Vietnam, the war which Fredric Jameson called the "first terrible postmodernist war,"[5] and most recently to the Gulf War. Although Vietnam is only one example of the way wars are being fought at the end of the second millennium, it has acquired a special place in global war discourse. Arab writers on their own postcolonial wars often invoke Vietnam as model or nemesis. In Sahar Khalifa's 1976 *Al-subar* (Wild thorns), a man refers to Vietnam as a new kind of war; he "mouthed the standard cliches, exciting no one but himself. . . . He held forth on the 'tide of revolution', on the Third World nations, on Vietnam . . . oh, how he talked of Vietnam!"[6]

. . . . .

The Lebanese Civil War in particular has challenged outsiders' labels that try to make sense of the senseless violence. It collapses notions of beginning and end: the war is not called war until after the outbreak and resolution of a quarrel. What is not this state of war becomes a new charged normality that lies on a continuum between war and peace, a constantly invoked absence. It subverts conventional categories: men and women are no longer definable in terms of the spaces they occupy and the roles they play. Front (male space) and home front (female space) are indistinguishable in a situation where war can break out at any instant in any place. Combatant (male) and noncombatant (female) are indistinguishable in a situation where civilians are drawn *nolens volens* into skirmishes, or when they are specifically targeted as noncombatants by snipers to ensure a reign of terror. Friend and foe even may become indistinguishable in a situation where brother and sister may be drawn into opposing militias because of personal reasons and needs. Post-1975 Lebanon, like William Broyles's Vietnam, was a place where "it was hard to tell friend from foe—it was too much like ordinary life." Ordinary life, violent life. Hanan al-Shaykh vividly renders the confusion between war and peace when she has her protaganist in *The Story of Zahra* say: "We did not dare to think or believe that fighting meant war any more than a cease-fire meant peace. We did not know what to think or say, even about the front being an inferno. Those were merely words, 'the front,' 'peace' and 'battle,' all meaning the same thing: war. But we didn't think of ourselves as being in a war: we evaded the truth."[7] Victory and defeat are meaningless categories in a setting where violence has become a way of life, its own justification. It is my own experience of the Lebanese Civil War that has given me a different understanding of the nature of war in the late twentieth century; it has also provided me with a prism for elaborating a theory of postmodern war.

The Algerian Revolution, the so-called Beacon of the African Revolution, was the first of these three wars to end. Within seven years, the Algerians had revolted and finally repulsed the French colonial presence. The story of the Revolution has become legendary, as has the role of the women in it. The women were heroines who had risked life and, even more, honor to fight for their country. The men were cads who used this new cadre during the emergency and then dispatched it back whence it had come once the crisis had passed. This metanarrative of exploitation is under current revision. Algerians were alleged to have been aware of the importance of women's participation in a military capacity, but current thinking contests this claim. Sociologists like Marie-Aimée Hélie-Lucas and writers like Assia Djebar are now correcting these estimates of women's perceived importance to the Revolution, even if at the time some of them may have concurred. A careful reading of women's and men's literature on the Revolution emphasizes the need for this revision.[8]

In *Les enfants du nouveau monde* (1962), the Algerian woman writer Assia Djebar follows a number of protagonists through a single day. Both men and women have been brought into the fray, but the women do not undergo radical textual transformations. The secluded and heavily veiled

Cherifa is the only one to experience some change during the narrative. When her revolutionary husband Yusuf is in danger, she crosses the city alone for the first time. The reader sees through her veil the new world with which she is coming into contact and realizes with her that this has been an empowering experience, but it is not shown to be transformative. The two women who have dedicated themselves to military endeavors are flatly portrayed, and the Westernized Touma is a traitor and a prostitute, a caricature of what "Westtoxification" can do to a Muslim woman. The male characters, on the other hand, are beginning to worry about the women's growing importance to the revolution. In her next novel, *Les alouettes naives* (1967), Djebar writes of three couples whose lives are intricately intertwined. The women, even if militarily involved, are more committed to their love than they are to the nationalist cause. The men are crippled by their relationships with the women. Although the women do not perceive a change in their status, the men are wracked with anxiety.

Are male and female characters' perceptions of women's significance as a result of their participation in the war as incompatible for men writers as for women writers? It would seem that they are. Algerian men have written about the war from the perspective of husbands and fathers. They write not from the vantage of the protected but of the protector, therefore, of the one who has much to lose by being deprived of control.

Malek Haddad's oeuvre displays a growing unease about women's power. In *L'élève et la leçon* (1960), the narrator, a medical doctor living in Paris, has to deal with his daughter, who has fought in the maquis. She comes to him with a devastating request: Will he abort her child by her lover? Not only does this woman have control over her own body but she is compelling the one who is supposed to be responsible for her to act out on her body the most disempowering of operations: the destruction of the fetus that is his only guarantee of survival. In *Le quai aux fleurs ne répond plus*, published the following year, Haddad's fear peaks into panic. While the writer-narrator was in Paris agonizing about his role as an intellectual in the war, his lovely, "loyal" wife Ourida was having an affair with a French officer. How does he learn of this betrayal? He reads a notice of their simultaneous death in the small print section of an Algerian newspaper.

Another male writer to describe women as transformed, in this case into Medusas and sirens, is Mohammed Dib, the man whose earlier works had described women so sympathetically within the sociorealist framework of Arab writing of the mid-twentieth century. *Qui se souvient de la mer?* (1962) traces through the nightmarish evolution of a submissive wife into a distant and threatening figure. The narrator comes to depend on her for everything, even his life. Dib associates Nafissa, the narrator's wife and his children's mother (*mère*) with the sea (*mer*). This homophonic association recalls the male fantasies and anxieties that Klaus Theweleit locates in fascist men's writings of the between–World Wars period.[9] Dib concludes his self-styled Guernicaesque creation with an anguished prognostication of the flooding of the sea. The narrator has externalized and projected his fear of dissolution, of loss of control, onto the woman/sea. She vehicles his fragile sense of self and appropriates his control of her. He can now only relate to her through desire.[10] Medusa-like, this *femme-soldat* turns him into stone, hardens him, and only she, of course, can depetrify or soften him. Quoting Freud's *Medusa's Head*, Theweleit writes: "For becoming stiff means an erection. Thus in the original situation it offers consolation to the spectator: he is still in possession of a penis, and the stiffening assures him of the fact." Theweleit adds: "soldier males freeze up, become icicles in the fact of erotic femininity. . . . By reacting in that way, in fact, the man holds himself together as an entity, a body with fixed boundaries. Contact with erotic women would make him cease to exist in that form." Nafissa is a terrifying specter representing the narrator's loss of potency, and although she does not have the snakes on her head, she does turn stone walls into snakes and people into stone. Nafissa gives him boundaries that she, however, can melt at will and thus make him dissolve into the flood which the narrator repeatedly invokes. Theweleit writes that such floods do not signify a Jungian "oceanic feeling," but rather a threat that "may be combatted with 'erections': towering cities, mountains, troops, stalwart men, weapons."[11] And these are precisely the scenarios Dib delineates. The coming flood presages the narrator's loss of control as the social boundaries around his dammed-up ego are eroded and undermined by a flood of feeling that will no longer allow him to distinguish himself from the woman, the wife as well as the vulnerable feminine in himself.[12] The loss of mastery over his woman represents the loss of the last bastion of power accorded to the colonized man.[13]

To the Algerian male writer, women's military participation was filled with significance, but to the woman writer it was not. Whereas the women wrote of multiple, generally undramatic roles for women in the revolution, the men described only one that was mythically terrifying. Political, sociological, and now this literary evidence affirms that during the Revolution the Algerian women were not conscious of their opportunities, and they had not thereafter "allowed" themselves to be disempowered. Consequently, it is not so surprising that they made no attempt to inscribe into the war text experiences that may have been transformative. When they had written, they had done so with little awareness of what military participation had meant. Since the women writers were not reading the men's writings to understand the men's fear of women's new visibility and activism, they were not learning—even only by proxy—how their image had changed. Without the registration of their voices and the interpretation of their experiences in the war, they had nothing to show. Later, they could only weep alone and in silence at the neglect of their achievements.

The Algerian Revolution came too soon in the history of modern Arab women's discursive activism to serve as a catalyst for the inscription of feminist issues into the nationalist agenda. That was achieved later and initially by outsiders, for example, Franz Fanon and Simone de Beauvoir. War was declared an opportunity that women had failed to exploit. Subsequently, other Arab women have turned to the Algerian Revolution so as not to replicate mistakes.[14] In Lebanon, Randa Berri, the wife of the leader of the Amal Shiite party, said that the difference between the Algerian and the Lebanese women who participated in their two wars was that the Algerian women did not have a feminist context, for example, no indigenous, independent feminist organization, within which to situate their struggle. She contrasts this situation with that of the Lebanese women, who had long organized women's, if not feminist, associations. Hence, as the Lebanese war progressed, "women became more aware of their abilities and the role they could play in their country's life."[15]

Such sociopolitical explanations may well be correct, but they are at best partial. What is more significant and all-encompassing is the historical, cultural logic of the revolution. The Algerian Revolution was an anticolonial war whose representation was still controlled so that only certain groups could speak about the war and even then in prescribed ways. For the sake of the story of the Algerian war, the front had to be "remembered" as the place where women were not, as Cynthia Enloe writes.[16] But the way to changing the conventional war story was being paved, because women in the Algerian Revolution were indeed represented, even if only heuristically as an absence. By the late 1970s, Lebanese and Palestinian women were making references to the Algerian war and the lessons it had to teach. One of the women in the 1980 novel *Abbad al-shams* (Sunflower), by Palestinian writer Sahar Khalifa, asks: "What happened to Algerian women after independence? Women returned to the rule of the harem and to covering their heads. They struggled, carried arms and were tortured in French prisons—Jamila, Aisha and Aishas. Then what? They went out into the light and the men left them in the dark. It was as though freedom was restricted to men alone. What about us? Where is our freedom and how can we get to it? They shall not deceive us."[17]

· · · · ·

The Lebanese Civil War erupted thirteen years after the end of the Algerian Revolution. It exploded out of the discontents of a postcolonial society that fed and fed off others' images. Lebanon generated a war for itself,

yet none knew who this Lebanon was beyond a construction responding
to individual needs. The prototypical postmodern war, it was a chaos
that jumbled and subverted war's archetypal binary structures. In her war
memoir written in the wake of the Israeli invasion of 1982, Jean Said
Makdisi is eloquent:

> Just when one thinks that the war is over, that, for better or worse, one has
> understood what it was all about, that one knows, to borrow the vulgar
> Lebanese phrase, on which stake one has been impaled; just as one gets
> one's political bearings after emerging from the bomb shelter in the latest bat-
> tle, and, looking around, blaming this or that faction for its arrogance, short-
> sightedness, cruelty, and treacherous alliance with this or that foreign power;
> just then the whole picture changes again. A new battle erupts, and new politi-
> cal realities appear. It is like looking through a kaleidoscope: Shake it, and a
> design appears; shake it again, and an altogether different one replaces it. Shifts
> happened so often that one wonders if they will ever end.[18]

Makdisi is describing the war the men were waging: male alliances that
form and transform with the speed of a twist of the kaleidoscope. All that
matters is the creation of a community that confers meaning and self-
worth on the lives of its individual members. When the group can no
longer satisfy the individual's needs, it is rejected. This process is evident
elsewhere and particularly at times of conciliation. Just as negotiations
seem to be producing progress toward cessation of hostilities, group co-
hesion often gives. Those who cannot see a significant role for themselves
in the new system refuse the second-tier spot assigned to them. The only
group that validates the individual is the one that is under stress or under
that individual's command.

However, the story of militias and campaigning and alliances is only
half the story. The other half tells of the bedrock on which these games
could be played out. This bedrock was made up of the women who maintained a semblance of normalcy throughout the bedlam. Unlike their Algerian sisters, Lebanese women wrote self-consciously about their role in
the civil war. Some had written before; others turned to writing as a ca-
thartic outlet for feelings caused by continual and senseless violence. The
Beirut Decentrists, as I have called a school of women writing in Lebanon
during the war,[19] wrote of a war in which women were the only rational
actors, the ones who made possible the country's survival against all
odds. The men had joined militias or left the country to find other means
for survival; the women had stayed because of traditional expectations of
behavior patterns, but also because many understood that their staying
was existentially important for Lebanon, but also for themselves. By
1980, the Beirut Decentrists were writing of a change wrought in women
who were realizing that they had been abandoned in a dirty war. They
were beginning to transform survival into resistance. Nuha Samara's

"Two Faces One Woman" (1980) recounts an almost paradigmatic experience of transformation.[20] A gentle, unfailingly obedient wife finds herself alone in Beirut after her husband has decided to take a post in Paris. Although she had not resented his departure, her neighbors' innuendos disturb her. Slowly, she begins to review her marriage. From this new vantage point, she realizes that he had always wanted to possess her and that she had always instinctively, unconsciously, but also unavailingly tried to resist this need to possess. Now, however, he has gone and she can act. She cuts off the hair for which she thinks that he married her. She bleaches it until she looks like a Nazi officer. She goes out to target training and excels. But then she masturbates, discovers her woman's desire, and pursues a lover. It is not clear what Samara thinks of this newly empowered housewife, because the reference to a Nazi officer would seem to be negative. But what is positive is the possibility the war has provided of manipulating her gender identity and role. Samara has created an ambiguity, or space of freedom, unavailable to those locked in social constructions.

This metamorphosis and emergence of the newly self-conscious woman into the public domain has become one of the Lebanese war's feminist stories. It is in the *Künstlerroman* of the late 1970s and early 1980s that this myth is honed. Umaya Hamdan's *The Blue that Comes with the Wind* (1980) works through the tensions in the life of the woman artist as she tries to balance what are often described as feminine and masculine conceptions of responsibility: the first involves duties to others and the second implies rights for oneself. As a mother and wife, the narrator has duties to her family, but as an artist, she is more like a man because she has rights for herself. Ultimately, she decides for herself, for it is only when she has taken charge of her own life, and thereby given it value, that she can effectively take care of others. The writings of the Beirut Decentrists expose the dangers inherent in women's socialized maternal "instinct" for protection of others that may involve self-sacrifice. They almost caricaturize the woman artist as representing self-interest and responsibility to the self. This stark contrast is heuristically effective because it allows for the definition of difference that can only be destroyed once it is discovered. They urge the need to destroy these differences and to integrate male and female senses of responsibility. Such an integration will result in a change in expected behavior for women and, by extension, for all Lebanese. If all men, like Radwan in Emily Nasrallah's *Flight against Time* (1982), could begin to think maternally, as Sara Ruddick writes, conflict would be resolved not in killing but in negotiating.

This feminization of Lebanese society as a whole challenges while not contradicting Sandra Gilbert's description of the crossing of gender lines in Western society during twentieth-century wars.[21] The Lebanese war's discursive hyperspace provided the inlets and outlets that were not previously available and that now characterize postmodern wars. Lebanese women, writers as well as activists, have recognized these transformed conditions. They have realized that for women to be able to resist and to retain agency, they may have to resort to what Jane Marcus calls the "Asylums of Antaeus," which are those "real and imagined places where the contradictions of her state-enforced roles drive woman mad. . . . She speaks out of the confusion and fear derived from this condition in a doubled voice."[22] This condition is an ambiguous space that allows the previously unspoken to be spoken. It is spoken by a doubled voice that belongs to the prewar woman who must submit to patriarchal prescriptions and to the wartime woman who finds herself in an anomic space where she has the freedom to begin to construct new norms of behavior. Women's madness in war can create new worlds.

One of the most compelling stories of women's madness in the Lebanese Civil War is Hanan al-Shaykh's 1980 novel *The Story of Zahra*. Zahra is an alienated woman whose attempts to relate to others through physical intimacy fail and are then turned against her. These experiences of exploitation render her constantly and painfully aware of her body as an object others use to achieve their own goals. Zahra elaborates her body's grossness until it becomes a thing that she can shake off when others' needs have become too invasive. The presence of the *qarina*, a spiritual guide or doppelgänger, makes explicit this separation of body from consciousness. Her repeated escapes to the bathroom, a place of cleansing, allow her the space and privacy to pull herself together. Such periods of silence and withdrawal are labeled madness because they are forms of behavior that none can understand and therefore categorize.[23] A woman who does not fit into society as a woman, who refuses to play its games, must be excluded and this exclusion must be signaled, in Zahra's case, by electroshock treatments.

The war brings change. Although Zahra remains other than people consider women should be, she is no longer in conflict with her environment and therefore with herself. As bullets fly and people cower in basements, Zahra blossoms. Unlike prewar society, this context does not alienate, and Zahra can structure herself in harmony with it. The sickness of society has made Zahra whole and allowed her to escape society's expectations: "When I heard that the battles were raging fiercely and every front was an inferno, I felt calm. . . . It meant that nothing which my mother wanted for me could find a place. . . . The idea of my marrying again was buried deep down by the thunder and lightning of the rockets" (107). The climax of Zahra's healing through absorption into the normless chaos comes in her sexual relationship with the sniper. Timid, self-absorbed Zahra decides that she will do her bit for humanity: she will offer her abused body to the local sniper, the quintessential symbol of abstracted violence, to distract him from his deadly job. For the first time, she initiates a sexual liaison and she experiences her first physical pleasure. By releasing resistance, Zahra no longer needs to separate herself from her offending body. She thinks she can use it for her own purposes.

However, the novel's denouement dispels hopes of implementing easy changes. Zahra becomes pregnant and conjures up images of domestic bliss. She goes to the sniper whom she now wants as a husband and father for their unborn child. He must no longer remain abstract. She demands his name. Now he is Sami, a man she wants and who will help her to achieve the kind of happiness others considered their right in prewar society. But Sami is no family man; he must eliminate the individual who needs to turn him into an individual. The possibility of pleasure and happiness deludes Zahra into believing that she can use the war against itself: to construct a woman in harmony with one environment, the war, who can then move into another, prewar, with different rules and expectations. Although Zahra is transformed by her relationship with the war, her individual transformation has not transformed others. The norms of society have not yet changed but have only been exceptionally modified in anticipation of a return to status quo ante. The only hope is the destruction of the previous ethos and the creation of a new one modeled according to transformed individual women like Zahra.[24] This destruction/creation cycle is the hope of postmodern war as it more and more comes to resemble and become part of the postmodern condition.

Like those of the Algerian Revolution, writings by Lebanese men and women reflect a differentiated experience and, hence, a different interpretation of events. The Lebanese Civil War as written by women subverts the binary system on which most cultures' war myths depend for their survival. All were free to create the war they had known without reference to an epic model. Yet Lebanese men's writings on the war fit the historically approved mold. They represent the war as conventionally self-evident in its waging, its constitution, its outcome, and its gendering. They were driven by commitment, by the need to justify actions in terms of ideology. Whereas the women's writings insist that each individual must assume responsibility for the chaos, the men's writings point the finger of blame at an enemy—some -ism or other—and thus exonerate themselves. They render logical and rational a war that was waged without clear cause against a mercurially changing enemy.

Like all postmodern wars, the Lebanese Civil War provided a discursive hyperspace that permitted women to pursue their own political and literary agendas, however opposed to the violence they might be. However, their radicalism fell at first on deaf ears. The Beirut Decentrists' literary feminization of Lebanese identity and society as an antidote to the war was scarcely, if at all, understood. Male writers did not take women's writings seriously enough to perceive their attack on the national, cultural, and above all patriarchal ethos that drove and continues to drive the war. And so the reader notices that in marked contrast with Algerian men's writings, Lebanese men do not write about women as terrifying. Their discursive participation did not threaten as the Algerian women's military participation had threatened because its subversiveness was quiet and invisible. It was only after 1982 that the writings of the Beirut Decentrists began to be translated and to gain currency abroad and at home. With hindsight, their discursive transformations of personal identity may play a political role in Lebanon and even beyond.

. . . . .

The Palestinian war is the longest lived in the region. It began in 1948 with the establishment of Israel and reached crisis in the defeat of 1967. The only hope has come out of the latest stage, the Palestinian Uprising, which was named the Intifada in 1987 but which arguably began in 1967. Palestinian literature is rich, and male writers in particular have attracted much critical attention. The women writers have been less acclaimed, although their political activism and the translation of their works into other languages have served to highlight their contributions. This is especially true of the West Bank woman novelist, activist, and professor Sahar Khalifa. Her urgent writings address major issues that other Palestinian women writers like the poet Fadwa Tuqan and the fiction writers Fadia Faqir and Raja Abu Ghazala have touched on but not always as explicitly. Because she has tried to make sense of the tensions underlying nationalist as opposed to feminist struggle and has tried to create strong women characters who might be instrumental in total social revolution, she has encountered resistance, particularly from those outside the occupied territories.

In 1976, Khalifa published *Wild Thorns*, a novel that was subsequently translated into seven languages, including Hebrew. This novel tells the double story of Palestinian resistance—from within and from without. Khalifa shows that neither of these two alternatives is satisfactory and suggests that there is no hope of resolution as long as action is male-driven and can be plotted only along a single line, with revolution fomented in exile being at one end and passive staying, with attendant compromises and sacrifices, at the other. In this early novel, which revolves around men's actions under oppression, Khalifa only hints at a new role for women in the conflict. In Khalifa's later works one can read that in Palestine, as in Lebanon, it is the women who remain on the land

and retain an understanding of what total revolution connotes. Their activism has conferred upon them a new social status.[25] In 1976, during the second year of the Lebanese war, when Palestinians in Beirut were coming under growing pressure to leave it was not clear whither, Khalifa seems to be predicting a third way that was gender- and age-specific: the revolution had to be accomplished by a new cadre—women and children—and not by the men who could see action and solutions only in binary terms.

Four years after the publication of *Wild Thorns*, Khalifa produced its sequel, *Abbad al-shams* (Sunflower). The novel describes a society torn apart by mutual suspicion, ideological and personal ambition, and in which only those who have nothing to lose, that is, women, dare to act. The men remain caricatures, mouthpieces for ideologies that range from a pure Arabism through an idealized internationalism to a romanticized collaboration with the Israeli intellectual Left.[26]

The women are more fully fleshed out, less iconically anchored and fixed. From the first page, women appear as powerful and rebellious, a far cry from the shadowy, symbolic figures of *Wild Thorns*. The journalist Rafif proposes a feminist solution to her paper's circulation problems: target women. On the face of it, the proposal sounds reasonable. And so it is tempting to ask whether Khalifa is advocating feminist activism, despite nationalist reluctance, as central to Palestinian self-affirmation when she writes: "The cause of the woman is a fundamental part of that of the nation" (17). Perhaps. For, whereas the Palestinian people are challenging those who rule them, Palestinian women are revolting against the system as a whole in an attempt to renew it from within. But Khalifa is keenly aware of the tensions inherent to the linking of these two causes, particularly when each has been highly abstracted and ideologized. Pious words about feminist revolutions are not enough and Khalifa criticizes feminists, like her protagonist Rafif, who are ultimately as simplistically ideological and programmatic as the men. Both novels reject action that is managed and articulated by ideologues, whatever their gender. More and more Khalifa's focus is on the construction of an activist feminism that can work with, and not alongside, the nationalist agenda.

The peasant mother and widow Saadiya is more effective because she works according to the rules of her society. She constructs herself as male to escape social expectations and to be able to take care of herself in a society that immediately condemns single women as invariably immoral. Manipulating gender roles gives Saadiya the same insight the protagonist of Samara's "Two Faces One Woman" achieves upon the departure of her husband: her beloved Zuhdi had not loved her but wanted to possess her. Saadiya will no longer tolerate any man's attempts to establish proprietorial control over her. During the Nablus uprising, when Saadiya's son is detained by the Israelis, she leads a spontaneous demonstration and, at the right moment, she kicks a soldier between the legs. Inspired by Saadiya's example, the other mothers in the demonstration start to throw stones and glass. The sons take advantage of the confusion their mothers have caused and escape. This description of Saadiya's instinctive politicization illustrates Sara Ruddick's contention that motherhood, and more specifically maternal thinking, is a powerful instrument in the resolution of conflict. "Typically, the point of women's politics is not to claim independence from men but, positively, to organize, direct and enact a politics that enables them to exploit their culture's symbols of femininity. . . . Insofar as they become publicly visible *as mothers* who are resisting violence and inventing peace, they transform the meaning of 'motherhood.' "[27] The difference between this form of maternal resistance and that of Saadiya is, of course, that Saadiya was driven to violence. But whatever violence that the women of the Intifada invented, which consisted primarily of stone throwing and kicking, was not so much violent, though it might be thus construed, as it was designed to incapacitate the violence of the other.

Another revolutionary model is Khadra, the prostitute. She has learned that for women to survive in a male-dominated world, they must use some of its instrumentalities, even if these include some form of violence. Again and again, Khadra asserts that she is no longer afraid of anything. She assures Saadiya that she should kick all men between the legs even if she can see no immediate benefit (84–86). As noted above, Saadiya put this lesson to good use. Khadra's daring is not empty bravado; it empowers the women to declare, "They say that we women are each worth five shillings. By God, each of us is worth ten men" (166).

The allusion to unfeminine behavior modeled on the actions and reactions of the widow mother Saadiya and the prostitute Khadra, women society marginalizes, anticipates questions Khalifa raises in her next novel: Must Palestinian women construct themselves as not-women so as not to be blocked by social expectations? Yet how can women fight and survive when they have created themselves outside the norms of social acceptability? Is there any other way to escape the limits imposed on women's possibilities of action? In *Memoirs of an Unrealistic Woman* (1986), Khalifa shows that each woman must become so self-conscious that she can distinguish between who she is in the eyes of society, who she thinks she is, and who she would like to become. The mythical quest for the active Palestinian female agent cannot be begun before those first two personas have been outlined and the gap between them recognized in order to make room for the third constructed persona.

Afaf, the protagonist whose name, meaning "chastity," serves as a constant reminder of what others expect of her, rejects a reality that is circumscribed by borders and boundaries that allow women no possibilities beyond commodification and black-and-white moral judgments. In art as well as in daydreams she pens fluid boundaries that allow her to re-configure identity. Like the peasant woman Saadiya in *Sunflower*, she rejects her femininity that she recognizes to be dangerous. She tries to create a new self outside a simple binary structure, a form of transsexuality that none can fix and that will escape the prison of easy labels. This self-structured androgyn inhabits the margin that links the oppositions defining her life.

Afaf takes the Lebanese Zahra's self-construction within a war logic a step farther because she is intensely aware of the splintering of her own identity between socialized construction, self-perception, and self-production. Unlike Zahra, she is not traumatized by others' abuse of her body. She does not need Zahra's self-alienating device of a *qarina* (see above) who concretely separates her mental from her physical self. She recognizes the female body as the site of the battle to co-opt women's agency, and so she tries to retain control of this body.

She controls her body through artistic perception, using poetry and paint to break down the boundaries separating people from people and people from things. Afaf refuses the destiny her body has imposed. She paints and paints and, with time, art becomes her madness. But madness is also a label others use against her: when her initiatives cannot be appropriated, they are named mad. Madness is her blessing and her curse. As long as social attitudes do not change, as was the case in Zahra's Lebanon, the transformed individual woman will be alienated, unable to inscribe her transformation into political action and discourse. Transcendent moments are always already labeled mad, and so the subject must dissimulate. Dissimulation for Afaf, as for Zahra, is silence or escape to a sanctuary to collect herself, and again, as for Zahra, this sanctuary is the bathroom: "I was always afraid of crying in front of people. Yet I did. . . . A thing I learnt during those years in prison was to control my sobs until I reached the bathroom. I didn't learn shame but fear. Fear of the word mad" (12). However, this definition of madness does not accord with accepted psychiatric notions of insanity, which Stan Rosenberg and Bernard Bergen have described as the experience of "being in the world as one of bondage and fraudulence. [The psychopath] fears that becoming himself is a danger to be avoided at all costs, and yet he is tortured in his inability to be himself."[28] In fact, such a definition allows us to read Afaf's "madness" as the opposite of insanity. For she constantly struggles to free herself from society's bondage and fraudulence. She does not fear becoming herself, but rather insists that if she does not, she will be reduced to the nonentity that society needs her to be. It is fear of this reduction that is her torture. *Memoirs of an Unrealistic Woman* delineates the opportunities that postmodern wars offer for manipulating, reconstructing, and then redefining gender identity and roles. However, because the time is not right, the novel cannot yet create the hyperspace where such a reconstruction and redefinition can fit and function.

This *Künstlerroman* echoes of Beirut Decentrists like Umaya Hamadan. Afaf has turned to art as a political tool. Whereas the Beirut Decentrists used art as a raison d'être that supersedes that of wife and mother so as to find a way to prioritize self above selflessness, Khalifa has Afaf turn to art to try to change reality. She must continually struggle to overcome the laws of a society that refuses to change or even only to recognize another's transformation. She is inscribing her newly conscious self into the political process in the hopes of thereby renewing it.

It was to be expected that Khalifa's next novel, which emerges out of the official Intifada, would provide the transformed context. The conditions would seem to be ideal because the Intifada is the most explicitly feminized of all postmodern wars. The Intifada battlefield can be described as a kind of hyperspace that welcomes some, just as it alienates and deterritorializes others. Clashes occur spontaneously and randomly and rarely in response to directives from a controlling agent. Women and children and, more recently, young men initiate confrontations with the military administration in the West Bank and Gaza. Soldiers trained to fight other soldiers have to improvise in the face of the unexpected. They have no rules, only the threat that if they do not act as soldiers, they will cease to be soldiers, cease to be completely masculine, may be reduced to the feminine level of their opponents. The combatant masquerading as a nonsoldier, as a woman or as a child,[29] threatens the soldier with his own dissolution should he not keep himself under complete control. The soldier must play the game according to rules he learned before this encounter. This battlefield would have seemed to provide the ideal conditions for women's activism and its interpretation to come together in a counterdiscourse that articulated a new social formation.

Bab al-Saha (1990) provides a sober warning to those, like me, who have understood this woman-defined war as a new way of unarmed fighting and mobilizing socially that might at last have an impact.[30] Women can never give up either the struggle to retain agency or the significance of their alternative approaches to the resolution of crises. It is ironic, or perhaps not, that this novel, which emerges out of the named Intifada, but named by men, should be the least optimistic not only about the outcome of the people's revolt but above all about women's effectiveness in this women's way of fighting. It is worth noting that *intifada* is a domestic term referring to the shaking out of dustcloths and carpets that illustrates so brilliantly the process of these women's almost twenty-five-year-old insurrection. When the men recognized the women's successes, they hailed their activities, which thus became official. The naming changed the nature of the war so that it began to parody other earlier civil conflicts. When the intifada acquired a capital *I*, it became worthy of men's participation. It was at that point, when it became politicized and male-defined, that the Intifada faltered.

Fourteen years after the publication of her first war novel, Khalifa returns to the theme of men's unsuccessful ways of fighting. The intervening years have changed nothing. The men have not learned from the models offered by the women and the children. They still leave for the Gulf and the United States with promises to return and restore Palestine. Their fathers, ironically, still condemn their staying as folly. They continue to score small victories that the Israelis quickly undo. Again, they are killed in ideological actions. Like Afaf's father in *Memoirs*, they care more about *sharaf*, or honor connected with women's chastity, than they do about *'ird*, or honor pertaining to dignity and reputation. They consider loss of *'ird* by working in Israel to be less heinous than loss of *sharaf*; a brother is more concerned to kill his sister who has been forced into prostitution than he is to recognize her contribution to the struggle. Despite all that the women have achieved, the men cannot see them except as transgressing bodies. A discouraging development in this novel is that, as in Algerian writings in the immediate postwar period, men's interactions with women are limited at best to romantic attachments. And when these women speak out and refuse to be symbols, the men will not listen.

Bab al-saha comes as a shock to the reader who has followed through the development in Khalifa's depictions of women's strength and self-assertion. It is not that the women are any less strong and assertive, it is just that the expected transformation in the social context has not taken place. The Intifada, which epitomized the postmodern battlefield, a hyperspace, and which thus seemed to provide interpretive options to its participants, was already in its waging being reformulated in the image of the conventional front. It was not a space that women should occupy except in archetypal roles.

The women recognize the travesty. They know that they have fought and are about to be forgotten even before the end. This somber and ironic novel proclaims that women have not been empowered and that the Intifada has changed nothing in women's lives except their level of anxiety (cf. 20, 73, 126). The prostitute Nuzha, like her predecessor Khadra in *Sunflower*, is the strongest and most perspicacious woman. But everyone, including the pious Zakiya, rejects her, and her brother comes back to kill her. Another woman is Samar. She is a tough fighter who has stood up to Israeli soldiers but she cannot stand up to her brother, Sadiq (136). Even when she is in a position of power, she does not exploit her advantage. A

patrol passes as Sadiq is dragging her back home after curfew forced her
to spend nine nights at Nuzha's house. Sadiq is afraid because he does not
have his identity card on him, and he turns, suddenly conciliatory in his
hour of need, to his sister. Samar is first gleeful, then sad, then gentle, and
finally protective: she stands in front of him so that the Israelis should not
see him. The man was saved by the woman's body, yet he will not remember because he did not notice. Attitudes in the family have not changed,
therefore social relations also cannot change.

The women may be strong but they are not united. Nuzha accuses
Samar of forgetting her when Husam courts her, even though he would
"sell his mother and father and even the love of his life" (203). Nuzha has
been so hurt that she refuses to return to Bab al-Saha, their neighborhood, because it and all in it have become so corrupt. She refuses to play
the game, to perpetuate the cycle of violence. She will not "rejoice" when
her brother is killed. The women are angry when she refuses to celebrate
the marriage of the cadaver with the earth. But she explodes in fury at
them and at Palestine, who "took mothers, fathers, brothers, land, honor.
You left nothing, Palestine" (21). All pronounce Nuzha mad. But she is
not so mad that she cannot show the women how to show the men how
to fight. Outside a riot has broken out. Some young men want to break
into the military compound, take over the command post, and burn the
Israeli flag. One by one, they climb to the top of the wall surrounding the
compound, where they are predictably enough shot. After twenty have
climbed to their deaths, become "grooms" to Palestine, Nuzha quietly
announces that she knows a better way to enter the square. She leads
them through her kitchen—a powerful domestic symbol—to an underground passage that leads into the heart of the square: "Within a few
moments, crowds of women poured out of the earth" (222). The young
girl who was in the lead with the flag in one hand and a Molotov cocktail
in the other is shot. Nuzha, as though in a trance, goes to the girl's body.
The novel ends with her lighting the cocktail "not for the she-ghoul [Pal-
estine] but for Ahmad" (222). Why did Nuzha turn this heroic suicide
into an act of revenge for a brother who had wanted to kill her? Was it
that family, however bad, matters more to women than does politics? Or
does this act represent her final capitulation to a male logic of violence?
Or is there another explanation?[31] Nuzha may have suspected that
women's activism is generally doomed to co-optation, and that her blowing up of the command post would eventually be called personal revenge.
By calling her act revenge, she could retain control of the naming process,
and then, perhaps, others might see that the personal alone could not
have provided sufficient cause, but that her act must also have a political
dimension. By being named against itself, the personal could thus finally
be recognized as political.

Khalifa's work paints the canvas of postmodern warfare on which men fight ideologically, fragmentedly, and schizophrenically; and women offer new cognitive maps. They are fully conscious of the power of war rhetoric that constantly strives to recuperate a threatened masculinity and to co-opt women's agency. They warn that without a revolution in men's attitudes, nothing will change. The nationalist revolution must work with the women's revolution because *neither can succeed without the success of the other*. As long as men continue to ignore women's ways of fighting, women's contributions to the national struggle, their cause cannot prosper. Indeed, Khalifa indicates that this obdurate negligence is disastrous for the community; if only the twenty men who had singly climbed to the top of the wall and been shot had paid attention to the woman they called a prostitute, they would have survived and learned how to fight effectively. Khalifa shows how men claim the ownership of women's successes, name them, and then empty them of meaning and, therefore, efficacy. It is up to women to reverse this process. They must take men's language and experience and redefine both from a feminist center.[32] Viewed from this perspective, it seems less likely that this novel presents a dystopic vision of an impasse the Intifada confronted, but rather that it is another attempt to inscribe women's agency into a war that would rather ignore it and pretend that whatever had been achieved had been achieved by men.

.   .   .   .   .

What do women in these three different wars have in common? I submit that they share a growing literary corpus that is beginning to make sense of their participations within the broader context of late-twentieth-century wars. All these wars are Arab. All are shaped by the colonial experience. But not all are postmodern. Preliminary analysis of this new literature indicates that it is only in postmodern wars that women begin to realize that feminist activism and theorizing, or the interpretation of that activism, are part of a single process. Writing is not an indulgence that can be weighed against activism as more or less important; each is necessary to the other.

The Algerian women who fought in the anticolonial war were the least aware of the function of writing in the action. Even a progressive writer like Assia Djebar could not at the time decode messages generated by the *femme-soldat*. It seemed enough that women had been there with the men; surely this "fact" did not need to be belabored to be understood. The Lebanese women fought in a postmodern war and quickly became aware of what was happening and what they should do: the men were playing militiamen or they were escaping and leaving behind the wives and children whom the War Myth told them they were supposed to protect. The women were staying no matter the cost. They recognized the reversal in gender roles, and they wrote about it in full knowledge that writing was part of their resistance. These texts went beyond awareness and rejection of male behavior to forge a utopian discursive activism. Staying and surviving—hitherto dismissed as woman-specific passivity—was construed to be active and exemplary for Lebanese national behavior and therefore identity. Finally, Palestinian women are in a war that in 1967 became postmodern. They see in the Intifada the occasion to urge a total social revolution. Their writings express disenchantment with men's ways of fighting that attempt to reconstruct the postmodern battlefield in the image of a simulacrum: a nonexistent originary male-defined model of revolution and heroism. Despite men's attempts to co-opt *their* resistance, the Palestinian women continue to demonstrate that it is only by means of women's ways of fighting that successes can be won. Women must fight men's needs to destroy them, even if only discursively, so that these men may be reborn as remasculinized heroes in the solidarity of an all-male enterprise which they need the war to be. Women's struggle to inscribe and then interpret their experiences is not an attempt to find in war a womb for a new birth but rather a matrix out of which a new reality for society as a whole may be produced.

Palestinian writers like Sahar Khalifa are aware of their literary and activist precursors. They have taken note of what women in anticolonial Algeria and postcolonial Lebanon have not and have written. Khalifa confronts both Algerian and Lebanese models: fear of the Algerian women's postconflict disempowerment, aspiration to the utopian inscription of feminist mobilization into Lebanese war discourse. However, Khalifa shows that the discursive activism that Lebanese women fashioned to counteract the debilitating effects of Algerian women's voicelessness was just that, discursive. She poses the further questions: How can discourse affect attitudes and thus change reality? How can women protect difference while enabling public action? How can activism and its interpretation become one so that discourse can be recognized as an agent of change? Is Alice Walker right when she talks of literature as being not so much about as integral to political struggle: "When I didn't write I thought of making bombs and throwing them. Of shooting racists. Of doing away—as painlessly and neatly as possible—with myself. Writing saved me from the inconvenience of violence"?[33] For Khalifa also literature is a way to participate in the nationalist movement as a feminist activist without using violence. Her protagonists, however, do not have this luxury, for they are drawn into the increasingly violent vortex of the struggle. Each of Khalifa's women protagonists tests ways of valorizing women's activism within the nationalist struggle without descending into violence. Each shows how hard it is to hold on to agency and to effect social change. Yet, each holds on to the struggle as double-edged, against an external enemy of their land and an internal enemy of their freedom.

. . . . .

This paper contains an irony of which I am not unaware. I have described the collapse of hegemonic discourse and the emergence of multiple discourses in the process of disengagement from a binary construct, and to this end I seem to have constructed a metanarrative. Yet, I would counter that the foregoing is not so much a metanarrative but rather a cautionary tale, or what Gayatri Spivak would call a "theoretical description." Although such a description may only "produce provisional generalizations,"[34] the "persistent production" of these generalizations is critical even if only to provoke the reader "to think of exceptions," as Jean Franco has said.[35] Mine is a framing story about the end of one kind of war with its own kind of space, participants, and interpretive discourse, and the emergence of another. I have tried to show how war discourse today participates in the deconstruction of a particular way of re-membering and representing war by deploying a new arsenal of war imagery. Such imagery undoes the conventional binarisms, for example, war/ peace, good/evil, victory/defeat, stability/instability, self/other, masculinity/femininity, soldier/civilian, front/home front. Above all, postmodern discourse undermines the reality/literary representation binary. This slippage is part of the effect of the experience and expression of postmodern wars. It heightens awareness of the proliferation of war stories, each one of which serves to administer yet another blow to the War Myth. Postmodern war discourse introduces ambiguity into a narrative that has needed clarity and certainty to survive.

Postmodern wars frame and give substance to a new counterdiscourse. What is new about this counterdiscourse, however, is not so much its expression as its reception. Women are among the new speaking subjects who are beginning to find an audience. They inscribe their actions and their words in a way that seems to make possible the production of a new world. It is not yet clear what such a new world might be. Would it be a postwar world? I doubt it. But it might be one in which conflict, a necessary part of human intercourse, would be resolved without resorting automatically to violence. It would certainly be a space in which women could restore the WO- to the woman who had always been there but who had not known how to make others remember her.

NOTES

I would like to thank members of the International Gender Committee at Duke University, especially Al Eldridge, Alice Kaplan, Jean O'Barr, Alex Roland, and Jing Wang for their helpful criticisms of earlier versions of this chapter. I owe a special debt of gratitude to Bruce Lawrence, Margaret Higonnet, Marianne Hirsch, Sally Ruddick, Bouthaina Shaaban, and Angela Woollacott, who were so generous with their time and energy: they read through various drafts and then wrote, telephoned, or talked to me at length about ways in which this work might be improved.

1. Fatah proclaimed: "Sacred violence will pave the way to a Palestinian national revival." John Laffin, *Fedayeen* (New York: Free Press, 1973), p.5.

2. For a discussion of the difference between postcolonial and postmodern, see Kwame Anthony Appiah, "Is the Post- in Postmodernism the Post- in Postcolonial?" *Critical Inquiry* 17, no. 2 (Winter 1991): 336–57.

3. Juan Corradi, "Our Violence: Terrorism as a Mode of Post-Political Self-Reference" (paper delivered at the "Talking Terrorism" conference at Stanford University, February 4–6, 1988), pp. 10, 14, 17, 18, 26.

4. Bush's threats made from golf carts, speedboats, and other sports venues emphasized the frame through which the war was to be contemplated: a sports spectacular. On January 26, 1991, a sports commentator talking about the precautionary measures being taken to safeguard the Superbowl noted reassuringly that "we are keeping civilians out of the stadium." In all news briefings, American military referred to the Kuwaiti theater. Hence, the early surmises that the Iraqis had built cardboard runways to eat up American and coalition forces' arsenal seem to make sense. Each side was building a set for the pleasure of the beholder.

5. Fredric Jameson, "Postmodernism, or the Cultural Logic of Late Capitalism," *New Left Review* 146 (1984): 84.

6. Quotations are taken from the 1985 English translation by Trevor LeGassick and Elizabeth Fernea entitled *Wild Thorns* (London: Al Saqi Books, 1985). Page references appear paranthetically in text. In Khalifa's *Memoirs of an Unrealistic Woman* (Beirut: Dar Al-Adab, 1986), Nawal describes the Intifada as being the final stage in a chain of wars that began with Vietnam (96).

7. William Broyles, Jr., "Why Men Love War," *Esquire* November 1984, p. 57; Hanan al-Shaykh, *The Story of Zahra* (London: Quartet Books, 1986), p. 106.

8. See Marie-Aimée Hélie-Lucas, "Women, Nationalism and Religion in the Algerian Struggle," in Margot Badran and Miriam Cooke, eds., *Opening the Gates: A Century of Arab Feminist Writing* (London: Virago; Bloomington: Indiana University Press, 1990), pp. 104–14. See also, Miriam Cooke, "Deconstructing War Discourse. Women's Participation in the Algerian Revolution," in Rita Gallin and Ann Millard, eds., *Women in Development* (East Lansing: Michigan State University Working Paper), 1989.

9. Quoting Sandor Ferenczi, Klaus Theweleit writes, "Mothers should actually be seen as symbols or partial substitutes for the ocean." He adds, "First comes

la mer, then *la mère*. First streams, then their lesser equivalent, incest" (*Male Fantasies* [Minneapolis: Minnesota University Press, 1987], 1:292), and "the coupling of erotic woman and water [happens with] the pure woman without boundaries" (1:420).

10. The presence of wild, mythical beings like the iriace intensifies this libidinous atmosphere. Theweleit quotes Freud's *Interpretation of Dreams* when he writes, "It might be said that the wild beasts are used to represent the libido, a force dreaded by the ego and combatted by means of repression" (ibid., p. 194).

11. Ibid., pp. 198, 244, 253, 402.

12. "He is afraid of falling back into a state of intermingling with the opposite sex—a state in which his own power would dissipate" (ibid., 321).

13. In *No Man's Land: The Place of the Woman Writer in the Twentieth Century* (New Haven: Yale University Press, 1988), Sandra Gilbert and Susan Gubar describe the same discrepancy in men's and women's assessments of progress made by women in the twentieth century. In "Rivers and Sassoon: The Inscription of Male Gender Anxieties," Elaine Showalter concludes that men's experiences of World War I led them to consider the war as a "ritual sacrifice to [women's] victorious femininity" (in Margaret Higgonet, Jane Jenson, Sonya Michel, and Margaret Weitz, *Behind the Lines: Gender and the Two World Wars* [New Haven, Conn.: Yale University Press, 1987], pp. 61–69). Their world had been upended and they took refuge in shell shock that involved impotence and mutism.

14. The editor of *Free Palestine* wrote in July 1970: "Among Palestinian women or those who support them in the larger framework of an Arab revolutionary movement, the relevance of the Algerian situation as described by Fanon in *A Dying Colonialism* remains a model" (vol. 2/3; 3).

15. Bouthaina Shaaban, *Both Right- and Left-Handed* (London: Women's Press, 1988), p. 110.

16. See Postscript to this volume, p. 320.

17. Sahar Khalifa, *Abbad al-shams* (Sunflower) (Beirut: Das al-Awda, 1980), p. 119. Hereafter, page references will be given in text.

18. Jean Said Makdisi, *Beirut Fragments: A War Memoir* (New York: Persea Books, 1990), 15.

19. See Miriam Cooke, *War's Other Voices: Women Writers on the Lebanese Civil War* (London and New York: Cambridge University Press, 1988).

20. In Badran and Cooke, *Opening the Gates*, pp. 304–13.

21. Sandra Gilbert, "Soldier's Heart: Literary Men, Literary Women, and The Great War" in Margaret Higonnet, et al., *Behind The Lines: Gender and The Two World Wars*.

22. Jane Marcus, "The Asylums of Antaeus: Women, War, and Madness—Is There a Feminist Fetishism?" in H. Aram Veeser, ed., *The New Historicism* (New York and London: Routledge, 1989), p. 135.

23. Hanan al-Shaykh, *The Story of Zarah*. Page references appear parenthetically in text. Stan Rosenberg and Bernard Bergen have written of the recourse to this kind of silence that it "represents an attempt to remove the self from the ongoing cycle of enacting depersonalized roles for the other while they reciprocate in kind. [It is] that movement out of the discourse which joins one to history.

[It is] the opening up of new possibilites. This movement does not guarantee an end to one's suffering . . . but it does move the self to a struggle which it can experience as more real. This new struggle is the attempt to know that part of one's sickness which he carries inside of him, that internal disquietude which the self seeks to place in the outer world. . . . In silence is a shutting off of the dialogue by which the self defines itself through culture's edicts and culture's response to him" (Stanley Rosenberg and Bernard Bergen, *The Cold Fire: Alienation and the Myth of Culture* [Dartmouth, N.H.: New England Press, 1976], pp. 178, 190–92, 196).

24. Another possible interpretation of the need for Zahra's death might focus on her instrumentality: by wanting the baby, she is becoming an accomplice in the propagation of the war. She has found in war sexual pleasure and has thereby accepted "the role of circulating sexual object crucial to the war effort. Contemporary feminist theory reveals that the contraceptive choice can be understood as life-affirming rather than life-denying. . . . Contraceptive choice can symbolize the refusal of complicity with the war system" (Helen Cooper, Adrienne Munich, and Susan Squier, *Arms and the Woman: War, Gender, and Literary Representation* [Chapel Hill: University of North Carolina Press, 1989], p. 20).

25. Edward Said has written that "because of the intifada, the role of men was altered, from being dominant to being equal" ("Intifada and Independence," *Social Text* 22 [Spring 1989]: 38). Dan Connell writes that the Intifada has caused the women's committees to go through "some very profound changes. . . . There has been a large move within the committees to address the position of women in Palestinian society, but there is a sensitivity to not dividing the movement" ("Building a Nation," *Mideast Monitor* 6, no. 1 [1989]: 3–6).

26. Adil was like all intellectuals who are "contradictory and vacillating, making generalizations without applying specifics" (17). Salim can only speak in slogans, e.g., "Total liberation, Partial liberation, Staged liberation. Tactics. Strategies Israel Begin. Likud. Likud is no different from Maarakh" (105). What is forgotten is that revolutions are waged by groups, not individuals; each tries to exclude the others by proclaiming him not politically correct.

27. Sara Ruddick, *Maternal Thinking: Toward a Politics of Peace* (Boston: Beacon Press, 1989), pp. 223, 241.

28. Rosenberg and Bergen, *The Cold Fire*, p. 95.

29. Some Israelis justify killing children by saying that the Intifada leaders use "children as foot-soldiers." A recent article quoted an anonymous official as having said, "We are faced with a situation where children are among violent demonstrators. It is not always possible for the soldier to discern the presence of children. Children are turned into martyrs and are engaged to confront soldiers" (*New York Times*, May 17, 1990).

30. Sahar Khalifa, *Bab al-Saha* (Beirut: Dar al-Adab, 1990). Page references appear parenthetically in text.

31. The comparisons with Shadia Abu Ghazala, who in 1968 died while exploding an Israeli military installation, are inevitable.

32. Khalifa told me that she "crippled" Husam so that he would be compelled to watch Nuzha and to learn from her. Stuck as he was in her house for days on end, he could no longer ignore her (interview, Nablus, May 27, 1991).

33. Alice Walker, "In Search of Our Mothers' Gardens," in Marianne Hirsch, *The Mother-Daughter Plot* (Bloomington: Indiana University Press, 1990), p. 193.

34. Gayatri Chakravorty Spivak, "Subaltern Studies: Deconstructing Historiography," in Ranajit Guta and Gayatri Chakravorty Spivak, *Selected Subaltern Studies* (New York and Oxford: Oxford University Press, 1988), p. 17.

35. Jean Franco, "Nation as Imagined Community," in H. Aram Veeser, ed., *The New Historicism* (New York: Routledge, 1989), p. 205.

Chapter 9

NOT SO QUIET IN NO-WOMAN'S-LAND

MARGARET R. HIGONNET

> Patriarchal Poetry is the same as Patriotic poetry is the same as
> patriarchal poetry is the same as Patriotic poetry is
> the same as patriarchal poetry is the same.
> (*Gertrude Stein*)

WORLD WAR I seemed to many contemporaries to defy linguistic formulation. Authentic speech, it has often been repeated, could come only from the trenches in the disabused words of a man who had "seen" combat. The very concept of a soldier-poet, which gained critical currency during World War I, privileges the lived experience of violence.[1] Because of mass mobilization, the Great War indeed produced many writers who had seen combat, some of whom, like Isaac Rosenberg, actually died during the war. We remember today many of these men who recorded the Great War—American, English, French, and German names are all familiar.

Can authentic words be found by a woman? After all, women too were officially mobilized in paramilitary and medical forces, starting in August 1914. These women gained firsthand experience of war, and not just in the ostensibly private roles of widow, mother, rape victim, or civilian casualty. Though only a handful, like Flora Sanders or Russian volunteers, cut their hair, cross-dressed, and fought, women were subject to violence as they actively served in liaison and the underground, and in medical, relief, and paramilitary organizations.[2] Yet Claire Tylee's *Great War and Women's Consciousness* (1990), which studies images of militarism and womanhood in British fiction, was the first general survey to address the theme of the Great War in women's prose. Even feminists have denied women's ability to find a voice sufficiently ironic to describe the war. Thus Jean Bethke Elshtain says, irony "is a voice largely foreign to women writers." She goes on: "When women have imagined war itself . . . it has frequently been in abstract, stereotypical tropes that bear little relation to war's realities."[3]

This essay identifies some of the misogynist barriers women had to overcome when they translated the war into words.[4] It focuses specifically on the ways they dealt with problems of language adequate to the experience. Many women self-consciously reflected on the way an imperialist, propagandistic "war of words" was anchored in stereotypes of a gendered battlefront. In turn, I argue, they investigate war as a discursive structure whose grammar disarticulates individuals, both men and women, in order to translate them into a uniformly polarized social system. They do so at the risk, however, of misreading and censorship.

The woman writer who trespasses onto the territory of war fiction transgresses many taboos. First and most important, she articulates knowledge of a "line of battle" presumed to be directly known and lived only by men. Women, many still believe, should remain "behind the lines" at the "home front," as the symbolic preservers of peace and of the race. A famous anecdote of the period tells us that when Dr. Elsie Inglis volunteered her services in August 1914 to the Edinburgh War office, she was told, "Go home and be still." In the words of a German song,

Die Waffen hoch! Das Schwert ist Mannes eigen.
Wo Männer fechten, hat das Weib zu schweigen.

Where *men* fight, *woman* should be silent.[5] They cannot be permitted to speak, because their knowledge has no official standing.

In *A Room of One's Own*, Virginia Woolf demarcates this linguistic frontier, specifically linking women's impoverished literary history to their exclusion from battle. She contrasts the situation of George Eliot, who retreated from public scandal into protective seclusion, with that of Leo Tolstoy, who could live freely with a gypsy or a great lady, "go to the wars," and pick up "unhindered and uncensored all that varied experience of human life which served him so splendidly later when he came to write his books."[6] According to Woolf, Eliot's narrow realm and diffidence about her own subject matter are inscribed in the limitations of her novels, while Tolstoy's masculine freedoms enabled him to write *War and Peace* with the "integrity" or authority of an eyewitness. Men's military service does them a special literary service, giving them "experience" to back up their style.[7] In this pessimistic view, women's social confinement constitutes an artistic disability. Whether they write about war or about more familiar, domestic scenes, their "tone of voice" may betray their diffidence, deflection of criticism, or a covert protest.

Second, rules of propriety applicable to women alone impeded their struggle to express the inexpressible. A century earlier, Anne Brontë had asked "why a woman should be censured for writing anything that would be proper and becoming for a man." There should be "less of this delicate concealment of facts," she thought, "this whispering 'Peace, peace,' when there is no peace."[8] The war gave acute meaning to the question of gendered gentility. To record soldiers' actual language and attitudes required the use of expletives, gross epithets, and an abandonment of literary refinements. Could a woman write with propriety about a "hell" never described before, certainly never described in words deemed acceptable for women?[9]

Related to the transgression of verbal proprieties is another more profoundly transgressive knowledge and language. Brontë probably could not have imagined describing the effects of gas gangrene, or stomach wounds. A woman war-writer faced the challenge of describing physical mutilation without violating an old taboo on women's naming the parts of a male body. To describe the material effects of war means to possess an anatomical knowledge and vocabulary from which women traditionally were excluded.[10]

Finally, a woman who undertook this topic might encounter hostility for trespassing on politically reserved terrain. If she wrote realistically, she could face official censorship for producing demoralizing, unpatriotic texts.[11] A veteran, who had risked and perhaps given his life for the nation, might be justified in holding the leaders of the nation to account for the bloodshed it had exacted. But a woman who had not been called upon to make parallel sacrifices, from this point of view, had no right to criticize the very system that protected her. Then again, in a characteristic double bind, patriotic discourse was "backed up," as Sassoon put it, by a soldier's actions, but emptied out by women's passivity. "The poet who gives his life in battle most certainly has the privilege of writing [nationalistic] verse. But has the civilian reader exactly the same right to confine his thoughts of war to such sentiments?"[12] This kind of argument against women's full citizenship in the republic of letters, of course, tends to be circular, just as the refusal to grant women the vote was often justified by their "exemption" from the full duties of citizenship, including bearing arms for the nation.[13]

These, then, are some of the obstacles female writers faced when they attempted to set the war down in words. The same obstacles have prevented readers from apprehending their ironies and insights. Changing perceptions of women and war in midcentury have permitted us in the last decade to rediscover novels and memoirs by the female half of the population. In addition, a recognition of the slippages between diary, testimony, autobiographical fiction, and novel has made it possible to reassess the "life/lines" women have drawn from war.[14]

It would be wrong, however, to accept the claim that an appropriate language for war can be found only by those who have actually witnessed battle. Indeed, who would claim that great literature of war like Tolstoy's novel records only what a single participant might have experienced? An important task has been to recognize the deficiency of a narrow definition of "war" literature as "authentic" autobiography produced by and about the trenches, a self-serving label circulated by soldier-writers like Robert Graves and Jean Cru. In order to recognize the fullness of women's contribution to this genre, we must reconceptualize war—and therefore the vocabulary of war—itself.

Only if we recognize that female writers have challenged the fundamental definition of war itself can we fully grasp their radical critique of the interplay between war and words. It is one of the premises of this paper that women's symbolic positioning "behind the lines" enabled some of them to question the insulation of war from social, historic, and economic realms, as well as the implicit anchoring of war in a segregation of public from private life, and of men's words from women's words.

.   .   .   .   .

Before we analyze in detail women's encounter with the language of war, we may review briefly the way men evoked the problem of finding adequate words, which has been extensively discussed by critics such as Peter Buitenhuis, Paul Fussell, Holger Klein, Eric Leed, and Martin Travers. The problem of truth bears directly on that of aesthetics: the "poisonous question" of literary value has typically turned on the avoidance of platitudes and propaganda. And women, in turn, have been thought by virtue of their distance from the war to be vulnerable to such literary sins.[15]

The verbal economy became a central issue for every writer who depicted the Great War, as body counts became mere words, and language a debased currency. By 1917 if not earlier, the discourse used to mobilize millions of soldiers came to seem obscene. Political rhetoric about the war to end all wars, about a holy war against a barbaric enemy, about the gallant sacrifice of shining knights for the mother country and Empire—all such phraseology became a mockery. However heroic the individual, the larger picture of the war in its physical and political context was filthy, stupid, futile, and evil as well.[16]

What kind of language could come out of such experience? In Pound's famous lines,

> frankness as never before,
> disillusions as never told in the old days,
> hysterias, trench confessions,
> laughter out of dead bellies.[17]

Scatological language seemed to some the only available code for experiences that one would like to eliminate from memory. A brief chapter of Henri Barbusse's novel *Under Fire* (*Le feu*, 1916) carries the title "Les gros mots." One of Barbusse's comrades, who is watching him jot things in a notebook, doubts whether their speech can be recorded—publishers will not accept it. "Hey, you guy who are writing, tell me: you're going to write later about the soldiers? you're going to talk about us, right? . . . will you make 'em speak they way they really do? . . . If you don't, your portrait won't look like 'em." The narrator responds that he will use expletives, "because it's the truth."[18] Similarly, in *All Quiet on the Western Front* (*Im Westen nichts neues*, 1929), Paul Bäumer reflects that three-quarters of his vocabulary is derived from the stomach and intestines; it will shock his family, "but here it is the universal language."[19]

Propaganda sharpened writers' fears of clichés. Ford Maddox Ford imagines two soldiers (who have met death in unheroic accidents) intoning the same cliché about having "done my duty to Society and the Fatherland!" Ironically, the politicians who sent them to their deaths "are saying the selfsame words" about their "exploit."[20] The sinister triumph of the cliché reduces to a common denominator heroic and trivial deaths, the exploits of soldiers and the "exploits" of politicians.

By contrast to the braggart civilian, the mark of the real soldier who has witnessed the war may be silence. Thus when Paul Bäumer in *All Quiet* goes home on leave, he does not want to recount to his father's circle of friends what he has witnessed. Paul reflects that his father "does not know that a man cannot talk of such things. . . . It is too dangerous for me to put those things into words" (183). Henri Barbusse's fellow soldiers are likewise suffocated by their experiences at the front, which break up their speech into "fragments." "It blocks your words." Only lists of names, men and places, remain: "nothing's left but the names, the words for the thing, like telegram" (272–73). Experiences have become like words stripped of the syntax that gives them contextual sense. Hemingway's Frederick Henry (who has read Barbusse) agrees: "I was always embarrassed by the words *sacred*, *glorious*, and *sacrifice*, and the expression *in vain*." "I had seen nothing sacred, and the things that were glorious had no glory and the sacrifices were like the stockyards at Chicago if nothing was done with the meat except bury it. There were many words that you could not stand to hear and finally only the names of places had dignity."[21]

In this binary world, then, we find "two languages . . . which represented two competing constructions of reality": civilian propaganda set against the soldiers' truth.[22] Corrupt language at the home front is a destructive weapon. Patriotic humbug and death are ironically juxtaposed by e.e. cummings in a poem spoken by a dead soldier.

aunt lucy during the recent
war could and what
is more did tell you just
what everybody was fighting
for
. . . my
mother hoped that
i would die etcetera
bravely of course;
. . . meanwhile my
self etcetera lay quietly
in the deep mud.[23]

In these male poets' version of the script of war, women and old men become, as Sandra Gilbert has eloquently shown, vampires feeding on the deaths of young men.[24]

If women's words help to make the war that destroys young men, how can a woman decently write about the war? If she frankly decodes the lies for which lives are being senselessly sacrificed, she may be accused of betraying the courage and dignity of the dead. Put this way, it becomes clear that her problem resembles a more general survivor's guilt. Male writers like Hemingway may circumvent their own survivors' guilt by insisting on "the big wound," the suffering that guarantees their brotherhood with the fallen. But it was widely held that a woman, who at least theoretically remained unwounded, should not attempt to describe this hell or the special masculine heroism it en/gendered.

.   .   .   .   .

Both male and female writers thus had to overcome feelings of guilt and impotence in order to write about the war. But for women, the taboos on knowledge of the military/masculine complex, on body language and scatology, and on political discourse without performative guarantees all had special force. Both poets and critics have assumed that women's lack of experience could explain their proneness to platitude or propaganda. But were they so prone?

The body of this paper traces in a range of women's texts the compelling evidence of their conscious artistic struggle to escape those taboos. Whether the issue is their "knowledge" of the "war," their familiarity with the language of soldiers, or their ability to represent men's bodies, they keep returning to the themes of propaganda and verbal abuse. They observe social disorder built on falsification of the meaning of words and of the truth about men's and women's experiences. They foreground the ideological functioning of language in the formation of war itself.

To escape stereotypes of passivity and political marginalization, women picked up their pens. By writing, they both affirm and make possible what we may call "knowledge" of the war. "Women wrote in an attempt not only to express what their varied war-experience was like, but also to publish opinions about the war, and to try to enter imaginatively into areas of war experience other than their own."[25] Their symbolic otherness may have helped them. Self-consciousness about the limits of one's knowledge enables a writer to begin the process of breaking the frame of socially or politically constructed knowledge. At the same time, our access to knowledge means escaping from the prison that prevents our being known ourselves. As a working woman noted, "I could make myself understand if I could only make myself understood."[26]

Many civilians, both men and women, felt excluded from the knowledge of the soldier. Edith Wharton explores this problem in *A Son at the Front* (1923) from the perspective of her protagonist, Campton, an artist working in Paris. When Campton's son returns from the front with a wound, the young soldier has moved to the margin of language. He lies plunged "in secret traffic with things unutterable."[27] Faced with mutilation and death, language finds itself in crisis. A friend of Campton reflects on "how the meaning had evaporated out of lots of our old words, as if the general smash-up had broken their stoppers" (187, see 128). War signs its own difference by silence. Yet Wharton does not suggest that the soldier's silent "traffic" with death is necessarily good or a marker of transcendent truths; rather, it imprisons him and baffles observers.

In a less tragic note, Willa Cather describes the rupture in knowledge and language as a historical shift in *episteme*. A core theme in *One of Ours* (1922) is the way war interrupts the social syntax. When war breaks out, it defies understanding. Families search out dusty books in order to locate the war on a map; they recall stories of Napoleon and the Civil War in order to locate the atrocities reported by the papers on some historical map of human capacity for evil. The sinking of the *Lusitania* and execution of Nurse Cavell seem to go beyond the old linguistic frame. "Nobody was ready with a name for it. None of the well-worn words descriptive of human behavior seemed adequate. The epithets grouped about the name of 'Attila' were too personal, too dramatic, too full of old, familiar human passion," she writes.[28] People rally to fill the discursive gap with propaganda and new (old) clichés. Breaks in knowledge cause breaks in language.

In their representation of a gulf between war and peace, Wharton and Cather reinscribe the gap between the silent "knowledge" of the battlefront and the ignorant wordiness of the home front. Through this reinscription they may seem traditional. Yet by assuming an apparently "feminine" narrative position from behind the lines, they make a political point: behind the gulf lies the commonality of an exploitative capitalist society that segregates, then overwrites knowledge of the battlefront. In Cather's novel, returning soldiers realize that the wrong men will wear medals; authentic heroes will be lost, unrecognized in the mud. The soldiers themselves will be unable to reframe their lives within the businesslike terms of those they left at home; confronted with such problems of translation, some will prefer suicide.

Cather's insistence on framing her French battle scenes within a critical analysis of American civilian society finds an analogue in Edith Wharton's decision to set her novel in Paris among socialites and artists who remain behind the lines. Wharton, who was awarded the Légion d'Honneur for her relief work in France, bitterly condemns the indifference of civilians, men and women alike, whose lives not only continue but thrive. She shows how patriotic speechmaking serves economic interests and relief work builds private power bases ("Refugees"). Her comic sketch "Writing a War Story" (1919) neatly satirizes the "literary" prettification, sentimentalization, and exploitation of the war record. When asked to write a "rousing war story" that is not too depressing, a pretty poetess pouring tea in a canteen ironically succeeds in cheering up the soldiers she cares for: they simply laugh at her product. Instead of drawing on her own confused perceptions ("she knew so much about the war that she hardly knew where to begin"), she has translated a diary into a dim echo of magazine fiction, creating a text that is at three removes from the front.[29]

A more complicated situation is inevitably recorded by some of the women whose experiences took them to the front. Wharton points to this distinction in "Writing a War Story" by contrasting the poet's pablum with its erased source, a "tremulous" but lifelike record by a nurse. Jane Marcus has argued that nurses became "forbidden, dangerous, polluted carriers of a terrible knowledge" that "separated them from the complacent, jingoist home front and the mobile battlefronts."[30] A delirious patient may clasp a nurse, shrieking, "Have nothing to do with a woman who is diseased!"[31] In this sexual perversion of medical logic, we recognize that the system is diseased; women as symbols of the stable order may "carry" that disease. Nurses are both of the system and not of it, both knowledgeable about the war and, as noncombatants, ignorant of it.

Ellen La Motte, a nurse who published standard studies of tuberculosis and opium addiction, worked with the French medical corps during the war. In *The Backwash of War* (1916), a collection of sketches about her work as a nurse, she plays ironically with this problem of knowledge. "The Hole in the Hedge" describes the hospital compound as a *hortus conclusus*, a protected world: "What went on outside the hedge, nobody knew. War, presumably." We are asked to imagine the reasons for this supposed insulation from knowledge about the war: the lack of (censored) news from the capital; the wartime fragmentation of institutions that disrupts communication lines and generates partial images of the fighting; or perhaps the intensity of work on the wounded that leaves no time to explore the world beyond the hedge. "The hospital was very close to the war, so close that no one knew anything about the war" (45).

The knowledge that soldiers bring, La Motte shows, must be suppressed within the sanitizing zone of the hospital. The hospital is so close to the front that any real reporting might damage the morale of those soldiers who could recover and return to combat. Repeatedly, La Motte contrasts what she sees and hears to the lies about the war reproduced in the newspaper, in plaques on the wall, or in the decorations officially "recognizing" the war effort. Against a backdrop of the sign Valeur et Discipline, she describes an operation on a morphine-drugged soldier whose pain will be stilled only by death: "discipline had triumphed. He was very good and silent now, very obedient and disciplined" (64). His silence is his virtue; no matter whether it is produced by "discipline," pain, or encroaching death. Ironic translation becomes a tool for interrogating social knowledge.

Women above all are a hazard at the front, La Motte explains in "Women and Wives." "The trenches are mostly reserved for men of the working class," but their wives must stay at home, since "the words home and wife were interchangeable and stood for the same thing" (107). Wives are not allowed into the war zone because they, "it appears, are bad for the morale of the Army. . . . They establish the connecting link between the soldier and his life at home, his life that he is compelled to resign" (109). There is no telling what "disturbing things" a wife might say, "so she herself must be censored" (110). As for the other kind of "women" at the front, they are "pretty dangerous," and certainly unmarriageable, since they are "all ruined." "It is rather paradoxical, but there are those who can explain it perfectly" (115, 111). La Motte's pretense that she cannot know about the war or understand military lines of gender division subversively argues that any officially constructed knowledge excluding women must depend upon censorship and relabeling.

A contrary way to convey women's actual (if impolitic) knowledge is to reinforce women's immersion through their work at the front in soldiers' argot, macabre humor, latrine scenes, and blasphemy. An instance that "breaks the sound barrier," as Jane Marcus puts it, is the memoir of ambulance driver Winifred Young, reworked by the novelist Evadne Price under the pseudonym Helen Zenna Smith and given the telling title, *Not so Quiet . . . Stepdaughters of War*. A self-proclaimed riposte to Remarque's masculine vision of the bestiality of war, which portrays male bonding to the exclusion of women other than mothers or prostitutes, this feminist vision insists on female bonding in the face of shelling, physical deprivation, and the ever-renewed task of cleaning ambulances caked with mud, vomit, excrement, pus, and blood. To lend satiric force to this other view of the war, "Smithy" employs battlefront argot. You line up at "7:30 ack emma." According to the new grammar of war, you are "hungry in varying degrees: hungry, starving, ravenous." You sleep in fleabags, you eat tack. You hate the "bloody guns" and "bloody war."[32] Knowledge of this language offers a guarantee that women knew life at the front.

In Price's fictionalized autobiography, these young women mark their rite of passage beyond the boundaries of the known feminine world by rebaptism with dirty nicknames, like "B.F." for nymphomaniac Bertina Farmer. Tosh, the most forceful and humorous of the drivers, invents a war alphabet: "B for Bastard—obsolete term meaning war-baby. . . . I for Illegitimate—(see B). . . . V for Virgin—a term of reproach" (160–61). The jargon demystifies war and marks a shift in the subject's gender position to one outside the traditional social order.

Underscoring their realignment, Price's drivers reject the verbal gender line between men and women; they reject propaganda, clichés, and "feminine" verbal screens. While the heroine's mother expects "women in France to have a womanly, refining, softening effect on the troops," they instead learn from the men on stretchers those abbreviated, jocular expletives that help to ward off horror and hysteria (80). Price brilliantly exposes the contrast by intercutting quotations from Helen Smith's mother or descriptions of a ladies' committee with fragmented descriptions of Helen's own labors: "Mother smug, saccharine-sweet . . . shelves of mangled bodies . . . filthy smells of gangrenous wounds . . . 'Proud to do her bit for the old flag.' Oh, Christ!" (33). Smithy describes the knowledge purveyed by newspaper clippings as "muck" and "rubbish" (60, 134). She may write cheery letters ("the only kind of letter home they expect"), but in truth, "You don't believe in God or them or the infallibility of England or anything but bloody war and wounds . . . and lice and filth and noise, noise, noise" (30).

Medical women at the front record the curses and wounds, as well as the wise if sometimes simple words of the men they served. La Motte transcribes the cries of those she tends in a French that gives an accent of authenticity while it separates the soldiers' language from her own reserve and irony. (An effect quite different, one might add, from Hemingway's cosmopolitanist ethnography.)

Nurses' diaries and testimonials acquire sudden life when they shift into transcription of conversations with the wounded. One of the best, by

Dr. Tatiana Alexinsky, a Socialist émigrée who returned from Paris to work on a Russian hospital train, vividly re-creates conversations with soldiers and prisoners of war, capturing their stoic realism amid pain, as well as her own critique of czarist society.[33] Nurses curtly tell us about epidemics of dysentery; the smell of sepsis; the difficulty of disposing of excrement when pipes freeze; maggots in belly wounds. These women's claim to knowledge thus leads them to cross the barrier between their own "refined" language and the "gross" language of men; the technique of citation legitimates the transgression.

Many women also sexualize their descriptions of war. Yet I think we may differentiate the most common functions of sexual metaphor in men's and women's war writings. Whereas Lovelace gallantly depicts honor as a rival mistress and Hemingway uses the aggressive masculinist metaphor of pregnant soldiers protecting their cartridges under their capes, La Motte and Mme. Colombel poignantly depict ambulances as wombs, or pain as a harlot in whose embraces men writhe. In a lower key, one of Price's heroines remarks of war, "It's like having a baby—you're trapped once you've started" (135). The theme of the desexing of both men and women, which recurs in many nurses' texts, concerns not so much sexual potency as the destruction of one's most intimate capacity for relationships with others and of a will to continue—since continuation so often means to go on killing.

A distinctive feature of many women's texts, however, is their asexual linguistic treatment of men's bodies. We do not find extensive descriptions of sexual organs (one nurse notes a soldier has been wounded in "la partie sacrée"). Nor do nurse-writers play with risqué innuendos about impotence. Instead, we find figures of dehumanization. Bodies have been turned into numbers, material functions, social signs. The organic, living being who has been wounded is split up and dismembered by the dysfunctionality of war. This disassembly and deliteralization of the body in war provides a creative solution to the taboos against a woman's writing the male body.

War creates a broken human syntax. Some of the most powerful evocations of men's reduction by military routine and medical triage into fragments of their former selves can be found in a remarkable set of sketches by an American, Mary Borden, who set up a mobile field hospital just behind the lines in what was called the "Forbidden Zone," winning the Légion d'Honneur for her work. She shows brilliantly how men are "deformed" by "the deformity of war," and by the way language operates on them as well. War reduces human beings to labels. A "luggage ticket" is tied to the bodies of the wounded, in case they forget their name or the nature of their casualty. When the men arrive at the triage center, where the living will be sorted from the dying, they become organ parts: "I've got three knees, two spines, five abdomens, twelve heads."[34] Borden repeatedly asks how her charges can be men—and how, confronting them, she can remain a "woman" and retain her sanity. These wounded soldiers have been deprived of individuality, wholeness, manhood—of everything that constitutes life. The men are no longer subjects, they have become mere synecdoches, lists of parts that stand in for the whole.

Ellen La Motte similarly describes anonymous wounded whom she cannot yet treat because a general has come to decorate them: "The beds in the Salle d'Attente . . . are filled with heaps under blankets. . . . Sometimes the heaps, which are men, moan or are silent" ("The Interval," 90). Medals precede medicine in a system where pain has purely symbolic value. The French nurse M. Eydoux-Démians introduces her patients by the number of their bed.[35]

Numbers alone suffice to turn men into matériel. Dr. Alexinsky, who describes her staff composed of eleven women and two orderlies as "truly a feminist train," returns insistently to the triple-stacking of men on litters in converted "goods" wagons, with many more packed on straw-strewn floors of the cars during the worst retreats (10, 112). Photographs of hospital boats show the same compacted confusion.

Mary Borden shows how the social institutions that thrive on war corrupt language. Language permits officers to casually sign papers that are death warrants for countless men; it permits us to translate human beings into sandbags to be "thrown in" to a breach; it permits us to treat killing as a business, like any other human activity; it turns medicine into the handmaiden of capitalism, like a modern Frankenstein who disassembles and reassembles bodies.[36]

These women represent the verbal reduction of men's bodies to Lego pieces in a large war game. They perceive a military and political play with words that disassembles the social order in order to exploit one sector for the benefit of another. Crucial to the successful waging of war is the rewriting of discourse at the home front. Theorists of war, from Schopenhauer and Clausewitz to Freud and Elaine Scarry, have stressed the role of strategy as feint, disinformation, encoding, camouflage, or cutting the enemy's lines of communication. Yet they too tend to insulate war from peace, to distinguish a specific propaganda effort from the general disinformation of realpolitik. By contrast, a number of these texts by women demystify the discourses of which they are the gendered object, discourses that assimilate all women to parasitical profiteers or to the camouflaged political "enemy" at home. The more subversive texts collapse the distinction drawn by Scarry between "casualties that occur *within* war" and "the verbal issues (freedom, national sovereignty . . .) that stand *outside* war."[37] Through the theme of language, they connect what happens at the front to the apparently remote concerns of metropolis and farmland. They demystify the binarisms of so much male literature about the war.

Cather and Wharton stress language both to expose jingoist hypocrisy and callousness and to raise the larger social issues cast up by linguistic change. How were people drawn into war? How did they use language to grasp the mechanisms of war? Cather meticulously outlines the transformations that must take place at home: hysterical propaganda against local German neighbors, fetishization of atrocities, and glimmers of economic gains to be won. By reproducing the seductive effect of propaganda, Cather exposed herself to charges of jingoism with "its literary reinscription of . . . jubilant innocence." Yet her irony, which has consistently been overlooked even by feminists such as Jean Elshtain and Sandra Gilbert, emerges patently from the contrast between her characters' beliefs and the narrator's commentary.[38] Her soldiers sail away "to die for an idea, a sentiment, for the mere sound of a phrase" (274). In fact, her soldiers succumb to disease—"Certainly not to make the world safe for Democracy, or any rhetoric of that sort," as Cather's spokesman David Gerhardt says (409).

In *A Son at the Front*, Wharton treats war as a discursive system that imposes itself as natural via a change in people's language. Like Cather, she has been misread as a jingoist. "People," Wharton writes, "were already beginning to live into the monstrous idea of it, acquire its ways, speak its language, regard it as a thinkable, endurable, arrangeable fact; to eat it by day, and sleep on it—yes, and soundly—at night." "A new speech was growing up in this new world. There were trenches now, there was a 'Front'—people were beginning to talk of their sons at the front" (111). A mother may boast of her son "at the front" (as in the title of the novel), even though she believes that she has secured a safe post for him. A polarized verbal system screens a more complex reality: if he is not "at home," he must be "at the front."

Many texts by women observe the propagandistic evacuation of bloody actualities into statistics and technicalities, mythically justified sacrifices, or naturalized events. Claire Tylee has shown that Rose Macaulay drew on her work for the Ministry of Information (Department of Propaganda) for *Potterism* (1920) and *Catchwords and Claptrap* (1926). Mary Hamilton's *Dead Yesterday* (1916) analyzes the functioning of propaganda, perhaps informed by her friend Irene Cooper Willis's pacifist study of propaganda or by her own contacts with the propagandist Philip Gibbs.[39]

A focus on propaganda characterizes not only pacifist novels but a politically wide range of women's fictions and memoirs. One possible explanation is that the distance of many women from the killing lines may have enabled them to focus their attention on the war of words. In Virginia Woolf's first war novel, war (a mowing down of almost invisible men "like blocks of tin soldiers") is described as driven by an accumulation of papers,

> inscribed with the utterances of Kaisers, the statistics of ricefields, the growling of hundreds of work-people, plotting sedition in back streets, or gathering in the Calcutta bazaars, or mustering their forces in the uplands of Albania, where the hills are sand-coloured, and bones lie unburied.

Red-faced men, she tells us, are "manfully determined" "to impose some coherency upon Rajas and Kaisers and the muttering in bazaars."[40] Aside from a brief, prophetic glimpse of naval and land battles, Woolf resolutely focuses on a social structure "at home" that includes the Empire, and where the words are written that constitute the war.

The construction of war through words typically requires "redescription," translation, and mystification.[41] In "Pale Horse, Pale Rider," Katherine Anne Porter mocks the volunteers at home who relabel every soldier's medical problem "rheumatism."[42] She describes the war-based economy as a new kind of "dusty story," a form of patriotic blackmail in which jingoists try to force the heroine to buy liberty bonds. Two well-nourished men recite clichés about "the Huns overrunning martyred Belgium" as they threaten Miranda with losing her job if she does not pay up. Reflecting on these salesmen of patriotism,

> Miranda wondered why nearly all of those selected to do the war work at home were of his sort. He might be anything at all, she thought; advance agent for a road show, promoter of a wildcat oil company, a former saloon keeper announcing the opening of a new cabaret, an automobile salesman—any follower of any one of the crafty, haphazard callings. (272)

Their debasement of language turns the "filthy" facts of the war into "moldy" speech. Their speeches are formulaic, and their fondness for cigars betrays the profiteering that lies behind their call for sacrifice by others. Behind the stated moral justification of the war lie more materialist calculations. Miranda asks silently, "Coal, oil, iron, gold, international finance, why don't you tell us about them, you little liar?" (193). Porter concisely denounces a collusion between the tycoons of capitalism and the manufacturers of patriotic language.

While Porter focuses on the economic intrication of propaganda with profits, nurse-writers expose the corruption of the pure profession of medicine. Borden insists on the power of medical terminology to turn pain-tormented reality into "magic hieroglyphic names" (113) that conceal the truth. When a man comes in, "We discuss his different parts in terms that he does not understand." She compares her task to fixing the mangled laundry of the politicians: "Just as you send your clothes to the laundry and mend them when they come back, so we send our men to the trenches and mend them when they come back again. . . . It is arranged that men should be broken and that they should be mended" ("Conspiracy," 117). War does not in fact cleanse its participants; it tears them apart. La Motte too explains in one of her most damning passages:

> By expert surgery, by expert nursing, some of these were to be returned to their homes again, *réformés*, mutilated for life, a burden to themselves and to society; others were to be nursed back to health, to a point at which they could again shoulder eighty pounds of marching kit, and be torn to pieces again on the firing line. It was a pleasure to nurse such as these. It called forth all one's skill, all one's humanity. ("Heroes," 19)

La Motte exposes an idealistic terminology of humanistic service built upon men's submission to destruction.

In a grotesque instance of translation, the mutilated body is proudly returned by the military to his family. The demobilized are "re-formed." Mutilated for life, they can be symbolically reincorporated into society. La Motte describes a barber's son, a blinded soldier with two artificial legs and arms who has been brought back to life by the new art of plastic surgery: "He was a surgical triumph," sporting on what used to be his face "a hideous flabby heap, called a nose, fashioned by unique skill out of the flesh of his breast." The wounded boy, however, refuses to become a mere sign of his former self: "the wreck, not appreciating that he was a surgical triumph, kept sobbing, kept weeping out of his sightless eyes, kept jerking his four stumps in supplication, kept begging in agony, 'Kill me, Papa'" ("A Surgical Triumph," 159–60). Evadne Price cites the most banal translation of all: "It isn't murder to kill your enemies in wartime" (55).

A critique of propaganda may have been particularly difficult for German women both during the war and in the Weimar period. Yet Meta Scheele, whose *Frauen im Krieg* (Women in war, 1930) satirizes older women and men at the home front, exposes the absurdity of linguistic nationalism as well as the slippage between defending the hearth ("Mutterland") and Germany's colonies. Propaganda pervades social communication: people screw up door plaques with the new motto, "Sei deutsch in Wort und Gruss"(Be German in word and greeting)—and thus ironically betray the ubiquity of such "foreign" phrases as "Adieu." Already at the end of the first year of war, tranquilizing lies have become the only acceptable topic of conversation, as middle-class families gather to hear poetic pomposities about bullets striking the soldier's heart.

Scheele's heroine Johanna Hell cannot communicate with her family or fiancé about her desire to work or her political views. She hopes to assuage her thirst for "activity and independence" by becoming a nurse. She bites her tongue, and tries to be still. To speak of going to work, of winning the right to vote, or even to read the papers—all these activities seem ridiculous to the traditionalist, patriotic mothers who collude in Johanna's silencing. "Here I can not mention what I think." In one of the rare metaphors marking Scheele's stripped narrative, "Silently buried in their thoughts, mother and daughter went home to their apartment."[43] Many kinds of "dead" work their way to the surface in the chaos of this world war.

Those who try to speak the truth—several attempted suicides in these texts try to write the truth on their bodies—must be silenced by the machine of war. In *Not So Quiet*, when one of the heroine's friends, nicknamed Bug, commits suicide, the "powers that be" prudently relabel her death as an accident. No shame for the family, no need to review discipline and work conditions or to reconceive the war itself as a form of suicide. Ellen La Motte describes operating on a self-wounded man to save him for execution. To keep him from screaming and ripping open his wound, he is bound. The gag they put on his mouth breaks his teeth.

Censorship rules the front. It also ruled publication behind the lines. La Motte's *Backwash of War* itself fell subject to censorship in 1918. It could not be printed in England and was suppressed when America entered the war in 1918. A favorable review in the *Liberator* was inked out. She reports the explanation offered by her publisher: "The pictures presented—back of the scenes, so to speak—were considered damaging to the morale." "In the flood of war propaganda pouring over the country, these dozen short sketches were considered undesirable." Enid Bagnold's *Diary without Dates* (1918) incurred her dismissal from the VAD (Volunteer Aid Detachment) hospital that she had described. Rose Macaulay's satire on wartime bureaucracy, *What Not: A Prophetic Comedy*, was held up by the Defence of the Realm Act and could not appear until the war was over.[44]

Censorship, both official and internalized—in part a response to the unspeakableness of what they had seen—gives an ironic stamp of modernism to many of these women's writings. In her afterword to *Not So Quiet*, Jane Marcus describes Price's text as a bombarded terrain. Smithy's communications are interrupted by the arrival of new convoys. In Marcus's words, "The reading experience is a reproduction of the ambulance driver's route, swerving to avoid obstacles and holes." The "body of the text is 'not whole'; it is a war casualty." Its gaps and "ellipses like the censor's black lines crossing out sentences" echo the heroine's inescapable process of self-censorship.[45]

To shocking effect, Marcelle Capy's pacifist set of sketches, *Une voix de femme dans la mêlée* (A woman's voice in the fray, 1916), with an introduction by Romain Rolland, was printed with blank pages and asterisks: "coupé par la censure" (cut by the censor). Even the titles of sketches have been left blank, so that the table of contents looks like a shelled cityscape, with gaps created by the war. Her text, like those of La Motte and Borden, takes the form of fragments broken up on the page and compressed into explosive bits.

. . . . .

I have used the phrase "female writers" to describe the authors under consideration here. I do not mean to universalize the sex of particular literary strategies. Not all women who wrote about this war confronted linguistic issues in the same way, or even in a politically awakened way. Nor were men incapable of the same insights. Yet the sustained bias of literary history against women who did write about the war invites us to reexamine the stereotypical identification of women with propaganda and cliché, which has been inadvertently perpetuated by Sandra Gilbert's brilliant study, "Soldier's Heart." Women's wartime involvements and depictions of war have been erased again and again from popular memory. The *New York Times* could celebrate the end of the war in the Persian Gulf (1991) as occasioning "New Twists" in "Old Tales": "They talk not just of men under fire but also of women under fire."[46] A review of women's writings about World War I shows us that women came under fire in other wars as well. More important, it reveals the "twist" many women chose to give to the tales of war constructed by men.

To varying degrees, the women cited here could be described as feminists; they criticize a social order that uses language to kill men and to repress dissent and difference. They assume a right to know and to write. To do so, they must confront a fetishization of battle-knowledge inscribed as a badge of manliness through injuries to men's bodies. They must challenge the notion that knowledge of the war can or should be the preserve of politicians and its shell-shocked victims. Giving a new twist to Juvenalian satire, they pick up metaphors of the scalpel and curette to justify a woman/nurse writing.[47]

Linguistic analysis permits these female writers to deconstruct the oppositions between battlefront and home front, public and private, war and peace, men and women. They expose these opposed fronts as parts of a hidden economy—political, verbal, and literal—whose profits depend on the meretricious divisions of war. Cather and Wharton, Woolf and Porter all see systematic interconnections between the manufacturers of language, imperialism, and capitalism. These interdependencies become manifest linguistically as a complicity between dusty patriotic blackmail and blood sacrifice. By accepting but reevaluating their traditional assignment to a domestic literary economy and domestic knowledge, women can recast the cost/benefit analysis of war.

The larger perspective, which denies the privileging of an encapsulated concept of war, goes hand in hand with an attack on the abuse of language to metaphorize death and injury away. Women's texts anchored in experience at the front put the blood and shit back into "bloody" expletives and explode the sexual glamour of war-tested and fragmented male bodies.

More important, in a striking reversal of norms, they redefine "dirty language" not as the language of the body or of sacrilege but as the debased currency of politics that masks the way war is paid for by both men's and women's bodies. La Motte's sketch "Women and Wives" has shown us how renaming plays a key role in fusing military censorship, political propaganda, and misogyny. The simplistic view that identifies all women at the front with prostitutes is part of the "dirty sediment" or "backwash of war." La Motte mockingly echoes the comforting discourse on female sexuality that exculpates men for their sexual violence and exploitation. Our soldiers do not make war on women's bodies, they "visit" little girls of fourteen. "It's not the men's fault that most of the women in the War Zone are ruined" (114). If they are not "professional prostitutes" from Paris (provided by the government), they have been "ruined" by the Boches, not by our men. "Any one will tell you that" (115).

The theme of language foregrounds the problems women face in inscribing their experience of war. They remind us that the male body is not merely a "text" or number, and that women's bodies, as well as men's, are at stake in war. A close examination of their prose shows that feminist writers were indeed conscious of the ideological and aesthetic problems of finding language for war. Those who served at the front learned a new language that left its mark on their work. Whether at the front or not, these women developed ironic devices of translation and substitution to expose the ideological underpinnings of the rhetoric of war. One of the major accomplishments in their texts is to show how what we call "war" is a discourse that mobilizes actions and beliefs, veils events, constructs gender, and both permits and inhibits understanding. When women violated the taboos surrounding male identification with the language of World War I, they redrew the lines of war itself.

Notes

This paper could not have been undertaken without the encouragement and example of several notable feminist critics of war literature: Gisela Brinker-Gabler, Sandra Gilbert, Susan Gubar, Jane Marcus, Sonya Michel, Susan Schweik, and Claire Tylee, who generously shared their resources (and Xeroxes!) with me, invited me to speak, and inspired me by their own clarity and force. I owe a special debt to the group at Dartmouth whose institute on gender and war led to this volume.

The lines from "my sweet old etcetera" are reprinted from *IS 5 poems* by E. E. Cummings, edited by George James Firmage, by permission of Liveright Publishing Corporation. Copyright © 1985 by E. E. Cummings Trust. Copyright 1926 by Horace Liveright. Copyright © 1954 by E. E. Cummings. Copyright © 1985 by George James Firmage. Reproduced by kind permission of HarperCollins Publishers Ltd.

1. Many studies of male writers have touched on the problem of language; for my work, the most important has been Paul Fussell, *The Great War and Modern Memory* (New York: Oxford University Press, 1975). The fetishization of combat experience has been effectively documented and eloquently challenged by Claire Tylee, *The Great War and Women's Consciousness* (London: Macmillan, 1990); and Susan Schweik, *A Gulf So Deeply Cut: American Women Poets and the Second World War* (Nebraska University Press, 1991).

2. See Arthur Marwick, *Women at War, 1914–1918* (London: Fontana, 1977) for the British situation; Françoise Thébaud, *La femme dans la première guerre mondiale* (Stock: Pernoud, 1986); for a comparative overview, see the introduction to *Behind the Lines: Gender and the Two World Wars*, ed. Margaret R. Higonnet et al. (New Haven: Yale University Press, 1987), pp. 1–17.

3. Jean Bethke Elshtain, *Women and War* (New York: Basic Books, 1987), p. 214.

4. Most of the women's texts to which I refer here are English, American, and German. I engage a broader comparative perspective including a few critically neglected French, Nigerian, and Indian writers in "Cassandra's Voice" (paper delivered at the 1991 International Comparative Literature Association meeting in Tokyo).

5. For the cultural symbolism linking women to peace and reproduction, as opposed to war, see Elshtain, *Women and War*; and Nancy Huston, "The Matrix of War," in *The Female Body in Western Culture*, ed. Susan Suleiman (Cambridge: Harvard University Press, 1985), p. 135. Marwick cites the Inglis story in *Women at War*, p. 127. Felix Dahn's song is cited by Gisela Brinker-Gabler, *Frauen gegen den Krieg* (Frankfurt/M: Fischer, 1980), p. 178 (my italics). Note the innuendo of the first line: "Weapons high! The sword is man's own." Susan Schweik links women's silence to their traditional role as *readers* of letters home and spectators of combat. She cites Lovelace's poem "To Lucasta" as a silencing of woman's complaints and a figuration of the pursuit of honor as erotic.

6. Virginia Woolf, *A Room of One's Own* (1929; reprint, San Diego: Harvest/HBJ, 1957), p. 74.

7. See Susan Schweik, *A Gulf So Deeply Cut*, pp. 54, 55.

8. Anne Brontë, preface to the second edition of *Tenant of Wildfell Hall*, ed. Herbert Rosengarten (Oxford: Clarendon Press, 1992), p. xxxix.

9. Claire M. Tylee calls attention to this problem in her brilliant essay "Verbal Screens and Mental Petticoats: Women's Writings of the First World War," *Revista canaria de estudios ingleses* 13–14 (1987): 144. In asserting, however, that the crude language of the front was not printed until after the Second World War, she forgets Barbusse, Price, and others.

10. For an exploration of these taboos and the intersection between the terms of *corpse*, *military corps*, and *literary corpus*, see Jane Marcus's afterword to Helen Zenna Smith's *Not So Quiet . . . Stepdaughters of War*, republished as "Corpus/Corps/Corpse: Writing the Body in/at War," in *Arms and the Woman: War, Gender, and Literary Representation*, ed. Helen M. Cooper et al. (Chapel Hill: University of North Carolina, 1989), pp. 124–67.

11. On the censorship of women's war writing, see Angela Ingram, " 'Unutterable Putrefaction' and 'Foul Stuff': Two 'Obscene' Novels of the 1920s," *Women's Studies International Forum* 9 (1986): 341–54. Jane Marcus also discusses self-censorship, a topic to which I return at the end of this paper.

12. Sassoon, introduction. Oscar Williams, Introduction, in *The War Poets: An Anthology of the War Poetry of the Twentieth Century* (New York: John Day, 1945), p. 15, cited by Schweik, *A Gulf So Deeply Cut.*

13. Jenny Gould reviews the "physical force" argument that the enforcement of law and national defense rests with the physically stronger sex, who must therefore retain political power, in "Women's Military Services in First World War Britain," in Higonnet et al., *Behind the Lines*, p. 116–17. Susan Schweik draws on Laura Mulvey and Margaret Homans to elaborate the misogynist assumption that women should be the bearers, not the makers, of meaning.

14. See Bella Brodzki and Celeste Schenck, eds., *Life/Lines: Theorizing Women's Autobiography* (Ithaca: Cornell University Press, 1988).

15. Tylee reviews the repetition of this accusation by men in "Verbal Screens," pp. 130–32. See also, surprisingly, Jean Elshtain, *Women and War*, p. 214, and Sandra Gilbert, "Soldier's Heart: Literary Men, Literary Women and the Great War," in Higonnet et al., *Behind the Lines*, pp. 208–11.

16. Such a reading of the war is the central premise of Fussell's *Great War and Modern Memory*. Disillusionment could go hand in hand with defeatism and the sense that the war was an "authorless" text, as Eric Leed has argued in "The Event as Text," *No Man's Land: Combat and Identity in World War I* (Cambridge: Cambridge University Press, 1979), pp. 33–38.

17. Ezra Pound, "Hugh Selwyn Mauberley," in *Poetry of the First World War*, ed. Maurice Hussey (London: Longmans, 1967), p. 158.

18. Henri Barbusse, *Le feu: Journal d'une escouade*, ed. Pierre Paraf (1916; reprint, Paris: Flammarion, 1965), pp. 141–42.

19. Erich Maria Remarque, *All Quiet on the Western Front*, trans. A. W. Wheen (London: Putnam, 1929), p. 15. Marcus draws an extended comparison between the language of body functions in *All Quiet* and *Not So Quiet* in "Corps/Corps/Corpse," pp. 164–66.

20. Ford, "That Exploit of Yours," in *The Penguin Book of First World War Poetry*, ed. Jon Silkin (Harmondsworth: Penguin, 1981), p. 146.

21. Hemingway, *A Farewell to Arms* (1927; reprint, New York: Scribner's, 1969), pp. 184–85.

22. Tylee, "Verbal Screens and Mental Petticoats," p. 135.

23. e.e. cummings, "my sweet old etcetera," in Silkin, *Penguin Book of First World War Poetry*, p. 140

24. Sandra Gilbert, "Soldier's Heart," pp. 197–226. For critiques of Gilbert's assimilation of most women writers to this view, see Tylee, "Maleness Run Riot,"

Women's Studies International Forum 11 (1988): 199–210; and Marcus, "The Asylums of Antaeus—Women, War and Madness: Is There a Feminist Fetishism?" in *The Difference Within: Feminism and Critical Theory*, ed. Elizabeth Meese and Alice Parker (Amsterdam: Benjamins, 1989), pp. 49–83. Fussell lays out the wartime binarisms of politics, class, time, and of course sex in chap. 3 of *The Great War*, pp. 75–113.

25. Tylee, "Verbal Screens," p. 128. Tylee argues that even "naive, sentimental, or blinkered" texts shed light on the socially set limits to women's "understanding of the world they lived in and of the part they might play in it." She therefore casts her net much wider in *The Great War and Women's Consciousness* than I do here. Miriam Cooke's essay in this volume addresses the constitution of women's political consciousness through writing.

26. Cited by Regina Barreca (paper delivered at a Modern Language Association special session on Women and World War II, Chicago, 1990).

27. Wharton, *A Son at the Front* (New York: Charles Scribner's Sons, 1923), p. 402.

28. Willa Cather, *One of Ours* (New York: Knopf, 1922), pp. 167–68. See Sharon O'Brien's study of the problem of knowledge, "Combat Envy and Survivor Guilt: Willa Cather's 'Manly Battle Yarn,' " in Cooper et al., *Arms and the Woman*, pp. 184–204.

29. In "Writing a War Story" this process entails the erasure of rustic speech and addition of sentiment. "Refugees" (1919) mocks relief workers jostling for power in their grasping hunt for nice (not filthy) refugees. *The Collected Short Stories of Edith Wharton*, ed. R. W. B. Lewis, vol. 2 (New York: Scribner's, 1968). Elshtain attacks Wharton for writing "patriotic doggerel" in texts she published as part of an appeal for relief funds; she does not note the different outlook of the pieces written a few years later (*Women and War*, pp. 214–15). Wharton could be parodying the newspaper exhortation cited by Fussell: "What can I do? How the Civilian May Help in this Crisis. Be Cheerful. . . . Write encouragingly" (*The Great War*, p. 17).

30. Marcus, "Corpus/Corps/Corpse," p. 124.

31. Ellen N. La Motte, *The Backwash of War: The Human Wreckage of the Battlefield as Witnessed by an American Nurse* (1916; reprint, New York: Putnam, 1934), p. 39.

32. Helen Zenna Smith [Evadne Price], *Not So Quiet . . . Stepdaughters of War* (1930; reprint, New York: Feminist Press, 1989), pp. 25–27, 29–30. Marcus analyzes parallel treatments of the body by Price and Remarque in her afterword.

33. Tatiana Alexinsky, *With the Russian Wounded* (London: T. Fisher Unwin, 1916), p. 96 and passim. Alexinsky also comments on her surprise at the falsehoods in newspaper accounts that she reads during a brief leave: "Where on earth do the journalists get all the stuff they write about the war?" (50). For typical transcriptions of conversations, see Mme. Emmanuel Colombel, *Journal d'une infirmière d'Arras, août-septembre-octobre* 1914 (Paris: Bloud et Gay, 1916), pp. 72–73, 100–102.

34. Mary Borden, "Blind," in *The Forbidden Zone* (London: Heinemann, 1929), 152. References in the text will include the title of the sketch. The same synecdoche can be found in many nurses' memoirs.

35. M. Eydoux-Démians, *Notes d'une infirmière, 1914* (Paris: Plon, 1915), 5–6.

36. See Jane Marcus and my essay, "Women in the Medical Corps during the Great War: Changing Attitudes towards Self and Society," *Le Monde du travail dans les pays de langue anglaise*, forthcoming.

37. Elaine Scarry, *The Body in Pain: The Making and Unmaking of the World* (New York: Oxford UP, 1985), p. 63.

38. Simplistically, Elshtain identifies Cather with Claude. She argues that Cather "unselfconsciously uses words of sacrifice, honor, ecstasy, freedom" (*Women and War*, p. 216–18). Gilbert writes in "Soldier's Heart," "Metaphorically speaking, . . . Edith Wharton and Willa Cather (in the United States) distributed white feathers to large audiences of noncombatant readers" (209). Jean Schwind corrects the simplistic readings of Cather by Hemingway and other critics and biographers in "The 'Beautiful' War in *One of Ours*," *Modern Fiction Studies* 30 (1984): 53–71. See also Raymond J. Wilson, III, "Willa Cather's *One of Ours*: A Novel of the Great Plans and the Great War," *MidAmerica* 11 (1984): 20–33.

39. Tylee, *The Great War*, pp. 111–120. Peter Buitenhuis, who acknowledges Wharton's depiction of an "unbridgeable abyss" and of war's transformation of language, nonetheless includes no women among those who demystify propaganda. *The Great War of Words: British, American, and Canadian Propaganda and Fiction, 1914–1933* (Vancouver: University of British Columbia, 1987), pp. 151–53.

40. Woolf, *Jacob's Room* (1922; reprint, San Diego: Harvest/HBJ, 1960), pp. 155, 172.

41. Scarry discusses the evacuation of pain and injury by renaming or metonymic transfer to abstract entities in *The Body*, 66–157 passim.

42. Porter, "Pale Horse, Pale Rider," in *The Collected Stories (San Diego: Harvest/ HBJ, 1965)*, 276.

43. *Meta Scheele, Frauen im Krieg* (Gotha: Klotz, 1930), p. 68.

44. Tylee, *The Great War*, pp. 121–22.

45. Jane Marcus, "Corpus," pp. 272–273.

46. *New York Times*, March 11, 1991, A1. Some twists in my own family's stories: a great-grandmother who refused to catch her high-spirited horse for marauding soldiers during the Civil War; an aunt who during World War I concealed refugees from rival parties in assorted closets of her apartment in Berlin; two cousins, women whose average age was forty, who went to the Gulf.

47. See Higonnet, "Women in the Medical Corps."

Chapter 10

WARS, WIMPS, AND WOMEN:

TALKING GENDER AND THINKING WAR

CAROL COHN

I start with a true story, told to me by a white male physicist:

> Several colleagues and I were working on modeling counterforce attacks, try-
> ing to get realistic estimates of the number of immediate fatalities that would
> result from different deployments.[1] At one point, we remodeled a particular
> attack, using slightly different assumptions, and found that instead of there
> being thirty-six million immediate fatalities, there would only be thirty million.
> And everybody was sitting around nodding, saying, "Oh yeah, that's great,
> only thirty million," when all of a sudden, I *heard* what we were saying. And
> I blurted out, "Wait, I've just *heard* how we're talking—*Only* thirty million!
> *Only* thirty million human beings killed instantly?" Silence fell upon the room.
> Nobody said a word. They didn't even look at me. It was awful. I felt like a
> woman.

The physicist added that henceforth he was careful to never blurt out
anything like that again.

.   .   .   .   .

During the early years of the Reagan presidency, in the era of the Evil
Empire, the cold war, and loose talk in Washington about the possibility
of fighting and "prevailing" in a nuclear war, I went off to do participant
observation in a community of North American nuclear defense intellectuals and security affairs analysts—a community virtually entirely composed of white men. They work in universities, think tanks, and as ad-
visers to government. They theorize about nuclear deterrence and arms
control, and nuclear and conventional war fighting, about how to best
translate military might into political power; in short, they create the discourse that underwrites American national security policy. The exact relation of their theories to American political and military practice is a
complex and thorny one; the argument can be made, for example, that
their ideas do not so much shape policy decisions as legitimate them after

the fact. But one thing that is clear is that the body of language and thinking they have generated filters out to the military, politicians, and the public, and increasingly shapes how we talk and think about war. This was amply evident during the Gulf War: Gulf War "news," as generated by the military briefers, reported by newscasters, and analyzed by the television networks' resident security experts, was marked by its use of the professional language of defense analysis, nearly to the exclusion of other ways of speaking.

My goal has been to understand something about how defense intellectuals think, and why they think that way. Despite the parsimonious appeal of ascribing the nuclear arms race to "missile envy,"[2] I felt certain that masculinity was not a sufficient explanation of why men think about war in the ways that they do. Indeed, I found many ways to understand what these men were doing that had little or nothing to do with gender.[3] But ultimately, the physicist's story and others like it made confronting the role of gender unavoidable. Thus, in this paper I will explore gender discourse, and its role in shaping nuclear and national security discourse.

I want to stress, this is not a paper about men and women, and what they are or are not like. I will not be claiming that men are aggressive and women peace loving. I will not even address the question of how men's and women's relations to war may differ, nor of the different propensities they may have to committing acts of violence. Neither will I pay more than passing attention to the question which so often crops up in discussions of war and gender, that is, would it be a more peaceful world if our national leaders were women? These questions are valid and important, and recent feminist discussion of them has been complex, interesting, and contentious. But my focus is elsewhere. I wish to direct attention away from gendered individuals and toward gendered discourses. My question is about the way that civilian defense analysts think about war, and the ways in which that thinking is shaped not by their maleness (or, in extremely rare instances, femaleness), but by the ways in which gender discourse intertwines with and permeates that thinking.[4]

Let me be more specific about my terms. I use the term *gender* to refer to the constellation of meanings that a given culture assigns to biological sex differences. But more than that, I use gender to refer to a symbolic system, a central organizing discourse of culture, one that not only shapes how we experience and understand ourselves as men and women, but that also interweaves with other discourses and shapes *them*—and therefore shapes other aspects of our world—such as how nuclear weapons are thought about and deployed.[5]

So when I talk about "gender discourse," I am talking not only about words or language but about a system of meanings, of ways of thinking, images and words that first shape how we experience, understand, and represent ourselves as men and women, but that also do more than that; they shape many other aspects of our lives and culture. In this symbolic system, human characteristics are dichotomized, divided into pairs of polar opposites that are supposedly mutually exclusive: mind is opposed to body; culture to nature; thought to feeling; logic to intuition; objectivity to subjectivity; aggression to passivity; confrontation to accommodation; abstraction to particularity; public to private; political to personal, ad nauseam. In each case, the first term of the "opposites" is associated with male, the second with female. And in each case, our society values the first over the second.

I break it into steps like this—analytically separating the *existence* of these groupings of binary oppositions, from the association of each group with a gender, from the valuing of one over the other, the so-called male over the so-called female, for two reasons: first, to try to make visible the fact that this system of dichotomies is encoding many meanings that may be quite unrelated to male and female bodies. Yet once that first step is made—the association of each side of those lists with a gender—gender now becomes tied to many other kinds of cultural representations. If a human activity, such as engineering, fits some of the characteristics, it becomes gendered.

My second reason for breaking it into those steps is to try to help make it clear that the meanings can flow in different directions; that is, in gender discourse, men and women are supposed to exemplify the characteristics on the lists. It also works in reverse, however; to evidence any of these characteristics—to be abstract, logical or dispassionate, for example—is not simply to be those things, but also to be manly. And to be manly is not simply to be manly, but also to be in the more highly valued position in the discourse. In other words, to exhibit a trait on that list is not neutral—it is not simply displaying some basic human characteristic. It also positions you in a discourse of gender. It associates you with a particular gender, and also with a higher or lower valuation.

In stressing that this is a *symbolic* system, I want first to emphasize that while real women and men do not really fit these gender "ideals," the existence of this system of meaning affects all of us, nonetheless. Whether we want to or not, we see ourselves and others against its templates, we interpret our own and others' actions against it. A man who cries easily cannot avoid in some way confronting that he is likely to be seen as less than fully manly. A woman who is very aggressive and incisive may enjoy that quality in herself, but the fact of her aggressiveness does not exist by itself; she cannot avoid having her own and others' perceptions of that quality of hers, the meaning it has for people, being in some way mediated by the discourse of gender. Or, a different kind of example: Why does it mean one thing when George Bush gets teary-eyed in public, and something entirely different when Patricia Shroeder does? The same act is viewed through the lens of gender and is seen to mean two very different things.

Second, as gender discourse assigns gender to human characteristics, we can think of the discourse as something we are positioned *by*. If I say, for example, that a corporation should stop dumping toxic waste because it is damaging the creations of mother earth, (i.e., articulating a valuing and sentimental vision of nature), I am speaking in a manner associated with women, and our cultural discourse of gender positions me as female. As such I am then associated with the whole constellation of traits—irrational, emotional, subjective, and so forth—and I am in the devalued position. If, on the other hand, I say the corporation should stop dumping toxic wastes because I have calculated that it is causing $8.215 billion of damage to eight nonrenewable resources, which should be seen as equivalent to lowering the GDP by 0.15 percent per annum, (i.e., using a rational, calculative mode of thought), the discourse positions me as masculine—rational, objective, logical, and so forth—the dominant, valued position.

But if we are positioned *by* discourses, we can also take different positions *within* them. Although I am female, and thus would "naturally" fall into the devalued term, I can choose to "speak like a man"—to be hardnosed, realistic, unsentimental, dispassionate. Jeanne Kirkpatrick is a formidable example. While we can choose a position in a discourse, however, it means something different for a woman to "speak like a man" than for a man to do so. It is heard differently.

One other note about my use of the term *gender discourse*: I am using it in the general sense to refer to the phenomenon of symbolically organizing the world in these gender-associated opposites. I do not mean to suggest that there is a single discourse defining a single set of gender ideals. In fact, there are many specific discourses of gender, which vary by race, class, ethnicity, locale, sexuality, nationality, and other factors. The masculinity idealized in the gender discourse of new Haitian immigrants is in some ways different from that of sixth-generation white Anglo-Saxon Protestant business executives, and both differ somewhat from that of white-male defense intellectuals and security analysts. One version of masculinity is mobilized and enforced in the armed forces in order to enable men to fight wars, while a somewhat different version of masculinity is drawn upon and expressed by abstract theoreticians of war.[6]

Let us now return to the physicist who felt like a woman: what happened when he "blurted out" his sudden awareness of the "only thirty million" dead people? First, he was transgressing a code of professional conduct. In the civilian defense intellectuals' world, when you are in professional settings you do not discuss the bloody reality behind the calculations. It is not required that you be completely unaware of them in your outside life, or that you have no feelings about them, but it is required that you do not bring them to the foreground in the context of professional activities. There is a general awareness that you *could not* do your work if you did; in addition, most defense intellectuals believe that emotion and description of human reality distort the process required to think well about nuclear weapons and warfare.

So the physicist violated a behavioral norm, in and of itself a difficult thing to do because it threatens your relationships to and your standing with your colleagues.

But even worse than that, he demonstrated some of the characteristics on the "female" side of the dichotomies—in his "blurting" he was impulsive, uncontrolled, emotional, concrete, and attentive to human bodies, at the very least. Thus, he marked himself not only as unprofessional but as feminine, and this, in turn, was doubly threatening. It was not only a threat to his own sense of self as masculine, his gender identity, it also identified him with a devalued status—of a woman—or put him in the devalued or subordinate position in the discourse.

Thus, both his statement, "I felt like a woman," and his subsequent silence in that and other settings are completely understandable. To have the strength of character and courage to transgress the strictures of both professional and gender codes *and* to associate yourself with a lower status is very difficult.

This story is not simply about one individual, his feelings and actions; it is about the role of gender discourse. The impact of gender discourse in that room (and countless others like it) is that some things get left out. Certain ideas, concerns, interests, information, feelings, and meanings are marked in national security discourse as feminine, and are devalued. They are therefore, first, very difficult to *speak*, as exemplified by the physicist who felt like a woman. And second, they are very difficult to *hear*, to take in and work with seriously, even if they *are* said. For the others in the room, the way in which the physicist's comments were marked as female and devalued served to delegitimate them. It is almost as though they had become an accidental excrescence in the middle of the room. Embarrassed politeness demanded that they be ignored.

I must stress that this is not simply the product of the idiosyncratic personal composition of that particular room. In other professional settings, I have experienced the feeling that something terribly important is being left out and must be spoken; and yet, it has felt almost physically impossible to utter the words, almost as though they could not be pushed out into the smooth, cool, opaque air of the room.

What is it that cannot be spoken? First, any words that express an emotional awareness of the desperate human reality behind the sanitized abstractions of death and destruction—as in the physicist's sudden vision of thirty million rotting corpses. Similarly, weapons' effects may be spoken of only in the most clinical and abstract terms, leaving no room to imagine a seven-year-old boy with his flesh melting away from his bones or a toddler with her skin hanging down in strips. Voicing concern about the number of casualties in the enemy's armed forces, imagining the suffering of the killed and wounded young men, is out of bounds. (Within the military itself, it is permissible, even desirable, to attempt to minimize immediate civilian casualties if it is possible to do so without compromising military objectives, but as we learned in the Persian Gulf War, this is only an extremely limited enterprise; the planning and precision of military targeting does not admit of consideration of the cost in human lives of such actions as destroying power systems, or water and sewer systems, or highways and food distribution systems.)[7] Psychological effects—on the soldiers fighting the war or on the citizens injured, or fearing for their own safety, or living through tremendous deprivation, or helplessly watching their babies die from diarrhea due to the lack of clean water— all of these are not to be talked about.

But it is not only particular subjects that are out of bounds. It is also tone of voice that counts. A speaking style that is identified as cool, dispassionate, and distanced is required. One that vibrates with the intensity of emotion almost always disqualifies the speaker, who is heard to sound like "a hysterical housewife."

What gets left out, then, is the emotional, the concrete, the particular, the human bodies and their vulnerability, human lives and their subjectivity—all of which are marked as feminine in the binary dichotomies of gender discourse. In other words, gender discourse informs and shapes nuclear and national security discourse, and in so doing creates silences and absences. It keeps things out of the room, unsaid, and keeps them ignored if they manage to get in. As such, it degrades our ability to think *well* and *fully* about nuclear weapons and national security, and shapes and limits the possible outcomes of our deliberations.

What becomes clear, then, is that defense intellectuals' standards of what constitutes "good thinking" about weapons and security have not simply evolved out of trial and error; it is not that the history of nuclear discourse has been filled with exploration of other ideas, concerns, interests, information, questions, feelings, meanings and stances which were then found to create distorted or poor thought. It is that these options have been *preempted* by gender discourse, and by the feelings evoked by living up to or transgressing gender codes.

To borrow a term from defense intellectuals, you might say that gender discourse becomes a "preemptive deterrent" to certain kinds of thought.

Let me give you another example of what I mean—another story, this one my own experience:

One Saturday morning I, two other women, and about fifty-five men gathered to play a war game designed by the RAND Corporation.[8] Our "controllers" (the people running the game) first divided us up into three sets of teams; there would be three simultaneous games being played, each pitting a Red Team against a Blue Team (I leave the reader to figure out which color represents which country). All three women were put onto the same team, a Red Team.

The teams were then placed in different rooms so that we had no way of communicating with each other, except through our military actions (or lack of them) or by sending demands and responses to those demands via the controllers. There was no way to negotiate or to take actions other than military ones. (This was supposed to simulate reality.) The controllers then presented us with maps and pages covered with numbers representing each side's forces. We were also given a "scenario," a situation of escalating tensions and military conflicts, starting in the Middle East and spreading to Central Europe. We were to decide what to do, the controllers would go back and forth between the two teams to relate the other team's actions, and periodically the controllers themselves would add something that would rachet up the conflict—an announcement of an "intercepted intelligence report" from the other side, the authenticity of which we had no way of judging.

Our Red Team was heavily into strategizing, attacking ground forces, and generally playing war. We also, at one point, decided that we were going to pull our troops out of Afghanistan, reasoning that it was bad for us to have them there and that the Afghanis had the right to self-determination. At another point we removed some troops from Eastern Europe. I must add that later on my team was accused of being wildly "unrealistic," that this group of experts found the idea that the Soviet Union might voluntarily choose to pull troops out of Afghanistan and Eastern Europe so utterly absurd. (It was about six months before Gorbachev actually did the same thing.)

Gradually our game escalated to nuclear war. The Blue Team used tactical nuclear weapons against our troops, but our Red Team decided, initially at least, against nuclear retaliation. When the game ended (at the end of the allotted time) our Red Team had "lost the war" (meaning that we had political control over less territory than we had started with, although our homeland had remained completely unviolated and our civilian population safe).

In the debriefing afterwards, all six teams returned to one room and reported on their games. Since we had had absolutely no way to know why the other team had taken any of its actions, we now had the opportunity to find out what they had been thinking. A member of the team that had played against us said, "Well, when he took his troops out of Afghanistan, I knew he was weak and I could push him around. And then, when we nuked him and he didn't nuke us back, I knew he was just such a wimp, I could take him for everything he's got and I nuked him again. He just wimped out."

There are many different possible comments to make at this point. I will restrict myself to a couple. First, when the man from the Blue Team called me a wimp (which is what it felt like for each of us on the Red Team—a personal accusation), I felt silenced. My reality, the careful reasoning that had gone into my strategic and tactical choices, the intelligence, the politics, the morality—all of it just disappeared, completely invalidated. I could not explain the reasons for my actions, could not protest, "Wait, you idiot, I didn't do it because I was weak, I did it because it made *sense* to do it that way, given my understandings of strategy and tactics, history and politics, my goals and my values." The protestation would be met with knowing sneers. In this discourse, the coding of an act as wimpish is hegemonic. Its emotional heat and resonance is like a bath of sulfuric acid: it erases everything else.

"Acting like a wimp" is an *interpretation* of a person's acts (or, in national security discourse, a country's acts, an important distinction I will return to later). As with any other interpretation, it is a selection of one among many possible different ways to understand something—once the selection is made, the other possibilities recede into invisibility. In national security discourse, "acting like a wimp," being insufficiently masculine, is one of the most readily available interpretive codes. (You do not need to do participant observation in a community of defense intellectuals to know this—just look at the "geopolitical analyses" in the media and on Capitol Hill of the way in which George Bush's military intervention in Panama and the Persian Gulf War finally allowed him to beat the "wimp factor.") You learn that someone is being a wimp if he perceives an international crisis as very dangerous and urges caution; if he thinks it might not be important to have just as many weapons that are just as big as the other guy's; if he suggests that an attack should not necessarily be answered by an even more destructive counterattack; or, until recently, if he suggested that making unilateral arms reductions might be useful for our own security.[9] All of these are "wimping out."

The prevalence of this particular interpretive code is another example of how gender discourse affects the quality of thinking within the national security community, first, because, as in the case of the physicist who "felt like a woman," it is internalized to become a self-censor; there are things professionals simply will not *say* in groups, options they simply will not argue nor write about, because they know that to do so is to brand themselves as wimps. Thus, a whole range of inputs is left out, a whole series of options is foreclosed from their deliberations.

Equally, if not more damagingly, is the way in which this interpretive coding not only limits what is *said*, but even limits what is *thought*. "He's a wimp" is a phrase that *stops* thought.[10] When we were playing the game, once my opponent on the Blue Team "recognized the fact that I was a wimp," that is, once he interpreted my team's actions through the lens of this common interpretive code in national security discourse, he *stopped thinking*; he stopped looking for ways to understand what we were doing. He did not ask, "Why on earth would the Red Team do that? What does it tell me about them, about their motives and purposes and goals and capabilities? What does it tell me about their possible understandings of *my* actions, or of the situation they're in?" or any other of the many questions that might have enabled him to revise his own conception of the situation or perhaps achieve his goals at a far lower level of violence and destruction. Here, again, gender discourse acts as a preemptive deterrent to thought.

"Wimp" is, of course, not the only gendered pejorative used in the national security community; "pussy" is another popular epithet, conjoining the imagery of harmless domesticated (read demasculinized) pets with contemptuous reference to women's genitals. In an informal setting, an analyst worrying about the other side's casualties, for example, might be asked, "What kind of pussy are you, anyway?" It need not happen more than once or twice before everyone gets the message; they quickly learn not to raise the issue in their discussions. Attention to and care for the living, suffering, and dying of human beings (in this case, soldiers and their families and friends) is again banished from the discourse through the expedient means of gender-bashing.

Another disturbing example comes from our relationship with what was then the Soviet Union. Former President Gorbachev was deeply influenced by a (mostly) young group of Soviet civilian defense intellectuals known as "new thinkers." The new thinkers questioned many of the fundamental bases of security policy as it has been practiced by both the United States and the USSR, and significant elements of Soviet defense policy were restructured accordingly. Intellectually, their ideas posed a profound challenge to the business-as-usual stance of American policy analysts; if taken seriously, they offered an exceptional opportunity to radically reshape international security arrangements. And yet, in at least one instance, American security specialists avoided serious consideration of those ideas through mindless masculinity defamation; for example, "I've met these Soviet 'new thinkers' and they're a bunch of pussies."[11]

Other words are also used to impugn someone's masculinity and, in the process, to delegitimate his position and avoid thinking seriously about it. "Those Krauts are a bunch of limp-dicked wimps" was the way one U.S. defense intellectual dismissed the West German politicians who were concerned about popular opposition to Euromissile deployments.[12] I have heard our NATO allies referred to as "the Euro-fags" when they disagreed with American policy on such issues as the Contra War or the bombing of Libya. Labeling them "fags" is an effective strategy; it immediately dismisses and trivializes their opposition to U.S. policy by coding it as due to inadequate masculinity. In other words, the American analyst need not seriously confront the Europeans' arguments, since the Europeans' doubts about U.S. policy obviously stem not from their reasoning but from the "fact" that they "just don't have the stones for war." Here, again, gender discourse deters thought.

"Fag" imagery is not, of course, confined to the professional community of security analysts; it also appears in popular "political" discourse. The Gulf War was replete with examples. American derision of Saddam Hussein included bumper stickers that read "Saddam, Bend Over." American soldiers reported that the "U.S.A." stenciled on their uniforms stood for "Up Saddam's Ass." A widely reprinted cartoon, surely one of the most multiply offensive that came out of the war, depicted Saddam bowing down in the Islamic posture of prayer, with a huge U.S. missile, approximately five times the size of the prostrate figure, about to penetrate his upraised bottom. Over and over, defeat for the Iraqis was portrayed as humiliating anal penetration by the more powerful and manly United States.

Within the defense community discourse, manliness is equated not only with the ability to win a war (or to "prevail," as some like to say when talking about nuclear war); it is also equated with the willingness (which they would call courage) to threaten and use force. During the Carter administration, for example, a well-known academic security affairs specialist was quoted as saying that "under Jimmy Carter the United States is spreading its legs for the Soviet Union."[13] Once this image is evoked, how does rational discourse about the value of U.S. policy proceed?

In 1989 and 1990, as Gorbachev presided over the withdrawal of Soviet forces from Eastern Europe, I heard some defense analysts sneeringly say things like, "They're a bunch of pussies for pulling out of Eastern Europe." This is extraordinary. Here they were, men who for years railed against Soviet domination of Eastern Europe. You would assume that if they were politically and ideologically consistent, if they were rational, they would be applauding the Soviet actions. Yet in their informal conversations, it was not their rational analyses that dominated their response, but the fact that for them, the decision for war, the willingness to use force, is cast as a question of masculinity—not prudence, thoughtfulness, efficacy, "rational" cost-benefit calculation, or morality, but masculinity.

In the face of this equation, genuine political discourse disappears. One more example: After Iraq invaded Kuwait and President Bush hastily sent U.S. forces to Saudi Arabia, there was a period in which the Bush administration struggled to find a convincing political justification for U.S. military involvement and the security affairs community debated the political merit of U.S. intervention.[14] Then Bush set the deadline, January 16, high noon at the OK Corral, and as the day approached conversations changed. More of these centered on the question compellingly articulated by one defense intellectual as "Does George Bush have the stones for war?"[15] This, too, is utterly extraordinary. This was a time when crucial political questions abounded: Can the sanctions work if given more time? Just what vital interests does the United States actually have at stake? What would be the goals of military intervention? Could they be accomplished by other means? Is the difference between what sanctions might accomplish and what military violence might accomplish worth the greater cost in human suffering, human lives, even dollars? What will the long-term effects on the people of the region be? On the ecology? Given the apparent successes of Gorbachev's last-minute diplomacy and Hussein's series of nearly daily small concessions, can and should Bush put off the deadline? Does he have the strength to let another leader play a major role in solving the problem? Does he have the political flexibility to not fight, or is he hell-bent on war at all costs? And so on, ad infinitum. All of these disappear in the sulfuric acid test of the size of Mr. Bush's private parts.[16]

I want to return to the RAND war simulation story to make one other observation. First, it requires a true confession: *I was stung by being called a wimp*. Yes, I thought the remark was deeply inane, and it infuriated me. But even so, I was also stung. Let me hasten to add, this was not because my identity is very wrapped up with not being wimpish—it actually is not a term that normally figures very heavily in my self-image one way or the other. But it was impossible to be in that room, hear his comment and the snickering laughter with which it was met, and not to feel stung, and humiliated.

Why? There I was, a woman and a feminist, not only contemptuous of the mentality that measures human beings by their degree of so-called wimpishness, but also someone for whom the term *wimp* does not have a deeply resonant personal meaning. How could it have affected me so much?

The answer lies in the role of the context within which I was experiencing myself—the discursive framework. For in that room I was not "simply me," but I was a participant in a discourse, a shared set of words, concepts, symbols that constituted not only the linguistic possibilities available to us but also constituted *me* in that situation. This is not entirely true, of course. How I experienced myself was at least partly shaped by other experiences and other discursive frameworks—certainly those of feminist politics and antimilitarist politics; in fact, I would say my reactions were predominantly shaped by those frameworks. But that is quite different from saying "I am a feminist, and that individual, psychological self simply moves encapsulated through the world being itself"—and therefore assuming that I am unaffected. No matter who else I was at that moment, I was unavoidably a participant in a discourse in which being a wimp has a meaning, and a deeply pejorative one at that. By calling me a wimp, my accuser on the Blue Team *positioned* me in that discourse, and I could not but feel the sting.

In other words, I am suggesting that national security discourse can be seen as having different positions within it—ones that are starkly gender coded; indeed, the enormous strength of their evocative power comes from gender.[17] Thus, when you participate in conversation in that community, you do not simply choose what to say and how to say it; you advertently or inadvertently choose a position in the discourse. As a woman, I can choose the "masculine" (tough, rational, logical) position. If I do, I am seen as legitimate, but I limit what I can say. Or, I can say things that place me in the "feminine" position—in which case no one will listen to me.

Understanding national security discourse's gendered positions may cast some light on a frequently debated issue. Many people notice that the worlds of war making and national security have been created by and are still "manned" by men, and ask whether it might not make a big difference if more women played a role. Unfortunately, my first answer is "not much," at least if we are talking about relatively small numbers of women entering the world of defense experts and national security elites as it is presently constituted. Quite apart from whether you believe that women are (biologically or culturally) less aggressive than men, every person who enters this world is also participating in a gendered discourse in which she or he must adopt the masculine position in order to be successful. This means that it is extremely difficult for anyone, female *or male*, to express concerns or ideas marked as "feminine" and still maintain his or her legitimacy.

Another difficulty in realizing the potential benefits of recruiting more women in the profession: the assumption that they would make a difference is to some degree predicated on the idea that "the feminine" is absent from the discourse, and that adding it would lead to more balanced thinking. However, the problem is not that the "female" position is totally absent from the discourse; parts of it, at least, albeit in a degraded and undeveloped form, are already present, named, delegitimated, and silenced, all in one fell swoop. The inclusion and delegitimation of ideas marked as "feminine" acts as a more powerful censor than the total absence of "feminine" ideas would be.

So it is not simply the presence of women that would make a difference. Instead, it is the commitment and ability to develop, explore, rethink, and revalue those ways of thinking that get silenced and devalued that would make a difference. For that to happen, men, too, would have to be central participants.

But here, the power of gender codes' policing function in the thought process is again painfully obvious. The gender coding not only marks what is out of bounds in the discourse and offers a handy set of epithets to use to enforce those rules. It also links that "subjugated knowledge" to the deepest sense of self-identity. Thus, as was evident with the physicist who felt like a woman, when men in the profession articulate those ideas, it not only makes them mavericks or intellectually "off base"; it challenges their own gender identity. To the degree that a woman does not have the same kind of gender identity issue at stake, she may have stronger sources of resistance to the masculinity defamation that is used to police the thoughts and actions of those in the defense community. She does not have the power to change the fact that her actions will be interpreted and evaluated according to those gender codes, however. And in the defense community, the only thing worse than a man acting like a woman is a woman acting like a woman.

Finally, I would like to briefly explore a phenomenon I call the "unitary masculine actor problem" in national security discourse. During the Persian Gulf War, many feminists probably noticed that both the military briefers and George Bush himself frequently used the singular masculine pronoun "he" when referring to Iraq and Iraq's army. Someone not listening carefully could simply assume that "he" referred to Saddam Hussein. Sometimes it did; much of the time it simply reflected the defense community's characteristic habit of calling opponents "he" or "the other guy."[18] A battalion commander, for example, was quoted as saying "Saddam knows where we are and we know where he is. We will move a lot now to keep him off guard."[19] In these sentences, "he" and "him" appear to refer to Saddam Hussein. But, of course, the American forces had *no idea* where Saddam Hussein himself was; the singular masculine pronouns are actually being used to refer to the Iraqi military.

This linguistic move, frequently heard in discussions within the security affairs and defense communities, turns a complex state and set of forces into a singular male opponent. In fact, discussions that purport to be serious explorations of the strategy and tactics of war can have a tone which sounds more like the story of a sporting match, a fistfight, or a personal vendetta.

> I would want to suck him out into the desert as far as I could, and then pound him to death.[20]

> Once we had taken out his eyes, we did what could be best described as the "Hail Mary play" in football.[21]

> [I]f the adversary decides to embark on a very high roll, because he's frightened that something even worse is in the works, does grabbing him by the scruff of the neck and slapping him up the side of the head, does that make him behave better or is it plausible that it makes him behave even worse?[22]

Most defense intellectuals would claim that using "he" is just a convenient shorthand, without significant import or effects. I believe, however, that the effects of this usage are many and the implications far-reaching. Here I will sketch just a few, starting first with the usage throughout defense discourse generally, and then coming back to the Gulf War in particular.

The use of "he" distorts the analyst's understanding of the opposing state and the conflict in which they are engaged. When the analyst refers to the opposing state as "he" or "the other guy," the image evoked is that of a person, a unitary actor; yet states are not people. Nor are they unitary and unified. They comprise complex, multifaceted governmental and military apparatuses, each with opposing forces within it, each, in turn, with its own internal institutional dynamics, its own varied needs in relation to domestic politics, and so on. In other words, if the state is referred to and pictured as a unitary actor, what becomes unavailable to the analyst and policy-maker is a series of much more complex truths that might enable him to imagine many more policy options, many more ways to interact with that state.

If one kind of distortion of the state results from the image of the state as a person, a unitary actor, another can be seen to stem from the image of the state as a specifically *male* actor.[23] Although states are almost uniformly run by men, states are not men; they are complex social institutions, and they act and react as such. Yet, when "he" and "the other guy" are used to refer to states, the words do not simply function as shorthand codes; instead, they have their own entailments, including assumptions about how men act, which just might be different from how states act, but which invisibly become assumed to be isomorphic with how states act.[24]

It also entails emotional responses on the part of the speaker. The reference to the opposing state as "he" evokes male competitive identity issues, as in, "I'm not going to let him push me around," or, "I'm not going to let him get the best of me." While these responses may or may not be adaptive for a barroom brawl, it is probably safe to say that they are less functional when trying to determine the best way for one state to respond to another state. Defense analysts and foreign policy experts can usually agree upon the supreme desirability of dispassionate, logical analysis and its ensuing rationally calculated action. Yet the emotions evoked by the portrayal of global conflict in the personalized terms of male competition must, at the very least, exert a strong pull in exactly the opposite direction.

A third problem is that even while the use of "he" acts to personalize the conflict, it simultaneously abstracts both the opponent and the war itself. That is, the use of "he" functions in very much the same way that discussions about "Red" and "Blue" do. It facilitates treating war within a kind of game-playing model, A against B, Red against Blue, he against me. For even while "he" is evocative of male identity issues, it is also just an abstract piece to moved around on a game board, or, more appropriately, a computer screen.

That tension between personalization and abstraction was striking in Gulf War discourse. In the Gulf War, not only was "he" frequently used to refer to the Iraqi military, but so was "Saddam," as in "Saddam really took a pounding today," or "Our goal remains the same: to liberate Kuwait by forcing Saddam Hussein out."[25] The personalization is obvious: in this locution, the U.S. armed forces are not destroying a nation, killing people; instead, they (or George) are giving Saddam a good pounding, or bodily removing him from where he does not belong. Our emotional response is to get fired up about a bully getting his comeuppance.

Yet this personalization, this conflation of Iraq and Iraqi forces with Saddam himself, also abstracts: it functions to substitute in the mind's eye the abstraction of an implacably, impeccably evil enemy for the particular human beings, the men, women, and children being pounded, burned, torn, and eviscerated. A cartoon image of Saddam being ejected from Kuwait preempts the image of the blackened, charred, decomposing bodies of nineteen-year-old boys tossed in ditches by the side of the road, and the other concrete images of the acts of violence that constitute "forcing Hussein [sic] out of Kuwait."[26] Paradoxical as it may seem, in personalizing the Iraqi army as Saddam, the individual human beings in Iraq were abstracted out of existence.[27]

In summary, I have been exploring the way in which defense intellectuals talk to each other—the comments they make to each other, the particular usages that appear in their informal conversations or their lectures. In addition, I have occasionally left the professional community to draw upon public talk about the Gulf War. My analysis does *not* lead me to conclude that "national security thinking is masculine"—that is, a separate, and different, discussion.[28] Instead, I have tried to show that national security discourse is gendered, and that it matters. Gender discourse is interwoven through national security discourse. It sets fixed boundaries, and in so doing, it skews what is discussed and how it is thought about. It shapes expectations of other nations' actions, and in so doing it affects both our interpretations of international events and conceptions of how the United States should respond.

In a world where professionals pride themselves on their ability to engage in cool, rational, objective calculation while others around them are letting their thinking be sullied by emotion, the unacknowledged interweaving of gender discourse in security discourse allows men to not acknowledge that their pristine rational thought is in fact riddled with emotional response. In an "objective" "universal" discourse that valorizes the "masculine" and deauthorizes the "feminine," it is only the "feminine" emotions that are noticed and labeled as emotions, and thus in need of banning from the analytic process. "Masculine" emotions—such as feelings of aggression, competition, macho pride and swagger, or the sense of identity resting on carefully defended borders—are not so easily noticed and identified as emotions, and are instead invisibly folded into "self-evident," so-called realist paradigms and analyses. It is both the interweaving of gender discourse in national security thinking *and* the blindness to its presence and impact that have deleterious effects. Finally, the impact is to distort, degrade, and deter roundly rational, fully complex thought within the community of defense intellectuals and national security elites and, by extension, to cripple democratic deliberation about crucial matters of war and peace.

NOTES

I am grateful to the John D. and Catherine T. MacArthur Foundation and the Ploughshares Fund for their generous support of my research, and for making the writing of this chapter possible. I wish to thank Sara Ruddick, Elaine Scarry, Sandra Harding, and Barry O'Neill for their careful readings; I regret only that I was not able to more fully incorporate their criticisms and suggestions. Grateful appreciation is due to several thoughtful informants within the defense intellectual community. This chapter was written while I was a fellow at the Bunting Institute, and I wish to thank my sister-fellows for their feedback and support.

1. A "counterforce attack" refers to an attack in which the targets are the opponent's weapons systems, command and control centers, and military leadership. It is in contrast to what is known as a "countervalue attack," which is the abstractly benign term for *targeting* and incinerating cities—what the United States did to Hiroshima, except that the bombs used today would be several hundred times more powerful. It is also known in the business, a bit more colorfully, as an "all-out city-busting exchange." Despite this careful targeting distinction,

one need not be too astute to notice that many of the ports, airports, and command posts destroyed in a counter*force* attack are, in fact, in cities or metropolitan areas, which would be destroyed along with the "real targets," the weapons systems. But this does not appear to make the distinction any less meaningful to war planners, although it is, in all likelihood, less than meaningful to the victims.

2. The term is Helen Caldicott's, from her book *Missile Envy: The Arms Race and Nuclear War* (New York: William Morrow, 1984).

3. I have addressed some of these other factors in: "Sex and Death in the Rational World of Defense Intellectuals," *Signs: Journal of Women in Culture and Society* 12, no. 4 (Summer 1987): 687–718; "Emasculating America's Linguistic Deterrent," in *Rocking the Ship of State: Towards a Feminist Peace Politics*, ed. Adrienne Harris and Ynestra King (Boulder, Colo.: Westview Press, 1989); and *Deconstructing National Security Discourse and Reconstructing Security* (working title, book manuscript).

4. Some of the material I analyze in this paper comes from the public utterances of civilan defense intellectuals and military leaders. But overtly gendered war discourse appears even more frequently in informal settings, such as conversations defense intellectuals have among themselves, rather than in their formal written papers. Hence, much of my data comes from participant observation, and from interviews in which men have been willing to share with me interactions and responses that are usually not part of the public record. Most often, they shared this information on the condition that it not be attributed, and I have respected their requests. I also feel strongly that "naming names" would be misleading to the extent that it would tend to encourage the reader to locate the problem within individual men and their particular psyches; in this paper I am arguing that it is crucial to see this as a cultural phenomenon, rather than a psychological one.

5. For a revealing exploration of the ways in which gender shapes international politics more generally, see Cynthia Enloe, *Bananas, Beaches and Bases: Making Feminist Sense of International Politics* (Berkeley: University of California Press, 1989).

6. See Cynthia Enloe, *Does Khaki Become You? The Militarization of Women's Lives* (London and Winchester, Mass.: Pandora Press, 1988); and Jean Elshtain, "Reflections on War and Political Discourse: Realism, Just War and Feminism in a Nuclear Age," *Political Theory* 3, no. 1 (February 1985): 39–57.

7. While both the military and the news media presented the picture of a "surgically clean" war in which only military targets were destroyed, the reality was significantly bloodier; it involved the mass slaughter of Iraqi soldiers, as well as the death and suffering of large numbers of noncombatant men, women, and children. Although it is not possible to know the numbers of casualties with certainty, one analyst in the Census Bureau, Beth Osborne Daponte, has estimated that 40,000 Iraqi soldiers and 13,000 civilians were killed in direct military conflict, that 30,000 civilians died during Shiite and Kurdish rebellions, and that 70,000 civilians have died from health problems caused by the destruction of water and power plants (Edmund L Andrews, "Census Bureau to Dismiss Analyst Who Estimated Iraqi Casualties," *New York Times*, March 7, 1992, A7). Other estimates are significantly higher. Greenpeace estimates that as many as 243,000 Iraqi civilians died due to war-related causes (Ray Wilkinson, "Back from the

Living Dead," *Newsweek*, January 20, 1992, 28). Another estimate places Iraqi troop casualties at 70,000 and estimates that over 100,000 children have died from the delayed effects of the war (Peter Rothenberg, "The Invisible Dead," *Lies of Our Times* [March 1992]: 7). For recent, detailed reports on civilian casualties, see *Health and Welfare in Iraq after the Gulf Crisis* (International Study Team/ Commission on Civilian Casualties, Human Rights Program, Harvard Law School, October 1991), and *Needless Deaths in the Gulf War* (Middle East Watch, 1992). For a useful corrective to the myth of the Gulf War as a war of surgical strikes and precision-guided weaponry, see Paul F. Walker and Eric Stambler, "The Surgical Myth of the Gulf War," *Boston Globe*, April 16, 1991; and ". . .And the Dirty Little Weapons," *Bulletin of the Atomic Scientists* (May 1991): 21–24.

8. The RAND Corporation is a think tank that is a U.S. Air Force subcontractor. In the 1950s many of the most important nuclear strategists did their work under RAND auspices, including Bernard Brodie, Albert Wohlstetter, Herman Kahn, and Thomas Schelling.

9. In the context of the nuclear arms race and the cold war, even though a defense analyst might acknowledge that some American weapon systems served no useful strategic function (such as the Titan missiles during the 1980s), there was still consensus that they should not be unilaterally cut. Such a cut was seen to be bad because it was throwing away a potential bargaining chip in future arms control negotiations, or because making unilateral cuts was viewed as a sign of weakness and lack of resolve. It is only outside that context of hostile superpower competition, and, in fact, after the dissolution of the Soviet threat, that President Bush has responded to Gorbachev's unilateral cuts with some (minor) American unilateral cuts. For a description and critical assessment of the arguments against unilateral cuts, see William Rose, *US Unilateral Arms Control Initiatives: When Do They Work?* (New York: Greenwood Press, 1988). For an analysis of the logic and utility of bargaining chips, see Robert J. Bresler and Robert C. Gray, "The Bargaining Chip and SALT," *Political Science Quarterly* 92, no. 1 (Spring 1977): 65–88.

10. For a discussion of how words and phrases can stop the thought process, see George Orwell, "Politics and the English Language," in *A Collection of Essays* (Garden City, N.Y.: Doubleday, 1954): 162–76.

11. Cohn, unattributed interview, Cambridge, Mass., July 15, 1991.

12. Ibid.

13. Ibid., July 20, 1991.

14. The Bush White House tried out a succession of revolving justifications in an attempt to find one that would garner popular support for U.S. military action, including: we must respond to the rape of Kuwait; we must not let Iraqi aggression be rewarded; we must defend Saudi Arabia; we cannot stand by while "vital U.S. interests" are threatened; we must establish a "new world order"; we must keep down the price of oil at U.S. gas pumps; we must protect American jobs; and finally, the winner, the only one that elicited any real support from the American public, we must destroy Iraq's incipient nuclear weapons capability. What was perhaps most surprising about this was the extent to which it was publicly discussed and accepted as George Bush's need to find a message that "worked"

rather than to actually have a genuine, meaningful explanation. For an account of Bush's decision making about the Gulf War, see Bob Woodward, *The Commanders* (New York: Simon and Schuster, 1991).

15. Cohn, unattributed interview, Cambridge, Mass., July 20, 1991.

16. Within the context of our society's dominant gender discourse, this equation of masculinity and strength with the willingness to use armed force seems quite "natural" and not particularly noteworthy. Hannah Arendt is one political thinker who makes the arbitrariness of that connection visible: she reframes our thinking about "strength," and finds strength in *refraining* from using one's armed forces (Hannah Arendt, *On Violence* [New York: Harcourt, Brace, Jovanovich, 1969]).

17. My thinking about the importance of positions in discourses is indebted to Wendy Hollway, "Gender Difference and the Production of Subjectivity," in *Changing the Subject*, ed. J. Henriques, W. Holloway, C. Urwin, C. Venn, and V. Walkerdine (London and New York: Methuen, 1984): 227–63.

18. For a revealing exploration of the convention in strategic, military, and political writings of redescribing armies as a single "embodied combatant," see Elaine Scarry, *The Body in Pain: The Making and Unmaking of the World* (New York: Oxford University Press, 1984): 70–72.

19. Chris Hedges, "War Is Vivid in the Gun Sights of the Sniper," *New York Times*, February 3, 1991, A1.

20. General Norman Schwarzkopf, National Public Radio broadcast, February 8, 1991.

21. General Norman Schwarzkopf, CENTCOM News Briefing, Riyadh, Saudi Arabia, February 27, 1991, p. 2.

22. Transcript of a strategic studies specialist's lecture on NATO and the Warsaw Pact (summer institute on Regional Conflict and Global Security: The Nuclear Dimension, Madison, Wisconsin, June 29, 1987).

23. Several analysts of international relations have commented upon the way in which "the state is a person" in international relations theory and in war discourse. For example, Paul Chilton and George Lakoff, distinguished linguists who study war, offer very useful explorations of the impact of the state-as-a-person metaphor on the way in which we understand the Persian Gulf War. Yet neither of them find it noteworthy that the state is not simply any person, but a *male* person. See Paul Chilton, "Getting the Message Through: Metaphor and Legitimation of the Gulf War" (unpublished paper, 1991); George Lakoff, "The Metaphor System Used to Justify War in the Gulf" (unpublished paper, 1991).

24. For a lucid and compelling discussion of why it is an error to assume an isomorphism between the behavior and motivations of individuals and the behavior and motivations of states, see Marshall Sahlins, *The Use and Abuse of Biology* (Ann Arbor: University of Michigan Press, 1977), pp. ix–xv and 3–16.

25. Defense Secretary Dick Cheney, "Excerpts from Briefing at Pentagon by Cheney and Powell," *New York Times*, January 24, 1991, A 11.

26. Scarry explains that when an army is described as a single "embodied combatant," injury, (as in Saddam's "pounding"), may be referred to but is "no longer recognizable or interpretable." It is not only that Americans might be happy to imagine Saddam being pounded; we also on some level know that it is

not really happening, and thus need not feel the pain of the wounded. We "respond to the injury . . . as an imaginary wound in an imaginary body, despite the fact that that imaginary body is itself made up of thousands of real human bodies" (Scarry, *Body in Pain*, p. 72).

27. For a further exploration of the disappearance of human bodies from Gulf War discourse, see Hugh Gusterson, "Nuclear War, the Gulf War, and the Disappearing Body" (unpublished paper, 1991). I have addressed other aspects of Gulf War discourse in "The Language of the Gulf War," *Center Review* 5, no. 2 (Fall 1991); "Decoding Military Newspeak," *Ms.*, March/April 1991, p. 81; and "Language, Gender, and the Gulf War" (unpublished paper prepared for Harvard University Center for Literary and Cultural Studies, April 10, 1991).

28. For a fascinating treatment of that issue, see Sara Ruddick in this volume.

PART V

THE POLITICS OF REPRESENTATION

Chapter 11

SEXUAL FANTASIES AND WAR MEMORIES:

CLAUDE SIMON'S NARRATOLOGY

Lynn A. Higgins

K ISS YOUR MOMMA GOOD-BYE" orders a United States Army
recruitment advertisement. Leave the soft life behind, join the
Army and become a real man. To replace the feminine comforts
of home, recruits are offered initiation into brotherhood: "these are your
buddies." War has traditionally been considered the quintessential proving ground for masculinity. The recruitment ad invokes the dominant
Western cultural understanding of masculinity defined as a flight from the
feminine.[1] The ad's imperative further implies that military behavior and
discourses do not *confirm* as much as they actually *construct* "masculinity."

In the literary domain, concepts of military masculinity are engaged,
often embodied, in war narratives. Now, the women left behind come
back into the picture. Whenever it is time to tell stories, women provide
someone to talk *about* (to other men, to pass the time in the trenches,
or in prisoner-of-war camps); and someone to tell stories *to* after the war
is over, when the returned soldier tries to make discursive sense of his
experiences.

These are the contexts in which Claude Simon's protagonists try (and
fail) to come to terms with their memories of war. It is not surprising that
many of Simon's seventeen volumes (in a writing career that began in
1946 and continues today) have circled around war memories,[2] since
Simon himself fought in two wars: at the age of twenty-three, he joined up
to fight on the Republican side of the Spanish Civil War. Then, as a cavalry officer in 1940, he witnessed the disastrous and surreal defeat of the
French army by the Germans. In addition, Simon's father, also a cavalry
officer, was killed at the beginning of World War I, and a family ancestor,
whose portrait hangs in Simon's home and whose avatars reappear (cum
portrait) in several of his novels, was a nobleman who betrayed his class
to participate in the Convention, voted to execute the king, and then became a general in Napoleon's army.

All of Simon's novels are richly woven with competing threads of fiction and autobiography, memory and invention, the desire to record the past and a conviction that history is no more than an entropic accumulation of meaningless events. Refusing even to recuperate meaning as tragedy, Simon's deeply pessimistic vision is embodied in an ironic prose, heavy with sensory imagery, that has often been described as unreadable because of its avoidance of either syntactic or logical causality. Paragraphs can run to thirty pages, sentences, including multiple parentheses, to five pages or more; characters overlap, blend, and refuse to be distinct; repetitive plots ensnare the reader into a hallucinatory web.

Accordingly, the novels have most often been read in the light of their radically disrupted narrative form, with primary focus on the backward quest for memory and understanding as it is frustrated by the forward movement of time and by the power of language to create its own reality.[3] Simon himself cites Faulkner, Joyce, and Proust as his precursors. Associated with the New Novel and French experimental writing of the 1950s and 1960s, Simon adopts the oft-repeated credo, coined by fellow novelist Jean Ricardou, that writing is not the story of an adventure but rather the adventure of a story. But Simon's value as a writer cannot, any more than that of other New Novelists, be accounted for as simply the sum of its language games. What has been largely overlooked by critics—and by Simon himself in his rare theoretical statements[4]—is the difficulty of taking into account both the novels' linguistic play and their status as historical fiction.

The Flanders Road (1960),[5] probably Simon's masterpiece, consists of a narrator's long (mostly interior) monologue in which he tries to bring order into his memories but manages only to achieve confusion, despair, longing, and befuddledness. The novel is probably the best exemplar of the qualities mentioned in Simon's 1985 Nobel Prize citation, where the Swedish academy described Simon's humanism as well as his despair and praised the ways in which the grimness of his writing is counterbalanced by elements of "tenderness and loyalty, of devotion to work and duty, to heritage and traditions and solidarity with dead and living kinsmen."[6]

Georges, the narrator of *The Flanders Road*, is not typical of what Klaus Theweleit calls a "soldier male" or a member of what Barbara Ehrenreich calls a "warrior elite," glorifying war as a means to masculine self-affirmation.[7] Rather, he is a disillusioned and broken veteran of the Second World War who has lost most of his war comrades (including his friend Blum and his cousin and commanding officer, de Reixach), who is losing his faith in the coherence of history and the power of language, and who has renounced a career as an intellectual to bury himself in farming. Nevertheless, his representation of women and of "Woman" (especially as seen in the case of one particular woman, Corinne) falls within the notions of masculinity suggested by the army recruitment poster I described above.

This essay will examine the importance of Corinne in the ruminations of Georges. Corinne plays two roles in Georges's narration. First, to pass the time of their captivity in a German prisoner-of-war camp after the fall of France in 1940, Georges and his buddies, Blum and Iglésia, fantasize her together and recount her real or imagined sexual adventures. Then, six years after the war's end, Georges spends a night of lovemaking and reminiscing with Corinne herself. Lying beside her, Georges relates (or thinks about) his experiences with death and destruction. His postwar quest is both erotic and epistemological: he wanted to find this woman around whom his wartime fantasies revolved; he also wants to solve the enigma of her husband's death. Georges's anguished desire to know the truth about the past circles around the question of whether de Reixach succumbed to a German machine gun as a sort of suicide, an honorable way out for a man faced with his wife's infidelities.

By shifting our attention from Georges to "the woman lying invisible beside him" (77) throughout his entire retrospective narration, and by listening to the few words Corinne does speak, it will be possible to ask what might unite Georges's twin quests to "know" in the two senses of the word. Why does he seek Corinne in the first place?—surely not for what she might be able to tell him, since his own monologue fills virtually the entire novel. Why is his epistemological quest embedded, so to speak, in an erotic one, and a military debacle framed within an amorous one?

Ultimately, though, I want to ask about the gendered nature of representation: What is the role of Woman in the construction of Georges's discourse both during and after the war? My argument will be that Corinne is important to Georges's war narrative not because of the lovers she might or might not have had, or because of what Georges does with or to her, or even why. What is crucial for our understanding of Corinne's role in the novel is what Georges says about her, in other words, how (and why) he represents her. Framed in these terms, Corinne can be read as a *mise-en-abyme* or privileged locus of Georges's signifying practices, a reading capable of taking into account the role of gender in war narrative.

My starting point is Corinne's angry departure near the end of the novel. Having spent the night listening to his memories, she accuses Georges of using her as a pornographic fantasy: "All I am for you is a soldiers' girl something like the kind you see drawn with chalk or a nail in the crumbling plaster of barrack walls" (204). He protests that he loves her, but she leaves him alone in the hotel room where, for a short while, he continues his musings unperturbed.

With her angry exit, Corinne places herself in a tradition of heroines who close the door on the men who represent them without their consent, a tradition that includes Ibsen's Nora and especially Freud's Dora. In his case study on Dora, Freud laments that hysteria produces symptoms not only in the patient's body but also in the narration—that whatever has been repressed can be detected in the patient's inability to tell coherent stories.[8] Leaving aside the question of whether Dora's or anyone else's narrative incoherence is an illness to be cured, we can observe that Freud's own story is anything but straightforward: it leaves gaps, digresses, circles back, and remains inconclusive. And if we read Dora as a case of Freud's own hysteria, as his desperate attempt to explain Dora in spite of her, the Freud-Dora couple begins to look a lot like Georges and Corinne: Georges (Freud) tells a story that depends on and originates in Corinne (Dora), but the pursuit of the story and the needs of the storyteller require the departure of the woman and the repression of her own voice.[9] Both Corinne and Dora leave the "analysis" incomplete and the male interlocutor unsatisfied. Pursuing this analogy, we might wonder whether Georges's story is incoherent because, while obsessed with Corinne, he has in fact silenced her throughout and finally expelled her from the novel. At least this far, his discourse constructs itself through suppression of the feminine.

Nevertheless, when Georges imagines Corinne and when he recounts his tale of war and survival, Woman is paradoxically both the stimulus and the object of his semiotic production, both the precondition and the goal of his quest. Georges's desire for Corinne is the foundation on which not only she, but also history itself are represented: the French national debacle of 1940 is brought by Georges into parallel with the Napoleonic wars, both stories plotted according to Georges's imaginings of Corinne's infidelities. Teresa de Lauretis's analysis of the role of women in the "Invisible Cities," a story by Italo Calvino, is thus equally applicable to Simon's novel: Corinne is "both the source of the drive to represent and its ultimate, unattainable goal"; Georges's narration is "a text which tells the story of male desire by performing the absence of woman and by producing woman as text, as pure representation." And the novel itself, with the history it produces, is "an imaginary signifier, a practice of language, a continuous movement of representations built from a dream of woman."[10] Simon's historiography, like Calvino's city, is shaped by masculine desire.

.   .   .   .   .

Jean Ricardou has enumerated the many levels at which Simon's novel represents war as disintegration.[11] Surprisingly, Ricardou does not ask about the function for the characters of their own semiotic production. I want to characterize the soldiers, fantasizing about Corinne, as so many Scheherazades. Like the heroine of the *Arabian Nights* , Georges, Iglésia, and Blum speak in order to re-create what has been destroyed and to postpone, outwit, or escape death. They speak in order to conjure away "the sickening stink of war" (13).

Georges represents himself and his buddies as victims. War shatters individual identity, rendering men indistinguishable from each other, from animals, from objects, from corpses. The novel teems with hybrids: de Reixach is a "man-horse," Iglésia has a nose like a lobster, a peasant is described as a goat. Piled upon each other in a cattle wagon, prisoners on their way to concentration camps crawl like reptiles. In the wagon, humans are no more than moving blotches, a sort of "blackish, viscous matter, noisy and moist from which emanated . . . voices" (56). In the mass of bodies, others' limbs cannot be distinguished from "one of your own, or at least something that you knew to be one of your limbs" (59). Georges experiences his own leg "as something inert, something that no longer really was a part of himself. . . . A series of bones strangely hooked together and connected to each other, a series of old clattering and grinding utensils, that's what a skeleton was, he thought" (56). In prison the men are so many "caged animals" (91), contemplating "their condition of victims, rubbish, debris" (128), overwhelmed by "a feeling of permanent disgust, of permanent impotence and permanent decomposition" (160). The known world "was actually falling apart collapsing breaking up into pieces dissolving into water into nothing" (16). These and literally hundreds of other examples of disintegration and blending evoke the terror of the uncanny,[12] as they transgress the boundaries between categories usually reassuringly distinct: self and other, men and animals, living and inanimate matter. War assimilates everything to the same color (the color of earth) and a single texture: a disgusting viscosity.

Put otherwise, war means a terrifying breakdown of *difference* accompanied by an erosion of the soldiers' human agency and subjectivity. Semiosis being a distinctly human activity, Georges, Blum, and Iglésia produce stories in order to reinstate their status as distinct from animals and objects (including corpses), in short, to survive as speaking human subjects.

In addition, their stories—and particularly their discourse about women—serve as a ritual of male solidarity. Georges produces his stories in collaborative authorship with Blum and Iglésia. The relationship between the men is a homosocial one, mediated by language and by the necessary absence and silence of the woman they share in imagination.[13] As the phrases (*membres* , in French) of the novel's sentences, interwoven and accumulating like the soldiers' limbs ("*membres* "), figure the loss of difference, so the slip from first- to third-person narration—with the dialogues spoken by "Georges (or Blum)" to "Blum (or Georges)"—is em-

blematic of this male bond.[14] But again it must be stressed that the fantasies these men generate are not those of typical "soldier males": their
desires do not feature brutality to women or the urge to kill or scapegoat
or even to protect them. Theirs are simply sexual stories . . .

Nevertheless, if, after the fashion of Scheherazade, the captured soldiers reestablish their own status as subjects by telling stories, the topic of
those stories is not arbitrary; and if their discourse functions to re-create
difference, they start with sexual difference (and hierarchy). Georges and
the boys thus also play the role of the Sultan, who conjures up a new
woman every night to supply him with pleasure and stories and then dis-
poses of her in the morning. In the process, the fantasmatic construction
of Woman ("not a woman but the very idea, the symbol of all women,"
34) functions to reinscribe masculinity and the masculine subject.

Moreover, Georges's fantasies about Woman produce a discourse
that is specifically pornographic. It is pornographic in the literal sense
(etymologically: description of harlots) in that Corinne is repeatedly described as a whore. More importantly for our purposes, it is pornographic not (only) in *what* it depicts but in *how* it sees, in *how* it represents—in what we can call, after Susanne Kappeler, its pornographic
structure of representation. According to Kappeler, pornography has as
its primary goal not sexual titillation specifically, but rather the more
general "feeling of life, the pleasure of the subject." Kappeler echoes de
Lauretis when she argues that this enhancement (construction, in fact) of
subjectivity is part of a broader male privilege of assuming the subject
position in patriarchal culture: "as the authors of culture, men assume the
voice, compose the picture, write the story, for themselves and other men,
and *about* women." Thus, in pornography, the woman is objectified in
two ways: "as the object of the action in the scenario, and . . . as object of
the representation," with the second of these being the more essential to
the construction of masculine subjectivity.[15] In these terms, what is significant is not whether Georges hurts Corinne (he does, twice), whether
or not he makes love with her (he does), whether or not he even touches
her. It is the nature of his fantasy alone—that is to say, his representations
of her—that suffices both to define his discourse as pornographic and to
serve his purpose of resuscitating that feeling of life, of pleasure, of subjectivity.

Corinne knows that Georges is attempting to marshal his own subjectivity at the expense of hers. She recognizes explicitly that the discourse
about her consists of pornographic "soldiers' jokes" (204), and that she
is not even present as a subject. Twice she castigates him for reducing her
to the kind of image that men scratch on the walls of cafés or pin up in
barracks. In both instances she emphasizes that "in those drawings you
see there they never show the faces it usually stops at the neck" (74, see

also 204). Being without a face means being unable to *see* (Georges insists that she not turn on the light and is uneasy that she seems able to see in the dark) and unable to *speak*. Georges has arrogated both of these powers to himself.

Further, Georges's discourse transforms Corinne in precisely the ways the soldiers themselves had been dehumanized: his fantasies figure her as an animal, as an object, as a corpse. First, her association and identification with animals (mostly horses) and descriptions of her as a hybrid creature seem to highlight her sexuality and the difficulty of taming her. An intricately written horse-race scene featuring de Reixach's competition with his jockey, Iglésia, over their prowess as lovers and horsemen is built by identifying Corinne with a racehorse. Horse and woman finally merge into one "woman-chestnut, the blond female" (137) to be mastered together by a horseman and by means of the puns with which the ambiguity is achieved:

> he thought that he would kill, so to speak, two birds with one stone, and that if he managed to mount the one he could control the other, or vice versa, that is if he controlled the one he would also mount the other victoriously to where he had probably never managed to lead her, would make her lose the taste or the desire for another stake (am I expressing myself clearly?) or if you prefer of another stick, that is if he managed to use his own stick as well as that jockey who . . . (138)

and so on.

This example is the most salient one of Corinne's capacity to transcend categories and subvert binaries, a feature that already renders her somewhat disturbing. She has an "inhuman or nonhuman character" (107) that places her among

> beings . . . of a hybrid, ambiguous nature, not quite human, not quite object, inspiring both respect and irreverence by the combination, the compromise in them of disparate constitutive elements (real or supposed)—human and inhuman—, which was doubtless why he talked about her the way horse dealers talk about their animals or mountain climbers about mountains, his manner both coarse and deferential, crude and delicate; (106–7)

her toilette is not exactly indecent, it is "beyond indecency, that is, suppressing, making senseless any notion of decency or indecency" (111); the most uncanny thing about her, according to Iglésia, is that she seemed to him a mere child, until he noticed that "she was not only a woman but the most Woman of all the women he had ever seen, even in fantasy." This child-woman Iglésia finds to be "monstrous, embarassing," and "one of life's most "sacrilegious and disturbing parodies" (106).

Secondly, as an object, Corinne is often edible, nourishing, and maternal. She is a communion wafer; her feet are apricot colored, and her dress is the color of a cherry-red gumdrop. A peasant woman glimpsed by the light of a lantern is described as a "bowl of milk" (96) and a "milky apparition" (205), and in similar fashion, Corinne is repeatedly associated with milk: her neck and breasts are milky white, and the touch of Georges's lips on them brings "the milk of oblivion" (193). Not surprisingly, then, it is his mouth that remembers her: "she was something he thought about not with his mind but with his lips" (174). Making love with her is a return to "that matrix the original crucible" whence soldiers originally came (35). As a simultaneously erotic and maternal object, Corinne is also uncanny in the sense that Freud, using the same imagery as Simon, spoke of female genitals as an "*unheimlich* [uncanny] place," which is "the entrance to the former *heim* [home] of all human beings, to that place where everyone dwelt once upon a time and in the beginning."[16]

It is important to remember that these are descriptions of soldiers playing Scheherazade to escape the surrounding menace of death and destruction. Their maternal fantasies send them back to "mother in the midst of terror," as one war poet put it.[17] Woman, especially in her maternal/comestible incarnation, therefore, is the one to whom the soldiers return to tell their tale. Accordingly, their escape route often leads toward childhood, resurrected in fairy-tale or Proustian fashion: huddled freezing in the German camp, they blow on their hands in the cold,

> while trying to transfer themselves by proxy (that is, by means of their imagination . . . summoning up the iridescent and luminous images by means of the ephemeral, incantatory magic of language, words invented in the hope of making palatable—like those vaguely sugared pellets disguising a bitter medicine for children—the [unspeakable] reality). (137)

And again, "the voices shouting now, like the voices of two boastful children trying to keep their courage up" (97–98). In this context, Corinne is the milky and maternal fantasy invented by young soldiers "sevrés de femmes" (literally, "weaned of women").[18] Kiss your Momma Good-bye.

But thirdly and finally, Woman (especially Corinne herself, lying beside Georges now) is associated with the most uncanny of hybrid objects: a corpse. Like death, she causes men to liquefy. She is several times described in terms of a gash or scar, until finally the female genitals are described as an "eternal wound" (142). Lying with her reminds him of his brush with death as he lay in a grassy ditch; by means of an interweaving of heterogeneous descriptions, Corinne becomes the earth, the maternal but also mortal "matrix, the original crucible" to which dead men return. At one point, his imagination transforms her into a cadaver lying heavily on top of him. Through these articulations, she herself actually comes to represent death. The erotic seems to be a displaced image of death, now the repressed. Or, I would rather say, keeping in mind Hélène Cixous's remark that death and the female genitals are the two unrepresentable things,[19] that whereas in the trenches, fantasies of Corinne kept the soldiers from thinking about death, after the war is over that connection is reversed, and she becomes for Georges a displaced means of reflecting on the dead. In fact, this is why he seeks her out.

Because even when he is in bed with Corinne, his stories are told for and with other men, and the function of his narration is still that of male bonding. Corinne is still the token in an exchange between men. Once again, she is the foundation supporting his representations; like language, she is a mediator allowing him to resurrect his dead buddies and, with them, his memories of the confusing and anguishing microscopic events that make up History. Put otherwise, she *is* the language with which he speaks about (and even speaks *to*) his lost comrades. In seeking her out, Georges in fact acknowledges that his war discourse depends on her, that she is the prerequisite for his representation not only of her but of his war experiences and friends.

If the masculine subject is the sole possessor of desire, he is also the owner of language. That Georges is the shaper of discourse is most evident in his (Simon's) use of puns and wordplay to produce the multiple fantasmatic images of Woman as I have outlined them, and to forge links between war and the feminine. Women have no access to discourse, and can only complain about the way they are used by it. Corinne herself claims that Georges's narration erases her in favor of Blum, and he muses that "maybe she was right after all maybe she was telling the truth maybe I was still talking to him, exchanging with a little Jew dead years ago boasts gossip obscenities" (205).

So after the war, even with her body touching his, Georges continues to create Corinne in her absence. Her presence is not necessary, in fact, it is her absence that is required; he expels her *in order* to create her. It is his remembered fantasy of her that he wants to recapture, and with it, the context of male solidarity and masculine identity which that fantasy constructed. The two layers of storytelling collapse into one. *The Flanders Road* is a story about love between men, a symphony in two voices— Georges's and Blum's, one alive and one dead—stimulated into narration by the presence of a feminine imago. Corinne's departure disrupts the narration, but it is not her presence that is gone, it is her absence. And Georges is then not only unable to tell coherent stories (we expect this of modern texts); after a short while he is unable even to continue, and the novel ends.

I think it has to be said that while Georges's narrative does not glorify war or heroism, and while thematically it makes of war a disgusting, destructive, pointless, even boring erosion of everything human including language, at a deeper level *The Flanders Road* cannot be considered an antiwar novel. What it deplores thematically, it nonetheless repeats in its structures of representation: Georges's discourse about women reenacts the very same dehumanization that victimized *him* in wartime. The road *from* Flanders is the same as the road *to* Flanders, and only the characters have changed places.

NOTES

This essay is dedicated to my son Julian.

1. See for example, Dorothy Dinnerstein, *The Mermaid and the Minotaur: Sexual Arrangements and Human Malaise* (New York: Harper and Row, 1976); Barbara Ehrenreich, *The Hearts of Men: American Dreams and the Flight from Commitment* (Garden City, N.Y.: Anchor, 1984); Klaus Theweleit, *Male Fantasies*, vol. 1, *Women Floods Bodies History*, trans. Stephen Conway (Minneapolis: University of Minnesota Press, 1987), and vol. 2, *Male Bodies: Psychoanalyzing the White Terror*, trans. Erica Carter and Chris Turner (Minneapolis: University of Minnesota Press, 1989).

2. Particularly notable for their portrayal of war are: *L'herbe* (1958); *La route des Flandres* (1960); *Le palace* (1962); *Histoire* (1967); *La bataille de Pharsale* (1969); and *Les georgiques* (1981), all published in Paris by the Editions de Minuit.

3. See for example John Sturrock, *The French New Novel* (London: Oxford University Press, 1969), and Leon S. Roudiez, *French Fiction Today: A New Direction* (New Brunswick, N.J.: Rutgers University Press, 1972). More recent criticism has explored a wider range of critical approaches; see especially David Carroll, *The Subject in Question: The Languages of Theory and the Strategies of Fiction* (Chicago: University of Chicago Press, 1982). Only recently has the fantasmatic dimension of Simon's writing been opened to debate, but without addressing the problems of gender: see Celia Britton, *Claude Simon: Writing the Visible* (New York: Cambridge University Press, 1987), and a review of it by Lynn A. Higgins, *Studies in Twentieth Century Literature* 14, no. 1 (Summer 1990): 131–33. Winifred Woodhull has described the ways in which gender issues have been systematically avoided in Simon criticism: "Reading Claude Simon: Gender, Ideology, Representation," *L'Esprit Créateur* 27, no. 4: 5–16.

4. See the preface to *Orion aveugle* (Geneva: Skira, 1970) and *Discours de Stockholm* (Paris: Editions de Minuit, 1986). The latter is Simon's speech accepting the Nobel Prize for literature in 1985.

5. Claude Simon, *The Flanders Road*, trans. Richard Howard (London and New York: John Calder Riverrun Press, 1985). Originally published as *La route des Flandres* (Paris: Editions de Minuit, 1960). Quotations will be taken from the translated edition. Modifications in the translation, when necessary, appear in brackets.

6. "Claude Simon of France Wins the Nobel Prize in Literature," *New York Times*, October 18, 1985.

7. Theweleit, *Males Fantasies*, vols. 1 and 2, and Ehrenreich, "Iranscam: The Real Meaning of Oliver North," *Ms Magazine*, May 1987, 24–27.

8. Sigmund Freud, *Dora: An Analysis of a Case of Hysteria* (New York: Macmillan, 1963), p. 31. Even Corinne's name, a variant of Cora (or Kore, patroness of agriculture, to which Georges also returns) aligns her with Nora and Dora.

9. Freud mentions Dora's complete loss of voice without seeing what this might signify in terms of the power dynamics of their interaction (*Dora*, p. 37). For explorations of Dora from a feminist perspective, see the essays in Charles Bernheimer and Claire Kahane, eds., *In Dora's Case: Freud-Hysteria-Feminism* (New York: Columbia University Press, 1985).

10. Teresa de Lauretis, *Alice Doesn't: Feminism, Semiotics, Cinema* (Bloomington: Indiana University Press, 1984), pp. 13–14.

11. Jean Ricardou, "Un ordre dans la débâcle," in *Problèmes du nouveau roman* (Paris: Seuil, 1967), pp. 44–55.

12. For a discussion of the uncanny and how it informs the novel's representation of history, see Lynn A. Higgins, "Language, the Uncanny, and the Shapes of History in Claude Simon's *The Flanders Road*," *Studies in Twentieth Century Literature* 10, no. 1 (1985): 117–40.

13. For a discussion of male homosocial bonds in literature, see Eve Kosofsky Sedgwick, *Between Men: English Literature and Male Homosocial Desire* (New York: Columbia University Press, 1985).

14. In their introduction to *Behind the Lines: Gender and the Two World Wars* (New Haven: Yale University Press, 1987), p. 14, editors Margaret Randolph Higonnet, Jane Jenson, Sonya Michel, and Margaret Collins Weitz suggest that the device of multiple protagonists implies a theme of male community.

15. Susanne Kappeler, *The Pornography of Representation* (Minneapolis: University of Minnesota Press, 1986), pp. 52–61 and *passim*.

16. Freud, "The Uncanny," in *Collected Papers* (London: Hogarth Press, 1953), 4:399.

17. Richard Eberhart's "Brotherhood of Men," cited by Susan Gubar in " 'This Is My Rifle, This Is My Gun': World War II and the Blitz on Women," in Higonnet et al. *Behind the Lines*, p. 247.

18. Original French edition, pp. 234 and 304. The translation as "young men's lusting flesh" (174) and "deprived of women" (224) fails to capture the simultaneously maternal and erotic nature of their fantasy.

19. Hélène Cixous and Catherine Clément, *The Newly Born Woman*, trans. Betsy Wing (Minneapolis: University of Minnesota Press, 1986), p. 69; see also Cixous' "The Laugh of the Medusa," trans. Keith Cohen and Paula Cohen, *Signs* 1, no. 4 (1976): 885.

Chapter 12

DANGER ON THE HOME FRONT:

MOTHERHOOD, SEXUALITY, AND DISABLED

VETERANS IN AMERICAN POSTWAR FILMS

Sonya Michel

ONE OF THE IRONIES of the wars of the twentieth century is that as weaponry became more deadly and efficient, medical science and the ability of the military to manage and treat casualties also improved. As a result, a lower proportion of casualties proved fatal, while the numbers of permanently disabled veterans increased.[1] The sight of veterans with missing limbs, in wheelchairs or walking with the aid of canes, crutches, and prosthetics, became relatively commonplace in all of the belligerent nations. At least one, France, visibly singled out wounded veterans for special treatment, reserving certain seats on public transportation for *les mutilés de guerre* (and even granting them priority over pregnant women).

Injuries—scars—disabilities serve as permanent reminders of war. In Elaine Scarry's words, they "memorialize [the fact] that the war occurred and that the cessation of its occurrence was agreed to." Yet, she contends, injuries memorialize without specifying winner or loser, and as the war and especially its final outcome recede in time, wounds lose their power as political symbols, becoming almost banal.[2] I want to suggest that political meanings do not, in fact, disappear but shift from a specifically nationalist register to one of gender.[3] Injuries, scars, and disabilities, once easily readable emblems of patriotic sacrifice, become signs of masculinity that indirectly evoke service to country by referring to a mode of sacrifice ostensibly available (until the war in the Persian Gulf) only to men.

As signs of either patriotism or masculinity, war injuries are unstable, particularly when soldiers have suffered permanent disability. On the level of the individual, these handicaps can be read as signs of weakness or failure, implying feminization and emasculation.[4] On the national level, such handicaps threaten to expose the entire political system, for they point to its vulnerability, its inability to protect all of its citizens. Even on the winning side, disabilities can signify the nation's betrayal of its most loyal adherents. Insofar as political skepticism and opposition are linked with feminization, postwar "normalization" requires a restoration of the veteran's masculinity so that his signification of national triumph does not simultaneously constitute an affront to hegemonic political values.[5]

The veterans' physical and psychological rehabilitation is carried on in home and hospital, but the work of cultural translation and restoration occurs in many sites. In modern times, popular novels and films have figured importantly in the process. The drama of disabilities—their troubling persistence and resistance to normalization—makes the disabled veteran a common character in the texts of war,[6] so much so that postwar novels and films of recuperation have become distinctive subgenres. Many such novels emerged from post–World War I Britain, France, Germany, and the United States.[7] During the same period, the Europeans and, to a lesser extent, the Americans also produced a number of films, several based on novels;[8] in the United States, two of the best known were The Four Horsemen of the Apocalypse (1921), with Rudolf Valentino, and King Vidor's Big Parade (1927).[9] After World War II, American films of recuperation appeared even more regularly.[10]

America's post-1945 films emerged in—and reflected—an intellectual and cultural climate that made women's role in the recovery of disabled veterans especially problematic. "Experts" generally instructed American women to defer to the men returning from war. Using a discourse suffused with popularized Freudian notions, journalists, counselors, and psychologists advised women to be tolerant and understanding in order to make their men feel secure.[11] Women were not only to surrender their jobs, but also to subordinate their own dreams, ambitions, and desires to those of the veterans.

These instructions unquestioningly assumed that all men would have difficulty in adjusting to civilian life, whether or not they had seen action or were visibly wounded or psychologically distressed. At the same time, the advice betrayed a nagging fear that women would not—or perhaps could not—readily yield their newfound freedom and sense of identity.[12] The war had disrupted gender roles, especially for women, which would have to be reconstructed if postwar social order were to be established.

Nowhere was this more evident than in the realm of sexuality. Though the soldiers' sexual longing was a persistent theme in wartime popular culture, most blatantly in the ubiquitous pinups,[13] women were instructed to temper expressions of their own sexual needs and behave submissively, at least during the early stages of postwar reunions. One military psychiatrist, Herbert I. Kupper, advised women to "submerge [their own] feelings and drives" and "attempt to conform to [their men's wishes]."[14] As historian Susan Hartmann notes, this advice "reflected a recognition of female sexuality as well as a perception of the threat it held for men."[15]

Kupper also suggested that some returning veterans might require mothering, but this, too, was problematic.[16] American mothers were already under attack for overpowering their children. The "pathology of maternal overprotection" was first identified in 1939 by another psychiatrist, David Levy;[17] in its popular form, the disease became known as "Momism." As social commentator Philip Wylie described it in *A Generation of Vipers* (1942), Momism was an exaggeration of the maternal role that allowed women to dominate their children, especially their sons, rendering them dependent and effeminate.[18] Wylie's indictment of mothers gained renewed scientific legitimacy in 1946, when psychiatrist Edward Strecker published the results of a study of the army's psychiatric rejects. He claimed that in a majority of cases, overprotective mothers were responsible for their sons' immaturity.[19]

Altogether, the experts' "prescriptions for Penelope" (to use Hartmann's phrase) presented an ambiguous and contradictory message. In terms of sexuality, women were to be responsive, but not assertive. In terms of mothering, they were to be nurturing and accepting, but not domineering. And somehow they were to embody the qualities of both sexual partner and mother,[20] even though the combination was obviously fraught with social and psychological taboos. The wealth of articles, pamphlets, and books thus presented conflicting messages for women seeking to aid veterans' readjustment.

Postwar movies, on the other hand, seemed to clarify the situation. Fiction films, particularly those that loosely fit the genre of the "woman's film,"[21] afforded screenwriters and directors space in which to dramatize the tensions of reunions and readjustment. They created characters whose motivation made psychological sense, at least according to the theories then current.[22] Like the prescriptive literature, the films showed that veterans needed both sexual and maternal attention. While depicting the dangers of excesses of either,[23] they simultaneously tried to mitigate the contradiction between the two female roles. Resolution frequently took the form of ministrations by wives and sweethearts who knew how to balance loyalty, deference, and support with a discreet sensuality.

In the case of disabled veterans, contradictions were heightened and the possibility for satisfactory resolution might have seemed remote. Yet filmmakers willingly took on the task of bringing their lives to the screen, for they recognized their rich dramatic possibilities. This was exactly the sort of impossible situation on which the melodramatic "Hollywood film" thrived.[24] Moreover, such films would have universal appeal, for disabled veterans rendered visible (and thus all the more cinematic) the battle scars other soldiers carried hidden.

One of the most highly acclaimed and now classical examples of post-war films of veteran readjustment and disability is William Wyler's 1946 production, *The Best Years of Our Lives*. In a carefully balanced, closely woven narrative, three men return from war, each with certain problems that prevent him from readjusting smoothly. But the film allows these problems to be played out and apparently resolved. The men and their families—and, by extension, America at large—could now put the harrowing war years behind them and enjoy the fruits of postwar prosperity.[25]

Throughout the film, recurring triptychs of the three men throw into sharp relief the special difficulties faced by the disabled veteran. Al (Fredric March), a banker turned sergeant, cannot reconcile his cushy postwar life with the memory of his horrific wartime experiences; moreover, he and his wife, Millie (Myrna Loy), must overcome their mutual suspicions before they can resume a trusting relationship.[26] Fred (Dana Andrews), a glamorous flyer who cannot find a decent job as a civilian, discovers that his hastily contracted wartime marriage will not survive in the peacetime doldrums. These problems are troublesome, but they can be worked out over time.

Homer's difficulties, however, are more intractable. A sailor who was maimed in a ship fire, he has lost both his hands. Homer is played by Harold Russell, a veteran who actually suffered such a loss and wears two prosthetic hooks. The realization that Russell's amputations are authentic, not a clever special effect, produces a double frisson in the spectator that garners even more sympathy for the character he plays.[27] Homer's sacrifice falls just short of the ultimate one. He has not given his life, but he has given his future—as a worker, as a lover, as a "normal" man. His disability is permanent and undeniable; he has been practically, if not literally, emasculated. How can the film possibly recuperate this?

Early on, it becomes apparent that Homer's girl, Wilma, will be the key. Homer can be redeemed only if Wilma—who is literally the girl next door—accepts him as he is and makes good on her prewar promise to marry him. She must match his sacrifice with one of her own. Neither Homer nor the film makes this easy for her. Homer repeatedly tests her loyalty in an effort to provoke her into rescinding her vow. The camera constantly monitors her reactions to his body. In the homecoming scene, for example, Homer's mother is allowed to shudder when she sees his hooks, but Wilma must keep her eyes on his face, fling her arms around his neck, and kiss him as though nothing has happened. Wilma must express the unquestioning acceptance of the ideal mother for her child and at the same time convey continuing erotic interest in Homer. She must somehow transcend the madonna/whore split in order simultaneously to restore him to wholeness and affirm his masculinity—to "resexualize" him.[28]

Because of the parallel structure of the film—the three couples, each struggling to renegotiate their relationships—the bond between Homer and Wilma will inevitably be compared with those between the other couples. For them, too, the war has created gender imbalances that must be corrected before order can be restored. Al's return to his all-too-civilized life clearly gives him the jitters. Still, he lets his glamorous wife know that although she has served as both father and mother in his absence, she must now step aside and allow him to resume his rightful place as head of the family. Like Wilma, Millie tolerantly "mothers" Al as he acts out his anxieties in repeated drinking bouts. But she also allows their old erotic relationship to be rekindled. (The bedroom scenes between the two, a suggestive mix of humor and low-key erotic play, fell well within the bounds of the Hollywood Production Code then in force and also adhered to prevailing sexual mores and marital expertise, which condoned sexual satisfaction within marriage, even encouraging it as an antidote to maternal overinvolvement.)[29] Al and Millie's mutual suspicions of infidelity cancel each other out when both hint that they may have been unfaithful during the war but still love one another.

The dashing Fred finds no such staying power in his marriage. A good-looking working-class fellow, he left a dead-end job as a soda jerk to join the Air Force, serving as a bombardier. While in training, he met and hastily married Marie, a flashy blonde played by Virginia Mayo. But, like many wartime unions, this one turns out to be a mismatch. Fred discovers that Marie is really a floozie who was only attracted to his uniform and whose loyalty quickly evaporates when he takes off his medals and returns to his humble job in the drugstore.[30] Fred's masculinity is jeopardized not only by his humiliating work but also by Marie's flamboyant philandering.

Their marriage reaches the breaking point on a night when Marie wants to go out on the town and Fred must tell her they are broke. Marie offers to pay for their spree out of her own savings, but Fred tells her to keep her money and insists that she stay home and eat the meal he prepares in their tiny kitchenette. She threatens to go out by herself. Fred's masculinity is on the line in this scene, but he manages to reassert it, even amid the pots and pans, by strong-arming Marie and telling her, "You're going to stay right here and eat what I cook and like it." His triumph is short-lived, however, for Marie soon leaves for good. The antithesis of the ideal postwar woman, she refuses to rein in her own sexuality and has no compunction about using it to get what she wants. Within the value structure of the film (and according to most contemporary prescriptive literature), her poor showing as a wife results directly from the imbalance between her maternal and sexual qualities.

Fred, meanwhile, has fallen in love with Peggy (Teresa Wright), Al and Millie's daughter. Unlike Marie, Peggy does not attempt to unman Fred, but rather treats him with a combination of respect for his wartime bravery and sensitivity to his plight—both as a drugstore clerk and as the husband of the heedless Marie. Though Peggy clearly returns his love, Fred is reluctant to act on his feelings for her, at first because he feels obliged to try to work things out with Marie and, when that proves futile, because he believes that he must make something of himself before approaching her. At the end of the film, Fred has finally found a job that looks promising—salvaging old air force bombers—and he allows himself to express his passion for Peggy, who responds with equal intensity.

Though both Al and Millie and Fred and Peggy must make adjustments, not all of them minor, both couples appear in harmonious cameo by the end of the film, constituting an intergenerational model of ideal marriage. Peggy and Fred radiate a progenitive sexuality, while Al and Millie offer contented testimonial to loyalty and endurance. Against this backdrop, Wilma and Homer are married.

On the surface, the wedding scene is all charm and tradition, as relatives and friends gather in the home of Wilma's parents while Homer's cousin Butch plays the wedding march on the family spinet. When the minister tells them to "join hands," Wilma takes Homer's hook and Homer, clearly well practiced, manages to slip the ring on her finger. But the image of hook and hand jars against the conventional prettiness of the scene. How can this marriage succeed? By what means will it be consummated?

The delicate psychological balance in their relationship has been established in a crucial scene between Wilma and Homer midway in the film. Until this point, Homer has been avoiding Wilma in the hope that she will finally give up on him. But Wilma persists. In this scene, she confronts him late at night in his family's kitchen. She asks him what his intentions are, parrying his charge that she does not want to spend her life with a disabled man. Finally, he challenges her to come upstairs with him and see for herself "what it's like." She watches while he removes his hooks and shoulder harness and struggles into his pajama jacket. Then she buttons it up and helps him into bed, folding the prosthetic apparatus and placing it neatly on a chair. The scene is paced with unflinching deliberation.

Wilma's behavior here is part maternal, part sexual. She tucks Homer in like a child and kisses him good-night like a lover. Though muted, the sexuality here is clear, but the maternal content is also quite explicit; Homer even admits that without his hooks he is "as dependent as a baby that doesn't know how to get anything except cry for it." Wilma has become his hands; his body has, in effect, merged with hers—not sexually, but functionally. They have achieved what amounts to a mother-child reunion.

Though Homer finally allows himself to surrender to Wilma and her ministrations, it is not surprising that he has resisted for so long, for union with Wilma carries the threat of assimilation by the feminine, a loss of adult masculinity. Notably, until now, it has been Homer's father, not his mother, who has helped him each night, symbolically enabling him to stave off the threat of maternal domination.[31] In assuming the position of the maternal, Wilma displaces the father, reversing the oedipal direction—indeed, drawing Homer back to a pre-oedipal state.

The exaggerated normalcy of the wedding suggests, however, that Homer and Wilma's marriage will not remain at the level of regressive chastity, but that the sexual element of their relationship will be allowed to flower. True, the entire event has been (literally) orchestrated by Uncle Butch—Hoagy Carmichael—who appears (as he so often does in forties films) as an apparently celibate emotional gadfly. If Homer takes Butch as a model, the marriage will, indeed, be sexless. Butch, however, has repeatedly pushed Homer (who would prefer to hang out with his service buddies) into the emotional fray, counseling him to open himself up to Wilma and the rest of his family. The image of the other two couples—Al and Millie with their wise, beaming smiles, and Peggy and Fred, eyeing each other hungrily across the proceedings—has the effect of deepening the disjuncture between the whole bodies and the maimed one. At the same time, however, their presence suffuses the entire scene with sensuality, endorsing the sexual as well as the legal union between Wilma and Homer.

There is no organic, physical reason why Homer cannot function sexually. It is, finally, up to Wilma to accept him—to accept his hooks or his stumps upon her body—so that Homer can be resexualized and restored to his proper masculine place in society. Whether or not she finds this repulsive, neither Homer nor the film permits her to say. For her sexuality, her desire, is never fully articulated but rather expressed through her demure, quasi-maternal affection toward Homer. The denial of Wilma's desire allows Homer's to monopolize the sexual field. Insofar as the film imagines their sexual union at all, it is almost exclusively genital, for there is little indication of the possibility of oral sex—Homer's obvious alternative for giving Wilma pleasure, given the loss of his hands.[32]

Such a suggestion, even in the mid-1940s, would not have been completely farfetched. The most popular and explicit marriage manual of the day, Theodore Van de Velde's *Ideal Marriage* (1930), recommended the "genital kiss" as one of several techniques for conjugal sexual satisfaction. Moreover, according to Alfred Kinsey, oral sex was commonly practiced among the younger cohorts of married adults who were sexually active during this period.[33] True, the Production Code would have prohibited all but the most veiled reference to such a practice on-screen. But *The Best Years* (like many "woman's films" of the period) takes other liberties with the code: the suggestive bedroom antics of Al and Millie; Fred and Peggy's passionate kisses, one of them while Fred is still married to Marie; and even the key scene between Homer and Wilma, in which two unmarried adults are shown together in a bedroom, and Homer's stumps are exposed. Why, then, does it stop short of suggesting the possibility of sexual satisfaction for Wilma?

While the film must, as I argue above, allow Wilma to become both mother and sexual partner to Homer, it cannot allow her to play either role to excess. Like that of all women of the forties, Wilma's sexuality is threatening, even more so because of the fragility of Homer's masculinity. The film therefore seeks to contain her sexuality within conventional terms, rejecting any form of satisfaction that might require "special treatment" on Homer's part and thereby privilege Wilma's desire. Instead she must tailor her satisfaction to his psychological, as well as physical, limitations.

My reading of *The Best Years* differs significantly from another recent study by Kaja Silverman. In her essay "Historical Trauma and Male Subjectivity," Silverman contends that the film not only fails to reach resolution but is actually quite unusual, within the Hollywood canon, in its willingness to leave its male subjects exposed and vulnerable. It "not only . . . inverts classic cinema's scopic regime (a regime which turns upon woman's castration) but . . . openly eroticizes male lack. . . . *The Best Years of Our Lives* makes no attempt to contain the negativity which it unleashes, nor does it at any point facilitate a phallic identification on the part either of its male characters or its male viewers."[34] Silverman links the film's sexual inversion with its pessimistic view of the postwar social order, a view that dismisses the trappings of military victory (like Fred's medal for distinguished flying) as "junk," and exposes the economic injustices many veterans had to face.

These critical elements are unquestionably present in the film, but, in my view, they become neutralized within its libidinal economy. Not only Wilma, but Millie and Peggy, too, must sacrifice their sexual and psychological autonomy in deference to their men. Millie yields her wartime place as head of the family to Al, though he is hardly up to the stress of the position. While her parents struggle to maintain the veneer of a conventional marriage, Peggy surrenders any hope for security she may have had when she pursues Fred. In the closing scene, he warns her, "You know what it'll be, don't you, Peggy? It'll take us years to get anywhere. We'll have no money, no place to live. We'll have to work . . . be kicked around." It is precisely this prospect that Marie has rejected, preferring to assert her independence and chance it on her own. Taking Marie's place, Peggy implicitly agrees to subordinate her own needs to Fred's and accept whatever he can offer.

Though acting with determination to win Fred—as does Wilma in pursuing Homer—Peggy ends up deferring to her man in order to prop up his sense of authority within the relationship. And she, along with Wilma and Millie, will learn to temper whatever sexual and emotional autonomy they have managed to achieve during the war. The film makes it clear that no matter how vulnerable, how threatened their masculinity, Fred, Al and Homer have nothing to fear from *their* women.[35]

. . . . .

The gender of recuperation is made explicit in the title of a 1950 film about a paraplegic veteran, *The Men*. Teresa Wright once again comes on the scene, this time as Helen, the fianceé of Lieutenant Bud Wilcheck (Marlon Brando), who is undergoing rehabilitation in a military hospital. As the opening flashback establishes, Bud had been a strong and active individual, boldly leading his men when he was struck down in action. When the film opens he is bitter and dejected, deeply pessimistic about his future. Helen assigns herself the task of helping him come to terms with his lifelong injury so that he can rejoin society. Like Homer, Bud tries the patience of the woman he loves by alternately withdrawing and lashing out; he is sometimes fiercely independent, sometimes hypersensitive and paranoid. And, like Homer, Bud wants to cling to the familiarity of an all-male social group, in this case his comrades in the veterans' hospital, rather than face the difficult challenges of marriage and civilian life.

For Bud and other paraplegics, more so than for Homer, marriage implies surrender to the feminine, reunion with the maternal without the possibility of rescue through sexuality, for their disability—paralysis from the waist down—leaves little hope for genital sexual functionality. When another patient marries a nurse, one of Bud's wardmates comments, "It should work out—after all, she's a nurse. She knows what she's getting into." But the nurse/wife role cannot be separated from the maternal, with its connotations of incest. One of the veterans baldly draws the connections as he jibes at an older, plain-faced nurse: "If you wasn't so sexy, you'd remind me of my mother."[36]

The prospect of spending the rest of his life with a nurse/mother is precisely what Bud cannot tolerate. The nature of his disability compels him to depend upon others both physically and emotionally, but his needs are overdetermined by the fact that he is an orphan. His unmet desire for parental affection heightens his susceptibility to maternal love.

Fearful of admitting this desire, he repeatedly denies it by rebuffing Helen's advances. Until he can find some way to restore his own sense of masculinity and autonomy, he cannot accept her love.

As in *The Best Years*, Bud's masculinity will be restored at the expense of Helen's sexuality. Again, the film never fully acknowledges the *woman's* sacrifice. In an early scene, the hospital's medical chief, Dr. Brock, lectures a group of veterans' wives, girlfriends, and mothers on the nature of paraplegia. He explains that most of the men will be "unable to have children"—the film's euphemistic synecdoche for sex. But what he fails to mention, either directly or by innuendo, is that it is still possible for the men *and their partners* to enjoy other forms of sexual pleasure; nongenital and female-genital sex lie outside his—and the film's—sexual imagination. The implication, then, is that if the man cannot function "normally," there will be no sex at all.

After the meeting, Helen approaches Brock and asks him to help her get through to Bud, who has been refusing to see her. The doctor parries, "Why don't you just leave it alone? It takes a pretty special kind of woman in a lot of ways." "Maybe I'm special," Helen retorts with spunk. Through persistence and strength of will, she earns the right to Bud's appreciation; by contrast, his resistance to coming to terms with his disability and accepting the responsibilities of marriage appear perverse and antisocial. But what gets lost in the momentum is Helen's sexuality—the fact that she is being consigned to a lifelong union that, however emotionally fulfilling (and even this is dubious), holds out little prospect of sexual satisfaction for her *or* Bud, at least within the erotic framework of the film.

Though unexpressed, sexual anxiety is the underlying cause of a quarrel on their wedding night, prompting Bud to retreat to the hospital. Taking cover once again behind his emotional wall, he rejects Helen's apology (a gesture that exposes her masochistic position within the relationship, since it was *he* who precipitated the quarrel). What finally breaks down Bud's resistance is not a recognition of Helen's sincerity (or her seemingly infinite supply of self-abnegation), but a conversation he has with Dr. Brock.

Brock is the focus of patriarchal power within the film. He gives orders to everyone, staff and patients alike, pronounces authoritatively on all medical questions, and even seems to hold the key to family happiness as he doles out prognoses to the veterans' loved ones. Throughout, his manner is inexplicably brusque and cynical; it is not until this conversation with Bud that we learn why. Years earlier, Brock's wife had become paraplegic as the result of a car accident. But medical science had not yet advanced to the point where such patients could be routinely saved, and she eventually died. Brock continues to mourn her, his sorrow the source of his unstinting devotion to his patients as well as of his abrasive manner.

When Bud complains that Helen does not really love him but married him only out of pity, Brock dismisses his suspicion. "I'd give anything in the world to go home and find [my wife]," he tells Bud, "—*in* a wheel-chair." In effect, Brock offers Bud an acceptable model of *male* sacrifice—one that allows him to come to terms with his own disability and also to believe that Helen's motives are sincere. The film's closing dialogue suggests that this step brings him into some kind of mutuality with Helen. As he drives up to her parents' home, where she has been staying, she observes, "You've come a long way." He replies, "I had a flat tire—fixed it myself." "Do you want me to help you up the steps?" "Please . . ." Helen seems to have the upper hand at this point (she is pushing his wheelchair), but it is clear that she will be continually challenged to uphold his masculinity at the cost of her own sexuality and ego. Once again, we are left with the image of a vibrant, healthy woman (intertextually, the same one who procreatively joined Dana Andrews in *The Best Years*) sacrificing herself for a disabled man.

These films are interested not simply in exploring the psychological subtleties and intrinsic drama of postwar readjustment, but in showing the possibility for alignment and mutual reinforcement between the gender and political orders. To confirm the political rectitude of the Allied victory, gender relationships were to uphold, rather than undermine, pre-existing gender arrangements. Throughout World War II, "the family" had served as the centerpiece of America's war goals—symbolic of all that was to be fought for and protected.[37] Accordingly, the family, with "proper" gender roles restored, became a centerpiece of postwar readjustment.[38] With their emotional as well as physical difficulties, disabled veterans potentially represented an ongoing affront to both familial and political normalcy. Through recourse to—and containment of—the maternal/sexual, these films manage the political as well as the physical and psychological recuperation of these men.

·   ·   ·   ·   ·

Films about disabled veterans underwent a renaissance during and after the Vietnam era. Though similar in some ways to the earlier examples, the later films vary the pattern we have seen so far in ways that confirm the linkage between patriotism and the maternal/sexual. Two bear closer analysis, *Coming Home* (1978) and *Born on the Fourth of July* (1989). In both, paraplegic veterans refuse at first to accept their disabilities or to allow themselves to recuperate through the maternal. For both Luke (Jon Voight) in *Coming Home* and Ron Kovic (Tom Cruise) in *Born*, coming to terms with their handicaps potentially means accepting the war and its politics. Renouncing the privileges of the returning hero, they instead begin to speak out against the war.

Both films open in Veterans Administration hospitals where, notably, conditions are depicted far less rosily than they were in *The Men*. Luke, face down on a gurney, is careening angrily around the ward, his bladder bag overflowing, when he meets Sally (Jane Fonda), who has come to volunteer as an aide. Reserved and conventional, Sally has just seen her husband, a marine officer, off to Vietnam. She is initially abashed by Luke's outburst, but soon befriends him. Though Luke accepts her help, he fiercely attempts to be self-sufficient. He is also explicitly sexual, at first with a prostitute, and then with Sally herself. Through cunnilingus, Sally even experiences orgasm with him, something she has been unable to do with her hyper-macho—and hyper-patriotic—husband Bob, played by Bruce Dern. In sharp contrast to the earlier films, *Coming Home* clearly indicates that disabled veterans can enjoy a range of sexual pleasures by looking at, touching, and satisfying their partners. In refusing to privilege (male) genital sexuality (though still unquestioningly heterosexual), the film opens onto a whole new realm of satisfactions for both the veterans and their female partners.

The sexual relationship between Sally and Luke is also an essential element of the film's political scheme, which traces the war to macho values and behavior while aligning antiwar politics with a new, *egalitarian* form of heterosexuality. Luke's willingness to speak out parallels his deepening relationship with Sally. Susan Jeffords reads Luke's behavior as "feminized," but I would contend that within the context of the film, his actions appear to be androgynous.[39] Though Luke repudiates his own behavior in Vietnam, he does so publicly; both this and his other antiwar acts of passive resistance demonstrate personal (but not explicitly heroic) courage. Luke's sexuality, demeanor, and politics all seem to carry the endorsement of feminism.

In linking antiwar politics to sexual and women's liberation, this late-seventies film indulges in a certain amount of hindsight, for it constructs associations that even movement activists were only dimly aware of during the Vietnam era itself. Though set in the late sixties, the film reflects a mindset rooted in values that did not converge in American culture until the late seventies. For it was not until that moment that the movement for sexual liberation began to incorporate feminist views of female sexuality. Along with its generally relaxed attitudes toward choice of partner and locale, prescriptive literature also began to expose the "myth of the vaginal orgasm" (a move dismissed a decade earlier as radical feminist screed), which established the principle that women's pleasure is centered in the clitoris, not in the vagina.[40] At the same time, many feminist ideas were gaining mainstream political and intellectual legitimacy. *Coming Home* offers evidence that feminist values had not only begun to permeate left-wing interpretations of the Vietnam war but had even made their way to Hollywood.

By 1989, however, antiwar sentiment and feminist values had become decoupled, as *Born on the Fourth of July* strikingly reveals. The film is rampantly misogynist. For example, in the retrospective prologue designed to expose the militaristic, competitive atmosphere of American boyhood in the 1950s, Kovic's mother is portrayed as the major source of his socialization. It is she, rather than his mild-mannered father, who eggs him on in high school athletic competitions, and she who plants in him visions of patriotic service and fame. When he returns home in a wheelchair, she is depicted as being unable to accept his condition, and it is his father (like Homer's) who assumes responsibility for his physical care.[41]

The film literalizes and completes the madonna/whore split when Ron goes off to a seedy Mexican watering hole that is a favorite with disabled veterans. The men even have a special brothel to cater to their needs. "Charlie from Chicago" (Willem Dafoe), the self-appointed guide to the place, initiates Ron into local sexual customs by indicating, with a thrust of his tongue, that most of the men practice oral sex. (His exaggerated gesture reads as a vulgar caricature of the sensual, almost reverential love scene between Luke and Sally in *Coming Home*.) Refusing Charlie's cynicism, Ron falls for the first pretty prostitute who plies her art upon him. Predictably, he becomes disillusioned when he discovers her lavishing her charms on another customer (shades of Marie in *Best Years*). Following a now-familiar pattern, Ron seeks comfort with his male buddy, Charlie.

The two men set out into the desert, but they soon fall into a bizarre form of macho one-upmanship, arguing over who committed the most outrageous atrocities in Vietnam (and, by implication, who should be the most guilt ridden). In a not-so-subtle homoerotic wrestling match that recalls a similar scene in the film version of D. H. Lawrence's *Women in Love*, the two wheelchair-bound men roll around in the sand for a while before eventually reconciling. They then decide to return to the States, where—somewhat inexplicably—they join the Vietnam Veterans against the War.

Ron soon becomes a leading spokesman for the movement. Notably, his role is highly individualistic, not unlike that of the classical veteran-hero, and his reference group is prominently devoid of women, either as mothers (real or role playing) or as lovers.[42] The film suggests that in the remasculinized culture of the 1980s, opposition to the war has found an acceptable niche, but women are once again viewed as threatening.[43] Wheeling his chair out onto a stage to face a cheering audience and the blinding lights of the national media, Ron is at once fulfilling and repudiating his mother's dream for him, and he does so surrounded by his fellow (male) veterans.

. . . . .

Taken together, these four films mark out a complex set of alignments between the maternal, the sexual, the patriotic, and the masculine. As a sacred national symbol, motherhood is something to be defended. But as maternal *power* (embodied in the bossy nurse or the overzealous mother like Mrs. Kovic), or when aligned with patriotism (mothers send men off to war, nurses repair them and send them back), motherhood is cast as a threat to masculinity.[44] In patriotic postwar films such as *The Best Years* and *The Men*, the maternal is tempered with sexuality, allowing for masculine recovery *and* resexualization. The *sexual*/maternal becomes a vehicle for political rectitude, as veterans resume full social participation and citizenship, now signified as masculinity. But, as I have tried to show, such films at the same time implicitly produce a recontainment of female sexuality and subjectivity.

The link between patriotism and the sexual/maternal is exposed and criticized in *Born on the Fourth of July*, which simultaneously manages to salvage a masculinity of sorts—homosocial, if not homoerotic—and link it to a specific kind of antiwar politics that now fall within the political pale. But both masculinity and opposition to the war exist at the cost of marginalizing all women, and specifically villifying both mothers and prostitutes.

The only feminist film of this group, *Coming Home*, does not depend on the sexual/maternal for recuperation. Sally is caring but not *caretaking*, and her sensuality is fully acknowledged. Interestingly, this is the only one of the four films that pays more than token attention to women's caring activities or is willing to portray their reactions to injuries and disability honestly and uncritically. The film not only shows Sally's hospital work in some detail, but allows her to express tentativeness and even revulsion when she first approaches the patients. She is granted far more emotional latitude than her ever-smiling predecessors, Wilma and Helen. By recognizing Sally's right to ambivalence, the film spares her both the self-denial and self-sacrifice that befell these earlier characters and the moral repudiation that would be Mrs. Kovic's fate.[45]

Indeed, *Coming Home* is as much about Sally's coming to personhood as it is about Luke's coming to terms with his disability and coming of age politically. The mutual respect that develops between them carries over into their sexual relationship, and this, in turn, allows Luke to oppose the war without becoming feminized. Neither his gender identity nor his politics wavers in the vicinity of women. Nor does the film require female sacrifice to achieve male recuperation.

The fact that *Coming Home* was succeeded by *Born on the Fourth of July* suggests that it is difficult to maintain such a delicate gender balance in modern American culture. Indeed, to Susan Jeffords, the cycle of "remasculinization" seems almost inexorable.[46] But the war in the Gulf appears to have reshuffled the pack, dealing caring responsibilities to men and military duties—with all of their attendant risks—to women. As a result, this conflict has carried the usual wartime destabilization of gender roles to a new level. There is at least a chance that "the new world order" will not bring back the old gender order in new political clothing.

NOTES

I would like to thank the members of the Dartmouth Institute on Gender and War for their provocative comments on an early draft of this paper. Wini Breines, Ramona Curry, Tom Doherty, Stephanie Engel, Lynne Layton, Kathleen McHugh, Sarah Minden, and Andrea Walsh offered many helpful comments and suggestions along the way. And working on the final version in the spring of 1991, I had the benefit of weekly discussions of wars past and present with the undergraduates in my seminar on gender and war at the University of Illinois.

1. On World War I, see John Keegan, *The Face of Battle* (New York, 1976), pp. 268–74. On American casualties during World War II, see Joseph C. Goulden, *The Best Years, 1945–1950* (New York, 1976), chap. 2. Over 400,000 American men died during this war, while over 500,000 returned with serious levels of disability.

2. Elaine Scarry, *The Body in Pain: The Making and Unmaking of the World* (New York, 1985), p. 114.

3. George L. Mosse discusses the mutual reinforcement between symbols of masculinity and of nationalism in *Nationalism and Sexuality: Middle-Class Morality and Sexual Norms in Modern Europe* (New York, 1985). He stresses that national ideologies incorporate only images of "respectable," correct sexuality—namely, heterosexuality—to represent the nation's goals and spirit.

4. According to Richard Holmes, emasculating wounds have been among those most feared by soldiers; see *Acts of War: The Behavior of Men in Battle* (New York, 1985), p. 182. These fears came to be expressed culturally; as Sandra M. Gilbert and Susan Gubar point out, literary representations of the devastating psychological and emotional effects of World War I frequently took gendered forms. A common figure in these texts is "that twentieth-century Everyman . . . [who] is not just publicly powerless, [but also] privately impotent. . . . Such effects of the Great War were gender-specific problems that only men could have," since women, "still struggling to attain public power, . . . could hardly worry about the loss of an authority they had not yet fully achieved" (Gilbert and Gubar, *No Man's Land: The Place of the Woman Writer in the Twentieth Cen-*

tury, vol. 2, *Sexchanges* [New Haven, 1989], p. 260). As I shall discuss below, the gender anxieties created by World War II were greater for both men and women, for by then women *had* achieved a certain amount of power, which simply compounded male anxieties.

5. On the postwar reconstruction of gender systems in general, see Margaret R. Higonnet and Patrice L.-R. Higonnet, "The Double Helix," in Margaret Higonnet, Jane Jenson, Sonya Michel and Margaret Weitz, eds., *Behind the Lines: Gender and the Two World Wars* (New Haven, 1987), pp. 31–47; for the United States after Vietnam, see Susan Jeffords, *The Remasculinization of America: Gender and the Vietnam War* (Bloomington, Ind., 1989).

6. According to Gilbert and Gubar, "maimed, unmanned, victimized characters are obsessively created by early twentieth-century literary men" (*No Man's Land*, vol. 1, *The War of the Words* [New Haven, 1988], p. 36).

7. I am not including texts whose protagonists suffer *only* from psychological disabilities, though their themes—and my interpretation—closely parallel those of texts of physical disability. In the latter category are novels such as Arthur Stuart-Menteth Hutchinson, *If Winter Comes* (Boston, 1921); Warwick Deeping, *Sorrell and Son* (London, 1925); Robert Keable, *Simon Called Peter* (New York, 1921); Jean Giraudoux, *Siegfried et le limousin* (Paris, 1922); Leonhard Frank, *Karl und Anna* (1926); Rebecca West, *The Return of the Soldier* (Garden City, 1925); Jacob Wassermann, *Faber; or, The Lost Years* (New York, 1925); Pierre Drieu La Rochelle, *Gilles* (Paris, 1939); and, of course, Hemingway's classic, *The Sun Also Rises* (New York, 1926).

8. Those based on novels include *As You Desire Me* (based on *Karl und Anna*; 1932); *If Winter Comes* (1923; remake, 1947); and *Sorrell and Son* (1927; remake, 1934).

9. These two films set up themes that will persist in later postwar films. In *The Four Horsemen*, Valentino plays a French soldier who returns blind from the war; his wife, who has been consorting with a German in his absence, is "punished" by being compelled to care for her disabled husband. In *The Big Parade*, the hero (played by John Gilbert) loses a leg while fighting overseas. After briefly returning to his family in America, he goes back to France to find his sweetheart, who readily embraces him, seemingly without concern about—or at least accepting of—his disability.

10. Kaja Silverman includes some of these films in the larger category of postwar films of historical trauma, in which "the male subject is constituted . . . [through] castration"; see "Historical Trauma and Male Subjectivity," in E. Ann Kaplan, ed., *Psychoanalysis and Cinema* (New York, 1990), p. 114.

11. For a comprehensive discussion of these instructions, see Susan M. Hartmann, "Prescriptions for Penelope: Literature on Women's Obligations to Returning World War II Veterans," *Women's Studies* 5 (1978): 223–39.

12. In a fascinating study of Australian women, Marilyn Lake argues that wartime conditions allowed women to express for the first time the latent sexuality and subjectivity that had begun developing before the war, and that was shaped, in large part, by the emphasis on "sex appeal" in advertising and film in the 1930s. See "Female Desires: The Meaning of World War II," *Australian Historical Studies* 24, no. 95 (October 1990): 267–84. A similar phenomenon could no doubt easily be documented in the United States.

13. See Susan Gubar, " 'This Is My Rifle, This Is My Gun': World War II and the Blitz on Women," in Higonnet et al., *Behind the Lines*, pp. 154–67.

14. Herbert I. Kupper, *Back to Life: The Emotional Adjustment of Our Veterans* (New York, 1945), p. 183.

15. Hartmann, "Prescriptions," p. 228.

16. "[The veteran] needs affection and mothering: not in a demonstrative and apparent way which threatens to overwhelm him but in an assured, very real manner of an intelligent wife. . . . He may appear to be too much of a 'man' on the surface, but within him he has the needs of a love-starved adolescent" (Kupper, *Back to Life*, p. 184).

17. Levy's work, in turn, had its roots in the theories of Helene Deutsch, Karen Horney, and Melanie Klein. For an excellent discussion of these theories and their impact on popular culture, especially film, see E. Ann Kaplan, "Motherhood and Representation: From Postwar Freudian Figurations to Postmodernism," in Kaplan, *Psychoanalysis and Cinema* (New York, 1990), pp. 128–42.

18. Wylie attributed specifically to mothers a charge that had been made earlier in more general terms by journalist Roy Helton. In "The Inner Threat: Our Own Softness," Helton had contended, "For twenty-five years the feminine influence on Western life has mounted into a dominance in every area but that of politics, and even there its power is absolute as to the direction of our purposes" (*Harpers* 181 [September 1940], 338).

19. Edward A. Strecker, *Their Mothers' Sons: The Psychiatrist Examines an American Problem* (Philadelphia, 1946). Kupper also alludes to this pattern in *Back to Life*. Strecker's charge gained added scientific legitimacy throughout the 1940s and early 1950s in the writings of Erik Erickson, Margaret Mead, and Geoffrey Gorer. On Levy, Wylie and Erickson, see Barbara Ehrenreich and Deirdre English, *For Her Own Good: 150 Years of the Experts' Advice to Women* (Garden City, N.Y., 1978), p. 208–14; on Strecker, see Susan M. Hartmann, *The Home Front and Beyond* (Boston, 1982), pp. 176–77; on Gorer and Mead, see Christopher Lasch, *Haven in a Heartless World: The Family Besieged* (New York, 1977), pp. 72–73, and on Levy, p. 109. Lasch notes that Ernest Groves and Gladys Groves had referred to "the dangerous mother" even earlier, in their 1928 volume *Parents and Children* (209, n. 43).

20. Robert Westbrook has shown that this combination also appeared in pinups. Betty Grable, the GI's favorite, was explicitly sexual and seductive, but, well known as the wife of trumpeter Harry James, she also evoked marital loyalty and even motherhood. See " 'I Want a Girl, Just Like the Girl That Married Harry James': American Women and the Problem of Political Obligation in World War II," *American Quarterly* 42, no. 4 (December 1990): 587–614.

21. Interpretations of this genre vary; see, for example, Andrea S. Walsh, *Women's Film and Female Experience, 1940–1950* (New York, 1984), esp. chap. 1; and Mary Ann Doane, "The 'Woman's Film': Possession and Address," in Doane, Patricia Mellencamp, and Linda Williams, eds., *Re-Vision: Essays in Feminist Film Criticism* (Los Angeles, 1984), pp. 67–82.

22. In comparing the films *Now, Voyager* (1942) and *Marnie* (1964), Kaplan makes an important distinction between texts that "[use] psychoanalysis as a narrative discourse, as a means for producing character-change and explaining [in

this case] mother-daughter interactions," and those that "*embody* the level of the psychoanalytic" ("Motherhood and Representation," p. 129). The postwar films I am discussing would fall into the first category.

23. Mary Ann Doane notes that wartime and postwar films not only frequently present both excessive mothering and promiscuous sexuality as "dangerous aspects of femininity," but also link them to unpatriotic politics, specifically isolationism; see *The Desire to Desire* (Bloomington, Ind., 1987), p. 81.

24. See Robert Ray, *A Certain Tendency of Hollywood Cinema* (Princeton, 1985).

25. For a rather different, but compelling, reading of this film, see Silverman, "Historical Trauma," pp. 110–27. Using a Lacanian framework, Silverman argues that the film does not succeed in resolving the postwar traumas it exposes. Below I will detail the ways in which my interpretation differs from Silverman's.

26. Sexual mistrust and jealousy on the part of both men and women were common themes in wartime and postwar "woman's films"; see Walsh, *Women's Film*, pp. 98–103 and chap. 5.

27. The use of nonprofessional actors was typical in American postwar films whose directors had been influenced by Italian neo-realism. Here Wyler takes the gesture one step further by using a veteran who had actually suffered the loss he depicts.

28. For a fascinating, psychologically astute treatment of another split, see West, *The Return of the Soldier*. In this novel, a shell-shocked veteran suffering from amnesia has forgotten his marriage to a cool, selfish, upper-class woman, and insists on being reunited with the sweetheart of his youth, a work-roughened but kind and generous lower-class housewife. The split here is not precisely along the madonna/whore line, but along the lines of class and respectability, for the sweetheart embodies both sensual and maternal qualities in an exquisite balance that restores the veteran's memory but, ironically, compels him to renounce her and accept his socially correct marriage. On the restoration of masculinity in post-Vietnam culture, see Jeffords, *Remasculinization*.

29. On the Production Code, see Walsh, *Women's Film*, pp. 32–34 and 206–17. On marital advice and sexual mores, see Estelle B. Freedman and John D'Emilio, *Intimate Matters: A History of Sexuality in America* (New York, 1988), 266–68; Ehrenreich and English, *For Her Own Good*; and Elaine Tyler May, *Homeward Bound: American Families in the Cold War Era* (New York, 1988), chap. 4.

30. In the typical mode of the Hollywood film, Fred's problem, dictated chiefly by his class position, is expressed—and resolved—at the level of the individual.

31. Kupper contends that mothers' attention to their veteran sons all too frequently slips into—and/or is perceived as—efforts to control them. Accordingly, he strongly advises mothers to hold back in their ministrations and expressions of affection (*Back to Life*, pp. 188–89).

32. Some viewers have suggested that the film does visually indicate the possibility of oral sex when Wilma buttons up Homer's pajama jacket, moving toward his mouth, while the demure V neckline of her crisp blouse points down to her breasts. But their kisses remain strictly above the neck, giving only the slightest hint of sexual ardor. In later films, as we shall see, references to oral sex become

completely explicit; see the discussions of *Coming Home* and *Born on the Fourth of July* below.

33. See Freedman and D'Emilio, *Intimate Matters*, pp. 267–69.

34. Silverman, "Historical Trauma," p. 127.

35. One might also construct an interpretation of recuperated male power in this film by following the line of argument developed by Christopher Newfield in his ingenious analysis of *The Scarlet Letter*, "The Politics of Male Suffering: Masochism and Hegemony in the American Renaissance," *Differences* 1, no. 3 (Fall 1989): 55–87.

36. Male attitudes toward nurses differed markedly from nurses' own perceptions of their work and affect. In examining World War I texts, Gilbert and Gubar note, "This education in masculine functioning that the nurse experienced as a kind of elevation was often felt by her male patient as exploitation: her evolution into active, autonomous, transcendent subject was associated with his devolution into passive, dependent, immanent medical object" (*No Man's Land* 2:286–87). For a different interpretation of some of these texts that stresses the nurses' devastation (as opposed to "elevation") by what they saw, see Jane Marcus, "Corpus/Corps/Corpse: Writing the Body at War," in Helen M. Cooper, Adrienne Auslander Munich, and Susan Merrill Squier, eds., *Arms and the Woman: War, Gender, and Literary Representation* (Chapel Hill, N.C., 1989), pp. 124–67.

37. See Sonya Michel, "American Women and the Discourse of the Democratic Family in World War II," in Higonnet, Jenson, Michel, and Weitz, *Behind the Lines*, pp. 154–67.

38. See Hartmann, "Prescriptions," and May, *Homeward Bound*, esp. chap. 6.

39. According to Jeffords, "the price of [Luke's] release from the hospital was his gradual containment of . . . anger and violence, now effectively neutralized (feminized/castrated)"; she seems to regard his confession of guilt as "feminine" (*Remasculinization*, pp. 146–47). The film's emphasis on Luke's sexuality and strength of character can hardly be read as castration; moreover, when Bob threatens Sally and Luke with his M-1, it is Luke who disarms him, removing the symbol of his phallic power along with the weapon. If anyone is "feminized" in the film, it is Bob, who commits suicide by drowning, that most female of all methods.

40. See Freedman and D'Emilio, *Intimate Matters*, pp. 330, 337. Sexual pleasure was condoned both inside and outside of marriage, and homosexuality was also gaining recognition and acceptance.

41. The portrayal of Mrs. Kovic as villain seems to be largely director Oliver Stone's invention, for she is presented more sympathetically in Kovic's 1976 book of the same title, on which the film was based.

42. Luke's style of sexuality apparently held no appeal for either the cinematic Ron or his actual counterpart; in his autobiography, Kovic remarks, "I gave my dead dick for John Wayne" (quoted in Holmes, *Acts of War*, p. 182).

43. Throughout her study, Jeffords, following the lead of Klaus Theweleit, argues that remasculinization entails the reestablishment of male bonds, almost always to the exclusion of women; see Theweleit, *Male Fantasies*, 2 vols. (Minneapolis, 1987–89).

44.   Here my argument diverges somewhat from that of Doane, who contends that the "strategy of imbricating the concept of the maternal with that of a nationalistic patriotism also succeeds in giving the woman a significant position in wartime which does not constitute a threat to the traditional patriarchal order" (*Desire*, 79).

45.   While rare in male-authored texts, the open-ended exploration of women's responses to pain, suffering, and dismemberment has been a central theme in women's wartime and postwar writing (especially those by and about nurses and ambulance drivers); female writers adopted several distinctive voices to express and contain their anguished perceptions, ranging from the heavily ironic to the unflinchingly frank. For excellent discussions of women's texts of caring, see Claire M. Tylee, *The Great War and Women's Consciousness* (Iowa City, 1990), esp. pp. 93–100 and 190–97; Jane Marcus, "Corpus/Corps/Corpse," pp. 124–67. In her study of fifty military nurses who served in Vietnam, Elizabeth Norman observed that they tended to "insulate themselves, build up a shield that allowed them to work" (*Women at War* [Philadelphia, 1990], p. 34). But neither irony nor emotional isolation was an option for the postwar cinematic wives of the 1940s and 1950s.

46.   See Jeffords, *Remasculinization*, esp. last chapter.

PART VI

INTERPRETIVE ESSAY

Chapter 13

THE BOMB'S WOMB AND THE GENDERS OF WAR

(WAR GOES ON PREVENTING WOMEN

FROM BECOMING THE MOTHERS OF INVENTION)

KLAUS THEWELEIT

RE-WINNING LOST WARS

"WAR IS BAD," the man said to the taxi driver. "*It's bad for the losers. If you lose the war, you lose everything.*"

The taxi driver nods. He knows what it means to have or have not a taxi (lost or won).

He's winning his war on the streets of La Paz.

The man he drives is a *warrior*. A warrior carries the war around with him like a thing. This one can't show it as openly as he wants to, because (once again) he has lost his war. They caught him. They'll bring him to the airport and put him on a plane. He's got no expectations . . . to find his war again.

"*If you lose the war, you have lost everything.*"

Two speakers are speaking this sentence. One is Walter Benjamin speaking about German soldierly men of the twenties, who were longing for the next war, which was to come as World War II, because they had *lost* the first one. They needed a war won, to get the lost one back. They then lost that second one as well.

The second speaker is one of those war-losers: Klaus Barbie, sitting in a Bolivian taxi talking to the taxi driver about what you lose when you have lost your war (again).

The French, the British, the Americans, the Russians took the war from him and his companions in 1945—a loss hard to suffer. They left him behind with nothing left. So he had tried it again, next year, some place; another year, another place; any year, any place: this time South America proved to be the best region for re-winning that lost THING.

Chorus of men carrying a war: "As long as we have lost, the war will not be over."

(To be sung in every interval of "peace." To be sung during wars. To be sung all the time.)

"Benjamin is right; Joyce is right," Klaus Barbie says (not knowing he is quoting anybody). He doesn't know anything about quotations. For he who has lost a war has lost everything. In the first place, he has lost his memory. When you lose a war, you lose your memory. That's the first thing to lose. The memory (of what one has done in the war) is replaced by the desire to change the old war into a new war, a war that still can be won, a war that doesn't yet belong to an enemy. If you have lost the war, your memory is replaced by something called "The Search." HE is transformed into a searcher. THE SEARCHERS are searching for a little girl who has been kidnapped by Indians, they say.

They are not interested in little girls. They are interested in how their bodies feel. They are searching for some part of their bodies that has got lost in the moment they lost their war. They have to find a war which will bring back to them the lost one as that thing you can carry around in your heartbeat, in your pocket like a key. A key for a world existing out of won wars only; wars totally won, which bring back to winners every lost war in the shape of the sure ability of winning everything that can be won; the ability of changing the world into the stage of AND HE WAR.

AND HE WON. Barbie at times was quite good at that (as many of his companions were, getting back lost wars as won ones in South America Crazy Banana).

America during the eighties was very busy trying to re-win the Vietnam War, Lynda Boose says. Re-winning lost wars means to *get back* everything. Does it mean even getting back a memory? Hell, no. Not memories of what a warrior has done (losing a war). A warrior doesn't "remember." Only people who didn't *fight* remember something. The others are getting back memories of the time they were *little innocent boys*. Innocent: without the knowledge of defeat. That's all a real grown-up searcher man wants to find, undefeated innocence.[1] In 1991 he calls it "a new world order." Will you please hand it over, Mr. Saddam!

To become innocent again, you have to kill. That's one of the giggling rules of male logic. Women give birth to something *different* from themselves. Men give birth to themselves living in New World Orders. Men are *re-born* by killing. They always stand up, re-erect out of something that dies around them. You have to deal with that logic or metamorphosis when dealing with war. WAR ranks high among the male ways of giving birth.

With a lost war in your hand you are sort of a woman, Susan Jeffords realized. You will have no resurrection, re-erection, re-election. You will not be a man again, you will not be in control of all the things that have to be in control to make you feel like a natural winner, unless you've got a replay on the war machine; a replay you win.

America's way of re-winning the Vietnam War was described by Susan Jeffords as *The Feminization of Loss*—a civil war. Its main rule: women lose, men don't. So, whoever made that mistake of losing the Vietnam War: he had to be brought into some humiliating connection with femininity. Jeffords called that civil war for re-winning the Vietnam War *The Remasculinization of America*.[2] Politicians and journalists, moviemakers and television people, novelists and church people, songwriters and generals, the media and Mr. President have been involved in winning this war, changing America's gender into "male" once again. All those Americans who were blamed for losing that Vietnam thing had to be turned into "women" wimps, who had not been able or willing to resist those yellow rapists, who stole the undefeatable feeling from America's pure innocent male virgin body.

Winning a war against the people you live with is one of the real ways of re-winning lost wars. WHO lost Vietnam: all those good Americans who made the individual mistake of letting themselves be turned into feeling human beings (= women) by those poor Vietnamese people; secondly, all those *not so good* Americans who didn't want to win: hippies, musicians, civil rights freaks, dems & fems.

The BIG SHE had to be defeated to make America feel like somebody carrying that *thing* again. The United States of America changed into the United States of Amnesia, admiring Jesus stepping down from The Cross with a machine gun, helping Mr. Stallone turn Mr. Reagan into a laughing little boy again. As a laughing little boy filled with innocence, Mr. Reagan made his departure.

Fighting femininity, simultaneously winning the COLD WAR, became the ways of getting back parts of the Vietnam War as a war won. Women and "the East" had to give back what had got lost in the swampy triangle of that Asian communist prostitute.

The war of genders is wonderful for re-winning lost wars because of its very certain result: men never lose, women have to. Though hot wars are better: you have real dying people as those to be kicked in the ass.

Not only in America. Though closely linked together, America and Western Europe don't know much about each other. That's part of the information war that is steadily won by newspapers and the TV. All they fear is having readers or viewers who are informed somehow about what's going on. (Not only when the military takes over the news reports.) So it was *not possible* to see from Germany that American politics in recent years had something to do with the attempt to re-win the Vietnam War. Nor that the attempt to re-win had taken the shape of a remasculinization of America's public spheres. I had to come to the States to learn about it.

The other way round was just the same. Returning to Germany from the United States in summer 1990, I saw the re-winning of World War II in high gear: German public spheres were being remasculinized. Germany, sharing the Western victory in the COLD WAR, is allowed by the Allied forces of World War II to re-win that lost Nazi war; I had seen *that*. What I hadn't seen, but learned back here: women politicians in both parts of the country complaining about the disappearance of women's issues from public discussions during unification.

A clear shift toward an aggressive antifeminism: legal abortions under threat; as industrial unemployment rises women are fired; decreased child-care budgets. Newspapers and magazines, so women reported, simply refused to print interviews or articles about such topics. They feel silenced.

Describing the gates broken into the Wall since November 1989 and its first passers-through, Antje Vollmer, spokeswoman of the Green party writes: "*At every breakthrough of the wall or the barbed wire the first ones to open their mouths were men, masters. The right of the first night was completely theirs—and then the common people were allowed to float and stream, kept thoroughly admonished by their rulers: Thou shalt be happy now!*" And, viewing the political situation as a whole: "*Men, wherever I look, an uncountable army of dark blue suits, men permanently coupling in male couples.*" (Re-winning lost wars.)

That song is a real Traditional. In Germany in 1919 and the following years, it was sung against women workers of the munition factories. They especially were blamed for having lost World War I, having organized several big strikes in 1917–18 to put an end to the war and to the starving of their children. These women were made a strong pillar of the stab-in-the-back legend. No *man* had lost the war (except for communists, wimps, dems & fems).

The Nazi party twenty years later took that point very seriously: up to 1939 they had reduced factory working women down to the lowest number in twentieth century Germany. The blitzkrieg was started and thought to be won *without* women having the chance of stabbing any man anywhere.

Toward the end of World War II two-thirds of all factory workers were women. Goebbels's diaries show his March 1945 plans to draft women batallions as a last weapon against Allied troops stepping onto German soil.

So (as everybody knows) the dying warrior waits until the last second of life to cry for Mammy or Sister. Until that second he fights them as the incarnation of LOSS. Only when he has real Arabs to fight, he starts loving women (from a desert distance). And only when dying, he allows himself to change sides, to become a deserter into the big army of women, of wimps, and of the dead. Peace to their ashes and asses.

What shall I do now with the re-won World War II that the newspaper spills every morning on my breakfast table as a present from history to

German men. I don't want it. I can't throw it out with that paper. It won't stay there.

To me, the lost war had always been a won war; that is from the time I was fourteen on. In Germany after 1945 there was a good opportunity to learn about the beauty of lost wars. The only thing I ever liked about that damned World War II was its existence as a lost one. It provided a possibility to win a reasonable life. A chance to escape from some common European despotisms to Western sounds and pictures, records and movies; that meant: finding the bodies of *women*, coming along with these sounds and pictures; that also meant escaping the bodies of soldiers and the rules of soldierly life.

Throughout 1990 I saw Western male politicians and businessmen hoping for a breakdown of the Soviet Union, with their trigger fingers and checkbooks itching. They wish "Moscow" to grow weak (into the "women's position"), and the forces, who demand the independence of their countries from the USSR to grow strong, thus risking wars from the Mediterranean and the Baltic Sea to the Pacific Ocean: the Lebanonization of Eastern Europe and the Soviet Union, as President Bush named the "threat" hanging over Gorbachev's head. Yugoslavia, Poland, and the USSR *re-stabilized* could stand for a future without wars in Eastern Europe and Asia.

A balanced East could vitalize public feminine feelings that are vanishing in the West now; feelings of care for the lives of people, respect for the integrity of human bodies and a trust in conference tables for solving political conflicts. Whereas a weak East opens the doors to wars. That's what I thought in summer of 1990; now we learn that it *is* the weakened position of the USSR in the UN that allowed the United States to bomb Iraq.

I didn't want to re-win World War II. I didn't want to win the cold war. I don't want to re-win the Final Solution by living in a country which is selling gas to deadly enemies of Israel.

Victories like that take away from my generation the war we had won when I was a boy (innocently liking girls, loving to have lost THE REICH). The war we had won (girls and boys), the lost Nazi war, looked for a while as if it could have been THE WAR TO END ALL WARS, at least for Central Europe, at least for the rest of this century, or a little longer.

"Chancellor Krauty is bringing it all back home," the taxi driver says. "To hell with him and his victories," Klaus Barbie murmurs. "Too late for *me*." (Not for some of his companions.)

For lots of German men, the victories are just in time: waving flags, singing hymns, they watch their trigger fingers (having been amputated for a while) re-growing. We'll see whether Middle European HUMALITY has grown beyond the possibility of AND HE WAR.

People who never learned how to love a loss are dangerous. It's one of the beautiful experiences they never shared. I still love it, having become the owner of a lost war. (A war I carry around with me like a key.)

Loving lost wars makes a change in the war of the genders. But which man wants to lose a war to possibly win a woman? HE WAR still prefers rubber dolls wrapped up in flags. Fighting the feminization of a society means taking three steps to heaven (that sort of heaven only warriors reach).

LABOR PAINS

"I'm still a Leninist," German music critic Diedrich Diederichsen says. *"The reason is: Lenin was the only one who wanted to give power to the intellectuals."*

Now that communism has lost the cold war, it's also the intellectuals who have lost. Whether they really had their chance or not: nobody will believe any longer in the capacity of intellectuals to win world wars by means of their war: authoritarian philosophy wrapped up in weapons. The breakdown of state socialism in the European East was the last death throes of Western philosophy (a dying forecast by Nietzsche; one hundred years later it came to an end in Gorbachev, Reagan/Bush, and Honecker).

The IRON CAGE for intellectuals who had tried to be part of the political power of their countries came tumbling down with that WALL. Joshua spoke the truth: It was Music, Rock Music against state composers, that brought down the Walls of Jericho. It was the Trombones of Electronics, and it was the Western way of working, advertising, selling, buying; or, more precisely, the Western way of showing it all on the television screen. The superiority of the pictures produced by Western labor has defeated the works and the intellectuality of the East.

Maybe Gorbachev will end up being the only one to have changed a won war into a lost one. If it happens like that, it will be seen as a result of the weakness of Eastern *labor*.

The Western labor-weapon has beaten the East. War is a possible part of the work of Western presidents, chancellors, prime ministers. They go on working. Working for them *is* a kind of war making.

But to talk about war also means to talk about ways of working: productions, destructions, male ways of working, female ways of working, ways of constructing a reality, consuming a reality, destroying a reality.

The female production of giving birth to children and taking care of them, of doing housework, appears under the term *reproduction* in this thinking about productivity. Even feminist women use that term *reproduction* for the sort of labor their mothers did for them.

The term *reproduction*, so seemingly innocent, goes on keeping the gender gap wide, goes on deepening it. I wish it would be dropped completely and be left to the ants. But it is kept running by trade unions, governments, house fathers, mothers themselves, and ahead of them all, the industries producing the real gross social product. Mothering doesn't *add* to the gross social product. That's it. War does. War is more reasonable—in terms of production—than mothering is.

Maternal Thinking

The term *reproduction* is kept going even in a text I read in America, which, more than any other, is able to criticize fundamentally the terms of production/labor as they are used in the Western world.[3]

Sara Ruddick, thinking about mothering, finds definitions of human labor that are based neither on the philosophical abstraction of "human productivity" nor on the practice of industrial work/war in Western societies. Her definition of labor has grown out of the conditions of women's daily ways of dealing with the things that have to be done. She calls that kind of labor *caring labor*. The product of caring labor is not measured in money (though it has, in certain ways, to match market conditions). It's measured in abilities and competencies a grown-up person owes to a woman's work: the abilities to be alive, to perceive, be able to listen, be efficient and clever in producing things like "peace," deal with people and their problems without being destructive, invent room and procedures for nonviolent life.

The basis of the special female ability for these kinds of labor Sara Ruddick sees is a woman's capacity to give birth to a new human being. "*Whatever the state of technology, a man engages in no activity that can match, in labor, a woman's pregnancy, with its anxieties, discomfort, intrusive testing, painful delivery, and unique excitements and pleasures.*" But this is not a precondition. You don't necessarily have to give birth to a child to start with "caring labor."

Out of that term Sara Ruddick develops a whole system of living and thinking. Caring labor is a way of living, of thinking, a way of producing reality that (though it can be or even has to be militant) disconnects with making war, disconnects with the common (male) ways of destruction, disconnects with the common (male) way of linking labor to a sort of productivity that expresses its worth or unworth only in money relations, in economic victory or defeat.

Everybody—women, children, men—is capable of maternal thinking and caring labor. Everyone can learn to distinguish between ways of making things and people grow or making them die. You can add life to things and people and you can take it away from them. It's not a "natural gift" to make the things you touch flourish or wither. It's the kind of labor you enact upon them. It's a very far-reaching term, if you *want* to use it like that. And a very practical one: it's not difficult at all to tell, for example, a caring architecture from a destructive one. Living conditions would change rapidly if they were put under the purview and procedures of caring labor. And it's easy to see that no economy would have to suffer breakdowns if "caring labor" were at work. Only the world of profit *distribution* would have to suffer, heavily.

I feel this to be a radical new, a revolutionary definition of labor: the *making* of peace, professionally working on the gender difference. This time it's not the public talk of war makers about their being peaceful to the core. Caring labor disconnects with making war—though it can be or even has to be militant. It's not *pacifism*; it's the hard work required to identify violences wherever they occur—in boardrooms, bedrooms, factories, classrooms, and battlefields. Peacemakers do not turn away from violence but ferret it out, asking in detail who is hurt and how.[4]

Male reader, you are not convinced—how could you be? You will laugh: true utopian thinking seldom tries to talk you into something. Caring labor and maternal thinking include the knowledge that it is an experience to be practiced that leads to them, not the believing or not believing in an "idea."

Sometimes it turns out to be a fundamental experience. Part of the self-knowledge of my body is the experience of the distance I had to maintain while watching my wife giving birth to a child; sitting at her bedside, trying to give signs of help that in a way reached her, but much more didn't reach her, because she was in a reality too far away and too alien for me to enter: she working, me watching the labor that threatened to tear her body apart. I could see her body change her "nationality" as she began to live in a country I could never inhabit in the same way.

It's not difficult to realize that, as a male witnessing a birth. You're witnessing a transubstantiation: a female body, who tortures herself into this new life, "child." I think women transform themselves through that labor into beings possessed by a deep-rooted unwillingness to take that life away again. Not only *that* life: a disgust with killing, taking life away from anybody. I have often realized it in women; not only women who had borne a child. Call it mysticism; call it biology.

I hadn't realized it in my body before, because it probably hadn't been there with such certainty: the feeling that it is deeply wicked to take lives away from anybody—war or not war—by any kind of violence. It probably started at that moment and continued growing in later moments, related to the work with our children and their friends. That was a strange discovery for someone who had believed in the possibility of "just wars" up to then. The parts of my body armor that had "seen" the world as something you could "free" by the use of weapons in "the right way" began to fall.

In a man, this unwillingness to take away life will take some time to grow, maybe years, until you really can speak of a self-transformation. But it happens. You realize this change in a growing distance from common male talk, walking, and speech, from the tempo of decision making, the gestures of hands, the change of that steady wise smile on men's faces, in a changing attitude to male hierarchies (so very, very important to them). You recognize most men's poorly developed capacity to listen as compared with their wonderfully developed capacity to talk and talk things down that are not compatible with their systems: different kinds of labor of the tongues and ears. Hard work to change. The disconnection of "work" and "war" is one of the preconditions of this change.

Over the last eighteen years I have made the strange (and horrifying) discovery that most of the men you meet haven't the slightest possibility of understanding what "caring labor" is about, unless they themselves have done some work in that field. Not necessarily with a child; it can be with anything you cherish and foster (. . . the clearly felt unwillingness to share any longer the pleasures of destruction). The labor you do *really* changes the self.

CARE, CRIME, AND MALE WAYS OF GIVING BIRTH

Through Western history giving birth has been a *despised* form of labor, of living. Western males learned to trivialize and fear birthing labor, which should "stand at the center of a maternal history of the flesh." In all Western philosophy, the roles of natality, sexuality, and mortality are diminished, due to the elimination of the body from philosophical and scientific discourse. This happened through practices that alienated bodies from their own feelings (like those bodies I tried to describe in *Male Fantasies*, esp. vol. 2).[5] In trivializing women's birthing labor, men got used to claiming for themselves a higher creativity. "*Accepting no presuppositions but those they stipulate, they sail away, disown what went before, begin anew as Fathers of themselves.*"[6] Men want to be the products of their own labor. (They don't want to be born by mothers. From Plato to Goebbels, men called that way of birth "the wrong way.")

Men "spiritually" produce things, which they feel belong to a higher order than the productions of the female body: "*Everyone would prefer children such as these to children after the flesh,*" as Sara Ruddick quotes Plato about "productions of the (male) soul" from the Symposion. Men have always led this war most aggressively: not hesitating to call their productions *children* and to compare them with the productions of their women, giving themselves the crowns of THE REAL CREATORS.

Not considering birth *the* basic human labor has become the fundamental distortion of Western culture and other male-dominated societies. Disowning the mothers is the basic expropriation. Alienating women from their labor, men are fighting the fact that it is not God who gives life, but women.

You wouldn't need a god construction if you accepted women in the position of creators. Where creation and reason walk "hand in hand" there's no need for any figures of transcendence. Men wage their wars with "God on their side." AND HE WAR.

"Caring labor" indicates that human productions happen between at least two people. The subject of traditional philosophical discourse (an individual, a male individual) is disappearing in the lucidity of caring thinking.

Care isn't paid for and is socially despised. It has no authority. Father's authority is not earned by caring, Sara Ruddick says. That means it's worth more. That makes it more powerful. It's closer to war. Here is one of the bridges children may cross to find their mother's labors contemptible. Children get used to dancing across this bridge from one shore to the other, blaming the mother's work when having adventures on father's side (Why else do they have two different parents? Who could blame them?). Walking across this bridge too often means slipping into the common worshiping of war and crime as paying better than caring does.

It *is* the basic crime between the genders, to accept as a rule that you need not care for care.

THREE KINDS OF LABOR AND THE BODY OF THE "I"

So we have three main complexes of labor. Firstly, the sum of all that labor contributing to the gross social product (in factories, on farms, in workshops, in offices, in universities, at airports, in film studios, etc.). Jean-Luc Godard proposed separating it into two great divisions: the industries of the days and the industries of the nights; wanting to add all the work that is done in connection with human pleasure and recreation, tourism, show business, prostitution, and so forth, as "industries of the night," to a definition of human industrial productivity.

Secondly, there is the complex of wasting the economic wealth that is accumulated by all the working people of a community (wasting it in military expenditure; in astro adventures; wasting it in wars; wasting it in the big destruction organized between nations to keep their own citizens poor, needy and greedy). It's very hard work, but regularly done in our history up until now at certain intervals. All nations have had special workers for that kind of work, simple soldiers, officer soldiers, scientists.

A third, definitely a different sort of work, is caring labor.

The first two ways of work are closely linked to wars and to male procedures of organizing life, especially to organizing forms of birth and rebirth that are independent of the bodies of women. Its basis is *the individual (male) person* involved in a struggle for permanent increase of power.

The third way is linked to peaceful ways of production. It is fighting war as a means of human productivity. It can be done by women and men. Its basis is the connection of at least two people of whatever sex or age, caring for the growth and welfare of the other.

Many men, stating that *war* has been a big productive force for the development of our societies, are completely right. But they avoid answering the question whether *wars* lead to new inventions, ventures, investments, and the like. And they avoid counting the costs of destruction. But they look at human lives as something to be converted into the abstractions of victories or defeats, as something they have the right to use for their special productivity. Each feels himself to exist in deep disconnection from other people, in a powerful I-solation.

The military body is the perfect incarnation of traditional philosophical thought, of the "I." (Being right. Being undefeatable. Being systematic. Being addicted to work. Being alone. Shining in a suit of armor. Bearing a head on the shoulders for seeing through and winning wars.)

So the rocket as the most perfect representation of the military body is the embodiment of Plato today (his present-day reincarnation). The nuclear load in the rocket's warhead is a transmutation of Plato's brain. The old boys' network of science and black magic has never stopped spreading since the days of the Plato/Socrates male couple.

Some Words about the Rocket in My Pocket

"We'll do the motherhood role—telemetry, tracking, and control—the maintenance," the control officer says. He's talking about a new communications satellite system that would resist the electromagnetic impulses set free by a nuclear explosion. (Not knowing that he's quoting anybody ... using a central term from Margaret Mahler's psychoanalysis of psychotic children ... "maintenance" for their struggle to find a state of balance for their disturbed bodies.) Carol Cohn, having spent some time among so-called *defense intellectuals*, learned about the explosive abstraction of male birth giving.[7] The first hydrogen bomb was saluted as a newly born boy (and Edward Teller as the mother who carried the baby;

not having needed to provide an egg, only a womb for that task). The bomb is male progeny. Males give birth to wonderful explosions.

You could take that as a "code," for example, when an American general cables his expressions of joy about the first successful testing of that nuclear boy to the secretary of war in the words "*I could have heard his screams from here to my farm*," and when that secretary, Henry Stimson, hands that information to Winston Churchill at the Potsdam Conference with the words "Babies satisfactorily born." Carol Cohn states: "*The entire history of the bomb project, in fact, seems permeated with imagery that confounds man's overwhelming technological power to destroy nature with the power to create.*"[8]

I read Carol Cohn's quotation from William L. Laurence, after he witnessed the Trinity test of the first atomic bomb: "*The big boom came about a hundred seconds after the great flash—the first cry of a new born world. . . . They clapped their hands as they leaped from the ground— earthbound men symbolizing the birth of a new force.*" Watching "*Fat Man*" being assembled the day before it was dropped on Nagasaki, he described the bomb as "*being fashioned into a living thing.*"[9]

Reading this repeatedly, I find that the whole event as described by Laurence *parallels* a birth process as it used to happen in normal hospitals. "A big boom" and a "great flash" were the first two things a baby experienced in the old, traditional form of birth: getting her or his head out into a world of noise, s/he was taken by the doctor, banged with a clap of his hand on the ass, and the great flash of light outside the womb broke into the baby's eyes. The newly born child started crying and the doctor said, Everything is okay. Then the people who had been waiting outside (a father, grandparents, friends, relatives) getting the great news, leaping off the ground, laughing with joy (like the men in the desert watching the explosion), admiring the newborn world and hailing it: "It's a boy."

Laurence's description of the birth of the bomb contains every little trait of that traditional "real birth." He's speaking out of the truth of bodies that never really had the chance to experience the differences of being dead or alive emotionally. That doctor's clap on their asses was followed by treatment that separated men from their bodily feelings as potentially enjoyable feelings: Laurence is speaking in the language of armor-suited soldierly men, that of the military documents of the Western world (not only those of German soldiers, whose writings I have analyzed to some extent).

These are no "metaphors." He writes down what he sees. And what he sees is not a bomb exploding. What he sees is the birth of a new world. So he salutes the explosion of the bomb in exactly those words and actions a doctor would use, holding the newborn baby in his hands. Thousands of soldiers have told a similar story describing their being reborn through the eruptions of a machine gun.

Commander Schwarzkopf, happily enjoying his high-tech-boy-scout's parade, is not able, or willing, to tell the number of the bombed (killed) people in Iraq. Who is newly born doesn't count the number of those who don't count.

In August 1945 military men handed their own unbirth over to some hundred thousand—were they "living"?—"Japanese."

It *made* them feel alive. It's not "language." It's not a figure of speech: they try to be *accurate* in the description of *their* bodily transformation. The overwhelming feeling of becoming alive through powers of unthinkable energy: being birthed by a powerful mother. (By NATURE HERSELF. By the controlled power of nuclear nature herself.) It makes them jump and cry.

HE, who has the power to destroy everything, HE, who is DEATH and LIFE in person, really can claim to have created HIMSELF. The makers of the bomb are the first men to have been really successful in bringing this oldest of male fantasies into material reality. They really proved themselves to have made themselves and to be *alive!* All the "Living Dead" (we), crawling around in never-ending interminglings, polluting the surface of the globe, disappear in the meltings of that evolving mushroom. Only the *eye* that belongs to the witness of that process belongs to a person who really lives.

They, too, are transformed by the experience of witnessing a *birthing labor process*. They just manage to do it better, without needing women. You don't need women when you are in the position of the CREATOR. "*It was as if we stood at the first day of Creation*," Oppenheimer says (to the taxi driver). The taxi driver doesn't answer. He is driving GODFATHER DEATH, the figure successfully surviving life. That demands some respect.

If the bomb's destructive power lies in the bodily structure of the men handling it, it would be right to say *they* are nuclear power; "defense intellectuals" waiting for the moment that the button will start LIFE. "*The enormous destructive effects of nuclear weapons systems become extensions of the self, rather than threats to it*," Carol Cohn perceives clearly.[10] (Continuing Marshall McLuhan's "understanding" of technical media as "extensions of the self.") Men are being extended, transformed, reborn through the use of new technical media. The bomb was a new medium, like television; it has become the ultimate medium of change through media: being (re)born without women.

Perhaps it's too impossible to imagine: that there are human beings for whom REAL LIFE starts in the moment which for "us" would be the moment of the biggest thinkable (or "unthinkable") destruction. But probably there have been moments when "we" and "they" have been just the same or similar persons. We are living on that thin line every second of our lives. "Powder keg" was the old term for it. But it's wrong to call it a powder keg. We had better call it a life-giving miracle machine. The bomb's womb will give life to a world that previously was dead.

Or, previously was uneducated, childish, toddlerlike, staggering through the Oriental universe, as we hear Mr. General Westmoreland eloquently speaking his "*Talking Vietnam Blues*": Life is cheap, life is not important in the "Orient," we hear him say. They are not really born down there. The Vietnam War somehow was dealing with a child, he says, a child crawling around, trying its first steps (that's a literal quotation from *Hearts and Minds*).

What was he doing there? He was caring for the future life of those half-born Orientals while bombing their living rooms.

Wars as Liberators

"Wars," Sandra M. Gilbert says, "especially World War I, often have been the precondition for the liberation of women."[11] Miriam Cooke states the same thing for many women in Beirut during recent years: even the most horrible forms of civil war, with children snipers on every second roof of half-burnt houses, provided the chance for a lot of women to escape from the totally dependent roles of normal Muslim-housewife lives. Some of them started writing; so we know something about their experiences of leading lives of their own, having work and money of their own, being independent from husbands, communicating both the liberation and the threat of living on that thin line to death; things no Muslim women were able to speak about before.[12]

Many (especially writing) women after World War I told the same story; so did working-class women, especially from the munition factories, who expressed similar statements that the war had given them an unknown freedom as Angela Woollacott shows.[13]

"The war was too good to last," Gertrude Stein stated. H.D. (who did not fit the type of woman warrior) made sort of a lover out of that HE-WAR: "The war was my husband."[14] That marks the relationship to her more human husband, Richard Aldington, and to male lovers like D. H. Lawrence, who both, as husbands/lovers, rarely tried to be as bewitching as a many-stringed, multitalented creative woman would have expected them to be.

Can those sentences be read as a vote for wars? Aren't they clearly written against soldiers and men being soldiers? *The war* revealed how crazy those men really were. The war took them away; not bad.

Didn't women have a chance of making THE WAR just because they *didn't* have to share the fighting? That adds a special touch to the words of women speaking in favor of "wars." I don't hear them say they would have liked the male activities that are called warmaking to be done by themselves. They speak in favor of wars because wars opened some of the traps they were caught in, in so-called peace times (= patriarchal normality of war against women).

Margaret R. and Patrice Higonnet try to give an answer to this dilemma by using the image of a double helix, by which the possibility of female liberation through wars is tied to male ways of controlling: the double strategy of making presents and taking them away again. Wartime changes are short-term variations, they argue; after wars there are backswings; so wartime change often turns out to be illusory.[15]

Obviously both arguments are good: there is liberation for many women through the changes in civil life caused by wars, and there is the attempt of men to put women back into their old roles and places after the war work has been done. I hear a woman's voice in an old Cole Porter song singing: *I want your love / but I don't want to borrow / to have it today / and give it back tomorrow*; LOVE ME OR LEAVE ME, she says,—if borrowing is all you want. But "leaving" is just what the man doesn't want to do: borrowing and taking back is one of the main means of HIS love policy. It's not only in use after wars and not only in love. As far as I see, it's one of the main techniques of male ruling.

So what? We need your sex . . . we *want it* to borrow . . . to have it today . . . give it back tomorrow. Tomorrow, when we need soldiers or factory workers or state officials, men of trade and of the law . . . today we're going to put a sack over your sex again. As Sonya Michel shows, even women's sexuality is suppressed in postwar representations of the process of healing for disabled veterans, particularly to help them regain their masculinity.

And history starts a new round more or less without her. It belongs to the nature of the game to change the rules permanently, especially to change the rules that have been valid between men and women, also between parents and children, at least every time a new generation arrives in the public field.

∠"War liberates women"; yes; but male institutions, making use of liberated women, have a reliberation ever after. They reshape their forms of dominance, constructing some special corners for some free women's specialties, and win *their wars* just when some more women start thinking it would become a lasting freedom for them all.

Only the war that *ends wars* would put an end to the male way of reshaping (or rebirthing) a society through wars. As long as men have the power of their civil insitutions, and all these weapons and superweapons for winning and re-winning everything that can be won or re-won, the chances for real female equality aren't overwhelming. The disarmament of men and the replacing of HE WARS with some thousand forms of caring labor are more likely to reach the utopian shore of women not being dominated than are any imaginable form of wars. >297-8

"Victory and defeat are meaningless categories in a situation where violence has become a way of life, its own justification," Miriam Cooke says about the Intifada. So violence is part of the life of the women and the children, too. Miriam Cooke's statement that the Intifada ceased to be effective "when it became male-defined and politicized"—a claim for the superiority of women in the making of certain wars—I wouldn't doubt, as I wouldn't doubt the capacity of women for fighting when they are forced to fight. But I think I will go on suggesting that Arab men will try to push them back from postmodernity to modern Islam "when that war is over."

But "the proof of the pudding is in the eating," my dictionary says. There should be some "proof" in recent history concerning the durability of wartime changes and peacetime changes. The German generation to which I belong had the opportunity to study for some years an older generation, a soldierly educated generation, which was *forbidden* to lead its war for a long while. As a result of the treaties ending World War II, there was a stabilized peace order in Western Europe; for the older generation it was a sort of *dictated peace* they had to keep. For the younger people it was the first chance, in several generations, to grow up outside the standards of soldierly life. Ocassionally I realized how lucky we had been from 1967 on: all the changes then made in sexuality, in the development of egalitarian behavior through feminism and fighting political hierarchies, in ecology, in music and clothing, in ways of living together and even in working places—changes of a rather high durability (still going strong) could happen only through the absence of a war. What would the political leaders of the country have done to fight and to control these developments, which they *hated so much* from the bottoms of their hearts, if—? What would they have done if they had had the chance to send us into some little cute war to have half of us or more being shot, being pulverized in military action, how they would have loved it. How they envied America, which seemed to have the chance to abort the powers of this generation through Vietnam.

That is a sort of a proof, I think: most evolutionary developments for men *and* women since the sixties in Europe have been made in situations of nonwar. Our ruling male military and political powers were subjected to strong restrictions that prevented them from aborting and from controlling new libertarian developments with a real war. *Many* of the changes made through and after 1968 would have come anyway, with a war, without a war. I'm sure that *with* a war's possibility to shape them, to dis-shape them, their influence on civil life as it is to be seen now in almost every social class or group would have been much weaker; the changes would have been encoded with traits of military life, and the resigned wisdom of the simple destructibility of the human body amplified. I am especially sure about the fate of the changes that happened in workplaces, in factories and offices: they would not have happened at all in case of a war; they are among the first things wars manage to keep under hierarchical control: *work as war*—the song they have charted as their superhit for the last two centuries in the evolution of the West.

Even in Germany, a country ranking high among the magnificent countries of war and work criminals, there are some grown-up, reasonable people now in public life who reject the idea that work/war is the undisputed center of a useful human life, as it has been to the preceding generations. It's a *peace*-time change. A nonwar situation opened some doors to the thinkability of caring labor (even to some men).

LOOK AT THE TORTURER

SOLDIERS SHOOT DEFENSELESS INDIANS

Guatemala City (German Press Agency). Guatemalan soldiers staged a massacre of unarmed Indians on Sunday night, when they shot at least eleven of the natives. Other reports speak of even more than twenty dead. More than twenty were said to be hurt. According to the report of Guatemalan human rights lawyer Ramiro de Leon Carpio the massacre took place when soldiers from the garrison in Santiago Atilan, about 150 kilometers west of the capital, started firing on more than 1000 demonstrating Indians. They were protesting the arrest of a native during a military raid some hours before. The Army expressed its regret for the "tragic event."

The tragic incident the army mourns is that they didn't manage to make that Indian a prisoner without witnesses to protest the arrest publicly right afterward. They had been *searching* for that man (or woman) for quite a while. That's what they do all the time: make *guerrilleros* prisoners, afterward torturing them publicly to death under the eyes of their relatives and other witnesses whom they force to watch the torturings. I learned that from Irene Matthews, when she introduced the narrative of the Guatemalan Indian woman Rigoberta Menchu, recorded and transcribed by Elisabeth Burgos-Debray.[16]

The small report I quoted above is from a newspaper in December 1990. The world is full of tragic events like that. Events you never quite notice when you let your eyes stray through newspaper countries, making sure that once again it is not you who's dead or imprisoned, but really alive, busy doing your information homework. Only if you know something about the place and the people mentioned there, bells may start ringing in your head. Knowing Rigoberta Menchu, I know that article is speaking of torture (without saying anything about torture). Torturing is a criminal act, taking the tortured persons to the edge of death, into zones of experience about which they can't later speak. Whoever has suffered torture will hardly accept anything that is written about the pains of being tortured. It will not contain them.

Not so with the torturers. They are acting, and those who act get a language. Also, there are witnesses who are forced to speak about what they have seen, at least partly to get rid of the mind-burning scenes. Rigoberta Menchu's narrative about the torturings of the bodies of Indian people, executed and exhibited by soldiers of the Guatemalan army, are the most horrible reports I have heard since the Nazi torturings in the camps. Having written about the Nazi torturers and the bodily structure of fascist violence as a special form of male violence, I may be allowed to look at the torturers of the Guatemalan army in relation to Nazi soldiers and German men of the SS, torturing women, torturing communists, torturing Jews.

Torture is a relationship between people, a very distorted sort of relationship, where one side has all the power and the other none. Nevertheless, the action is not one-sided: to understand the work of torture, it is not only necessary to comprehend what the torturer does to his victim but what he does to himself. The effect of torture is double-sided: to destroy the victim, to eliminate a "threat" the victim embodies; and to construct the torturer as a new person. The production of a dead person on the one hand is matched by the production of a newborn person on the other. The torturer gets a new body while the body of the tortured is brought into shapes of vexation, the view of which the torturer needs for his own transformation.

At the heat of violence Canetti discovered the obsession with surviving: still to be there where others have vanished. To be standing where others are lying. To be a *single* survivor where the dead are piled up.

In terms of bodily countenance: the torturer (like all professional survivors) psychophysically is not balanced enough, is not strong enough to make his living without consuming the lives of others. Like a lover he needs another person for his own growth; but where a lover makes the other person grow, the torturer tries to annex this other: he transforms the other person into *a part of his own body; a part of his body he wants to get rid of.* The tortured thus are treated as parts of the body of the torturer: parts of his body the torturer doesn't have under control; parts of his body the torturer hates; parts of his body the torturer feels himself forced to kill.

The trancelike state most torturers bring themselves into while torturing—starting with "rational" questions, wanting "information" or "confessions" of guilt and so forth, then getting into a frenzy, becoming addicted to the act of torturing—has to do with that process of the disappearance of the borders between the body of the torturer and the body of the tortured person. In the perception of the torturer, he becomes "a whole," a whole that the torturer survives by cutting all destructive and hurting parts out of himself. He then feels balanced, undisturbed, guiltless, happy.

To describe this process I used a term developed by Margaret Mahler in the psychoanalysis of so-called psychotic children. These children manage to achieve their feelings of bodily wholeness through destructive acts Mahler understood to be acts of maintenance. "Maintenance drives" rule the bodies of people who, because of certain violence their bodies had to suffer, never achieve a bodily state where the drives are working according to what Freud called the pleasure principle.

You could call it a "pain principle," according to which these bodies have been brought up.

I described three main aspects to the acts of torturers: acts of "maintenance" (getting feelings of being "whole" by torturing every disturbing movement of other people, coming into touch with one's own body, to death); secondly, the act of doing to others what was done to oneself (but never doing it to the persons who did it because they are in master positions of the respective hierarchy); thirdly, acting out this "doing to others" from the position of a mighty figure in one's own hierarchical system: the position of a "parent," a "commander," a "teacher," a "god." Torturers speak as godlike *teachers* when speaking to their victims. Torturers are great correctors.

The maintenance actions of the German soldiers/torturers were aimed at three special perceptions of the bodily states of the victims. I name them according to the view the torturers desired of their victims and the special sort of trance this view inspired: "empty place," "bloody miasma," and "blackout." Are these terms peculiar to Germany of a certain time and military culture, or can they be applied to torture in other countries and cultures? Is torturing a male activity? An activity conducted by male bodies during certain states of *psychical fragmentation*, defining torture as one of the "healing forces of the universe" for the torturers' bodies?

Torture as Teaching. Torturing Men Having Fun

The brother of Rigoberta Menchu, sixteen years old and accused of being a *guerrillero*, was captured by the Guatemalan army in September 1979. Among twenty other men and one woman he was tortured for weeks to give the soldiers "information" about the hiding places of *compañeros* and about their actions. In the end he was killed with the others under the eyes of relatives and other village people who were forced to become witnesses to the killing, as a lesson: learning what would happen to them if they joined the "guerrillas."

What is this lesson/performance for? To teach the Quiché Indians something about governmental power? To present the captain as the army's Big Star? All the spectators, though crying, are filled with rage, Rigoberta Menchu says. As a result, they will all join the guerrillas in the next few days. That's what the captain is working for: to keep increasing the number of enemies he will be able to kill. To keep his daily work as a necessary job for which the government pays him. It wouldn't make any sense just to turn the Indians into "democratic Guatemalan people." That would mean his being just one among others. He teaches the Indians how to become guerrillas and he demonstrates to himself and to his soldiers their own invulnerability, their own supreme power, their own godlike state compared to the state of their victims and of the audience of his death theater.

"*He said that they had all kinds of weapons that we could choose to be killed with. The captain gave a panoramic description of all the power they had, the capacity they had. We, the people, didn't have the capacity to confront them. This was really all being said to strike terror into the people and stop anyone from talking.*"

—all capacities of the world gathered in the captain, the Indians silenced and weeping—

"*The officer called the worst of his criminals—the Kaibiles, who wear different clothes from the other soldiers. They're the ones with the most training, the most power. Well, he called the Kaibiles and they poured petrol over each of the torutred. The captain said, "this isn't the last punishment, there's another one yet. This is what we've done with all the subversives we catch, because they have to die by violence. And if this doesn't teach you a lesson, this is what'll happen to you.*"

Then the soldiers set fire to each one of them, making the half-dead tortured persons jump and cry for a last time. That's the moment the soldiers (the "teachers") start laughing. And it's the moment the watching Indians start getting out their machetes and other weapons, recklessly forgetting about caution and about the soldiers' guns and about the helicopters flying over the village all the time (to keep guerrillas who possibly could have been hiding in the nearby woods from bringing help to the village people).

The captain doesn't give an order to fire into the Quiché population. Not *this* time. That would be a simple act of war. It would mean turning the wonderful situation of funny teaching into a fight; fighting at this moment would mean destroying the essence of the whole action. Fighting now would disturb the experience of being transformed by an act of art

into bodies of giant power; it would disturb the sensations of the maintenance action the soldiers feel their bodies in: happily laughing, finding a
balance against the threats of bodily dissolution they usually live in. They
retreat.

"Well, the officer quickly gave the order for the squad to withdraw.
They all fell back holding their weapons up and shouting slogans as if it
were a celebration. They were happy! They roared with laughter and
cried, 'Long live the Fatherland! Long live Guatemala! Long live our
President! Love live the army, long live Lucas!' "

This moment of happiness and laughter, that is to be found at the very
center of so many torturings, is no accident at all. It's the boyish way of
feeling like "a man" all over the world, it seems. Guatemalan soldier-
kids; Tim O'Brien's American boy soldiers in Vietnam, laughing at their
slaughtering of an animal ("revenging the death of a friend");[17] German
Freikorps soldiers (mostly farmer boys) laughing about those dirty Ruhr
Valley workers (see how they run!); Gestapo people or SS men: we see
them teaching, correcting, lecturing on "the Truth," that means torturing, killing, loving their miraculous powers, giving death while starting to
live, feeling happy, having fun, completely unable and unwilling to grasp
the least bit of the reality of the suffering. The elimination of threats
within one's own body is pure pleasure: killings are a pleasure that leave
no room for any other feelings. Argentine soldiers, in the reports of Alicia
Partnoy, administer narcotics to prisoners "to calm them down," because
they are to be transported to other camps or prisons. They are joking:
they know their injections are the overture to death; the prisoners will be
shot. Obviously they are playing ("staging") Nazi doctors before the eyes
of their victims. They have big mirrors in their torture rooms, reflecting
themselves in great shape. And the newspaper next day will report people
having been killed "in armed confrontation" with the military forces—
ha ha!!

Or, reading the reports of some of the young snipers in Beirut, we hear
them talking about the pleasure of reaching the evening as survivors of
the shooting; there's no difference between "surviving" and "fun."
Guards dislocate the shoulders of a prisoner, then hang him by the arms
in a well of water; isn't that crazy, isn't that reason enough for hearty
laughter?

Inflicting pain on others diminishes the pain in the torturers' bodies;
that seems to be common to every act of torturing. Watching Marcel
Ophuls's film Hotel Terminus I hear a Frenchwoman talking about Klaus
Barbie's actions as a torturer: He just liked to inflict pain, she says. He
didn't care what he asked. No, they never care. They are busy waiting for
the feeling. The torturer, while torturing, is constructing himself as a
pain-free person. The more pain he is inflicting on the bodies he is de-

stroying, the easier he feels himself. It isn't a "cynical" act at all: it's his way of self-liberation, his way of body-psychoanalysis. Torturing is how tortured bodies find happiness. Rigoberta Menchu's description of the killing of her brother and other Quiché Indians by the army reveals that once again with horrible clarity.

In this case, the torturers are not reported by the tortured persons themselves, because the tortured are dead. But there are cases where the tortured persons survive and nevertheless are unable to *speak* in an "explaining" or in a "descriptive" way about the tortures they suffered. There are only two kinds of voices relating torture: the voices of the torturers (more or less happily) "confessing," and the voices of persons forced into being witnesses of torturings, speaking with tears and helpless rage. The voice of the tortured body mostly remains in silence. We know this silence from many victims of the concentration camps as well.

What happened to their voices? Do they "refuse" to speak for lots of understandable reasons, or "can't" they speak, having been robbed of their voices by the tortures they had to suffer?

Elaine Scarry in her book on "pain" suggests the answer: they can't speak.[18] Pain is not speakable; the experience of being injured, of being tortured, is not expressible in language; "pain" excludes "language about pain" from existing in the same body. Pain, of the intensity inflicted by torture, transcends the capabilities of the human body to be "felt" or to be "kept" by this body in memory; the body is deleted as a living body when tortured; the still-living body becomes part of the world of the dead. No language can articulate that experience of sudden deadness. The possibility of language becomes "tilt." The same thing happens to people who have suffered a shock which turned them (for moments or longer) into persons suddenly dead (finding themselves among the living afterward). Tortured persons carry that death experience as the absolute inability to "report" that experience; they carry it as an objectlike silence. "Death" has no language. It speaks through this objectlike silence out of the tortured person.

"When you lose your war, you lose everything," but you don't lose the ability to re-win that lost thing and you haven't lost your language. On the contrary, warriors change their language into an instrument to re-win lost wars; having lost a war is not a total loss. Having lost a war is not torture.

Having been forced into losing one's body in torture, to give it away to the dead and to the power of the torturer, is a loss much harder, a loss much deeper. It robs the tortured body even of the history of the torture; of the torture as having been something that *happened* to the tortured body. The torturer takes the whole *event*. He becomes *the owner* of the tortured body, the *owner of the capacity to have feelings*, which is robbed from the tortured body during the torture he or she suffers. That could explain the difference between the descriptions of torturings given by the torturers and the tortured. Jean Amery, who was tortured by SS people, saw them "working" on his body in a sort of concentrated earnestness. He didn't see them on that road to happiness the torturers so often see themselves on. Jean Amery, like many other tortured persons, tries to speak as a subject in full control of his perceptions. But when the pain transcends the brain's capacities to remember, to "store" the "feelings," the "subject" ceases to exist. The waves of the burning pain wipe out the controlled perception of the ego.[19] *That's* the moment of the torturers' happiness; the tortured person, sent off to another state of being, will not see this.

The spectacle of torture by the ruling political powers of a country is something like the "surplus" of the torturer's work going to the state that pays for this work: the public threat to members of the community that they will have to die by means of one of the tortures exhibited if they don't obey the commands and demands of the ruling forces. Every terroristic state, every dictator, every Mafia gangster, every leader of a criminal society is completely aware that torture must not be executed in secrecy: it has to be exhibited to be effective. Where there is absolute power there is no lack of tortured bodies shown in public.

The state takes over the theater, Diana Taylor realizes of the South American situation. Torture, terror, theatricality: the state takes over the spectacle, infantilizing a people. Actors are men. A public male identity is constructed under a female gaze, watching it admiringly or in fear. Some Argentine women, the mothers of the disappeared at the Plaza del Mayo, took it back from the government and gave the "theater," the art of acting for freedom in public, back to the people again.

The *shared knowledge* of being allowed to commit open criminal acts elevates the feelings of joy to unexpected heights or intensities. Rigoberta Menchu named the special troopers who set fire to the bodies of the tortured Quiché Indians (the *Kaibiles*) criminals. That's exactly the word. They enjoy the ritualized knowledge of being allowed to act in the regions of the utmost transgression of human laws. The biggest joy on earth is acting in total criminality, and *not being punished* for it. On the contrary: being a criminal in the name of justice, sheltered by the power of THE LAW. That seems to be the (boyish) sensation at the heart of all torture actions all over the world: kicking it all off, making it all the bloody mash that is the real shape of being; being the absolute criminal and being a good boy at the same time, teaching lessons about "Good and Evil." Good good boy who'll get some sticker from a Godfather when back home. Torture is the beloved thing at the center of male criminality: its shared open secret.

No Female Culture of Torture

The lust to become alive while torturing, cutting, tearing apart a body, then touching it "sexually," is male: not just "common" to men, but possible in men.

Do the comparably few women we know as torturers, in concentration camps or in war situations, demand another way of thinking about this?

Reading Marguerite Duras's confession of having tortured a traitor in her book *The War*, I see and hear that women of course are capable of committing cruel acts—being torturers, murderers, or in the camps, beastly criminals; but at the same moment it becomes clear that "the woman as a torturer" hardly is obsessed by the formation of feelings that we find at work among male torturers. The torturing as described by Marguerite Duras happens within a system of emotional *control*; reason is a ruling method. The torture will have an *end* after a while, after its "result," the "confession" or whatever, is to be seen. It is not directed toward the total destruction of the victim. It is not executed as work *primarily done* on behalf of one's own body. On the contrary: some women leave the room during torture that they feel to be without sense (and without *sensation*). They don't want to see this act of "justice"; it's no fun to them. They accept that it may be necessary to do things like that in certain situations. The surplus of lust achieved by male ways of torturing is completely lacking. The scene leaves the torturer crying (not laughing).

"Which way is it?" Lynn Higgins asks. "Is there no 'female culture of torturing' because torture doesn't do to/for the female body/identity what it does to/for the male torturer? Or is it the other way around: because women don't lust for torture, there is no female culture of torture?"[20]

I'd be happy if I knew. As women haven't had the power to act violently as men mostly could, there can't be final proof whether there is or is not a gendered essence. The problem would not be the "hot feminist potato" it still is if there were an answer. There are dominant and resistant cultures within the genders; so learning, bonding, working together, changing relations remain the main issues, and not an essential gendered nature.

Although, for my part, I have experienced life in a way that suggests the answer: there is an essential difference; I feel a sort of violence spreading from male bodies at all places of the planet I've been, which have no parallel in what female bodies are "telling" me. It's not proof at all, only my persuasion (fed by some bits of experience).

MEMORIES ARE MADE OF—WHAT?

The memory is a weapon for re-winning lost wars: what one person claims to "remember," another will not "believe." It may contain a "truth," but only accidentally.

MEMORY & MEMORY: we have an abstract memory, making our lives look quite similar; and a "personal" memory, which is the agent of our interests and feelings. The abstract memory is a storer and agent of institutions and all other things belonging to the official powers which rule us. It constructs an abstract person out of us. Whereas the storer and anarchist of the personal memory is a lone warrior, fighting the storage of all other memories as "wrong."

Warriors' memories go like this: "We waited till we could see the whites of their eyes . . . then we fiiiired," as Alec Guiness on the screen and all the front hogs at home told us in 20 billion abstract narratives, each as like the other as one pine needle resembles another.

Who stores? Who speaks? Who is speaking and what has been stored in the narrative of the Vietnam bomber pilot telling his interviewer, Dr. Stan Rosenberg, that "the first ten flights" are those you really fear? Then the fear ceases. "If you survive the first ten flights, you'll survive the next hundred." Got it? We can hear all the pilots sneering in their graves who have been shot down between flights forty to seventy. That doesn't make any difference to the narrator. His narration is not meant to be "true"; it's meant to drive away a fear. The fear felt during the flights in combat; the fear possibly appearing in the narrator now. He's neither lying nor telling "the truth," nor is he "remembering" something. He's constructing a reality he needs for his balance in this very second of life. He uses his "memory" to *construct a history he can live with now*. The abstract "memory" *rarely* talks about things that happened. It uses the names and events of the "past" to construct the sort of present the constructor now wants to live in. He's writing or talking like a *program* for himself and for others, which he/they can act out. So the reports of soldiers, "remembering" something, can't be taken as documents about what *happened* or what they did; but they tell a lot about bodily structures, wishes, fears, goals, the "program" of the speakers for the present moment.

The "abstract pilot," conditioning us with his story about the fear ceasing after the "tenth flight," speaks like that just *because* he survived. He carries the structure of a survivor as his program: wanting to make us survivors too (people of the same race). The more you survive (after the tenth flight in talking down your wife you've reached the state of invulnerability), the nearer you draw to the core of power; the more you survive, the more abstract (the more *programmatic*) your "memory" grows. The survivor's memory, speaking from the pole of anesthesia, has stored the tested invulnerability (blood proof) of its owner. Who speaks? A power without feelings wanting to make you a person according to its own image.

A body-snatching system wanting to produce layers, anesthetic against the differences of persons and genders.

.   .   .   .   .

What are technical media doing to the structure and working mechanisms of "the memory"?

Everything people of the twentieth century "remember" having *heard* during their lives is coshaped by the existence of tape recorders, radios, record players. Some say *totally* shaped by the media in use; it's not necessary to decide that debate here. This much is sure: our *inner* memories (the abstract one, the individual anarchist, the keeper of the traces of wounds and caressings) not only connects with the archives and methods of the outer memories (libraries, museums, tapes, photographs, movies, computers); to a certain degree the bodily memories have been programmed by the technical ones. Musicians play in ways they have heard on discs or tapes. Painters in 1910 tried to make use of Van Gogh's recording technique, then Picasso's. It's not *imitation*. People carrying ghetto blasters get a transistor growing in their bodies for the sudden amplification of their feelings. The Walkman changes the nervous system into a battery-driven *perpetuum mobile* (including autoreverse).

Politicians, or other public people who are forced to hide away their "private lives" or obsessions, have exactly the kind of past that has been recorded in a file by an institution. The memory of East German politicians like Lothar de Maiziere or Ibrahim Boehme, having cooperated with the STASI (the CIA of the former German Democratic Republic), is exactly coextensive with the recordings in the archives that are found or not found. As Foucault liked to put it: the person is defined by what is kept in the files of a documentary center. So is the memory of the "person." No other memory exists. Being programmed by STASI or the CIA, you only remember about yourself whatever some spy wrote, tape-recorded, or photographed.

"Remembering" or "not remembering" simply means making decisions about the reality to be produced. This history-*producing* trait of memory work is very interesting; especially interesting when combined with the question whether "memories," in their work of producing actual realities, can be understood to be gendered. Are there male as opposed to female ways of constructing a memory, and how are they related to the different forms of making wars or avoiding wars by men and women?

I started thinking about this while listening to Marianne Hirsch and Leo Spitzer speak about Claude Lanzmann's refusal to have Jewish women represented in *Shoah*. At first, I felt it to be unseemly to talk about Lanzmann's film like that. I had seen *Shoah* as an extremely moving and adequate effort to give the victims of the Holocaust a presence in our minds; a presence so needed in Germany.

But the parts of the film that Marianne Hirsch and Leo Spitzer showed and talked about proved their perception not only to be accurate but necessary for people who want to learn something about gendered ways of constructing "history."

Hirsch and Spitzer argue that Claude Lanzmann, constructing and cutting his huge material, didn't make use of the narrations of Jewish women even when he could easily have done so. Reviewing the film, it became clear that Lanzmann preferred men to be his "witnesses"; it also became apparent to me that almost every part of the film is centered around a *male couple*; male couples, reconstructing parts of the history of the holocaust.

What does that mean for the sort of "memory" at work in that film; and what are "male couples?" In *Book of Kings*, vol. 1, I have described how several artists, who felt themselves to be an "Orpheus of their times," sacrificed a woman, a Eurydice; Orpheus-man needs a dead woman, sent into Hades (by Orpheus's turning back on the "stairs") as a connection to the "past," which is "stored" in Hades. Another couple is part of the production game: not Orpheus coupling with another woman, but with another man, who knows the rules and secrets of his productions and who understands and helps. Quite often that man appears as a person living at the other end of a stream of letters, as in the cases of Gottfried Benn/W. F. Oelze, or Sigmund Freud writing to Wilhelm Fliess while step by step, letter by letter, discovering psychoanalysis. The strict exclusion of women from that level of producing artificial realities in art or science belongs to the rules (or laws) of male production in our societies.

As Lanzmann often stated, he could not have made his film without the research of historian Raul Hilberg. Lanzmann screened himself with Hilberg clearly as a couple of *two wise men* looking through the secrets and mysteries of history: *looking through and caring for them*; caring for the memory of the burnt Jewish people. The camera is close to Lanzmann's and Hilberg's faces studying documents; it circles around their faces. An eye, opening wide, a head, nodding severely toward the face of the other, a slow deep knowing smile, "understanding" silent movements of closed lips, eyes meeting eyes, all of it in the closest close-up, camera movements creating a male couple before our eyes; a couple filled with knowledge; doing its best to give us the truth; hardly speaking; and *if* speaking, it is in slow, heavy, well-pondered words.

Lanzmann took this coupling with Raul Hilberg as a model to construct his documentary of the holocaust; a "documentary," which he (with full right) wants to be seen as a work of art. What sort of art?

Lanzmann couples, in the different sequences of the film, with Simon Srebnic, then with the "old man" sitting on the stairs in front of his house in Chelmno, with the locomotive driver Gawkowski in Treblinka, then with Filip Müller, with Abraham Bomba, with Rudolk Vrba, with Richard Glazar, with Jan Karski. Every sequence has one or two chief witnesses with whom Lanzmann's camera constructs a special intimacy.

Would the presence of the female voices whom Hirsch and Spitzer name have made any difference? Does it matter that it is a woman or a man in front of the camera telling what she or he "remembers" of the holocaust? Marianne Hirsch and Leo Spitzer draw our attention to two narratives in *Shoah* that tell something about just that difference. The narratives are about two Jewish leaders who committed suicide when they could no longer bear the responsibilities for their people. Knowing they were all bound to die, knowing they wouldn't be able to help them, they chose to kill themselves. Both appear in the roles of *caring men*, one of them in Theresienstadt, the other one in the Warsaw ghetto. Their suicides are presented by Lanzmann as models of "responsible fathering."

Der Spiegel asked moviemaker Wim Wenders to write a eulogy for Fritz Lang the day after he died. Wenders wasn't so sure what to write, except that Lang's death reminded him that German postwar movie makers like himself had not had moviemaking *fathers* to admire. They had all worked in exile. So he was discovering Fritz Lang as a possible father now. He got the idea of phoning up Sam Fuller in Beverly Hills (or Santa Monica), to ask what his friends were going to do about Fritz. O yeah, Sam Fuller told him, we'll have a night watch. He and some friends would sit down with a bottle all night long and have Old Fritz remembered. That's fine, Wim Wenders closed his article; some old men would be sitting with a whiskey bottle caring, and things would be all right.

In both cases, we have the Old Jewish patriarchal tradition of *two wise men* (rabbis, or an assembly of wise men) congregating and thinking through and solving the problems of the world. This form of caring in *Shoah* works, as Hirsch and Spitzer say, as a gendered translation.

Maybe it's unintentional, unconscious, maybe even against the filmmakers' will; but they are using a narrative structure which says, "Two

old men will tell you how it was. . . . This time it's Raul and me giving
you the bitter truths. . . . Another time there will be two other men, caring." Additionally, Lanzmann encodes the women, who appear, as
Hirsch and Spitzer show, with threats of destruction and death. Men caring; women in the role of "Cassandras."

It is a gendered memory structure, producing the history of the holocaust as a history to be "remembered" and kept in mind as a history of
Jewish male caring. Male survivors of the camps are put together in positive or "good" couples with Lanzmann, to have the history of the camps
reconstructed. There are some "bad" couples, also—Lanzmann together
with survivors of the killer side, for example, with SS-Mann Franz Suchomel—but it's the same intimate, coupling structure.

The memory of events is a *production* by (at least) two people. It's
simultaneously a reconstruction and an artifact. So it's not possible to tell
the reconstruction of a "past" from the construction of a momentary
presence. In the case of *Shoah*, "memory" reaffirms an institutionalized
male aesthetic of male responsibility and vitalizes it to construct present
historical thinking. Women are not messengers from history, but from
Hades.

. . . . .

European writer-politicians like E. Juenger or A. Marinetti pioneered the
path of encoding the term "beauty" with warmaking around the time of
World War I. It struck me forcefully to see Tim O'Brien digging that same
passage through the heads of American readers now. "*It can be argued,
for instance, that war is grotesque. But in truth war is also beauty.*"

That far the text could have been copied from the European right-wing
futurists. What is the word *beauty* doing in sentences like that? There isn't
any *written law* to decide what is beautiful and what is not. You cannot
argue about it. Nobody is able or entitled to tell another person what she
or he should find "beautiful." So it's no use giving Tim O'Brien the answer: "No, an artillery barrage isn't beautiful to me at all." He knows
that, "smiling." But I *can* say that the word *beauty* simply doesn't belong
in the context of killing. Whoever uses it there is a criminal, wants to be
a criminal and *knows* it. The same is true for "morality" and "purity."
Killing is not a question of morality or purity, but of the written laws of
a country. Where the written laws say that killing in war is necessary and
legal, you can't argue that it is illegal. You can only detest it. Just the
same, it's not a matter of warfare to find the sounds and colors of the
killing "beautiful." That sentence is not covered by any law. It makes out
of the killing in war an act of pleasure. That's not demanded by law. It's
only a personal predilection. A personal predilection for killing and de-

struction would be a matter of simple criminality. And not a matter of aesthetics. Neither is a matter of war. Saying that you find the colors in Monet or Matisse "beautiful" is a different thing: you aren't destroying anything or anybody. To connect the term "beauty" with war and destruction is a mean act of robbery. *War is beautiful*: the complete distortion, "not speakable," like pain is not speakable.

Male language doesn't care about the unspeakable. It feels itself powerful enough to speak about everything. It can do so by cutting the cord between the voice and the body. The human voice, in Elaine Scarry's definition, is "the unreliable narrator of bodily events." The result of cutting it off is that death is life, that pain is pleasure, that napalm is something to feed the eyes with, that the end of the world is a beginning, that the Eve of Destruction is the Morn of Creation.

You can't argue about it. You can't discuss it. The only thing to say would be, "Swallow your shit, man. It's delicious."

That's exactly what the sentence *But in truth war is also beautiful* is all about.

You don't believe me? (You're quite intelligent for a guy with two brains.) "But in truth the brain is also a football."

After a firefight there is always the immense pleasure of aliveness.[21] A TRUE WAR STORY would contain this sentence only, five thousand times this sentence on three hundred pages.

Once again it's the emptiness at the bottom of the well. He who knows nothing teaches the lessons. If you aren't experienced in anything, war will appear as the great promoter. *Immense pleasure . . . aliveness . . . beauty*: yes, if you have been kept dead and ugly before. And then you have a *reason* to kill.

A woman could write and can write the sentence "War was too good to last."

I can't imagine a woman having written or writing the sentence "War is beautiful" (except in a TRASH MOVIE directed by a man). It's a gendered sign. A sticker, to be shown proudly. That sentence somehow marks the surface line of that abyss known as the "gender gap."

TECHNOMUSCULARITY

Who really wins wars? Rarely the people who fight them. Rarely the people who get this or that short-term liberation or short-term fun. Most of them simply will be dead before the war is over.

Wars are won by certain technologies. World War I produced the victory of the radio, of electricity, of the motor car, of military aircraft, and of the chemical industries.

World War II produced the victory of concrete, of rockets, of the hydrogen bomb, of spaceships. It developed civil aircraft; tourism for everyone and the victory of TV over the cinema.

World War III, some people say, is urgently demanding entrance into OUR WORLD because of the need of electronics to get into control and rule the earth. Defeating KING OIL and his dictatorship of the GULF, Mr. President is pioneering the possibility of turning The Fire in the Bush into an electronic revelation.

All revolutionary technical inventions (McLuhan says, Friedrich Kittler says) came into life and power through wars. Probably they are right.

Do we have to draw the conclusion (as McLuhan and Kittler fear we have to) that the ongoing and every further revolution in the technical fields necessarily will occur—"that's the way evolution works"—with new world wars? The Presidents of Evolution in the West and in the East are damned near giving their applause to that spectacle.

The old—the mechanical—techniques of the nineteenth century used transmission systems like toothed wheels, hydraulics, belts, crankshafts, and universal joints, which can be compared to the ways the human body works. Muscles, tendons, joints, and the lung can be seen as blueprints of the transmission systems of mechanics, kinetics, pneumatics. But there is no analogue to the brains or nerves in these technologies. The oil, circling inside the machines, stands for the blood circulation, not for the central nervous system.

Is the electronic technology of today (into which our central nervous system, tortured by the mechanical world, has long since emigrated, as McLuhan says) already emancipated enough to resist the crude procedure of "war" on its way to power? That's not easy to answer. But it's possible to see the superhuman flexibility and capacity of electronics; it's possible to realize that it is a sort of technology *not necessarily* calling for the bomb; it is prone to the consequences of strong nuclear radiation.

"Mankind" (at least its male components) will not put the world into the state of "peace"; if somebody/something will do so, it will be—the skills of technologies?

I don't see a race between "humans" on one side and "technologies" on the other side. What I see is the rat race between different technologies: the primitive, brutish, megalithic war-bound technology of nuclear fission in competition with the precise, subtle, nerve-processing microelectronicity (though it's true that the rockets with the nuke on top can find their way only by microelectronic subtleties).

Nuclear fission has no side where it could touch civil lifegame procedures of people in highly technical societies like ours who are trying to deviolate life. Electronics have many. They call for the transformation of life (even of working life) into a life of "playing the game."

Caring labor plus electronics—in that direction something like a formula for POE (Peace on Earth) could perhaps be found. (Or am I absolutely crazy?) That would mean a change from the "technomuscularity" (Lynda Boose's word) which has been poisoning the screens, books, and political scenarios of recent years and at the moment of writing this conducts its war in the GULF, to a technohumanity, in which the traditional adversity of women and "machines" had vanished and the traditional interchange of technology and weapons on the male side as well.

It's a male game to sell weapons to unarmed nations, then put them into local wars, supporting their military leaders as dictators, then turn the dictators into enemies of one's own country, so finally having a reason to unleash one's own huge weaponry on them and their people. It's a male game to talk about "trade controls" for chemical weapons, rockets, planes. As long as they are produced, they will be sold and used. Their production has to be banned to give life a chance.

Pushing the button on my remote control, taking a look at MTV, I see Janet Jackson. She's saying what she thinks America's problems are. "It's a country between education and chaos," she says, with a smile on her lips under her blue baseball cap. People consider her a workaholic, she says. She doesn't feel that she is. Smile. Working hard isn't a drug addiction, I understand. Nor is it an education. It's a form of caring for "chaos" to disappear, this time in dancing shoes.

Pushing the button again, I catch Commander Schwarzkopf, busy transforming the TV screen into a rocket's eye: a camera, installed in a missile's brain, is broadcasting a picture of the explosion it causes. That's the start of REAL TIME—the identity of a computed reality with a reality happening somewhere—as part of our everyday lives. With a BIG BANG these pictures are exploding in our heads. WE are the goal of Commander Schwarzkopf's Video Games. THE MEDIUM IS THE ROCKET. That's the ultimate (male) NEWS. (For an answer see Thomas Pynchon, *Gravity's Rainbow*, p. 760.)

NOTES

This essay is dedicated to all the participants at the Dartmouth Institute on Gender and War. Particular thanks for the inspiration and the wonderful time we had there go to Lynn Higgins, Brenda Silver, and Marianne Hirsch, who made the initial contact. Special thanks to Miriam Cooke, Angela Woollacott, and Fredric Kroll for work on my written English to make it printable "American." This essay is an abbreviated version of a longer piece.

1. Winners of lost wars have lost their memories also: they don't speak. Their memories, kept as secrets, turn out to be instruments of power. The winner as

the owner of the won war owns his lost memory as a power technique. He is beyond guilt.

2. Susan Jeffords, *The Remasculinization of America: Gender and the Vietnam War* (Bloomington: Indiana University Press, 1989).

3. Sara Ruddick, *Maternal Thinking: Toward a Politics of Peace* (Boston: Beacon Press, 1989).

4. Ibid., p. 137.

5. Klaus Theweleit, *Male Fantasies*, vol. 2 (Minneapolis: University of Minnesota Press, 1989).

6. Ruddick, *Maternal Thinking*, p. 192.

7. Carol Cohn, "Sex and Death in the Rational World of Defense Intellectuals," *Signs: Journal of Women in Culture and Society* 12, no. 4 (1987): 687–718.

8. Ibid., p. 701.

9. Ibid.

10. Ibid., p. 707.

11. Sandra M. Gilbert, "Soldier's Heart: Literary Men, Literary Women, and the Great War," *Signs: Journal of Women in Culture and Society* 8, no. 3 (Spring 1983): 422–50.

12. Miriam Cooke, *War's Other Voice: Women Writers on the Lebanese Civil War* (Cambridge: Cambridge University Press, 1987).

13. Angela Woollacott, *On Her Their Lives Depend: Munitions Workers in the Great War* (forthcoming).

14. Quoted in Gilbert, "Soldier's Heart."

15. Margaret R. Higgonet et al., eds., *Behind the Lines: Gender and the Two World Wars* (New Haven: Yale University Press, 1987).

16. Elisabeth Burgos-Debray, ed., *I, Rigoberta Menchú: An Indian Woman in Guatemala* (London: Verso, 1984).

17. Tim O'Brien, *The Things They Carried: A Work of Fiction* (Boston: Houghton Mifflin, 1990).

18. Elaine Scarry, *The Body in Pain: The Making and Unmaking of the World* (New York: Oxford University Press, 1985).

19. Jean Amery, *At the Mind's Limits: Contemplations by a Survivor on Auschwitz and Its Realities* (Bloomington: Indiana University Press, 1980).

20. Seminar presentation at the Dartmouth institute, May 30, 1990.

21. O'Brien, *The Things They Carried*, p. 87.

POSTSCRIPT

Miriam Cooke and Angela Woollacott

THROUGHOUT THE SPRING OF 1990, we talked about war as an abstraction. We hypothesized, theorized, dissected others' memories and interpreted their stories in a closed, safe environment. Then in August we found ourselves at war and having to apply these abstractions to the Kuwaiti theater of operation. It was impossible for the two of us as editors working on the compilation of this volume to ignore the implications of the war unfolding before us. Together we tested the hypotheses and issues raised during the institute against this latest war. Our reactions have been shaped by the essays in this volume. We offer them as a Postscript, though we emphasize that they reflect the view of the editors, not of all contributors to the volume.

We do not propose to deal here with the Gulf War in all its dimensions. We do not even pretend to cover the geopolitical or economic aspects of the war, all its causes or consequences. Our concern is with the gender issues: how the war was propagated through gendered representations and within a discourse of gender roles and behavior.

One of the most immediate issues we had to confront was the question of language and how it was shaping our experience of the war. Throughout the ten weeks of the institute we questioned and analyzed the role of textual, filmic, and media discourse in the representation of war and in the construction of the war story. We debated whether war exists independently of its telling. We thought about how it might be told without the war story falling into old molds. We kept coming back to the latest form of war telling: media coverage. And it is here that the Gulf War was so graphic an illustration of what we had observed to be the case in other mid- to late-twentieth-century wars. More than any other war, the Gulf War was waged on television. Deliberate distortion through sanitized metaphorization distanced the reality of a war that had to be seen as morally and cleanly prosecuted. In March 1991, Carol Cohn decoded military newsspeak in terms of its domestic allusions and its disturbing obfuscation: "It appears that the only things that get 'killed' on these sorties are Iraqi missiles and other military targets. Iraqi people do not get killed; civilian casualties are referred to as 'collateral damage'—a stunningly abstract and sanitized way to refer to mangled human bodies. The word 'collateral' serves to remove moral responsibility from the attacker; the deaths are 'collateral,' secondary, not at all what we intended. The word 'damage' serves to turn human beings into objects: *things* are 'damaged'; *living beings* are 'hurt.' "[1] ⟩317-18

We believe that unlike wars prior to Vietnam, this cyberwar went beyond the use of media for propaganda to implicate the media in the warfare itself. The military strategies and tactics seemed always to retain awareness of their media-tion. Now, a year after the war and inside the calm of walls of ivy, the editors are tempted to conclude that the only consistency of motivation in this highly personalized war lay in the media's projection of two male leaders, disabled (even if not physically) by previous wars, who needed to give new birth to themselves so as to recuperate a lost masculinity.[2] Each was living up to his culture's expectations of the ideal man: Bush was patronizingly uncompromising, the tough but good American Dad; Saddam Hussein was defiantly uncompromising, the tough Arab male leader who exemplified the cultural maxim that the first to raise his voice loses the argument.

Each leader needed the phallomilitary display to enhance his poor image and to defuse tensions caused by domestic fiasco. In Bush's case, it was the economic and political implications of the devastating savings-and-loan scandal and crisis in which his son, Neil Bush, was involved; it was also the specter of disarmament following the end of the cold war that threatened to render redundant a whole class of elite technocrats and to exacerbate unemployment. More generally, for Bush the diplomatic and military crisis (masculine domain) was the perfect alibi for yet again evading the feminized domain of "domestic" policy issues such as the economic recession, unemployment, education, health, and the environment.[3] In Hussein's case, it was the overwhelming cost in lives and national wealth of the Iran-Iraq war that he had launched to "construct a new Babylonian empire."[4] To this end, each leader adopted a particular profile that the media diligently projected. George Bush remained cool and calm in Maine, making his claim to masculinity with his speedboat and his many sporting skills. Saddam Hussein, always in uniform, modeled himself on the ruthless sixth century B.C. proto-Iraqi, Nebuchadnezzar. Three weeks after the invasion, he had himself filmed for international media as, in Lloyd deMause's term, the Terrifying Parent.[5] He was in Western attire, talking with some terrified hostages, whom he called "heroes of peace," and embracing one of their children. In an unequal contest for hegemony in different spheres, the one regional and the other global, two uncharismatic men staked their nations' all for personal glory and a shored-up sense of machismo. Desert Shield-Storm allowed for the assertion of these leaders' masculinity and, in the process, exposed the mechanisms at work in the construction of gender. It is not only the leaders of nations who have lost wars who desperately seek to be remasculinized; it is also their veterans and, indeed, their countries.

As Theweleit writes, no war is waged in isolation from other wars; lost wars beg to be won; won wars must be continually re-won so as to hold on to the victory. At the end of their revolution, the Algerians expressed their solidarity with the Palestinians by announcing that their revolution would have truly succeeded only when the Palestinians had won theirs. Early into the Iran-Iraq war, Saddam Hussein confirmed the significance of his "victory" against the Iranians by celebrating it as a renewed Qadisiya, in memory of the first Arab victory against the Persians in the seventh century. Yet the victory was won at a cost so great that its moral aspect must be continually emphasized lest the economic fiasco take precedence. Another, clearer war had to be won so that the Iran-Iraq war could be acknowledged as an unquestionable victory. Since 1975, Americans have been rewaging the war in Southeast Asia. In *The Remasculinization of America*, Susan Jeffords has shown how by the 1980s the successive defeats sustained by the Americans had been recuperated through the imagery of Vietnam films and literature: a remasculinizing of soldier heroes. The Gulf War provided the climax for this rewinning of a lost war. As Boose writes, there were countless ceremonies to welcome home the troops and ubiquitous displays of the American flag; television advertising invoked fit male bodies to represent America. All shared in this orgasm of recuperated manhood. And, adding the dimension of the paternal to this refound manhood, General Norman Schwarzkopf was named Father of the Year. Among those awaiting the first troops returning home were some Vietnam vets in wheelchairs. The soldier boys on whom the media immediately pounced declared, and apparently without false modesty, that it was not they but the 'Nam vets who were the real heroes of this war.

It is particularly significant that this celebration of a remasculinized America is happening at a time when women constitute an unprecedentedly large proportion of the military and increasingly are playing combat-related roles. John Nordheimer pointed out: "The American public, watching the Persian Gulf war on television, got its first eyeful of American women in expanded military roles despite policies that technically restrict women to non-combat functions."[6] A year later, women in combat remains a burning issue. During the Gulf War–Just War conference convened at Vanderbilt University in January 1992, Jean Bethke Elshtain pleaded for the withdrawal of mothers from combat positions. A uniformed man in the audience remonstrated that changes in attitude were called for: the American military was no longer made up of conscripted young men but of families. Room must be made for all women and men who enlist and who equally commit themselves to fighting for their country.

During this past year the military leadership has sought to erase the importance of women's participation. Women have come forward and demanded the right to name the nature of their participation.[7] The role of women troops in the invasion of Panama had set the scene for what was to come. It had shown that America could win a little war while allowing women a front-line role. It was time to try something bigger, to choreograph a "real war" against a Third World state with a military structure suddenly touted as the third strongest in the world. Victory being virtually assured, it was time to be to arrogant and to flaunt the vulnerability of the overwhelmingly superior American forces—women, blacks and particularly black women,[8] and not fully trained reservists. These untraditional soldiers, with their loved ones at home, were assumed to be more battle ready than the soldiers, undifferentiated, of the impudent states that dared to defy American notions of international proper conduct. By having such troops sent against them, the Iraqi military was effectively feminized.[9] As Carol Cohn writes in her essay, one aspect of this feminization was depictions of Saddam Hussein being anally penetrated by the United States. The American military had been so remasculinized that it could afford to salute its women recruits. Can it now, when the "victory" seems less absolute, keep them in the war story?

Cynthia Enloe describes the discursive process whereby women may continue to be denied access to the front. Women, she writes, "*as women* must be denied access to 'the front', to 'combat' so that men can claim a uniqueness and superiority that will justify their dominant position in the social order. And yet because women are in practice often exposed to frontline combat . . . the military has to constantly redefine 'the front' and 'combat' as wherever 'women' are not."[10] Part of the military's mechanisms for redefining space was exposed in the Gulf War: the war was really won by air superiority. Thus the pilots enjoyed the starring role; these most "masculine" (cool, skilled, in control) of the fighting forces were represented as having really won the war, despite women's contributions—even as pilots! As Stan Rosenberg demonstrates, the godlike pilots define themselves by supposedly masculine traits such as bravery and denial of danger.

Women have always been a part of war, but only now is their presence being explicitly represented. Since the invasion of Panama in 1989, when women combatants were chosen for special media focus, interest in female soldiers has been high. When American troops were dispatched to the Arabian desert, the media made much of the "Women Warriors," as a front-page story for the September 10, 1990, issue of *Newsweek* was headed. It was as though it was the first time that American women had been in military combat. Yet, as Laura Flanders writes, "women have taken part in every U.S. military crisis since the Revolutionary War." However, she points out that the Gulf War had "several special aspects. For one, women have never before served on such a large scale (11%

worldwide and 6% in the Gulf) or taken on such broad responsibilities. . . . Far more important, they are a perfect media story."[11]

In the twentieth century, women have gone beyond their time-honored military roles as camp followers, cooks, laundresses, nurses, and warriors passing as men in men's clothing.[12] They have entered the armed forces of numerous countries as women warriors. In Euro-American forces, the route to warrior status was circuitous, involving the establishment of the women's auxiliary corps in the First World War to relieve men from support services. In other parts of the world, women have been involved in nationalist wars, anticolonial movements, and civil wars.[13] The fact that women were in combat during the Gulf War, despite technical restrictions on their involvement, has already had repercussions. With the 1992 Defense Authorization Act, Congress has repealed the law excluding women from flying combat aircraft. While the Pentagon has not yet changed its policies on women in combat, a blue-ribbon presidential commission on the issue will report at the end of 1992. Policy will probably change.[14] The induction of women into the most prestigious and masculinist of military occupations, combat pilot, will leave little room for symbolic gendering of military roles.

The admission of women to official, recognized combat status in the late twentieth century challenges the Euro-American gender system. As women swell the regular ranks, they create a new myth by naturalizing the notion of women warriors.[15] On August 5, 1991, *Newsweek* published a poll indicating that 53 percent of Americans believe women should get combat assignments if they want them. The only area of skepticism was over infantry front-line duty. It is significant that women are increasingly present in the mainstream military forces and are no longer relegated to separate female forces, which are so readily marginalized after a conflict or during peacetime.[16] We are not trying to suggest that increasing the proportion of women in the armed forces is a feminist goal. But we believe that breaking the nexus (real or assumed) between military service and masculinity on the one hand and pacifism and femininity on the other will weaken the social pediments on which militarism rests.

The Gulf War provided a battleground for two cultural systems and, above all, for two gender systems. The media exploited these differences in their attempt to project dichotomized factions: us versus them; the West versus the Arab world. But it soon became apparent that the neat stereotyping would not serve international political purposes. After all, we did have to distinguish between Kuwaitis and Iraqis, between Iranians and Arabs, and even between neighbors like the Saudis and the Kuwaitis. But for many it was necessary to distinguish between national polities only; it was not necessary to differentiate these different nations' cultures as represented by their women. Suddenly, the press and the media zeroed in on Arab women. They represented them as uniformly veiled and segregated, passive and oppressed. In an excess of zeal, NOW President Molly Yard announced on December 4, 1990, that American lives should not be sacrificed on behalf of regimes that practiced "gender apartheid."[17] When on November 7, fifty Saudi women drove across Riyadh, reporters crowed at the coup for American cultural imperialism. Then, after the war was "over," the cultural victory continued to be feted.[18]

Yet, at the beginning of the crisis, there were moments of awareness of a somewhat more complicated reality for women in the Arab countries involved in the crisis. Just after the invasion, the Kuwaiti women's demonstration against the Iraqis—the first of its kind—was reported. In early September, *Time* showed a picture of women soldiers in the Iraqi army. It remains unclear whether their subsequent occlusion was due to censorship on both sides or lack of information. As mentioned above, in November the press reported the driving incident. But then when the war broke out, the images of the women reverted to their undifferentiated oppressed facelessness. This vacillation in representing the women of the Other, friend or foe, corresponded to the media's ambivalence in assessing this Other's strength relative to that of the United States. One of the most curious examples of change in reporting was in relation to Iran. Whereas until February, Iranian women had been consistently shown to be veiled and thus representative of an oppressive, backward, and patriarchal system, when Iraqi planes were flown to Iran, as though defecting, their media representation changed. The American public was suddenly presented with images of sophisticated, Western-attired Iranian women. If the Iranians were to become our friends, then their women had to be represented as compatible with American women.

This ambivalence has been less marked in the case of reporting about the women in the U.S. military. Stories were told about women who were actually in combat and who, during the ground war, flew support aircraft in the battle zone.[19] There were 32,340 American servicewomen in the Gulf:[20] 15 American women died, 11 in combat and 4 otherwise.[21] These women were depicted as tough but also as subject to both professional and sexual harassment.[22] Part of the harrassment consisted of exaggerated public claims of pregnancy among women sailors and troops. This charge has been used to intimidate women in the military throughout the twentieth century, starting with the women's auxiliary military corps of World War I. Are women tough enough and thus acceptable as ideal soldiers? Or are they playthings? Which pinup will last as the dominant image of the American woman in the military: the masculinized policewoman with the erect gun, reported as the favorite of the American male soldier in the Gulf, or Gary Trudeau's drawing of a semistripped, frightened woman soldier?[23]

Thus did the media construct the images of women in the military. But will the actual women soldiers on both sides of the line in the sand fit into the war story, and, if so, how? What will the media do about the women "combatants" who came home in body bags? And what of those taken as prisoners of war? Will such events help or hinder in the struggle to allow women to retain agency? Who will name the experiences and functions of these women? Women are challenging stereotypical notions of gender and the military. The challenge now extends to the home front. Can we call the space where men are left by the soldier wives home front? Is it okay to say that women go off to protect and defend men and that men stay at home and wait patiently, if anxiously, for the return of the warrior? Or will this agency be co-opted as usual? Even though the Gulf War was a "victory," will America once again need to remasculinize in the wake of war? If so, will it be necessary to eliminate the women who complicate the heroic story? A year later it is less and less evident that the war was "won," and as this awareness dawns, the story needs to be retold.

The Gulf War damaged received notions of masculinity and femininity. The women who fought, who were injured, and who died participated in an arena quintessentially masculine. They simultaneously subverted concepts of the masculinity of the men who fought beside them and of their own femininity. This disturbance of gender arrangements at the front was reflected at home. The collision of gender roles and representations produced a crisis that served to demonstrate the permeability of the concepts of war and gender. It is our hope that the destruction of the myth of the masculinity of soldiering will participate in the undermining of the erotics that have historically undergirded the re-presentation of war.

For the many dimensions of war and gender opened up by the volume, we would like to thank participants in the Dartmouth Institute. Their reactions, criticisms and suggestions have been represented, we hope, in the volume as a whole and also in this Postscript. Without their commitment to the project, their enthusiasms, outrages, insights, and energy, we would not have been able to produce this book or to begin to understand the war that was its sequel.

March 1992

NOTES

1. Carol E. Cohn, "Decoding Military Newsspeak," *Ms.*, March/April 1991, p. 88.
2. Susan Jeffords, *The Remasculinization of America* (Bloomington: Indiana University Press, 1989).

3. The fact that these issues have been shown by polls to be of greater concern to women and minorities than to white men was underscored by the gender gap in support for the war. According to columnist Ellen Goodman, polls found gender gaps of 18, 19, 24 and 25 percentage points. *Cleveland Plain Dealer* December 7, 1990.

4. Maxime Rodinson, "The Mythology of a Conqueror," *Merip* 168 (January/February 1991): 13.

5. Lloyd deMause, *Nation*, March 11, 1991, 300.

6. "Women's Role in Combat: The War Resumes," *New York Times*, May 26, 1991, 1, 13. Nordheimer quotes Representative Patricia Schroeder: "The Persian Gulf helped collapse the whole chivalrous notion that women could be kept out of danger in a war. We saw that the theater of operations had no strict combat zone."

7. Nordheimer also quotes Carolyn Becraft, director of a project on the military for the Women's Equity League: "This whole issue is about power, and whether women will be allowed to displace men in high-ranking positions" (ibid.).

8. "—Approximately 22% of U.S. military recruits are African-American: the Army, the branch most likely to suffer heavy casualties in ground combat, is 29.8% African-American—more than double the representation in the general population; 48% of the women in Desert Storm are African-American" (*Plain Dealer*, February 9, 1991).

9. The *Nation* ran a spoof entitled "The Beast within the Beast," in which Alexander Cockburn referred to representations of Saddam Hussein in the *National Examiner* that rendered him effeminate (*Nation*, April 1, 1991, 403).

10. Cynthia Enloe, *Does Khaki Become You? The Militarization of Women's Lives* (Boston: South End Press, 1983), p. 15.

11. Laura Flanders traces through the media coverage of American women's participation in the troop mobilization in an article entitled "Military Women and the Media," *New Directions for Women* 19, no. 6 (November/December 1990).

12. See Barton C. Hacker, "From Military Revolution to Industrial Revolution: Armies, Women and Political Economy in Early Modern Europe," in Eva Isaksson, ed., *Women and the Military System* (London: Harvester Wheatsheaf, 1988), for a concise account of women's roles in early modern armies and their subsequent exclusion due to industrial, technological, and military changes.

13. Julie Wheelwright, author of the valuable study of women passing as male soldiers, *Amazons and Military Maids: Women Who Dressed as Men in the Prusuit of Life, Liberty and Happiness* (London: Pandora, 1989), reported that women have made up more than a third of the Eritrean People's Liberation Front forces, just as women fought in the Algerian war aginst the French, and fought in both the North Vietnamese and Nicaraguan armies. See "Battle of Both Sexes," *Guardian* (Manchester and London), June 11, 1991, p. 17.

14. *Congressional Quarterly*, December 28, 1991, p. 3774. In February 1992 the first women were assigned to a combat-equipped U.S. navy ship (*New York Times* March 1, 1992).

15. For a discussion of the mythological and representational meanings of the Amazons and Boadicia, see Sharon Macdonald, Pat Holden, and Shirley Ardener, eds., *Images of Women in Peace and War: Cross-Cultural and Historical Perspectives* (Madison: University of Wisconsin Press, 1988).

16. See Macdonald's introduction to *Images of Women in Peace and War*, particularly her discussion of women in anticolonial struggles, in the Sandinista forces in Nicaragua, and in the Israeli army (9–12).

17. *Durham Morning Herald*, December 5, 1990. Similarly, Joan Lowry described the life of women in Saudi Arabia as unacceptable (*Plain Dealer*, April 10, 1991).

18. See, for example, Anna Reifenberg, "Saudi Women Remain under Cover, but. . . "*San Francisco Examiner*, March 10, 1991. Jacqueline Frank's title for her August 29, 1990, *Chicago Sun Times* article on the crisis in the Middle East also toots the cultural imperialist horn: "Women Soldiers' Key Role Forces Arabs to Bend Tradition."

19. Philip Shenon, "At Combat's Doorstep, She Confronts Peril and Male Doubt," *New York Times*, February 24, 1991; Jeannie Ralston, "Women's Work," *Life*, May 1991.

20. Marlee Miller, "AAUW Members in the Gulf War," *American Association of University Women Outlook* April/May 1991, 5.

21. *Facts on File*, July 18, 1991, p. 528A1.

22. Sergeant Cheryl Stewart of Flint, Michigan, was quoted as saying of her husband that he "had a problem with his male ego: He felt he should have been here and I should have been at home. . . . The Army is still very sexist. A lot of men advanced in ranks see women as a problem to be dealt with and an obstacle they have to consider." "War Puts U. S. Servicewomen Closer Than Ever to Combat," (*New York Times*, January 22, 1991).

Teri Bernside in the National Guard: "I'm in a unit with all men and four women. You have to put up with a lot of derogatory remarks. You also have to fight to work: it's very patronizing." "Feminists Tackle Military Issue," *Plain Dealer*, February 3, 1991.

Capt. Carol Barkalow and Andrea Raab, *In the Men's House* (New York: Simon and Schuster/Poseidon, 1990) discuss the profound and destructive sexism of the American military.

See Enloe's discussion of the paradoxical uses of women's images on both sides of the line in the sand, in "Womenandchildren," *Village Voice*, September 25, 1990.

23. Robert Rheinheld, "Policewoman in Denim Is Betty Grable of Gulf," *New York Times*, February 15, 1991; Gary Trudeau, "The Operation Desert Shield Emergency Pin-Up," *Durham Morning Herald*, January 7, 1991.

SELECT BIBLIOGRAPHY

Cooke, Miriam. *War's Other Voices: Women Writers on the Lebanese Civil War*. Cambridge: Cambridge University Press, 1988.

Cooper, Helen, Adrienne Munich, and Susan Squier, eds. *Arms and the Woman: War, Gender and Literary Representation*. Chapel Hill: University of North Carolina Press, 1989.

Ehrenreich, Barbara. *The Hearts of Men: American Dreams and the Flight from Commitment*. Garden City, N.Y.: Anchor Press/Doubleday, 1983.

Elshtain, Jean Bethke. *Women and War*. New York: Basic Book, 1987.

Elshtain, Jean Bethke, and Sheila Tobias. *Women, Militarism, and War: Essays in History, Politics and Social Theory* (Savage, Md.: Rowman and Littlefield, 1990).

Enloe, Cynthia. *Does Khaki Become You? The Militarization of Women's Lives*. Boston: South End Press, 1983.

Fogel, Joshua A., ed. *Chinese Women in a Century of Revolution: 1850–1950*. Stanford, Calif.: Stanford University Press, 1989.

Fussell, Paul. *The Great War and Modern Memory*. New York: Oxford University Press, 1975.

———. *Wartime: Understanding and Behavior in the Second World War*. New York: Oxford University Press, 1989.

Gioseffi, Daniela, ed. *Women on War: Essential Voices for the Nuclear Age from a Brilliant International Assembly*. New York: Simon and Schuster, 1988.

Harris, Adrienne, and Ynestra King. *Rocking the Ship of State: Toward a Feminist Peace Politics*. Boulder, Colo.: Westview Press, 1989.

Higonnet, Margaret R., Jane Jenson, Sonya Michel, and Margaret C. Weitz, *Behind the Lines: Gender and the Two World Wars*. New Haven: Yale University Press, 1987.

Isaksson, Eva, ed. *Women and the Military System*. London: Harvester Wheatsheaf, 1988.

Khan, Nosheen. *Women's Poetry of the First World War*. Lexington, Ky.: University Press of Kentucky, 1988.

Macdonald, Sharon, Pat Holden, and Shirley Ardener, eds. *Images of Women in Peace and War: Cross-Cultural and Historical Perspectives*. Madison: University of Wisconsin Press, 1988.

Peters, Cynthia, ed. *Collateral Damage: The "New World Order" at Home and Abroad*. Boston: South End Press, 1992.

Reilly, Catherine. *Scars upon My Heart: Women's Poetry and Verse of the First World War*. London: Virago Press, 1981.

Ruddick, Sara. *Maternal Thinking: Toward a Politics of Peace*. Cambridge, Mass.: Beacon Press, 1989.

Schneider, Dorothy, and Carl J. Schneider, *Sound Off! American Military Women Speak Out*. New York: Paragon House, 1992.

Stiehm, Judith Hicks. *Arms and the Enlisted Woman*. Philadelphia: Temple University Press, 1989.

Theweleit, Klaus. *Male Fantasies*. Vol. 1, *Women Floods Bodies History* (Minneapolis: University of Minnesota Press, 1987); vol. 2, *Male Bodies: Psychoanalyzing the White Terror* (Minneapolis: University of Minnesota Press, 1989).

Tylee, Claire M. *The Great War and Women's Consciousness: Images of Militarism and Womanhood in Women's Writings, 1914–1964*. Iowa City: University of Iowa Press, 1990.

Weil, Simone. *The Iliad; or, The Poem of Force*. Wallingford, Pa.: Pendle Hill, 1956.

Wheelwright, Julie. *Amazons and Military Maids: Women Who Dressed as Men in the Pursuit of Life, Liberty and Happiness*. London: Pandora, 1989.

Wolf, Christa. *Cassandra*. New York: Farrar, Straus, Giroux, 1984.

INDEX